TRAINED CAPACITIES

Studies in Rhetoric/Communication
Thomas W. Benson, Series Editor

John Dewey, Rhetoric, and Democratic Practice

TRAINED CAPACITIES

Edited by

Brian Jackson and Gregory Clark

Afterword by Gerard A. Hauser

The University of South Carolina Press

Published by the University of South Carolina Press
Columbia, South Carolina 29208

www.sc.edu/uscpress

Manufactured in the United States of America

23 22 21 20 19 18 17 16 15 14 10 9 8 7 6 5 4 3 2 1

Library of Congress Cataloging-in-Publication Data

Trained capacities : John Dewey, rhetoric, and democratic practice / edited by Brian Jackson and Gregory Clark.
pages cm.—(Studies in rhetoric/communication)
Includes bibliographical references and index.
ISBN 978-1-61117-318-5 (hardbound : alk. paper)—ISBN 978-1-61117-319-2 (ebook)
1. Dewey, John, 1859–1952. 2. Rhetoric—Philosophy. 3. Democracy—Philosophy. I. Jackson, Brian, 1932– editor of compilation. II. Clark, Gregory, 1950– editor of compilation.
B945.D44T58 2014
191—DC23 2013028736

CONTENTS

SERIES EDITOR'S PREFACE

In *Trained Capacities,* editors Brian Jackson and Gregory Clark have brought together a group of leading rhetorical scholars to consider the contexts of John Dewey's work as it contributes to rhetorical theory, rhetorical practice, and rhetorical education. The American philosopher John Dewey (1859–1952) has long been of interest to teachers of rhetoric and communication. The essays in *Trained Capacities* explore broad themes of Dewey's reflections on science, religion, pragmatism, war and peace, education, knowledge, theories of the public, and democratic practice.

A key feature of the book is found in essays exploring Dewey as compared with and in conversation with other thinkers on these themes—some of them his contemporaries, some not: Kenneth Burke, William Jennings Bryan, Randolph Bourne, Thomas Jefferson, Jane Addams, W. E. B. Du Bois, Walter Lippmann, and James Baldwin. The contributors also examine the reception and interpretation of Dewey by his successors and offer a balanced and informative introduction to recent scholarship on the work of John Dewey by rhetorical scholars.

ACKNOWLEDGMENTS

We acknowledge our debt to those who authored the essays in this volume for their interesting and insightful work. We have learned much from them in the process of completing this project.

We also acknowledge the College of Humanities at Brigham Young University and express gratitude for the support and encouragement they have provided as the project moved along. We are grateful to the people at University of South Carolina Press and those involved in the production of this volume whose work has been both essential and encouraging.

Introduction

John Dewey and the Rhetoric of Democratic Culture

Brian Jackson and Gregory Clark

Every once in a while, long-dead and oft-forgotten philosophers rise from their graves and walk their way into public conversations. Take John Dewey, for instance. In the spring of 2010 a group of concerned parents in a school district not far from where we both live gathered to oppose what they thought was a socialist education philosophy, expressed in the mission statement of the school district. They called it a "poison agenda," one conceived by none other than John Dewey (Warnock).

Though he may be considered the patron saint of U.S. education, it is not every day—alas—that local school board meetings debate John Dewey's ideas. Even academic interest in Dewey comes and goes. It died out after World War II, rose again in the early 1990s, and then waned again. Once presidential candidate Barack Obama worked in the Senate to pass the Emergency Economic Stabilization Act of 2008 to help a crippled economy, we began to hear strains of that perpetual national debate about the proper role of government in the United States, strains that summon Dewey's key ideas even if his name is not mentioned.

Dewey's post-Obama resurrection has been explained by the conservative political scientist Tiffany Jones Miller, who argues that Dewey did more than anyone to "repackage progressive social theory in a way that obscured just how radically its principles departed from those of the American founding" (Miller). Unlike the Founding Fathers, who argued for limited government and individual liberty against government encroachment, Dewey did indeed advocate an explicitly "positive" reading of the concept of freedom—as "freedom to" rather than "freedom from." For him, freedom offers individuals opportunities to develop their own capacities, opportunities that are often provided most reliably by the democratic state. Consequently by asserting that Dewey's work represents a "thoroughgoing reconstruction of the American way of living, primarily by means of the positive state," Miller identifies a political ideology that has been contested in the United States since the Progressive Era. Indeed to many—such as those who object to the idea that public schools might be "enculturating the young into a social and political democracy," a phrase that used to hang in the halls of the school district offices just north of us—such a "positive state" looks precisely like the enemy.

But this is not a book about political theory, nor even about democracy. Rather it is a book about the essentially rhetorical way of life—one we are calling here *democratic culture*—that we believe Dewey imagined in his work. For us, democracy describes the kinds of human interaction that must follow when individuals or groups choose to, or discover that they must, treat each other as equals. This assumption, or presumption, of mutual equality renders interactions within a community of equals necessarily, though often not happily, cooperative. Democracy extends well beyond government systems to include the prior and fundamental work of ensuring that "all adults are free to chime in, to join the conversation on how they should arrange their lives together," in the words of the philosopher Paul Woodruff (3). A democratic culture comprises the sum total of the values and attitudes as well as habits and behaviors that enable people to practice what amounts to responsible expression. Such a practice is inherently rhetorical, in the sense of requiring both assertion and response to be accountable to others with whom one is engaged.

Rhetorical practice is the kind of "practice" that Alasdair MacIntyre described in *After Virtue: A Study in Moral Theory* as foundational to community and culture: "By a 'practice' I am going to mean any coherent and complex form of socially established cooperative human activity through which goods internal to that form of activity are realized in the course of trying to achieve those standards of excellence which are appropriate to, and partially definitive of, that form of activity, with the result that human powers to achieve excellence, and human conceptions of the ends and the goods involved, are systematically extended" (187).

Persuasive communication is one of the most essential practices constituting democratic culture—one in which individuals are expected to express themselves constructively within a community and at the same time to judge rigorously the expressions of others on those same constructive criteria. When rhetorical practice enables people to solve particular problems or advance particular projects, they succeed in achieving what MacIntyre would consider "external goods," such as material prosperity. But rhetorical practice also establishes, and emerges from, the "goods internal" to democratic practice, such as the values, attitudes, habits, and behaviors that serve as the normative forces behind practice.

It has become commonplace in rhetorical studies to say that a vibrant, progressive democratic culture—the kind MacIntyre imagined was necessary for achieving "excellence"—depends on rhetorical engagement by individuals, and by as many individuals as possible. Nearly a century before John Dewey's richest work on democratic culture, Alexis de Tocqueville addressed the engagement problem for American democracy in prescient language: "When social conditions are equal, every man is apt to live apart, centered in himself and forgetful of the public. If the rulers of democratic nations were either to neglect to correct this fatal tendency or to encourage it from a notion that it weans men from political passions and thus wards off revolutions, they might eventually produce the evil they seek to avoid, and a time might come when the inordinate passions of a few men, aided by the unintelligible selfishness or the pusillanimity of the greater number, would ultimately compel society to pass through strange vicissitudes" (2, 256).

There is no doubt that Americans have passed, and will continue from time to time to pass, through "strange vicissitudes" due to their own disengagement from civic rhetorical practice. Since Tocqueville, America's political narrative has provided citizens many reasons, moral or otherwise, to remain disengaged. Paul Woodruff argues that of all political arrangements, democracy "faces human limitations" most honestly because it "balances distrust against distrust" and casts a critical eye on its own imperfections (21). Impurity, in fact, is not a condition of democracy only but of the "human scene" generally (Woodruff 21).

Impure as it is, democratic culture has had few more enthusiastic advocates than John Dewey. His capacious mind was fixed intensely on that human scene as he imagined it at its best. He imagined a culture of common values and attitudes, of shared habits and behaviors, that would enable individuals to engage constructively, together, in the rhetorical work of improving the conditions of living together—he called it the "task" of "creative democracy." Indeed he not only imagined that culture but also set out in his work both the content and the form of a civic education—curricular as well as extracurricular—that might prepare individuals to perpetuate and enrich it. That work seems almost to be a direct response to the plaintive call of Walt Whitman, a poet Dewey admired, for a "moral and artistic" community held together by "a common skeleton" (Whitman 10). Throughout his work Dewey imagines how that identity might be realized—how not only politics but also philosophy, aesthetics, and of course education might teach people ways of engaging rhetorically in the rocky collaborative project of democratic life *together.* What Dewey describes as a "public" comprises people who choose not only to tolerate each other but also to cooperate in generating collective progress from perpetual conflict, a project that relies on individual rhetorical practices of the democratic sort. From their experience of democratic culture, those people learn the essential elements of those practices and—returning to Whitman—to value them as matters of morality and even of art.

We intend in this collection of essays to accomplish two things. First, we want to explore how John Dewey's scholarship has influenced and can continue to influence the thinking of rhetoricians on the relationship between rhetoric and American democracy. Though Dewey was not actively engaged in the superdiscipline of communication, his work as a professional philosopher and public intellectual continues to serve as a well that rhetorical scholars draw from when they study rhetoric as the constitutive democratic practice. The essays that follow demonstrate Dewey's wide-ranging influence on rhetoric in an American intellectual tradition that addresses this national culture's fundamental conflicts between self and society, freedom and responsibility, individual advancement and the common good. We see this influence at work both in America's enduring abstractions (such as science, pragmatism, and religion) and in Dewey's interlocutors (such as Jane Addams or Walter Lippmann). Second, we want also to establish Dewey as an essential source for those engaged in the project of teaching others how to compose timely, appropriate, useful, and eloquent responses to the diverse and often contentious rhetorical situations that develop in a democratic culture. At stake here is not just instruction in traditional modes of public discourse because, by our definition, democratic culture encompasses a variety of situations, private or public, civic or professional, where people must cooperate more or less as equals in the work of advancing a common project. What prepares people to intervene constructively in such situations is instruction in those rhetorical practices of democratic interaction that we find at the center of Dewey's work.

We should mention one more intention: to make a collection that is itself a locus of collaboration among rhetoricians of various disciplines, particularly those scholars concentrated in English and communication studies who are united in their commitment to rhetoric. Though in his intellectual maturity he left Hegel behind, Dewey was infected, as William James wrote, with the "Hegelian bacillus of reconciliation" (in Westbrook 101), and we hope this collection of essays on his work might encourage a more thorough rapprochement of scholars who are concerned with these matters but find themselves divided, artificially, by disciplines, programs, and departments.

In this introduction we argue that Dewey's writing provides a rich framework upon which a distinctly American tradition of democratic rhetorical practice can be built—a tradition that combines the most useful concepts of classical rhetoric with those of modern progressive civic engagement. We say "distinctly American" because we believe Dewey takes us beyond our traditional emphasis on the democratic culture of classical Athens and provides connections to rich veins of American thought such as individualism, liberalism, progressive education, collectivism, pragmatism, and postindustrial science and communication. In this way his voluminous work is a modern and democratic expression of *paideia* or, if we can be forgiven for whimsy, *paideweya* (Jackson 183), expressing the interdependent elements of a civic education that is essential to the sustenance of a democratic culture. For Dewey, human potential is best realized in the free flow of artful communication among the individuals who together form a dynamic social organism. Because in America people are, at least in principle, more or less equal, each is responsible to be ever learning, ever growing, ever adapting to the problems that develop when diverse and divergent individuals must together construct and maintain their society. In his rendering (even though, again, he is a philosopher rather than a rhetorician), these practices of individual learning, growing, and adapting, as well as the contentious collaborative work that is their context, are essentially rhetorical.

DEWEY, DEMOCRATIC CULTURE, AND RHETORIC

Our point is that Dewey's work describes a democratic culture emerging from exchanges of "symbolic means of inducing cooperation" in others—Kenneth Burke's definition of rhetoric (43). That culture is democratic to the extent that it is, in Charles Tilly's terms, characterized by relationships that "feature broad, equal, protected and mutually binding consultation" (13–14) by citizens who are free to make their views known—to consult with each other or with representatives about how things should be (Dahl 37–38). Put perhaps more bluntly by Paul Woodruff, democracy engages its participants in two collaborative rhetorical projects at once: a "positive" effort that would "engage everyone's good will on behalf of the state so that it could grow and defend itself against its enemies without worrying about internal divisions"; and its necessarily "negative" mirror image, "to prevent the rise of tyrants and to ensure that money or aristocratic birth never conferred high privilege on anyone" (31).

These are descriptions of a democratic *state,* and while democratic culture is most often imagined as a state, it need not be. Constituted of democratic interactions, democratic culture takes many social forms—professional as well as civic, private as well as public. There are many situations in which people must cooperate in their self-government and so find themselves—happily or not—engaged with others in work that, however individual one's motivation, is necessarily a common project. A healthy democratic culture would provide individuals with perspectives and practices that, even in the face of conflict, enable constructive communication with divergent others.

This is familiar ground: democracy is "forged in political rhetoric," as Russell Hanson writes, through "arguments over the desirability of particular institutions and practices" (23). So democratic culture *is* rhetorical culture since democratic culture is created through rhetorical back-and-forthness. This has been discussed in rhetorical studies in recent years through a growing literature on deliberative democracy, inspired by Habermas and refined by a number of scholars interested in fleshing out the normative and descriptive dimensions of how citizens reason together through what Gerard Hauser calls "vernacular exchanges" in various public spheres (Hauser 74; see also Fontana, Nederman, and Remer). Deliberation springs from and creates democratic culture. The same can be said for public address, social movements, mass media, blogs, architecture, popular culture, Internet memes, commemorations, symbolic observances, and myriad other artifacts we may study.

RHETORIC AS "TRAINED CAPACITIES"

Dewey has been understood as a prime contributor to this conversation for some time now, though only in the last twenty years has his work received the sustained attention it deserves. In 1991 two engaging intellectual biographies were published—Robert Westbrook's *John Dewey and American Democracy* and Steven Rockefeller's *John Dewey: Religious Faith and Democratic Humanism*—just as Richard Rorty and other neopragmatists were beginning to make Dewey studies fashionable again after the post–World War II decline. For Rockefeller, Dewey's vision of democracy is a spiritual one, a craving for a unifying force to overcome those dualisms of modernity "that oppress life, restrict growth, and obstruct social progress" (2). Dewey, therefore, should be read as "the prophet of a new spiritual attitude" intended to "clarify and realize the religious and moral values inherent in natural experience and democratic culture" (Rockefeller 4, 22). Westbrook is more interested in seeing Dewey as the neglected articulator of a radical new liberalism, one in which, as was pointed out earlier, the business of democracy is the active development of its people—*all* its people. Dewey envisioned a "common democratic culture suffusing schools, factories, political parties, and other institutions" (Westbrook xvi), and he maintained a democratic faith amid withering criticism from all major points on the political spectrum.

Born in Burlington, Vermont, in 1859, the year Charles Darwin published *On the Origin of Species* (as everyone takes pains to note), John Dewey grew up in an intellectual environment aflame with ideological conflicts first sparked by the Enlightenment, such as the interminable debate between science and faith. He grew up in a family of Congregationalists who practiced a brand of liberal but pious faith that Dewey abandoned by the mid-1890s. He earned a degree from the University of Vermont in 1879 and taught high school for a few years in Oil City, Pennsylvania, though apparently he could not control his students and his most memorable attribute was his overlong morning prayers (Westbrook 8). At Johns Hopkins University, the first American institution to offer graduate studies, he studied philosophy with George Sylvester Morris, a philosopher who, like Dewey, found in the works of G. W. F. Hegel, the German idealist, a unifying principle, a principle that satisfied what Dewey decades later called "an intense emotional craving" to unite the modern divisions "of self from the world, of soul from body, of nature from God" (*Later Works* 5:153). In 1884 he followed Morris to the University of Michigan for his first academic post, and after a brief year at the University of Minnesota, he was head of the philosophy department at Michigan until 1894, when he transferred to the University of Chicago to head its philosophy department. In 1904 he moved to Columbia University, where he remained until he retired in 1930 with some of his best work still ahead of him (for example, *Art as Experience, Liberalism and Social Action,* and *Experience and Education*).

As Nathan Crick points out, though Dewey gushed that "of all affairs, communication is the most wonderful" (Dewey, *Later Works* 1:134), he used the term "rhetoric" maybe once in his voluminous work (in an encomium of one of his students, Fred Newton Scott, a founding compositionist) and never seems to operate explicitly in the rhetorical tradition handed down by classicists with whom he would have been familiar (Crick, *Democracy and Rhetoric,* 9). Even more challenging for a project like ours, Dewey's own rhetorical style, then as much as now, underwhelms. After reading *Experience and Nature,* Oliver Wendell Holmes quipped that Dewey wrote as "God would have spoken had He been inarticulate but keenly desirous to tell you how it was" (in Westbrook xiii). One of Dewey's sharper critics, Lewis Mumford, thought that the great philosopher's prose was "as depressing as a subway ride" (in Westbrook 381). He was ever changing his mind about key terms such as "instrumentalism," "culture," "experience"; nothing seemed to catch on.

His speaking style fared no better. Even Sidney Hook, who, as Alan Ryan writes, "admired Dewey only slightly this side of idolatry," recognized his mentor's shortcomings (Ryan 38). Dewey, writes Hook, made "no attempt to motivate or arouse the interest of his auditors, to relate problems to their own experiences, to use graphic, concrete illustrations in order to give point to abstruse positions," nor did he provoke "a lively participation and response" (Hook, *Out of Step* 82). The world-famous intellectual spoke "in a husky monotone," and "there were pauses and sometimes long lapses as he gazed out the window or above the heads of his audience" (Hook, *Out of Step* 83). One of his students said that his first experience in Dewey's class left him with "a shock of dullness and confusion" (in Westbrook 378). Hours after the bombing of Pearl Harbor, one of the most dramatic moments in world history, Dewey gave a plodding lecture on philosophy and completely sidestepped the *kairos* for which his pragmatism should have been keenly suited (Danisch 1). When compared to the luminous prose of William James, sure, Dewey's rhetorical style falls short; yet he articulated over and over a clear progressive vision of democratic culture that put back-and-forth communication at the center of a way of life whose ultimate goal was the growth of every person, what Nathan Crick calls the "arts of becoming" essential to the democratic project—one in which individuals and their groups can hope to progress together.

Did Don Burks exaggerate, then, when he wrote in 1968 that "perhaps no philosopher since Aristotle has more to offer the rhetorician than does John Dewey" (Burks 126)? That depends on whether or not we can successfully integrate the different strands of his thinking into a rhetoric of democratic culture that yields both theoretical insights and practical strategies, especially for teaching young people. Rhetoric is a *dynamis,* a power to do things with language in collaboration with others. As we practice rhetoric, we learn how to interpret, analyze, invent, and perform in dynamic social relationships that call forth ever more innovative responses to recurring situations. Dewey believed that the ultimate Good is the growth of a person as he or she interacts in social situations, building "social intelligence" and "social power" through "trained capacities of control" (*Early Works* 5:75). We believe that this idea of *trained capacities* is capacious enough to cover everything that makes rhetoric morally essential to democracy. Rhetoric, if we paraphrase Dewey, "educates"; it "enlarges and enlightens experience; it stimulates and enriches imagination; it creates responsibility for accuracy and vividness of statement and thought" (*Middle Works* 9:9). Rhetoric—both as theory and as practice—is necessary for our growth as human beings, and practicing it gives us trained capacities just as much perhaps as learning it in formal schooling.

This orientation to trained capacities leads us to go beyond the usual starting point for talking about Dewey and rhetoric: *The Public and Its Problems,* his most thorough statement of political philosophy (Westbrook 300). As important as that work is for rhetorical studies, we do not get a full view of Dewey's contribution unless we begin with his writings on ethics, which provide key underlying assumptions for his perspectives on education, aesthetics, and finally communication, which taken together express Dewey's *paideia* for democratic culture.

AN ETHICS OF DEMOCRATIC PRACTICE

Woven into Dewey's progressive vision of teaching, creating, and communicating is an ethics that guides the rhetorical practice of a democratic culture. Shaping this ethics are two moral principles learned from his mother, Lucina: the inestimable value of the individual and the spiritual longing and need to share a life with others. Absorbed from the evangelical pietism of his Congregationalist mother, these principles inspired Dewey long after he had abandoned the faith of his youth. For him, these principles were manifest as conflicting desires, for autonomy *and* communion, essentially—a conflict experienced as an "inward laceration" for a young, serious Vermont boy who, in his own words, had "an intense emotional craving" for their resolution (*Later Works* 5:153). While an undergraduate student in a physiology course at the University of Vermont, Dewey read T. H. Huxley's *Elements of Physiology* and was struck with the conceptual power of "organism" as a governing metaphor for life as an "interdependence and interrelated unity" among parts (*Later Works* 5:147). Indeed, in an early paper on the ethics of democracy, he wrote that citizens should not be "isolated non-social atoms" but part of a "common will," possessed "of unity of purpose and interest" (*Early Works* 1:231–32). So democracy becomes inherently "an ethical conception" because it holds as its "highest ethical idea" the active growth of each individual, wherein lies "an infinite and universal possibility" (*Early Works* 1:240, 244, 246). Eventually he would abandon this Christo-Hegelian language, but the kernel remained.

As "an account of human action," ethics, for Dewey, meant "practice and action, conduct viewed not partially, but in connection with the end which it realizes" (*Early Works* 3:241, 242). If the "end of action" is "the developed or satisfied self," then the end of social life is to create the conditions under which individuals may grow through interaction with others (300). Early in his thinking on ethics, he used the inelegant term "function" to describe the "two sides of individuality": the relation between "power of doing, on one side, and something to be done on the other" (303). Individuals exercise their "function" in response to the needs of their surroundings, and their surroundings should be transformed, as a "moral duty," to suit what becomes apparent as shared needs of individuals (313). A moral life, then, consists of constitutive adjustments that align the will of individuals with "the ends and demands of the social situations" in which individuals find themselves (*Middle Works* 5:199). The "satisfaction of the entire moral order" is contingent on the power of each person to find personal purpose in action among and with others (*Early Works* 3:321). Consequently individuals have a moral obligation to "*identify* our happiness with the happiness of others, to find our good in their good, not just to seek their happiness as, upon the whole, the most effective way of securing our own" (*Middle Works* 5:268, italics in original). At some point during his tenure as chair of philosophy at the University of Michigan, Dewey came to believe—perhaps with the help of his wife Alice's liberalizing social consciousness—that democracy, rather than the church, was the best system for enabling people to enact for themselves this account of the full and fulfilled human who, through interaction, develops trained (that is, learned, habituated) capacities for engaging in democratic practice.

One can see easily how this ethics provided the groundwork for Dewey's particularly American blend of liberalism and socialist democracy (see Westbrook 430); less readily evident, however, is its connection to rhetoric. But it should be clear that the adaptations, transformations, and social adjustments that make this kind of individual growth possible can happen only through rhetorical exchange—its symbol-making, its reason-giving, its back-and-forthness (Dewey called it "social give and take" [*Later Writings* 1:135]). Additionally we readily recognize rhetoric as the practice by which societies come to collective judgments, or what Dewey called the "social intelligence" we use to help us make changes necessary to remove roadblocks to growth (*Later Works* 11:39). Christopher Lyle Johnstone connects social intelligence to the Aristotelian concept of *phronesis,* or the "practical judgments" that enable us to predict or anticipate consequences "based upon insight into the tendencies of actions to bring about certain results" (Johnstone 188). Intelligent choices are "guided by open-minded and impartial inquiry and deliberation," the conclusions of which are regarded as "tentative, flexible, and capable of modification" (191). Johnstone concludes that "if a contemporary art of rhetoric is to contribute to the quest for wisdom, theorists must formulate artistic principles that will aid in the generation of discourse capable of fostering the growth of moral selves. These principles derive from an understanding of how communication in its pragmatic functions contributes to the growth of persons, and in particular to the development of those features of selfhood that constitute practical intelligence" (193). "Rhetoric" is, then, "the primary agency of moral growth" (193). We will have more to say about this conclusion when we examine communication as an expression of Dewey's ethics of democratic practice.

In *Democracy and Rhetoric: John Dewey on the Arts of Becoming,* Nathan Crick gives us a full account of Dewey's "ontology of becoming"—or, in other words, an ethics of rhetoric bound up in the historical, *kairotic* contingencies of situations that ultimately lead to new selves with broader capacities (77). Like Robert Danisch, Crick aligns Dewey with the Sophists in that he saw public life as an intellectual play, of sorts—a play of contingencies, discontinuities, challenges, crises, and transformations, all situated in specific historical moments that require creative practice. Rhetorical acts direct "experience within problematic situations" for which "long-term happiness" is contingent on an individual's ability to say what is most powerful, most fitting for the occasion, or at least to learn how to do so (22). Rhetoric has "progressive value," writes Crick, when it can "transform experience such that one emerges as a new self in a new world" (25, 33). Rhetoric is what keeps the organism active and responsive to the needs of its constituent parts. For Dewey, the moral life is a continually reconstructed life, fueled and formed by our ability to act creatively in "the new and serious situations which call out new vigor and lift [our lives] to higher levels" (Dewey, *Middle Works* 5:540).

Those "higher levels" are reached only in *democratic* interactions with others. As Gregory Fernando Pappas explains in his *John Dewey's Ethics,* it is in those interactions, rather than a contemplative process of "working downward from rules to situations," that Dewey locates the practice of a moral life (7–8). So Dewey's ethics prescribes an interpersonal enactment of, in Pappas's terms, the "underlying moral commitments and visions and fortifications of the soul that empower and inspire a democratic way of living in the world" (8–9). He describes Dewey's conception of individual moral development as a process of "democratization" that must, for every person, "grow from within" (10). That kind of growth occurs only in the context of what amount to rhetorical interactions—with the term "rhetorical" broadly defined to encompass a spectrum of communicative encounters that work toward the end of enabling common understanding and cooperation. This is how rhetoric sustains democratic culture.

In Dewey's own moralized words, as articulated in his *Ethics,* anything short of other-directed democratic practice is in fact immoral: "If the vice of the criminal, and of the coarsely selfish man is to disturb the aims and the good of others; if the vice of the ordinary egoist, and of every man, upon his egoistic side, is to neglect the interests of others; the vice of the social leader, of the reformer, of the philanthropist and the specialist in every worthy cause of science, or art, or politics, is to seek ends which promote the social welfare in ways which fail to engage the active interest and cooperation of others" (*Middle Works* 5:276). At the foundation of Dewey's ethics, then, is the principle that any "pursuit of the 'common' end" must involve intimately "the freely cooperative activities of others." Though in practice it "seems slow; it seems to postpone accomplishment indefinitely," the reality is that "this cooperation must be the root principle of the morals of democracy" (276). Much earlier in *Ethics*—a textbook, rather than a theoretical treatise, that he coauthored with James H. Tufts—Dewey defines that key term: "Cooperation implies a common end. It means that each is interested in the success of all. This common end forms then a controlling rule of action, and the mutual interest means sympathy" (46). Later in the work he returns to the concept of cooperation as a dialectical counterpoise to sociological applications of evolution (that is, the market use of the phrase "survival of the fittest"), writing that finally, "cooperation and sympathy prove stronger forces for progress than ruthless competition" (477). Ruthless competition can take many material forms, but cooperation and sympathy emerge from communicative interactions among people who must treat each other more or less as equals, willing at the very least to settle disagreements symbolically through discourse. Without such ethical interactions, the democratic practice of rhetoric cannot achieve the public goods that make for a good life for all.

EDUCATION AND DEMOCRATIC PRACTICE

Dewey's assumptions about education follow from this essentially democratic conception of ethical action. For him, education should provide for each individual, in the words of Robert Westbrook, "whatever is necessary to enable him to put his powers thoroughly at the service of society" (93). This involves instruction that supports individual development toward the end of meaningful participation with others in all layers of social life. Essentially schooling should reflect and organize "the fundamental principles of community life" (Dewey, *Early Writings* 5:63). Education should foster "habits of social imagination" in its students, and Dewey suggested what he called a "moral trinity of the school" that reflected the desired outcomes of education at every level: 1) *social intelligence,* meaning "the power of observing and comprehending social situations"; 2) *social power,* or "trained capacities of control"; which ultimately lead to 3) *social interest,* or the desire to engage with others in the cooperative social enterprise (75). Dewey wanted teachers to develop an active, pragmatic social consciousness in their students that would move them from awareness of the social situation in which they found themselves to their own self-motivated practice as agents endowed with new capacities to respond to those situations. As he said elsewhere, adapting human powers to the needs of social situations was "the supreme art" of instruction (94). Again, while Dewey does not use the term to discuss this adaptive art, we recognize that what we call "rhetoric" is central to that enterprise.

However, this does not mean that Dewey considered schooling as primarily a preparation for citizenship in the sense of knowing something about the Old Yellow Documents (for example, the Constitution) and the voting process (see *Later Works* 9:164). Rather he argued that schools' allegiance was to "society," democratically conceived as a network of individuals living and working together with the potential for political activity as one of many cooperative social practices in which they find themselves together engaged (Jackson and Miller 104). Schooling would invite students into the "fullness of sharing in the intellectual and spiritual resources of the community" by which they would come to understand the culture behind what we would call their various rhetorical situations (Dewey, *Middle Works* 2:93). Writing in an era of dizzying industrial expansion and immigration, Dewey placed schooling, as the educational historian Lawrence Cremin writes, at "the center of the struggle for a better life" as "an adjunct to politics" (119, 88). By the time he wrote *Democracy and Education* in 1916, this vision had made Dewey the leading voice of progressive education in America.

It was a vision that had, and continues to have, its critics: in Sidney Hook's phrase, Dewey's conception of education for some is "social, all too social" (in Dewey, *Middle Works* 9:xxi). Indeed sometimes he seems to use the word "social" as often as grammatical articles, leaving his readers feeling an Ayn Randian kind of social claustrophobia. One early reviewer of *Democracy and Education* argued quite precisely in the *Nation* that in Dewey's world "there is no room for any individual who wishes to lead his own life in the privacy of reflective self-consciousness" (in Cremin 126). It is true that the vestiges of Hegel remaining in Dewey led him to adopt the attitude that "the individual" qua individual outside society "was an abstraction" (Hook in Dewey, *Middle Works* 9:xxi). But this "too social" stance on education sprang from his reasonable conviction that learning to think *and* to act is indeed a social affair, one enacted in the context of schooling as a collaboration among peers with a more experienced mentor. If the educational project of schools is conceived as providing ongoing individuals with opportunities for their "continual reconstruction of experience," schooling should prompt students to analyze situations, make assumptions, and then experiment with some kind of consequent action—such as making an argument to others (Dewey, *Middle Works* 9:86). In democratic culture individual educational progress is not an end in itself but a means of rendering individuals contributors to the development of the larger societies to which they belong.

Students of rhetoric have long drawn on Dewey for support for teaching young people how to think, write, and speak effectively in the social situations in which they find themselves. Early in the twentieth century teachers of writing published articles in the *English Journal* using Deweyan language to argue that writing courses should teach writing in the context of democratic living (Gallagher 20). In the first half of that century, as David Russell has explained, this sort of "language instruction in general education became a rallying point for reformers searching for a common denominator to weave together the disparate threads of an increasingly complex polity" (Russell 136). Dewey's work was read in ways that offered teachers a "sound alternative" to the positivism of administrative progressives and the elitism of partisans for liberal culture (Russell 199). Though these Deweyan progressives did not prevail in the curricular debates, they did manage to articulate a vision of higher education that set "improved communication" at the center of a mission to "heal the divisions in industrial democracy" (Russell 200). Likewise speech and debate teachers early in the century leaned on Dewey to help them construct a political vision for teaching critical thinking and speaking. As William Keith notes, Dewey's apotheosis as public intellectual coincided with, and contributed to, advances in teaching systematic methods of discussion as a means of collaborative inquiry for civic ends.

Given all this, it is easy for us to locate Dewey's work at the center of an education that sees constructive rhetorical interaction, with both assertion and criticism as essentially cooperative acts, as the foundation for training people in the capacities of democratic practice. Just as Dewey rarely used the term "rhetoric" in his various discussions of education that we find fundamentally rhetorical, educators in rhetoric discuss education in light of what Stephen Fishman has called a "tacit tradition" that is fundamentally Deweyan (Fishman 315). Students imitate the back-and-forthness of public life when they write or speak in ways that assert or respond, when they do the work of criticism. As an obliterator of unnecessary dualisms, Dewey helps rhetoric teachers move beyond the impasses between expressivism and constructivism (Crick, "Composition as Experience"), agency and subjectivity (Jones), individual and society, knowledge and playful indeterminacy (Flower, Long, and Higgins), production and criticism (Fishman and McCarthy), public and professional knowledge, even speech and writing. This last dualism has been particularly damaging to rhetoric teaching at the undergraduate level, since the conventional university curriculum tends to separate instruction in writing and instruction in speaking. Dewey's rendering of a democratic education breaks down those disciplinary differences and, indeed, denies disciplinarity itself as he proposes an education that enables individuals to advance their capacities to contribute the essentially cooperative and collaborative project of "individuality operating in the common interest" that is his structural concept of democracy (Westbrook 93).

In the late spring of 1901 Dewey traveled to the enclave of the Mormons, fast against the west face of the Rocky Mountains in a state that had been a state for a mere five years, to give a series of lectures on education at a new normal school, the Brigham Young Academy, in Provo, Utah. The tenth and last of those lectures was titled "Some Elements of Character." Here Dewey explained that "the kind of character that we wish formed by education [is] something more than moral passability, or even more than freedom from evil tendencies" (*Later Works* 17:336). Rather the kind of character he had in mind is "a complicated thing" that involves, finally and fundamentally, a capacity to act in cooperation with others in effective and influential ways (337). Democratic culture is made from people of such character. Dewey concluded that lecture, and the series, with this:

> The three great factors in the formation of character are first good judgment, or the sense of the values of things about us; second the executive disposition, or tendency not to stop with intentions, but to be positive, self-assertive, and have a reasonable amount of aggressiveness in one's make-up. I think it was [Andrew] Jackson who said he had only contempt for the man who could not get angry. We do not want to cultivate the habit of getting angry; but there is a certain kind of assertiveness, of positive aggressiveness, in hanging to an idea and not being contented until we have made the effort to put it into execution which is necessary to character; and the third factor is that of delicate susceptibility of feelings which shall give poise to this executive tendency which in itself is likely to be a little hard and inconsiderate. (347)

What better description of the enactment of rhetoric—of what is required of the discourse of people who, sharing the status of political equals, can and must work together to determine the direction of their common life?

A RHETORICAL AESTHETICS

In this same lecture on schooling a democratic character, Dewey described the "training of the feelings [as] one of the most important parts of the training of character," noting that "feelings are the tune of our experiences" and that "seeing that the child has the proper kind of experience, and then letting him manage his feelings as he naturally will" is an essential element of a democratic education (*Later Works* 17:346). Dewey closed this series of lectures by exhorting his audience of apprentice teachers to "see to it," with him, "that our schools really become homes for the training and building up of men and women who are both noble and beautiful in the make-up of their own personalities" (347). Individuals enact that nobility and beauty aesthetically, in Dewey's expansive sense of that term. Art is often seen as something transcendent, separated from experience and entombed in New York museums or appreciated mostly by a cultural elite. Dewey's approach to aesthetic theory is to see art as a result and reflection of normal experience and in fact to see daily living, as Michel de Certeau has also imagined, as artful practice.

In *Art as Experience,* Dewey describes living as an ongoing project of composition. Simply stated, conscious life is constituted of experience, but that experience must be *made* meaningful. Dewey locates "experience" in "the interaction of the live creature and environing conditions," an interaction that, as it generates "conditions of resistance and conflict," is given shape by "emotions and ideas so that conscious intent emerges" (*Later Works* 10:42). We experience many things that are neither memorable nor meaningful. But when thoughts and feelings combine to give what we experience both form and meaning—a beginning, an end, and a significance—we recognize ourselves as living. Dewey's project in *Art as Experience* is to redefine the aesthetic, and indeed art itself, as the method by which individuals of democratic character—the creators of democratic culture—live their lives. Here is how Dewey describes this art of living: "[A]rt, in its form, unites the very same relation of doing and undergoing, outgoing and incoming energy, that makes an experience to be an experience. Because of elimination of all that does not contribute to mutual organization of the factors of both action and reception into one another, and because of selection of just the aspects and traits that contribute to their interpenetration of each other, the product is a work of aesthetic art" (54). Fundamentally important to that process is the attitude—indeed the identity—that an artist must assume: "The artist embodies in himself the attitude of the perceiver while he works" (55). In other words, artful living is other-directed, from the first moments of cognitive invention to the act itself.

Dewey did not, of course, have what we call "rhetoric" in mind when he wrote this. Nevertheless this transactional model of experience seems to us like the essential rhetorical act: to make one's experience accessible and meaningful to/for someone else. For Dewey, this transaction is the essential aesthetic act as well. It is an act of rendering an inchoate flow of events understandable, meaningful, and thus usable. "That which distinguishes an experience as esthetic," he writes, "is conversion of resistance and tensions, of excitations that in themselves are temptations to diversion, into a movement toward an inclusive and fulfilling close" (*Later Works* 10:62). This conversion, as every storyteller and orator and arguer readily knows, is what is required to communicate in ways that wield the powers of affect, of persuasion, of demonstration. Uniquely, Dewey concludes that aesthetic experience is constitutive of democratic practice: "Works of art that are not remote from common life, that are widely enjoyed in a community, are signs of a unified collective life. But they are also marvelous aids in the creation of such a life. The remaking of the material of experience in the act of expression is not an isolated event confined to the artist and to a person here and there who happens to enjoy the work. In the degree in which art exercises its office, it is also a remaking of the experience of the community in the direction of greater order and unity" (87).

That last point—remaking the experience of the community in the direction of greater order and unity—describes concisely the primary project of a democratic culture, even if a phrase such as "greater order and unity" perhaps provokes more questions than it answers. The aesthetic-democratic project he imagines progresses through the communicative actions of individuals, actions that are at once aesthetic in their form and rhetorical in their function. Dewey's aesthetics renders art and rhetoric the communicative warp and weft of democratic life. We make sense of our aesthetic experience through communication. Ultimately art is "expressive" in a far more meaningful way than simply "spewing forth" a narcissistic "self-expression" comprehensive (or enjoyable) to no one but the artist (*Later Works* 10:68). Rather for Dewey an expression "constitutes" an experience for those it addresses just as much as it does for the artist (91). Art is transactional. It does not simply state a concept; it enables an encounter with concept, a habitation of it (110). His vision of democratic culture involves the sharing of experiences, of ideas *and* feelings, of abstract principles *and* intensely social practices. "Because objects of art are expressive, they communicate," he writes. The meaning-making work they do "lives only in communication when it operates in the experience of others." This description of the communicative capacity of art is also an instructive description of the power of rhetoric. "In the end," Dewey declares, "works of art are the only media of complete and unhindered communication between man and man that can occur in a world full of gulfs and walls that limit community of experience" (110). Given all this, it seems that as we engage in the rhetorical and aesthetic work of carefully composing individual experience to render it accessible to others—in a manner that surprises or delights or provokes or inspires—we engage in the kind of ethical practice that democratic culture requires.

A profound and historical tension can be conceived between rhetoric and aesthetics. We have two books from Aristotle presenting separate subjects: a rhetoric and a poetics. It is also common to trace this tension back to the Enlightenment and the advance of logic and the new science, when it seemed to some that using eloquence or any kind of art to stir the passions was either dangerous, deceptive, or beside the point. Rhetoric has also been separated from aesthetics by the assumption that rhetoric's principle manifestation is in deliberative rather than poetic discourse. Yet in *Rhetoric and Poetics in Antiquity,* Jeffrey Walker shows how in the classical world poetic discourse was just as "rhetorical" (deliberative, argumentative) as an assembly speech because it made arguments—however implied—about the values, beliefs, and traditions that served as a cultural foundation for political life. Combining with Kenneth Burke's scholarship (that is, in *Counter-Statement* and other works), this argument expands the realm of the rhetorical to take into consideration artifacts traditionally ignored by rhetoricians such as novels, paintings, architecture, or films that represent the artifacts of rhetorical aesthetics.

Dewey delivered *Art as Experience* as a series of lectures at Harvard University in 1931 at a time when his creative energy was focused on discovering "the religious quality of experience" (Rockefeller 494). Though Dewey had long abandoned the reformed pieties of his youth, he saw in spirituality an ecology of feeling, an emotional vitality, that he believed was essential for a good life—a good social life, that is. As supernatural experience creates sacred space and renews life in those whom we say have been born again, so art suffuses life with "the wonder of the new," as Dewey writes in *Experience and Nature,* "making the world a different place in which to live" (*Later Works* 1:270, 272). "Any activity" that leads to "further consummatory experiences" or "refresh[es] and enlarge[s] the spirit" should be considered art (274). With all this emphasis on experience, Dewey moves aesthetics into the realm of rhetoric by situating artful communication properly in its "experiential conditions," in Westbrook's words, rather than leaving it at the level of "product" (Westbrook 390).

The phrase "experiential conditions" resonates with rhetoricians who view communication not only as addressed but *situated.* In *Democracy and Rhetoric,* Nathan Crick, fixing Dewey's sentiments within the "Emersonian tradition of eloquence" (133), argues that though aesthetics and rhetoric share a common telos for consummatory experience, rhetoric goes further by seeking in the audience "a common identification that extends beyond the immediate qualitative moment and results in action" (Crick 141). Dewey wants to see democratic culture cultivated by aesthetic acts that not only please but also commit audiences and publics to new ways of living through ever-expanding capacities for communicating effectively. Crick writes that for Dewey, "rhetoric embodies the spirit of movement" that leads us into a contingent future "with a new understanding and a shared hope" (186). This hope, we suggest, is an orienting attitude and capacity for democratic practice through artful communication.

COMMUNICATION

Rhetoric and aesthetics come together for Dewey in the consummatory experience of communication itself. As Scott Stroud points out, Dewey shows how even ordinary communication becomes artful when "subjective orientation" is taken into account (Stroud 165). What Stroud means is that communication goes beyond the mere pragmatic when participants orient themselves toward an experience and "*attend* to a situation" by focusing on "what they *value* in that situation" (165). Language for Dewey is not only "the essence of consciousness" but also the "instrumental and consummatory" tool of all meaningful relationships (Dewey, *Later Works* 1:147, 144). Communication gets things done in the world; it is also an end in itself, "immediately valuable," as Stroud puts it, for instantiating "harmony and coordination with others" (Stroud 168). In *Experience and Nature,* which Sidney Hook called Dewey's "most suggestive and most difficult" work (in Dewey, *Later Works* 1:vii), Dewey argues that the coordinated transaction of discourse leads to "imaginative identification," the "sharing and merging" of individuals, and finally "concerted consensus of action" (*Later Works* 1:145). Obviously it is central to democratic culture, and it can be improved through criticism and teaching.

For Dewey, ethical action takes the form of interpersonal *interaction* of a certain sort: it engages others—in capacity if not in achievement—as equals; it proceeds upon an educated understanding of principled and practical shared knowledge and need; and it does so by putting individual "powers," in Robert Westbrook's terms, "thoroughly at the service of society" (93) as when what an individual can offer to others is made accessible to them in the form a shareable aesthetic experience. These are the rhetorical elements of democratic communication as John Dewey envisioned them.

As a pragmatist, Dewey invites us to work to improve communication—surely a necessary "trained capacity of control"—in a technically advanced democratic state whose problems require the wisdom that comes from effective discourse. Democracy endures by choices, and choices are wise or intelligent when they are "guided by open-minded and impartial inquiry and deliberation" (Johnstone 191). As a foundational principle of democratic culture, according to Woodruff, "the wisdom of ordinary people" guides the ship of state between the aristocratic overreach of expert opinion and the rash actions of the mob (Woodruff 154). But democratic life was simpler for Demosthenes than for the modern citizen. In 1927 Walter Lippmann, Dewey's colleague at the *New Republic,* wrote *The Phantom Public,* a sequel to his earlier work *Public Opinion* and an eloquent critique of the dubious virtue of citizen wisdom in a technocratic age. Instead of "making good citizens," the citizen wisdom model of democracy creates a "mass of amateur executives," stumbling about the public talking "such nonsense about politics" because they lack the requisite knowledge to deal with modern problems (Lippmann 148, 150).

In his response to Lippmann, written in *The Public and Its Problems,* Dewey acknowledged democracy's flaws (for example, large and heterogeneous republic, indifference of its citizens, power of special interest, polarizing effect of parties, countless diversions, and the complexities of technology). His democratic faith rests in our power to refine "the tools of communication" in order to create what he calls, vaguely, the "great community" (*Later Works* 2:323–24). The great community will be achieved when "an organized, articulate Public comes into being" through "the highest and most difficult kind of inquiry and a subtle, delicate, vivid and responsive art of communication" (350). In one of the most quoted parts of *The Public and Its Problems,* Dewey writes that "the essential need" for improving the "methods and conditions of debate, discussion and persuasion" is "*the* problem of the public" (365). Effective deliberation creates a "flow of social intelligence" through the "direct give and take" of citizens—or in Dewey's more nostalgic mood, *neighbors*—willing to engage each other in a sustained swap of symbols (371).

This thesis has long been appealing to students of rhetoric engaged in the task of articulating the relationship between rhetoric and democratic culture. In 1968, in the journal *Western Speech,* Don Burks showed how Dewey's theory of communication leads us to see social consciousness and intelligence as products of effective discourse rather than "a self-subsistent reality" (122). Likewise Johnstone in 1983 wrote what we believe to be the first comprehensive treatment of Dewey's theory of communication as a synthesis of ethics, practical wisdom, and eloquence. It could be said further that Dewey's essays, especially *The Public and Its Problems,* are, or at least should be considered, the founding documents for what has been called public sphere theory or publics theory in rhetorical studies (see, for starters, Goodnight; Asen and Brouwer; Stob).

The "public sphere" entry on Wikipedia puts the German critical theorist Jürgen Habermas at the center of public sphere theory, but Dewey predates him and, as other rhetoricians have noted, adds useful correctives to Habermas's overemphasis on pseudo-Enlightenment rationality functioning in a single, monolithic bourgeois public sphere. Rather, as Gerard Hauser notes in *Vernacular Voices,* Dewey argues that reasonableness is revealed and refined in the very act of communication. A rhetorical model of publics is "discourse based" and "replaces the norm of critical rationality with the rhetorical norm of *reasonableness*" settled through local dialogue (Hauser 61). Robert Asen, building on a trend begun by Nancy Fraser and Hauser, shows how Dewey calls for enhancing the coordination of the "multiple publics and permeable borders" of dynamic democratic practice (Asen 179). Paul Stob provides a "postmortem dialogue" between Kenneth Burke and Dewey to lead us back to language and "the possibilities of language" as the central concern for "problem-solving and community-building" (Stob 228–29). In a complicated world, language will serve this problem-solving role best when science (or technology) and communication can be reconciled and together put in the service of public life. In *Pragmatism, Democracy, and the Necessity of Rhetoric,* Robert Danisch makes this case strongly by showing how Dewey's philosophy of communication essentially invents "contemporary American rhetorics" in its search for a refined art of communication in a postindustrial democratic culture (Danisch 63).

Dewey's conception of communication, finally, is founded upon his ethics, supplied with materials by his concept of democratic education, and enacted in exchanges of aesthetically expressed experiences that interlocutors can share. This democratic kind of communication begins with individuals—individuals whose clear sense of self is at once distinct and generous, confident and teachable, assertive and attentive. Those individuals proceed to communicate as a project that encompasses both teaching and learning, helping and being helped, self-realization and community building—a project in which each composes what Dewey calls "an integrated individuality" (*Later Works* 5:122). He concluded his *New Republic* series on *Individualism, Old and New* in 1930—as the economy of the United States ground to a halt and the collective life of almost all Americans sank—with this extended metaphor: "To gain an integrated individuality, each of us needs to cultivate his own garden. But there is no fence about this garden: it is no sharply marked off enclosure. Our garden is the world, in the angle at which it touches our own manner of being" (122–23). That manner of being must be enacted, inherently, in our communication.

As teachers, critics, historians, and scholars of rhetoric, we are delighted to present this collaboration in order to confirm John Dewey's place as a productive source of our enduring traditions, our *paideia,* constituted in democratic practice, embedded in culture, and informed by his "democratic faith"—an obviously and unashamedly idealistic faith—that we can create a "freer and more humane experience in which all share and to which all contribute" (*Later Works* 14:230). Our ability to do so is contingent on how well we use rhetoric to enhance our collective "power of social agency" through research, criticism, and teaching (*Early Works* 5:78). Perhaps there is no better way to describe what rhetoric, as *techne* and *paideia,* has to offer than the prospect of *trained capacities,* or as Dewey wrote in 1895, the "volitional command of one's own powers" as a "social agent" (*Early Works* 5:225). In the spirit of the great progressive educator, we learn by doing the things our capacities fit us for as scholars, critics, and teachers.

At its best, rhetorical criticism *instructs* those who read it. Our "critical sense and methods of discriminating judgment" must keep pace with the immense outchurn of rhetorical messages, recently accelerated by the self-publishing capabilities of the Web in a global message ecology (*Later Works* 2:337). As "investigators and artists" with a particularly useful "expertise," rhetoricians have a unique role to play in democracy if they choose to so orient their work (*Later Works* 2:365). In light of this calling, it is instructive to perform a little harmless vandalism to one of Dewey's most powerful statements, substituting "rhetoric" for his term "philosophy":

Rhetoric becomes meaningful "when it ceases to be a device for dealing with the problems of [rhetoricians] and becomes a method, cultivated by [rhetoricians], for dealing with the problems of [everyone]" (*Middle Works* 10:46). Rhetoricians can develop a trained capacity to see their historical and critical work as a labor of inquiry meant to improve democratic culture. We must imagine ourselves as public intellectuals and cultural workers more than we do now, and we should work to make our scholarship appealing to broader audiences.

Finally, in the spirit of Dewey's faith in the "educative" power of democratic practice (*Later Works* 14:229), we must embrace our roles as teachers of trained capacities such as invention, argument, style, storytelling, collaboration, figurative reasoning, debate, multimodality, arrangement, and contingent thinking. While scholars and teachers of rhetoric reproduce themselves through graduate programs in English and communication studies, we often neglect cultivating sleeper cells of rhetors in business, government, and the sciences through rigorous undergraduate teaching across the curriculum. Arguably one of the most important courses a student takes in college is either a speech or a writing class, and as James Aune has argued, these courses are our "base" of operations for teaching young people how to make and support claims (in Zarefsky 32). Dewey contended that students develop effective habits of action as they learn to be *plastic*—to "modify actions on the basis of the results of prior experiences" (*Middle Works* 9:49). The more experiences we give students to inhabit and respond to rhetorical situations, the better they will develop the trained capacities necessary for social power. We must tend to the undergraduate curriculum with rigor and Deweyan vision.

Democratic culture is sloppy. Dewey knew that. The anecdote we opened this introduction with seems to illustrate the challenges we face in our public interactions. In district meetings, in newspapers and Web sites, and on television, a handful of angry parents in a relatively remote corner of this republic associated that simple school district slogan about enculturating students in democracy to Marx, Lenin, Stalin, Hitler, and to John Dewey. These kinds of arguments challenge us as we exercise democratic faith in the deliberative process of the polis. Yet since democratic culture is constituted through rhetorical practice, it is not too far-fetched to suggest that we cannot only interpret the world rhetorically but also make it better through rhetoric.

THIS COLLECTION REPRESENTS an attempt to articulate how Dewey helps us understand how democratic culture is constituted through rhetorical practice in the context of the United States. We have divided the book into three parts: Dewey and Democratic Practice, Dewey and His Interlocutors, and Dewey as Teacher of Rhetoric. In Part I the contributors explain how Dewey's work on science, philosophy, and religion provide the architectonic assumptions of democratic practice. William Keith and Robert Danisch combine Dewey's notions of deliberation with his broad-based understanding of science as the ordinary process of human inquiry.

They argue that by uniting science and deliberation, Dewey provides a "sociology of rhetoric" that "amounts to a set of recommendations for developing a democracy in which specific forms of communication guide decision and judgment." Scott Stroud provides "a *reconstructive* account of pragmatist rhetoric" by showing us how Kenneth Burke's scholarship on orientation complements Dewey's implied rhetorical framework, all in the service of articulating what pragmatism offers rhetorical studies. Though early in his professional life Dewey forsook the religious tradition he was raised in, Paul Stob argues that Dewey constructed his own unique brand of religious rhetoric that somehow separated religious symbols from their more "problematic tendencies" in order to integrate them "into the discursive fabric of a pluralistic, democratic, cooperative culture."

Part II puts Dewey into dialogue—both analogically and literally—with five interlocutors on issues related to democratic culture. Jeremy Engels sees Thomas Jefferson—rather than Ralph Waldo Emerson, as Cornel West suggests—as the primary interlocutor for Dewey's rhetoric of democratic culture. Dewey turned to the historical Jefferson to articulate the moral dimensions of controversy during public crisis. In similar fashion, Dewey's dialogues with his contemporary Jane Addams, the Chicago reformer, led him to develop a more nuanced, pragmatic approach to public deliberation, as Louise Knight explains. Knight and Engels both show us how war challenges democratic culture and rhetorical practice, and Dewey was prominent in debates on the subject during both world wars of the twentieth century. Keith Gilyard presents W. E. B. Du Bois as one of Dewey's interlocutors who worked, with Dewey, to establish a rhetoric of education capacious enough to include the interests of underprivileged social groups such as African Americans. Dewey and Du Bois worked closely together as progressives engaged in social justice for all races, but Dewey did not fully grasp, as Du Bois did, that the educational system he so lauded had been "racially constructed."

Two other figures conclude the section on Dewey's interlocutors: Walter Lippmann and James Baldwin. As explained above, Dewey worked with Lippmann at the *New Republic* in the post–World War I heyday of American realism when social psychologists were publishing research studies on the mass stupidity of democracy's agents (see Westbrook 280–86). As Jean Goodwin explains, Walter Lippmann, unjustly constructed as an enemy of democracy, actually complemented Dewey's understanding of deliberation with a realist's perspective that emphasized debate over deliberation, casting citizens as competent outsiders who sit in judgment of *whom* to trust more than *what* to trust. Walton Muyumba proposes an essential connection between James Baldwin's radical cultural criticism and Dewey's claim that the enterprise of democracy is always essentially radical. Cultural critics such as Baldwin work rhetorically to form "the public spheres in which radical democracy is engineered."

In Part III the contributors explore various aspects of John Dewey's influence on teaching rhetoric in our day. Each essay argues that Dewey provides useful propositions for teaching students how to develop skills as arguers and inquirers. By connecting Dewey's teaching philosophy to a sophistical tradition in language arts, Nathan Crick shows how Dewey lays groundwork for experimental pedagogy in the teaching of rhetoric. Crick argues that Deweyan experimentalist pedagogy complements, even corrects, the approach taken by critical pedagogues who teach rhetoric in the tradition of the Sophists without fully exploring the *laboratory* aspect of invention in rhetoric. Brian Jackson, Meridith Reed, and Jeff Swift use Dewey's concept of public inquiry to understand how Aristotle's distinction between artistic and inartistic proof is unproductive when trying to teach students how to write arguments supported by grounded evidence, especially in light of how blogs have changed the way sources are used in political argument. Donald Jones challenges the traditional taxonomies we use to teach argument to undergraduates, arguing for a more inductive approach that leads students through their own experiences to develop an understanding of the way arguments work. In his afterword Gerard Hauser describes how contemporary political forces challenge us to lean even more forcefully on Dewey's notion of experience as a rhetorical response to democracy's challenges.

WORKS CITED

Asen, Robert. "The Multiple Mr. Dewey." *Argumentation and Advocacy* 39 (Winter 2003): 174–88.

Asen, Robert, and Daniel C. Brouwer. *Counterpublics and the State.* New York: State University of New York Press, 2001.

Burke, Kenneth. *A Rhetoric of Motives.* Berkeley: University of California Press, 1969.

Burks, Don M. "John Dewey and Rhetorical Theory." *Western Speech* 32.2 (1968): 118–26.

Certeau, Michel de. *The Practice of Everyday Life.* Berkeley: University of California Press, 2002.

Cremin, Lawrence A. *The Transformation of the School.* New York: Vintage, 1961.

Crick, Nathan. *Democracy and Rhetoric: John Dewey on the Arts of Becoming.* Columbia: University of South Carolina Press, 2010.

———. "John Dewey on Creative Expression and the Origins of 'Mind.'" *College Composition and Communication* 55.2 (2003): 254–75.

Dahl, Robert A. *On Democracy.* New Haven, Conn.: Yale University Press, 2000.

Danisch, Robert. *Pragmatism, Democracy, and the Necessity of Rhetoric.* Columbia: Uni—versity of South Carolina Press, 2007.

Dewey, John. *The Early Works, 1882–1892.* 5 vols. Ed. Jo Ann Boydston. Carbondale: Southern Illinois University Press, 1969–72.

———. *The Later Works, 1925–1953.* 17 vols. Ed. Jo Ann Boydston. Carbondale: Southern Illinois University Press, 1981–91.

———. *The Middle Works, 1899–1924.* 15 vols. Ed. Jo Ann Boydston. Carbondale: Southern Illinois University Press, 1976–83.

Fishman, Stephen M. "Explicating Our Tacit Tradition: John Dewey and Composition Studies." *College Composition and Communication* 44.3 (1993): 315–30.

Fishman, Stephen M., and Lucille McCarthy. *John Dewey and the Challenge of Classroom Practice.* New York: Teachers College, 1998.

Flower, Linda, Elenore Long, and Lorainne Higgins. *Learning to Rival.* New York: Routledge, 2000.

Fontana, Bendetto, Cary J. Nederman, and Gary Remer, eds. *Talking Democracy.* University Park: Pennsylvania State University Press, 2004.

Gallagher, Chris W. *Radical Departures.* Urbana, Ill.: National Council of Teachers of English, 2002.

Goodnight, Thomas G. "The Personal, Technical, and Public Spheres of Argument." *Journal of the American Forensic Association* 18.4 (1982): 214–27.

Hanson, Russell L. *The Democratic Imagination in America.* Princeton, N.J.: Princeton University Press, 1985.

Hauser, Gerard. *Vernacular Voices.* Columbia: University of South Carolina Press, 1999.

Hook, Sidney. *Out of Step.* New York: Carroll and Graf, 1988.

Jackson, Brian. "Cultivating Paideweyan Pedagogy: Rhetoric Education in English and Communication Studies." *Rhetoric Society Quarterly* 37.2 (2007): 181–201.

Jackson, Brian, and Thomas P. Miller. "The Progressive Education Movement: A Case Study in Coalition Politics." In *Active Voices: Composing a Rhetoric for Social Movements,* ed. Sharon McKenzie Stevens and Patricia M. Malesh, 93–113. New York: State University of New York Press, 2009.

Johnstone, Christopher Lyle. "Dewey, Ethics, and Rhetoric: Toward a Contemporary Conception of Practical Wisdom." *Philosophy & Rhetoric* 16.3 (1983): 185–207.

Jones, Donald C. "Beyond the Postmodern Impasse of Agency." *JAC* 16.2 (1996): 81–102.

Keith, William M. *Democracy as Discussion.* Lanham, Md.: Lexington, 2007.

Lippmann, Walter. *The Phantom Public.* New York: Macmillan, 1927.

MacIntyre, Alasdair. *After Virtue: A Study in Moral Theory.* London: Duckworth, 1987.

Miller, Tiffany Jones. "John Dewey and the Philosophical Refounding of America." *National Review Online,* accessed December 31, 2009; Web (accessed December 13, 2010) http://www.freerepublic.com/focus/f-news/2424305/posts

Pappas, Gregory Fernando. *John Dewey's Ethics: Democracy as Experience.* Bloomington: Indiana University Press, 2008.

Rockefeller, Steven C. *John Dewey: Religious Faith and Democratic Humanism.* New York: Columbia University Press, 1991.

Russell, David R. *Writing in the Academic Disciplines.* 2nd ed. Carbondale: Southern Illinois University Press, 2002.

Ryan, Alan. *John Dewey and the High Tide of American Liberalism.* New York: W. W. Norton, 1995.

Stob, Paul. "Kenneth Burke, John Dewey, and the Pursuit of the Public." *Philosophy & Rhetoric* 38.3 (2005): 226–45.

Stroud, Scott R. "John Dewey and the Question of Artful Communication." *Philosophy & Rhetoric* 41.2 (2008): 153–247.

Tilly, Charles. *Democracy.* New York: Cambridge University Press, 2007.

Tocqueville, Alexis de. *Democracy in America.* Vol. 2. New York: Vintage, 1990.

Warnock, Caleb. "Concerned Parents Decry 'Socialism' at Alpine District Meeting." *Daily Herald* [Utah County, UT], March 10, 2010; Web (accessed October 3, 2010).

Westbrook, Robert B. *John Dewey and American Democracy.* Ithaca, N.Y.: Cornell University Press, 1991.

Whitman, Walt. *Democratic Vistas: The Original Edition in Facsimile.* Ed. Ed Folsom. Iowa City: University of Iowa Press, 2010.

Woodruff, Paul. *First Democracy.* New York: Oxford University Press, 2005.

Zarefsky, David. "Institutional and Social Goals for Rhetoric." *Rhetoric Society Quarterly* 34.3 (2004): 27–38.

PART I

Dewey and Democratic Practice— Science, Pragmatism, Religion

Dewey on Science, Deliberation, and the Sociology of Rhetoric

William Keith and Robert Danisch

John Dewey's career-long exposition of and commitment to democratic culture still commands praise and admiration. Contemporary philosophers, social theorists, historians, and others committed to pragmatism still commend Dewey's faith in the democratic experience. Richard Rorty, Cornel West, and Robert Westbrook, to name just a few, all explain Dewey's towering importance in American intellectual history by way of his political activism and social theorizing about democracy. At the same time, however, Dewey's commitment to the importance of science seems to have become outdated. Rorty suggests that the main difference between first-generation pragmatism and contemporary pragmatism is that recent philosophers and social theorists have all read Thomas Kuhn and thus dismiss Dewey's apparently risible belief in positivism and scientific thinking (95). Thus Dewey's philosophy of science has been sundered from his larger theory of democratic culture. This, we argue, is a mistake. It is a mistake in terms of intellectual history and in terms of the usefulness of Deweyan social theory for contemporary democratic life.

Dewey's philosophy of democracy was participatory through and through. It required an involved community of inquirers capable of reflective thought regarding pressing problems and collective action aimed to improve difficult conditions. At the same time scientific thinking, for Dewey, was a refinement of the ordinary procedures for reflexive and practical problem solving by a community. There was no difference in kind between scientific thinking and ordinary popular problem solving. The difference was a matter of subject and formal procedure. This essay demonstrates the close affinity between Dewey's commitment to discussion as an engine of participatory democracy *and* his understanding of and faith in science as a central instrument in contemporary democratic culture. We argue that Dewey's belief in science is the other side of the same coin on which his belief in deliberation and discussion is inscribed. This represents a heretical interpretation of Dewey, given neopragmatism's present preoccupations.

Such a reading of Dewey is made possible by, and is alert to, issues within the rhetorical tradition. Our analysis of the relationship between Deweyan deliberation and philosophy of science, instead of seeing them as opposites, reveals the manner in which rhetorical communication shapes, improves, and constitutes democratic culture. By this we mean that within Dewey's outline of deliberative participation one finds a commitment to particular forms of rhetorical practice and particular social structures that make those forms of rhetorical practice possible. In addition within Dewey's philosophy of science one finds the rejection of traditional realist epistemologies and a rhetoric of science capable of outlining both how communicative acts are constitutive of scientific practices and the manner of incorporating scientific knowledge into public decision-making. Both of these considerations produce what we call a *sociology of rhetoric.* As such, we claim that the best way to understand Dewey's twin commitments to science and deliberation is in the light of his attempt to create a social democracy in which specific kinds of rhetorical practices become possible and useful. The search for a "social democracy" amounts to a search for the practical and intellectual conditions in which appropriate and timely communicative acts can guide public deliberation, and where public deliberation simultaneously considers both ends/values and means/technologies/knowledge.

Dewey does not offer a rhetorical pedagogy, a way of practicing rhetoric. Instead he offers a sociology of rhetoric—a systemic account of the theoretical and normative ways in which social structures, institutions, and forms of individual agency are both guided by and constituted by communicative practices. Rhetoric's traditional concern with specific interactions (as typified by a focus on speeches) is displaced by a structural account of what makes such interaction possible and meaningful. Dewey's sociology of rhetoric amounts to a set of recommendations for developing a democracy in which specific forms of communication guide decision and judgment. These forms are largely modeled on science. In other words, science is critically important in this sociology of rhetoric, and Dewey provides us with a way of understanding science as a form of rhetorical practice uniquely fit to American democratic culture. Only in the light of specific practical and intellectual conditions can scientific thinking be thought of as rhetorical practice that makes democracy possible. We aim to show, therefore, just how Dewey endorses a rhetorical way of life built on his twin commitments to science and deliberation. This provides the ground for a uniquely American democratic rhetoric, and Dewey is a key resource for articulating and endorsing such a rhetoric.

This essay first explains what a sociology of rhetoric is, why Dewey ought to be thought of as offering such a theoretical concept, and what the payoff of such an idea might be. Second, we explain the link between science and deliberation and show how the two preoccupations parallel and reinforce one another. This work is carried out in light of the rhetorical perspective outlined in the first part. Third, we explain the kind of rhetoric of science that can be gleaned from Dewey's work and show how it is different from other, more traditional versions of a rhetoric of science. Furthermore we argue that this rhetoric of science is a uniquely pragmatist contribution to democratic theory. Finally we argue that Dewey grounds a particularly American orientation to rhetorical practice, one that emphasizes and makes possible a specific set of practices different in kind from other orientations to rhetoric. The aim of this essay is to reconsider Dewey's preoccupation with science from the perspective of rhetorical theory. By such a move we hope to show how our own democratic society can still be enriched and improved by using the resources of pragmatism, but only if those resources are married to the rhetorical tradition.

A SOCIOLOGY OF RHETORIC

Among American liberal intellectuals, Dewey is perhaps the most important advocate of participatory democracy. We might loosely describe this as the belief that democracy calls upon men and women to build communities in which opportunities and resources are available to every person to realize their full potential *through* participation in political and social life. Dewey's belief in participation rested on a "faith in the capacity of human beings for intelligent judgment and action if proper conditions are furnished" (Dewey, *Later Works* 227). The stipulation of "proper conditions" is an essential feature, then, of participatory democracy, and Dewey spent considerable time concerned with these conditions, especially in *The Public and Its Problems.* His philosophy of education, in some way, could be read as an attempt to formulate such conditions in a formal school setting. In this essay we argue that one way to understand Dewey's search for the conditions within which participatory democracy is likely to flourish is to read him as explicating a "sociology of rhetoric." In many ways a sociology of rhetoric is deeply important to the development of a democratic culture and can reveal much about the constitutive features of particular democracies.

What, then, do we mean by a sociology of rhetoric? This is not Dewey's phrase, nor is it a phrase used by any other pragmatist. We are using it to highlight a feature of Dewey's work and to theorize the manner in which Dewey's work is useful for advancing both the rhetorical tradition and contemporary democratic theory. A sociology of rhetoric attempts to understand and explain how, on the one hand, social structures are products of specific communicative acts and how, on the other hand, those social structures affect human attitudes, actions, and beliefs by conditioning the kinds of communicative practices available to us as agents within larger groups. It is a way of exploring the role of communication in constructing, maintaining, and altering social organization, and a way of showing how social organization conditions the possibilities of human agency. This phrase is designed to synthesize several strands of Dewey's legacy. First, Chicago pragmatism was intimately related to critical work in the development of American sociology. Second, Dewey's often-cryptic comments on communication hint at how important Dewey thought communicative practices were to democratic and social life. Third, participatory democracy, for Dewey, often required deliberation, discussion, or some form of face-to-face interaction designed to solve pressing problems. These three strands of Dewey's legacy offer some insight into how he saw the relationship between structure and agency, a relationship that has, for an enduring period, been central to sociology. The phrase "sociology of rhetoric" is meant to highlight the ways in which such a relationship is managed by communication and to suggest that rhetorical practice gets conditioned in important ways by social structures. A "sociology of rhetoric" concerns the practical, intellectual, and social conditions within which communicative practices become possible.

Both Dewey's work and our argument are prescriptive and descriptive. Every democratic society presumes and instantiates a sociology of rhetoric. By that we mean that every democracy has a set of social structures that are maintained by specific communicative practices and that recommend the cultivation of specific rhetorical habits for the maintenance of that democratic society. We might, for example, describe a classical Athenian sociology of rhetoric, in which specific forms of speech acts were made possible and privileged by the intellectual, practical, and social conditions of that moment in time. Many historians of rhetoric and rhetorical theorists have labored to show how rhetoric was made possible at this unique moment in history and how rhetoric guided political deliberation. But classical Athenian rhetoric was particularly fit for that place and that moment, and not necessarily for ours or for Dewey's. The prescriptive argument is that if we alter the social structures of a democratic society, we alter the kinds of rhetorical practice available and acceptable in that society. Such acts of alteration require transformative rhetorical practices. If we wish to improve our democratic culture, we must assess the sociology of rhetoric that conditions and organizes communicative practices within that culture. Dewey had both of these tasks in mind within his consideration of "social democracy."

When Dewey arrived in Chicago to the unrest of the Pullman strike, he was alerted to the actual, practical machinations of democratic culture. This both sparked an ongoing social and political activism and drove his more speculative, philosophical projects. In other words, Dewey saw firsthand the conditions of the operative sociology of rhetoric in Chicago and then sought to articulate a different but still potentially achievable sociology of rhetoric that could improve decision-making and incorporate a greater number of citizens into the life-affirming participatory process. This is how one ought to read Dewey's proclamations about communication. On the one hand, they were descriptions of what he witnessed as central experiences within his democratic culture. On the other hand, they were prescriptions for how to improve the conditions for communication within American democracy with the hope that those improvements would ultimately have positive consequences for both individual citizens and the well-being of the state. Take, for example, his statements about communication in *Democracy and Education:*

"Men live in a community by virtue of the things which they have in common; and communication is the way in which they come to possess things in common . . . Communication is a process of sharing experience till it becomes common possession. It modifies the disposition of both the parties that partake in it" (4, 9). Here is a general description of the coordination of social action and the sharing of experience. But it also states, at the same time, an ideal.

The famous proclamations from *The Public and Its Problems* are similarly both descriptive and normative: "The essential need . . . is the improvement of the methods and conditions of debate, discussion, and persuasion. That is *the* problem of the public. We have asserted that this improvement depends essentially on freeing and perfecting the process of inquiry" (208). Thus *The Public and Its Problems* is an attempt to outline the practical and intellectual conditions for community-based inquiry, both descriptively and normatively, as a method of channeling communicative practices for the benefit of democratic society. The details of this particular sociology of rhetoric will be described in the next section. At its core, however, lie two methods of inquiry: inquiry that requires deliberation and discussion; and inquiry based on the methods of scientific thinking. These two prescriptions would improve American democratic culture, or so Dewey thought. It may be useful to consider what this sociology of rhetoric is not. It is not a commitment to the centrality of public address (as an Athenian sociology of rhetoric might be). It is not an agonistic model of rhetoric—it seeks the cooperation necessary for community-based inquiry, upon the model of scientific work. It is also not a mediated rhetoric of symbols, icons, or images—it seeks the face-to-face in an effort to leverage the knowledge of each participant in a deliberation. In other words, Dewey prescribes a unique sociology of rhetoric.

The Public and Its Problems centers on a vision of a "great community," a community whose success would rely on the "perfecting of the means and ways of communication of meanings so that genuinely shared interest in the consequences of interdependent activities may inform desire and effort and thereby direct action" (155). Accordingly, Deweyan pragmatism seeks methods of communication that would allow individuals in a democracy to participate in decision-making and realize the interconnectedness of the community to which they belong. Dewey, therefore, suggests a sociology of rhetoric that makes communion and cooperation possible and desirable. As we show in the next section, the details of such a sociology of rhetoric are related to Dewey's view of scientific work. In any case, democracy and community are tied together for Dewey by the belief that a specific version of communication as rhetoric is the primary means by which individuals become self-actualized and politics becomes a melioristic instrument of change: "The highest and most difficult kind of inquiry and a subtle, delicate, vivid, and responsive art of communication must take possession of the physical machinery of transmission and circulation and breathe life into it. . . . Democracy will come into its own, for democracy is the name for a life of free and enriching communion. . . . It [democracy] will have its consummation when free social inquiry is indissolubly wedded to the art of full and moving communication" (*Public and Its Problems* 184).

This is no doubt one of Dewey's most famous proclamations about communication. It is an endorsement and a prescription, as is all of *The Public and Its Problems*, of a sociology of rhetoric that conditions a specific form of communication (communal inquiry, discussion) and is brought into being by specific rhetorical acts (art, moving communication oriented to communion and cooperation).

Rhetorical practices do not happen in a vacuum but instead are made possible by a particular context. The challenge posed by Dewey is to account for what kinds of rhetorical practice exist within specific political cultures *and* what kinds we want to exist in our political culture. Where are we, and where should we go? Dewey's desire was to establish a sociology of rhetoric that made deliberation, discussion, communal inquiry, and cooperation possible, and he thought the possibility of it already existed, waiting to be actualized and universalized. Such a sociology of rhetoric would facilitate the growth of the individual citizens of the political culture *and* leverage the knowledge of all of the members of a political culture in order to improve decision-making. In scientific work and scientific thinking, Dewey saw a concrete model of this kind of sociology of rhetoric at work, and that is why science lies so close to the heart of deliberation in a Deweyan democratic culture.

SCIENCE AND DELIBERATION

The approach we advocate here finds the essence of rhetoric in the *ground* rather than the *figure*. The rhetoric we see all around us—in print and electronic media, in conversation, in governance—is the figure, and for the most part the rhetorical tradition has attempted to indicate how to manage this discourse and its effects; the handbook tradition, writ large, attempts to train people to create it. Rhetorical theories have generally focused on explanations of what language and people are like such that language could influence people. We think that Dewey teaches us that important explanations are to be found in the sociological conditions that make possible the idea that one can create psychological influence through language. As a theoretical move, this is a historicized parallel to Kant's transcendentalism, though instead of asking, What are the ultimate logical conditions for the possibility of X?, Dewey invites us to ask, What are the social conditions for the possibility of a certain kind of discourse? As an analysis it is parallel to Charles Taylor's concept of the social imaginary, a linked set of concepts about personhood, identity, agency, relationships, social action, and governance that undergird any moral order. Taylor tries to show that social and cultural changes in the north Atlantic states are explained by the specific evolution of an underlying social imaginary. Dewey is somewhat more radical than this: he approaches his analysis with a robust normative framework: How *should* we imagine the possibilities of our relationship to others? What would it take to create a society in which those possibilities were realized?

In this section we examine the way in which Dewey's account of thinking prefigures an account of both science and deliberation. We first look at his conception of thinking as a problem-solving practice, then show how the private act of thinking is modeled on the social practice of deliberation, and finally explain why Dewey's obsession with education is a peculiarly American response to the normative dimension of Dewey's sociology of rhetoric.

How We Think

While one might initially agree with Steve Fuller that the title *How We Think* is indeed "presumptuous" (12), with Dewey seeming to speak for the human race, closer inspection reveals that Dewey is engaged in a normative project.[1] Notwithstanding his elision of the normative/descriptive distinction in his reconstruction of "thinking," this is the best window into Dewey's larger theory. We will not claim that Dewey is giving (as he sometimes suggests) an account of the "actual" practice or micropractice of science; a large literature shows that to be a heterogeneous collection of practices indeed. Rather, Dewey wants to ask and answer a more systemic question: What is "scientific thinking" as a social practice, independently of whether it is embodied in laboratory science or governance?

His argument proceeds in several steps. First, he needs to detach thinking proper from merely "having thoughts"; thinking is characterized by "acceptance or rejection of something as reasonably probable or improbable" (*How We Think* 4). Dewey makes three important moves here. First, people do not just passively "have" beliefs but perform the action of accepting or rejecting; consistent with pragmatism, thinking and believing are both doings. Second, what they accept or reject is "something," a placeholder for a state of affairs, *not* merely a mental entity, making it more difficult to get a wedge in between rational thought and the way the world is (a difficult problem for the logical tradition that takes logical relations as prior to referential ones). Third, he eschews "true" for "reasonably probable." As we will see, this is not a Bayesian or subjective probability but a recognition of the essentially defeasible nature of human reasoning "in real life," so to speak.

His next moves are the ones that set the form for the rest of his analysis. Dewey wants to answer the questions, Why do people think, and why do they care about their beliefs? His answer is twofold. On the one hand, commitments are related to each other, so that a change in one commitment requires revisions of others; even modest and local consistency will create pressure for belief revision (Gärdenfors 1–20).[2] On the other hand, this is a matter not of logical consistency but of the ability to act at all: thinking is a precondition to action. As a pragmatist, Dewey is committed to the idea that actions are not "purely impulsive or purely routine" (*How We Think* 14) but rather are predicated on the "basis of the absent and the future"; predating Burke's "invention of the negative," Dewey points out that action as reasoned choice cannot be simply a response to current conditions (perceptual or otherwise) but must include nonpresent states of affairs (some in the past) and some conception of possible/desired futures (which he calls "systematized foresight" [15]). Now the more famous aspects of this book can come into focus. Dewey's examples for thinking include the following ("taken, almost verbatim, from the class papers of students" [68]):

1. *A case of practical deliberation:* Will the streetcar or subway get me to my destination more quickly?
2. *Reflection on an observation:* What is the function of the pole that projects from the ferryboat?
3. *Reflection and experiment:* Why are soap bubbles sucked inside an inverted tumbler?

The difference in behavior between hot and cold tumblers provides the answer.

Dewey then writes that these cases form a series, in that they begin with an immediate problem (How can I get to my appointment on time?) and progress to subtler notions of problems (Why is there a pole sticking out the front of the ferry? What mechanism pulls the soap bubbles into the glass?). The mechanisms of reflective thinking (or logic, for that matter) are in service of the solution to problems, because problems, *directly or indirectly,* are the occasions for action. Action must follow the perception of a need for it; that perception, as well as the possibilities for action it implies, is the product of a systematic reflective process. Unfortunately for Dewey, almost any way of putting this point misstates it, by making it seem as if there is a linear or sequential relationship between problems, thoughts, and actions. We would do better to think of it as a complex ecology, a densely interconnected system in which the connections are complicated and dense enough that any purely sequential description is an arbitrary one, which may serve a particular purpose but is not the only "true" description of that part of the system: one can legitimately reconstruct relations between problems, thinking, and action by starting with any of them.

So thinking, for Dewey, is a form of life, a set of practices involving multiple, overlapping language games, in Wittgenstein's words, "the language and the actions into which it is woven" (5e). It is neither simply an interior psychological process nor an abstractly logical one; thinking begins and ends in the texture of lived experience. So what, then, is the relationship between thinking, science, and deliberation?

"Science" and Deliberation

For a committed Deweyan, epistemology and democracy turn out to be two sides of a coin: every instance of knowing (directly or indirectly) implies a relationship to others (which may be democratic or authoritarian), and every relationship is implicated in knowledge by way of action, thinking, and problem solving. Science, properly understood, is a democratic enterprise, and democracy is a scientific one. Before going on, we need to distinguish between epistemology, science_1, and science$_2$. Epistemology is the theory of knowledge, and Dewey, in his account of reflective thinking, offers a pragmatist epistemology (albeit with some violence to more traditional notions of what constitutes knowledge). We would call science$_1$, then, the professional practices of those who pursue knowledge, not so much for its own sake but as a professional occupation: scientists, whether "laboratory" or field scientists in the natural sciences or even social scientists. Here Fuller would be quite right: Dewey's account of reflective thinking, especially taken as a simple sequence, would be a poor description of what goes on in science, of what scientists do.

However, Dewey's account is a better one for understanding science$_2$, which is the term we will use for the cultural understanding of a variety of practices having a strong family resemblance to the professional science and its epistemology. When Dewey talks about "science," he is usually talking about science$_2$. Dewey's inclination, throughout his writings, to refer to a variety of institutions and practices as "scientific" is really a measure of how scientific$_2$ he thinks they are: do they constitute a reflective, systematic practice of responding, individually or corporately, to perceived problems? Physicists are scientists, not historians, but both physics and history are scientific$_2$, in that they provide ways of systematically thinking through problems. In addition it will always be the case that both science$_1$ and science$_2$ are "team sports" in the sense that one could not do them alone.

Dewey's latent Hegelianism is evident in his view that reflection is fundamentally a property of groups of people, properly organized—which means properly communicating. Dewey wants to understand reasoning, writ large, at the cultural level. At the end of Dewey's *Logic* he says, "[The] failure to institute a logic based inclusively and exclusively upon the operations of inquiry has enormous cultural consequences. . . . Since scientific methods imply exhibit free intelligence operating in the best manner available at a given time, the cultural waste, confusion, and distortion that results [*sic*] from the failure to use these methods, in all fields in connection with all problems, is incalculable. These considerations reinforce the claim of logical theory, as the theory inquiry, to assume and to hold a position of primary human importance" (535).

"Deliberation," therefore, is the term we want to apply to logic, reflection, or science$_2$ when we are speaking of a group rather than an individual. While a person reflects on a situation, a group deliberates. So the democratic moment grows out of the social requirements of reasoned thought. In the introduction to an argumentation textbook in the 1930s, Dewey comments, "The security of democratic ideals depends on the intelligent use of the method of combined and unified honest effort to come to consciousness of the nature of social and political problems and their causes" (*Argumentation and Public Discussion* vii.).

I may reflect on *my* problems, but *we* must reflect on *our* problems, or both the description of the problem and the consideration of solutions will be morally and descriptively inadequate. Dewey seems to have been quite justified, from his point of view, in thinking that the method is the same, and scientific$_2$, in both cases: a solitary thinker's reflection allows her to see the connections between actions, inferences, outcomes, and goals, while a group's deliberations allow them to see the connections between their actions, inferences, outcomes, and goals. His use of "consciousness" in that passage is striking, and it connects to the story he wants to tell in *The Public and Its Problems,* in which he tries to dislodge the persistent realism that made Lippmann so despondent about the possibilities of democracy in a technocratic society. Lippmann's epistemology required him to think that there were "real" problems, and causes for them, "out there" and that only trained scientists could figure out what they were. Since Dewey thought that what constitutes a problem, what constitutes a cause, and what constitutes a desired goal are ecologically interdependent, the "real" social problem or cause will be the outcome of a deliberation in which *we* decide the best way to understand how they are related to one another. To the extent that we require the evolving joint consciousness to follow a pattern of reasoned inference, then, the deliberative process is scientific_2, without needing to be science_1. In fact, turning it over to scientists_1 would be doubly unproductive: for the result to be a truly joint and deliberative one requires the participation of (in principle) all those who perceive themselves to be affected by it. The validity of a solution is necessarily relative to a complex negotiation about what the relevant values are, and if everyone has not had a chance to think through and contribute to the values, it is not a valid solution for those who have not. This is why deliberation produces better decisions, even though from a realist point of view it does not.

Realist: The lake is not cleaned up.

Pragmatist: The lake is cleaner, through a process that balances the interests of everyone involved, taking account of costs and tradeoffs.

Here is where vulgar pragmatism and philosophical pragmatism meet up: the pragmatist solution is the more likely one to be implemented in a democracy because it is democratically a better decision. It also results in a cleaner lake.

What might be peculiarly American about this account is the way in which, as a social imaginary, it positions people "democratically." It does so in two senses, equality and engagement. The dreaded Platonic objection to democracy is that it is rule by the ignorant, and certainly in Dewey's vision (which as a social imaginary is abstracted from specific governmental setups), everyone's input is treated as equal. While it is true that in some parts of the reflective process expertise matters (scientists know more than I do about why and how the lake is polluted), in other parts, relative to values and interests, we should all be treated as equal (what trade-off in lost jobs should we accept for a marginally cleaner lake?). And of course the value commitments that people bring to a deliberation are not fixed: the values, their interpretation, and their application may all change as a result of the interactions. This is exactly the reason, from a democratic point of view, that deliberative engagement should be as universal as possible; not only do we owe it to people to give them a voice, however small, in the deliberation, but we would be foolish to think that technocrats could not lead us in a wrong direction—"wrong" in hindsight for not taking a sufficiently broad sense of our values into account.[3]

Why Education Matters

We claimed earlier that Dewey's sociology of rhetoric was a distinctly American one, and we would like to gesture at the kind of case we could make for it. Dewey believed in a version of the American experiment that was much more radical than that of the Founding Fathers: he believed in radical democracy, that everyone was capable of participating and in fact had a moral duty to do so. In the by-now-familiar way this is simultaneously a descriptive and normative claim. Yet while all are created equal, all are not equal—or are they? Let us look briefly at a somewhat parallel problem about status and difference and the "American" solution to it.

In *Common Courtesy: In Which Miss Manners Solves the Problem That Baffled Mr. Jefferson,* Judith Martin takes on a quintessentially American problem: what should American etiquette be? European etiquette (as amply proved by Norbert Elias) served explicitly to mark the differences between social classes, and these differences came with a heavy normative burden; the contempt of the English or French gentry for peasants or shopkeepers is strikingly similar to Plato's dismissal of hoi polloi—by nature they are not capable of anything better. If America was to be a democratic country, we would have to have democratic manners, ones that did not distinguish between class but somehow set up a new form of relations, of communication, between farmers, landowners, businessmen, and so on. Jefferson's solution was to distinguish people only by gender and nothing more; instead of lining up by rank, all men would be together as would all women, and they would proceed *pêle-mêle,* pell-mell, with no order at all. Martin claims that this represents no solution at all and in particular does not address the underlying function of etiquette, which is "[to] admit the possibility that people might be separated by basic, deeply held, genuinely irreconcilable differences—philosophical, religious or political. Thus the effort to trivialize etiquette, as being a barrier to the happy mingling of souls, actually trivializes the intellectual, emotional and spiritual by characterizing the difference between one person's and another's as no more than a simple misunderstanding, easily solved by frank exchanges" (12).

The correct American solution, she believes, lies not in pretending that everybody is equal in the sense of being the same but in deserving the right to "differ with dignity," "not just equal opportunity, but being considered 'just as good as anyone else'" (Martin 54). We have not all come to understand each other in a way that leads to agreement or unity, but to live in an equality that respects our differences, in capacity, experience, and commitments. This radical egalitarianism has been discussed in various ways since the founding of the republic, but it is Dewey who builds it into his social imaginary in a deeply philosophical way. The operative word is "good," as in worthy of engagement, in a public sense. Clearly not everybody brings the same skills, knowledge, and ability to the table when they engage. But that does not mean they do not have a stake in the larger conversation and a right to be a part of it.

Dewey had to believe in the democratic ($scientific_2$, deliberative) capacity of *everybody* to participate: not just the right by virtue of being human but potentially the ability. A follower of Dewey, Harrison Elliott asserted this with surprising directness. Elliott defined the goal of democracy this way: "The aim of true democracy is to secure the active participation of every individual up to the limit of his capacity in the conduct of all his social, vocational, and political affairs . . . [including] the immature child, the moron, and even the criminal" (Elliott 11).

The key term here is "capacity." It is not that everybody automatically is a good deliberator by virtue of being human; it is a capacity that must be developed through education. Until we have tried to educate everyone *in the right way,* we will not see the kind of deliberative practices that would realize democracy in its fullest form. In essence, in the American context, then, the empirical commitment follows from the moral one, and for Dewey, the great experiment is an educational one: can we design a system that will educate students for democracy? Our novel claim is that as a rhetorical education, this would involve not the typical materials from the handbook tradition but rather a full appreciation of rhetorical democracy as a mode of daily living, of constituting relationships. Rhetoric would be not a set of skills, in the usual sense, but a deeply lived appreciation of the consummatory moment, the fullness of engaging another in a democratic mode. According to Dewey's pedagogy, as exemplified in his work at the Chicago Laboratory School, learning is a mode of social engagement for any subject matter. Whether students are learning geography or history or chemistry, he places them in projects where they have to solve problems together (a pedagogy we have rediscovered as "collaborative learning"). Once again we see that knowledge and deliberation are two sides of a coin. To come to know or understand a subject matter is at the same moment to gain skill in developing relationships and communication skills that allow for solving problems and decision-making. In classroom group work, students should be introduced, in microcosm, to the picture of human relations that Dewey wished to see activated throughout society.

The professional mode of $science_1$ thus has to be understood in the context of $science_2$ and the deliberative communication that is at the heart of democratic life. Of course there are deep historical reasons for seeing science as the instantiation of the perfect democracy of the intellect. But contemporary philosophy of science and of science, technology, and society (STS) have instead insisted that science either has no social dimension (philosophy) or is reducible to merely its social dimension.

A DEWEYAN RHETORIC OF $SCIENCE_1$/$SCIENCE_2$

Richard Rorty is right to point to the enormous influence of Thomas Kuhn and Paul Feyerabend on the manner in which social theory now understands scientific practice. The rhetoric-of-science project has certainly tapped into the work of people such as Kuhn and Feyerabend in order to make a set of arguments about scientific practice. At the core of these arguments lies a critique of realist epistemology tied to the assertion that scientific work is available for interpretation in a similar manner to other kinds of texts. We have no objection to these basic insights, but Dewey's interest ran the opposite direction: he was interested in the effects of scientific thinking on social and political affairs. In our view, the practical effect of his continued ambiguity about the meaning of science was to bring $science_1$ and $science_2$ into productive tension and concord with each other.

Dewey certainly advanced his own critique of realist epistemologies throughout his career and thus could be read as a key contributor to work in what might be called "social epistemology." One could also find resources within Dewey's work to support some of the basic theoretical insights of the rhetoric-of-science project regarding interpretation and epistemology. Particularly in *The Quest for Certainty* Dewey dismantles realist epistemology and prefigures some of the arguments made by Kuhn, Feyerabend, and others. However, this is not the only way in which Dewey's work can be linked to the rhetoric-of-science project. In *The Problems of Men* (1946) Dewey laments philosophy's mistaken concern with the "foundations" or "conditions" of scientific knowledge. Instead he claims that philosophy ought to be concerned with the "actual and potential" consequences of scientific knowledge (*Problems of Men* 7). This amounts to the claim that we should not focus just on epistemology or hermeneutics but also on the effects of scientific claims and commitments. Accordingly, Dewey juxtaposes wisdom and knowledge: "philosophy is wholly that part of the historic tradition called the search for wisdom—namely, search for the ends and values that give direction to our collective human activities"; and the method of science "provides the means for conducting this search" (11). Here, as in the above section, Dewey does not use science to describe the formal procedures of physicists conducting experiments. Instead he means something similar to the reflective, scientific thinking described above. According to Dewey, two recent advances in $science_1$, Heisenberg's "Uncertainty Principle" and Einstein's "Theory of Relativity," demonstrate the impossibility of the quest for epistemic or $scientific_1$ certainty and the role that practical activity plays in scientific understanding. These advances indicated that knowledge no longer referred to the changeless attributes of natural substances. Instead the focus of $scientific_1$ inquiry was on "the deliberate institution of a definite and specified course of change" in an object. More specifically, "*the* method of physical inquiry is to introduce some change in order to see what other change ensues; the correlation between these changes, when measured by a series of operations, constitutes the definite and desired objects of knowledge" (*Quest for Certainty* 84).

Long before *Philosophy and the Mirror of Nature,* Dewey rejected the conception of an independent observer able to represent findings in an objective manner and replaced that view of scientific work with a more action-oriented view. The change in the method of "scientific" work, implied by Heisenberg and Einstein, recommended a "complete reversal in the traditional relationship between knowledge and action." To cling to traditional assumptions about the mind and the organs of knowing is to ignore the fact that "science advances by adopting instruments and doings of directed practice, and the knowledge thus gained becomes a means of the development of arts which bring nature still further into actual and potential service of human purposes and valuations" (*Quest for Certainty* 85). Science$_1$ is a method of acting with and on objects, according to Dewey. This extends his view of deliberation and scientific thinking, and it adds an attention to questions about the rhetorical practices of science$_2$.

The major implication of Dewey's argument is that "knowing is itself a mode of practical action and is *the* way of interaction by which other natural interactions become subject to direction." In other words, "the experimental method" is a "way of operating upon and with the things of ordinary experience" so that we can "control" those "things" and "direct their changes as we desire" (*Quest for Certainty* 106–7). In technical terms this means that data act as a substitute for objects because data are used by, and for, people. In addition data signify "subject-matter for further investigation" and ultimately the source of further problems for scientists to solve. In short, modern experimental science$_1$ becomes "an art of control" (99–100). The use of the word "control" here signifies the transformation of a realist epistemology as the basis of "scientific" work to a "pragmatist epistemology." By this we mean roughly that knowledge is, in and of itself, a form of action, just as thinking is a form of action. "Control" is probably not a word that helps us understand Dewey here, since it promises more than he can or wanted to deliver; "making a difference to" is closer to the pragmatist tradition and what he intended for the role of science$_2$ in our lives.

If we follow Dewey's understanding of science$_1$ as a method of practical action whose goal is to control our experience and direct changes in the natural world, we are perhaps not as far from the rhetorical tradition as one might think. Two aspects of rhetorical theory, invention and arrangement, emerge as tools for producing effects, for making interventions in the world. Dewey's rhetoric of science$_1$ commands our attention because the deliberative, discussion-oriented sociology of rhetoric he recommends shapes the kinds of effects that can and ought to be produced by a rhetoric of science$_2$. Dewey's grounding of rhetoric in deliberation prefigures rhetorical practice in specific ways, and it means that rhetoric *is* a kind of science$_1$ and science$_2$ and has as specific a role in managing decision-making, depending on problem and context, as chemistry or physics or implementing new water policy.

Invention is that part of rhetoric concerned with discovering what might be communicated about a subject to persuade an audience. Gerard Hauser offers a clear definition of "invention" that parallels Dewey's discussion of science$_2$: "we may define invention as the method of finding 'sayables' (symbols) with the potential to transform some matter or question of an indeterminate nature into one that is determinate in the mind of the audience"; this implies that rhetorical inventions "provide frameworks that aid us in interpreting novel, conflicting, or ambiguous" events (Hauser 109). In this sense both science$_1$ and science$_2$ are a matter of inventing methods or symbolic acts that transform the subject matter of experience in order to cope with a particular exigency. The very idea of "data" is just this kind of symbolic invention because the "data" scientists invent provide a framework to think about particular problems, to create further uncertainty, and to use in acting upon the objects of science in new ways. No longer is science$_1$ just a matter of observing the natural properties of objects. It is now a question of inventing the best ways to act upon such objects so as to produce an effect that works to demonstrate control over the object acted upon and to solve the scientific problem at hand. That project is, in part, a form of symbolic action, in addition to being the product of scientific$_2$, deliberative thinking. It is not a poetic form of symbolic action that issues from a solitary genius but a collective form grounded in the kind of scientific thinking characteristic of community-based deliberation.

The results of the process of invention must then be organized or arranged. It is the need for social action that prompts the organization and arrangement of the knowledge acquired through invention—"the need for direction of action in large social fields is the source of a genuine demand for unification of scientific conclusions" (*Quest for Certainty* 312). According to Dewey, "scientific" conclusions are "organized when their bearing on life is disclosed" (312). Both invention and arrangement are useful because they act in response to rhetorical situations. Arrangement points to the aesthetic and logical dimension of rhetoric and the necessity of shaping discourse into a form for maximum effect. In *Experience and Nature* Dewey tries to demonstrate the artistic aspect of the scientific$_1$ method: "Only action, interaction, can change or remake objects. The analogy of the skilled artist still holds. His intelligence is a factor in forming new objects which mark a fulfillment. But this is because intelligence is incarnate in overt action, using things as means to affect other things" (158). Scientific$_1$ discovery and invention create a "transformation of both meanings and the existences of nature," and for this transformation to work it must be given an intelligent form by the scientist. Therefore the results of experimentation are arranged in such a way that they can transform the object and our understanding of the natural world. Both kinds of arrangement require artistic skill just as arranging a speech to disclose a perspective on a specific situation requires artistic skill.

Viewed from a Deweyan perspective, rhetorical action is both a kind of scientific$_1$ and scientific$_2$ activity. By acting on, inventing, and arranging the objects of science, one engages in the constitutive task of developing and disclosing a particular perspective on the natural world. Such a view grounds Dewey's claim that the activity of science$_2$ is best directed toward the "problems of men" because it is scientific$_1$. This is not necessarily a radical departure from arguments advanced by Deirdre McCloskey or Alan Gross, but grounding the rhetoric-of-science project in Deweyan pragmatism does have different consequences, as we show below. When investigating physical phenomena, the scientific$_1$ method can operate with great precision, carefulness, and thoroughness and thus produce knowledge that more accurately yields expected results. Dewey's goal is to bring science$_2$ to bear on problems in the social world so that "the operations in which physical science is used" can transform "distinctively human values in behalf of a human interest." The greatest benefit of such a transformation is that "knowledge of the things of ordinary perception, use and enjoyment" can be understood in a "genuine and fuller and deeper" way compared to "the scientist in his laboratory" (*Quest for Certainty* 199). In other words, both kinds of science are most beneficial when used in response to everyday, social, or rhetorical situations and become knowledge by virtue of their communication and practical action, not their reflection of some objective reality.

What, then, does a Deweyan sociology of rhetoric teach us about science$_1$ and science$_2$? In the light of the account of deliberation and scientific thinking from above, it seems clear that both science$_1$ and science$_2$ are rhetorical in that rhetoric is an emergent response to a particular situation and problem. Furthermore both proceed by way of invention and arrangement and in so doing operate as a kind of symbolic action through and through. Scientific work (in both senses of science) can be read as a unique form of rhetorical invention. In addition Dewey points to the manner in which scientific thinking and scientific work produce effects. This is one of the outcomes of redescribing scientific work as a form of action, a typically pragmatist insight. Actions have consequences, and scientific work, as a special form of action, has particular, identifiable consequences; the rhetorical question is not so much What did scientists say or mean in a given text? but How did what they said become part of problem solving, deliberation, and inquiry? Dewey authorizes, therefore, a turn from the hermeneutic task of interpreting a scientific text to the pragmatic task of evaluating the effects of scientific claims and commitments, and insists that evaluation must, crucially, invoke his meliorism. Dewey's commitment to community, inquiry, and deliberation rests on his beliefs that these can all improve social and political conditions. In other words, incorporating people into a participatory process is essential for democratic culture, and it is productive of positive change. When scientific work is the outcome of a community-based deliberative process, one insures that that work will have positive consequences for the members of the community participating in deliberation.

Dewey's rhetoric of science, therefore, issues from the sociology of rhetoric that he outlines *and* his commitment to deliberation as the practical realization of that sociology of rhetoric. Science$_1$ and science$_2$ are mutual reflections of each other; laboratory science and large-scale social experimentation share a common logic. It follows that they share a common need: a set of background conditions that make them possible. Dewey (as many people did) celebrates the accomplishment of those conditions for science$_1$ while urging the creation of the conditions for science$_2$, which are, in our view, also the conditions for a flourishing democratic rhetoric.

A Deweyan rhetoric of science has certain features. First, it points to the conditions within which scientific knowledge, scientific work, and scientific thinking are produced. Social, institutional, situational conditions form the context within which scientific work proceeds and produces effects. Second, Dewey recommends a normative, prescriptive account for the best available sociology of rhetoric for science, and it is the same sociology of rhetoric that describes his version of democratic culture. The central features of this sociology of rhetoric are that it is participatory and community-based and relies on scientific methods but not only expert scientists. Furthermore it seeks, as a goal of effect, improvement, reconciliation, and self-realization. Third, artful practices of invention, both symbolic and technological, and arrangement are essential within the deliberative process. Artfully directing change through invention and arrangement is the key method of engaging in deliberation and discussion, and it is a key feature of scientific work (a feature often ignored by other philosophies of science). This reiterates the position advanced in *The Public and Its Problems,* and that should not be a surprise given how closely aligned the deliberative process is to scientific work.

Fourth, wisdom and prudence are outcomes of community-based, scientific deliberations. The circulation and use of knowledge in action is what the community of inquirers seeks and makes possible, and this is what is generative of wisdom and prudence (critical rhetorical values) within a Deweyan democracy. Furthermore wisdom and prudence are more important to democratic culture than knowledge because both allow for effective decision-making and both produce melioristic effects for the community. This is the proper end and value of scientific work. Dewey's rhetoric of science leaves the preoccupations of epistemology and hermeneutics behind for the ethical project of scientific-minded, community-based deliberation. Such a rhetoric of science is made possible because of his commitment to a particular sociology of rhetoric and a particular vision of thinking and democratic participation. The pragmatic advantage of such a position is that it turns our attention to assessing the effects of scientific work and the conditions within which scientific work happens. We can then ask deeply rhetorical questions: What effect has some kind of scientific work or scientific thinking had on community life? What were the conditions in which some scientific work happened, and were those conditions deliberative in the best sense possible? Such questions, and Dewey's general position, provide grounds for a uniquely American rhetoric.

CONCLUSION

Josiah Ober has done a wonderful job illustrating the context within which Athenian citizenship was practiced, its sociology of rhetoric. In *Democracy and Knowledge: Innovation and Learning in Classical Athens,* he argues that the Athenians crafted an institutional design for their democracy that emphasized the values of aggregation, alignment, and coordination. In other words, the Athenians sought the best means to tap into the knowledge of the community by setting up networks and teams, by designing rules and commitments for deliberation, and by codifying the outcomes of deliberations. It was within this context that the practice of rhetoric emerged. Thus rhetorical action was fit to the grounds of what we have been calling in this essay a sociology of rhetoric. Communication as "rhetoric" mattered for Athenian deliberative democracy, and it matters for American deliberative democracies. But the two different contexts provide different grounds from which rhetorical practice emerges. Dewey's "American-ness" cannot be ignored, and his stipulations about the conditions within which communication ought to happen and communities ought to be built can be read as the grounds for a uniquely American rhetoric. He does not, however, offer anything close to the kinds of concrete pedagogical suggestions and programs that Athenian teachers of rhetoric articulated. This is one of the limitations of pragmatism: it directs our attention to the ways in which communication shapes deliberative decision-making, but it actually does not offer a handbook on practicing and mastering rhetoric within such a context. But that was not Dewey's concern.

Dewey's concern was with outlining the conditions within which American democracy could flourish. Those conditions were predicated on coping with the social and political context of the time. For the most part that meant massive immigration, urbanization, pluralism, the great achievements of the scientific revolution, and the great destruction wrought by the Civil War. The Athenians would not have been strangers to the influence of war and violence on democratic culture, but the other central contextual factors indicate the extent to which Dewey was living in a moment that required and figured a different set of rhetorical practices. Dewey sought a sociology of rhetoric that cultivated community-based inquiry and participation. He believed that this was essential to the improvement of American democracy *and* that it required specific forms of communication. He also believed that scientific thinking was a model for this kind of inquiry and could therefore serve as an important resource for building a better democratic culture. He was committed to a belief in the meliorism of scientific work if it emerged from a democratic society. Thus he grounds a rhetoric of science attuned to the deliberative context from which scientific claims emerge and intent on assessing the consequences of scientific claims by virtue of their effect on democratic communities. Dewey teaches us that different grounds provide for different kinds of rhetorics and that if we change the grounds we can improve the chances of rhetorics leading to cooperation, meliorism, community growth, and individual self-actualization. Furthermore he leads us to ask how we might change those grounds. His normative and descriptive project can be used to justify and support the articulation of a unique American rhetoric. This is a project that pragmatism has not attempted to this point.

NOTES

1. The favored term for picking out normatively acceptable thinking has evolved over the last one hundred years. For Dewey and his peers, the term was "reflective thinking," and so the process described in *How We Think* is the "reflective sequence" (cf. Columbia Associates in Philosophy, *An Introduction to Reflective Thinking* [New York: Houghton Mifflin, 1923]). Sometime in the middle of the century this gave way to "straight thinking" (whose opposite was "crooked" thinking; cf. Monroe Beardsley, *Thinking Straight: A Guide for Readers and Writers* [New York: Prentice-Hall, 1950]). By the end of the 1960s "critical thinking" was the standard and became the name for a movement.

2. Oddly this picture-reasoned belief does not return to Anglophone philosophy until, prompted by Otto Neurath, Quine and Ullian (*Web of Belief*). Margolis gives a good explanation of why: for many philosophers, if the world is "one," and could not contract itself, if we get our beliefs square with the world, then they cannot possibly contract each other (*Historied Thought*). Brandom gives a highly articulated version of such a theory (*Making it Explicit*).

3. The literature on the Vietnam War (*Best and Brightest, The Fog of War,* etc.) makes abundantly clear that technocratic rule of the war erred not just realistically (war does not work the way the Rand Institute thought) but also by not taking into account a broad enough sense of the values at stake. Dewey's response to World War I shows that he thought this was exactly the disastrous effect of war plus patriotism on national deliberation.

WORKS CITED

Brandom, Robert. Making it Explicit: Reasoning, Representing, and Discursive Commitment. Cambridge, MA: Harvard University Press, 1994.

Dewey, John. *Democracy and Education.* New York: Macmillan, 1930.

———. *Experience and Nature.* Mineola, N.Y.: Dover, 1958.

———. *How We Think.* Charleston: Bibliolife, 2009.

———. Introduction. In Angelo Pellegrini and Brents Stirling, *Argumentation and Public Discussion.* Boston: D. C. Heath, 1936.

———. *The Later Works of John Dewey.* Vol. 14. Carbondale: Southern Illinois University Press, 2008.

———. *Logic: The Theory of Inquiry.* New York: Henry Holt, 1938.

———. *The Problems of Men.* New York: Philosophical Library, 2007.

———. *The Public and Its Problems.* Athens, Ohio: Swallow Press, 1954.

———. *The Quest for Certainty.* New York: Capricorn Books, 1960.

Elliott, Harrison. *The Process of Group Thinking.* New York: Inquiry, 1928.

Fuller, Steve. *Science: The Art of Living.* Montreal: McGill-Queens University Press, 2010.

Gärdenfors, Peter. *Belief Revision.* Cambridge: Cambridge University Press, 1992.

Hauser, Gerard. *Introduction to Rhetorical Theory.* Prospect Heights, Ill: Waveland Press, 2002.

Margolis, Joseph. *Historied Thought, Constructed World: A Conceptual Primer for the Turn of the Millennium.* Berkeley: University of California Press, 1995.

Martin, Judith. *Common Courtesy: In Which Miss Manners Solves the Problem That Baffled Mr. Jefferson.* New York: Scribner, 1985.

Ober, Josiah. *Democracy and Knowledge: Innovation and Learning in Classical Athens.* Princeton, N.J.: Princeton University Press, 2010.

Quine, W.V. and J.S. Ullian. *The Web of Belief.* New York: McGraw-Hill, 1978.
Rorty, Richard. *Philosophy and Social Hope.* New York: Penguin, 2000.
Taylor, Charles. *Modern Social Imaginaries.* Durham, N.C.: Duke University Press, 2003.
Wittgenstein, Ludwig. *Philosophical Investigations.* Trans. G. E. M. Anscombe. New York: Macmillan, 1953.

John Dewey, Kenneth Burke, and the Role of Orientation in Rhetoric

Scott R. Stroud

As a practicing orator or rhetorician, John Dewey seemed an abject failure. Regardless of the prescience of his ideas, his speaking ability was often dull and far from captivating. It transcended mere responses of apathy, as it was good-naturedly ribbed in the national forum of *Time:* "To his classes he lectured in a monotonous voice, made no rhetorical effort whatever to interest his audience. Once, after droning on to graduate students for three solid hours on the meaning of the word 'this,' he concluded: 'I think this is a little clearer to me now'" ("Education"). When he was given the stage in China in 1919, one American professor in the audience commented that "Dewey's lectures were dry as dinosaur bones; one chap who heard him said that if this educator should be announced to speak in the average American university, it is doubtful if fifty noses could be counted when the head of the department of education arose to announce the distinguished speaker" (Wang 42). Despite Dewey's failure to *practice* the arts of rhetoric, many see in his thought the seeds of what could be abstracted as a (though perhaps not the only) "pragmatist rhetoric." What are the prospects for finding such a doctrine or theory behind the less-than-expert rhetorical practices of John Dewey?

Initially one might think that such a quest will be extremely difficult. American pragmatists such as Dewey continue to frustrate scholars of rhetoric by the compatibility of his thought with concerns in rhetorical studies and his refusal to engage the conceptual tradition of rhetoric. For instance, Robert Danisch's interesting work argues for theoretical compatibility between the Sophists and the American pragmatists, even though the latter group did not use the term "rhetoric" in any significant or sustained sense. Dewey, for instance, did not seem to notice the Sophists as a viable, sustained tradition of thought concerning the powers of communication. Perhaps there is another way to "find" a pragmatist rhetoric in such figures as

Dewey. Instead of attempting to *locate* a pragmatist rhetoric, where would one start if one wanted to *construct* a pragmatist rhetoric? This question builds on the points Danisch makes and also facilitates new projects in pragmatist rhetoric. The present essay takes this pragmatist approach to theorizing pragmatist rhetoric. What I seek to construct is a *Deweyan pragmatist rhetoric,* not necessarily the account of rhetoric that Dewey held (or failed to hold).

This sort of project will be of great scope, and this essay can contribute only a small part to it. Elsewhere I have discussed how pragmatism would include rhetoric and communication in the potentially artful realm of activity, and that pragmatist views of criticism will foreground its artful engagement with many of the activities of everyday life (Stroud, "Artful Communication"; Stroud, "Artful Criticism"). My strategy in this essay is to continue to flesh out the core of what pragmatist rhetoric would consist of, especially in regard to its practices of criticism. Pragmatist rhetoric, taken here in the sense intimated by John Dewey, would emphasize individual interest in the critical act, the applicability of critical habits to all individuals, and the role of orientation in criticism. All three of these commitments place my reading of pragmatism in line with much of the early thought of a well-known rhetorical theorist, Kenneth Burke (for example, *Attitudes; Permanence*). Focusing on these sorts of commitments in framing what is at stake with a pragmatist rhetoric also would bring Dewey's way of approaching the issues of human communication closer to that of Burke's. Of course, Dewey and Burke differ on a variety of important issues, ranging from disparate instantiations of leftist politics (Stob, "Kenneth Burke") to differing evaluations of the promise of science in the 1930s (Hildebrand). I envision my project as a *reconstructive* account of pragmatist rhetoric, as opposed to a *descriptive* account that captures the historical relation between Dewey and Burke. Thus, I sidestep issues with Burke's reception of Dewey and Dewey's apparent lack of engagement with Burke's thought. The relation that I explore between these two thinkers is *conceptual,* as opposed to *historical.* Using the constructive methodology entailed by pragmatism, I ask the question, How can we use resources in the work of Burke to flesh out a Deweyan pragmatist rhetoric, the sort of rhetorical project that Dewey left uncompleted?

I argue that the crux to providing an account of a pragmatist rhetoric will be with the concept of orientation, or the deep-seated habituation of an organism toward its environment. This is also the point at which Dewey and Burke converge in complementary fashion. Much of Burke's *Permanence and Change* revolves around an explicit notion of "orientation," so this study will focus on that point in Burke's extensive writing as something that can help us construct a notion of pragmatist rhetoric. Why focus here on *Permanence and Change*? There are three reasons. First, this work by Burke begins with an analysis of orientation and ends with ways orientation can be changed. This serves as one of the most explicit discussions of orientation per se in Burke's corpus. Second, *Permanence and Change* was written in the early 1930s, as Dewey was presenting and publishing the material in his

Art as Experience. Both of these works, in their own way, were reacting to economic, technological, and humanistic concerns in U.S. society. One can even see both as answering the question of art's relation to politics and morality, a question that Ann George and Jack Selzer note as highlighted by aesthetes/formalists and Marxists in their struggles over the use of art to push "moral" ends. Third, focusing on the work that contains the majority of Burke's utterances on orientation helps refine our constructive use of this concept in a Deweyan view of rhetoric. As I will argue, Dewey hints at a general concept of orientation, but Burke's notion will allow us fully to flesh out the relation of orientation, habit, and language in the "rhetorical Dewey" we wish to create.

My efforts will focus on the following questions in constructively engaging Dewey and Burke with this project: 1) How do Dewey and Burke conceptualize orientation in their writings? Are such readings complementary? 2) What role will this emergent concept of orientation play in a Deweyan pragmatist rhetoric? These questions are essential not only to putting Burke's thought in some sort of relation to Dewey's thought but also in being specific about what pragmatism has to offer theories of rhetorical activity. Answering these questions will highlight the contributions that a Burkean notion of orientation can add to Dewey's rumination on this concept. The emergent concept of orientation will then be shown to have an important role to play in understanding rhetorical phenomena and their melioration through acts of criticism.

WHAT IS ORIENTATION?

A vital point in Dewey's work in aesthetics concerns the dispositional aspect to our aesthetic experiences. If one approaches some object in its environment in a certain way, it could possibly engender aesthetic experience, the sort of experience that hits a qualitative high point. If one orients herself differently, the object could be seen as merely a good or bad investment, something to waste time, and so on. Dewey points out this sort of dispositional quality in an example of students taking a test—one sees the test as an integral part of the "end" of education, whereas the other sees it as something to get through in order to get what he really desires (a degree). The experience of the former is said to be higher in experiential integrity, the sort of unity that characterizes the aesthetic. Thus one could argue that any experience could be aesthetic given a certain orientation that is conducive to this sort of integration (Stroud, "Orientational Meliorism"; Stroud, *John Dewey and the Artful Life*).

This is getting ahead of our specific, and necessary, inquiry here. Before one can recommend a specific orientation, more can and should be said on the concept of orientation in general. Indeed if this term is to function as a term of art in a general pragmatist rhetoric, it must have a sense separate from any specific employment. What, then, is orientation in general? Dewey's first mention of this term indicates the direction his later thought would take. In discussing Leibniz in an early work, Dewey talks about the former's "new spiritual picture of the universe" and "new conception of the world" as a "new mental orientation" ("Leibniz's Essays" 268–69). This gives us our first clue—orientations concern the world and are located in the mind. Yet Dewey was no dualist, so "mind" will feature in his account in a particularly Deweyan way. In Dewey's work on aesthetics, *Art as Experience,* "mind" can be linked to the term of "orientation." One can easily see that he is referring to the same sort of dispositional point in both Leibniz's way of engaging and thinking through the universe and the ways individuals can experience works of art.

Dewey's later work moves away from his early idealism but remains committed to an integrative view of human experience. This typically takes an organic or Darwinian form, with the unity formed between a growing or flourishing organism and some specific environment. What I find particularly interesting about this emphasis is the notion of habit, a way to account for the dispositional or orientational relation of an organism to its environment. In *Art as Experience,* Dewey paints a conception of mind that is much more active than substance-based accounts. Instead of taking "mind" to be a noun or as denoting a substance, Dewey points out that mind "is always used with respect to situations, events, objects, persons and groups" (*Art as Experience* 268). It is used instead as a verb, in the sense of "to mind" one's situation. Thus mind "denotes an activity that is intellectual, to *note* something; affectional, as caring and liking, and volitional, practical, acting in a purposive way" (268). "Mind" concerns the ways we engage the various situations we find ourselves in, instead of denoting a soul or substance that makes us up as individuals. It is used to indicate the sort of attention one gives to a situation, whether it is a relational situation or one that calls for certain skills of problem solving. One can see Lloyd Bitzer's "rhetorical situation" as involving this sort of concept as well. When a situation is problematic, when it calls for a rhetorical response to some exigency within that situation, then one is faced with "minding" that situation and all its details. *How* one minds it will differ in important ways depending on culture, experience, and certain personal capacities. Thus "mind" is an individuating term of sorts, allowing one to differentiate how differing people "mind" the same situation.

I argue that "mind" is simply another way of saying "orientation," as both involve the individual's approach to situations and activities. Mind and orientation shape our individual consciousness of objects (including a situation in general). For instance, one who is constantly fearful for her car's safety may have her experience of a movie toned by ruminative worries of what could be happening out in the parking lot. She could also say "no" to various date requests, as they might involve her car in some problematic parking situations. In other words, her orientation foregrounds the interests connected with her vehicle, and this consequentially tones her experience. A better example of orientation affecting experience in this way would be that of the radical egoist—one who thinks and perceives things in line with his interests. Mind or orientation is the sort of background filter that gives meaning to stimuli that one is consciously experiencing.

To determine the rhetorical implications of such a concept, we can extend Dewey's view of orientation with Kenneth Burke's account. Burke's description of "orientation" is similar to this notion of "mind" in Dewey. In *Permanence and Change,* Burke explicitly discusses orientation in light of Thorstein Veblen's notion of "trained incapacity," a concept stemming from Veblen's *The Instinct of Workmanship.* In this work Veblen briefly uses the term to refer to a sort of "business mind" that was being cultivated in American society. Burke sees this term as important, as it highlights two points: 1) humans have orientations that differ toward activities; and 2) these orientations involve both enabling and constraining features. In Veblen's terms, one's training and attention both help and hurt one's possible courses of action. Being great at math, say, could be an incapacity in noticing non-quantitative aspects of a situation. Burke glosses this concept as "that state of affairs whereby one's very abilities can function as blindness" (*Permanence and Change* 7). Orientation as trained incapacity arises in light of some environment. In a Deweyan fashion Burke argues, "The problems of existence do not have one fixed, unchanging character. . . . They are open to many interpretations—and these interpretations influence our selection of means. Hence the place of 'trained incapacity' is means-selecting" (10). For Burke, one's orientation integrally involves the ability to see events as like other events (such as past events), as well as the ability to match up means relevant to certain interest-driven goals in a given situation. At another point he claims, "Orientation is thus a bundle of judgments as to how things were, how they are, and how they may be" (14) and that "orientation is a reading from 'what is' to 'what may be'" (15). Thus orientation not only enables and disables in certain situations but also shapes our expectancies in light of certain meaningful events.

At this point one can see that Dewey's notion of "mind" from his 1934 aesthetics is similar to Burke's notion of "orientation" from 1935. Both involve personal dispositions that are 1) often under the reach of consciousness, 2) affect individual experience, and 3) come from the past experience of that individual. There is another term that can capture this emerging notion of orientation: the Deweyan concept of "habit." Orientations are habits, albeit wide habits that govern a variety of our actions and reactions in thought and body. The first step in understanding Dewey on habit is to realize that he is not merely referring to unthinking, mechanical, and limited forms of physical repetition. This is a notion of habit, but not that which Dewey believes describes the majority of human habit taking. As Nathan Crick (*Democracy and Rhetoric*) puts it, the Deweyan notion of habit "is a pattern of experience that comes into existence as a way of adjusting to persistent environmental conditions" (48). For Dewey, habit is broader than mere repetition and involves four important characteristics: "But we need a word to express that kind of human activity [1] which is influenced by prior activity and in that sense acquired; [2] which contains within itself a certain ordering or systematization of minor elements of action; [3] which is projective, dynamic in quality, ready for overt manifestation; and [4] which is operative in some subdued subordinate form even when not obviously dominating activity. Habit even in its ordinary usage comes nearer to denoting these facts than any other word" (Dewey, *Human Nature* 31).

Dewey's notion of "habit" involves these factors of history: systematicity, projective force, and constant presence. Thus a businessperson has certain habits of body and mind that orient her toward profit and personal gain. These arose in a historical process—perhaps from past experience in competitive social environments. This person's habits will also organize some amount of subordinate habits (say, the use of math in ledgers, skill in speaking, and so forth). These defining habits of this businessperson will also orient her toward certain activities, given the relevant situation and stimuli. This is a more detailed way of saying (as Burke does) that orientation qua habit involves us in means/ends selection. It orients us toward certain interests and projects certain ways as the "best" means of getting to those end points. Last, the habits of the "business mind" are still there when other habits are explicitly operative. One notices this when a friendly game of tennis with one's habitually competitive friend turns fierce after the score draws to a tie. Given this rich notion of habit, one sees why Dewey demurs at the putative use of habit to mean merely repetitive or unthinking acts. Instead he explicitly allies it with the more general, mental terms of "disposition" and "attitude." He ends his chapter on habit in *Human Nature and Conduct* by indicating, "The essence of habit is an acquired predisposition to *ways* or modes of response, not to particular acts except as, under special conditions, these express a way of behaving. Habit means special sensitiveness or accessibility to certain classes of stimuli, standing predilections and aversions, rather than bare recurrence of specific acts" (32). Thus habit can be quite broad in what it refers to. Dewey even equates it with our agential self by simply claiming, "It means will" (32). "Habits" can refer to specific actions such as nail biting, or they can refer to larger "ways of thinking" about the world. All these senses of habit, of course, are an important part of Dewey's mature organicism. Habit is the way that an organism is disposed to engage with some environment offering rewards and challenges to future growth.

It is in the larger sense of general, mental habits that we see the linkage to the notion of "mind" as an orienting habit. In his work on political philosophy, Dewey refers to different kinds of "minds" as habits, going so far as to argue, "Thinking itself becomes habitual among certain lines" (*Public* 335). Like Veblen, Dewey points out that habit enables certain ways of acting and thought in line with frequent occupations:

> The influence of habit is decisive because all distinctively human action has to be learned, and the very heart, blood and sinews of learning is creation of habitudes. Habits bind us to orderly and established ways of action because they generate ease, skill and interest in things to which we have grown used and

> because they instigate fear to walk in different ways, and because they leave us incapacitated for the trial of them. Habit does not preclude the use of thought, but it determines the channels within which it operates. Thinking is secreted in the interstices of habits. The sailor, miner, fisherman and farmer think, but their thoughts fall within the framework of accustomed occupations and relationships. (335)

This is another way of putting the earlier Deweyan point of "occupational psychosis" (as Burke labels it)—one's dominant form of occupation or activity has a strong formative power over one's disposition in general. This includes not only patterns of action but also wide-ranging ways of thinking through certain problematics.

Burke most likely took the idea of "occupational psychosis" (if not those specific terms joined together) from Dewey's essay "The Interpretation of Savage Mind." Here Dewey tries to place the thought of more "primitive" people not in a developmental context (which tended to denigrate nonmodern patterns of thought) but instead in relation to their dominant social activities. He argues that "mind has a pattern, a scheme of arrangement in its constituent elements" (41), and that occupations such as subsistence hunting can inculcate these habits of mind. He illustrates the way that these larger, occupationally influenced habits can organize and constitute subordinate habits, desires, and ends:

> Occupations determine the fundamental modes of activity, and hence control the formation and use of habits. These habits, in turn, are something more than practical and overt. . . . The occupations determine the chief modes of satisfaction, the standards of success and failure. Hence they furnish the working classifications and definitions of value; they control the desire processes. Moreover, they decide the sets of objects and relations that are important, and thereby provide the content or material of attention, and the qualities that are interestingly significant. The directions given to mental life thereby extend to emotional and intellectual characteristics. So fundamental and pervasive is the group of occupational activities that it affords the scheme or pattern of the structural organization of mental traits. Occupations integrate special elements into a functioning whole. (41–42)

Occupations are important for comparative psychology because they are widespread ways of shaping individual habits into powerful, integral wholes. In other words, occupations can form fairly consistent groupings of orientations across a social group. These orientations in turn involve and project desire (in the form of value and ends), mediate through the selection of means (what seems appropriate given some sort of value), and affect our judgments of others. In addition, since orientations govern how one thinks about things in general, they also are value-laden in terms of what counts as a good reason for this individual's patterns of inquiry. This is why Dewey makes it a point to focus on *habits* of thinking and problem solving in his educational work (for example, Dewey, *How We Think*).

Burke's notion of orientation can be constructively combined with Dewey's notion of mind and habit. This section has added additional detail to past accounts of orientation that related it to ontology and value determined at the individual level (Stroud, "Constructing a Deweyan Theory"). Orientation can be said to be a wide-ranging mental habit that governs an individual's response to a variety of objects, situations, and activities. Being a habit, an orientation forms in the light of past experience, both individual and group (namely, through socially encouraged occupations). It involves systematicity—it organizes subhabits of body and mind toward greater ends and interests. It is also projective insofar as it readies the agent for certain types of activities and "incapacitates" them in regard to other lines of action. This can even have an attentional importance—one's habits foreground certain environmental features and background others. One "minds" certain aspects as dictated by their orientation and tends to overlook ones noticed by someone of another orientation. This Deweyan notion of habit is one that extends William James's embodied notion of habit and one that fits well with Burke's later emphasis on the body (Hawhee). It therefore serves as an advance to see Burke's notion of orientation through the lens of habit in a pragmatist rhetoric, since it would cover both animals and humans (which Burke seems concerned with in his first section of *Permanence and Change*) as well as provide a way to meliorate human experience (through the modification of dominant habits of mind and body). This latter project seems to be evident in Burke's comments to his students at Bennington College, where he constantly pushed them to develop certain habits of critical text consumption (Wible). Thus there should be a fundamental compatibility between the two sources of this emergent notion of orientation. Yet one still may question the usefulness of orientation as a concept for a pragmatist *rhetoric*. Burke's own distinctive emphasis in his reading of language and orientation proves valuable in answering this question.

BURKE ON LANGUAGE AND ORIENTATION

Burke shares an interesting relationship to pragmatism. He clearly read Dewey (George and Selzer), and many of his commentators "called him a pragmatist, even if there has not been much consideration of all that this designation means for extensions of the Burkean system or of how this assessment might color attempts to reread and thus reconsider the pragmatic aspects of his rhetoric" (Blakesley 87). Yet it is not clear that Dewey read Burke. We also know with some certainty that they never corresponded. We can still constructively juxtapose their thought in our own attempt to think in a new way concerning how pragmatism might view rhetoric. I argue in this section that Burke's reading of language and its role in orientation can expand Dewey's habit-based notion of orientation. This extension will clearly move

Dewey's ethical and evaluative concerns with orientation into the realm of rhetoric—the purposive use of language among human agents. I consider two points in this explication: 1) Burke's rhetorical reading of motive and its relation to a Deweyan scheme of orientation; and 2) how Burke and Dewey can be used to enunciate the enigmatic concept of an "art of living." This latter point will clearly link issues of orientation to rhetorical methods of *orientational persuasion*, a potentially rich project for future study in pragmatist rhetoric.

Rhetoric, Motive, and Orientation

Burke's reading of orientation shares similarities to Dewey's in that the former clearly grounds human judgment and language use in the body (Crusius 37). As argued in the previous section, Dewey's flexible notion of habit can be another, more detailed way of explicating, as Burke puts it in his 1983 afterword to *Permanence and Change*, such "Bodies that Learn Language" (295). Yet Burke extends the habits involved in orientation in an interesting way. In *Permanence and Change* he clearly ties orientation to expectancy—"orientation is a reading from 'what is' to 'what may be'" (15). This is the sort of projective force of habits characterizing the Deweyan reading, the ability of habits to shape our experiences and activities in certain constrained channels. Burke explicitly links this expectancy from one's orientation to the sort of means selection (or marshaled subordinate habits) involved in reaction. Certain stimuli in an environment stand out or have meaning because our orientation puts it there. Furthermore our orientation tells us what to expect from those objects as part of that meaning. We then navigate—consciously or unconsciously—toward the interests and values enshrined in our orientation through seemingly consistent means selection.

All of this is readily compatible with the Deweyan notion of orientation provided previously. What Burke adds to this story is the next step—the claim that "in the human sphere, the subject of expectancy and the judgment as to what is proper in conduct is largely bound up with the subject of motives, for if we know *why* people do as they do, we feel that we know *what* to expect of them and of ourselves, and we shape our decisions and judgments and policies to take such expectancies into account" (*Permanence and Change* 18).

In the *human* or social environment, much of our orientation toward objects is that of being related to other human beings. These beings, according to Burke, do more than simply act or move. They act with *purpose.* This much is clearly aligned with Dewey, for whom all human action is interested and purposive at some level. Yet for Burke, motive becomes inherently connected to linguistic ways of "cutting" the world up. Burke ties motive to language and thereby renders orientations (which ground our notions of motives) *rhetorical.* This is clearly an advance on Dewey, who ruminated about the importance of language, yet often stopped with cryptic or overly laudatory proclamations about its value (for example, Dewey, *Experience and Nature*).

How are motives linguistic for Burke? Put simply, they are the terms that we use to label (or name) our reactions to certain situations. A situation is "suspicious" or "angst-filled," and so on. These words are powerful and meaningful because they foreground certain parts of the situation as major causal features, as in Burke's example of someone's *contextualized* behavior making us suspicious (*Permanence and Change* 31). An agent uses the word "suspicion" in regard to a personal reaction, but the agent really uses it to refer to "the situation itself—and he would invariably pronounce himself motivated by suspicion whenever a similar pattern of stimuli recurred" (*Permanence and Change* 31). The situation—meaning those contextual factors of self, other, environment, desires, and so forth—all add up to that term being applied. Furthermore once that term is applied, we have a path for action. Our orientations tell us certain ways to behave when confronted with "suspicious situations." Perhaps one behaves in a guarded, wary fashion. The important point is that the term attached to the motives involved in that situation comes from one's orientation and channels (consciously or unconsciously) one's reaction in that situation. Thus motive can provide a meeting point for interest and the projective forces involved in the Deweyan notion of habit that undergirds the idea of orientation.

Motives are inherently tied to our orientational responses to certain situations and are intrinsically linguistic. Burke points out that "motives are distinctively linguistic products. We discern situational patterns by means of the particular vocabulary of the cultural group into which we are born" (*Permanence and Change* 35). We are not born with certain concepts, least of all the rich, socially interesting ones that characterize human action and its judgment. Thus orientation or mind must be socially inflected, and the primary way this occurs is through the learning of a language. Burke is supportive of this way of reading human habituation—"Our minds, as linguistic products, are composed of concepts (verbally molded) which select certain relationships as meaningful. Other groups may select other relationships as meaningful" (*Permanence and Change* 35). Burke is clearly making the Deweyan point that "mind" is not a substance; instead it is a culturally formed orientation toward the range of experiences we undergo. Cultural diversity is related to orientational diversity, and the primary way this is enforced and transmitted is through language. Dewey (*Logic*) shares this view of language in its general themes, noting that while it is only one of many cultural institutions, language is the way "other institutions and habits are *transmitted* . . . it permeates both the forms and contents of all other cultural activities" (51). What Dewey does not provide is the sort of link between language and motive and situational responsiveness that Burke can provide.

This point must be explained, as some may object that Dewey clearly makes this move in his own work, and without needing a comparative engagement with Burke. Dewey clearly indicates the sociality of language by highlighting its inherently perspectival and imaginative nature (Alexander; Crick, "John Dewey's Aesthetics"; Dewey, *Experience and Nature*). Dewey also clearly points out that reflection or reasoning "is defined by development of symbol-meanings in relation to one another" (*Logic* 60) and is what lets us abstract from the immediate, particular contents of some present situation. Yet he leaves the ways that communication can develop unclear, save for talk about communication being "the making of something common" (52). But this reading leaves it unclear how communication could be manipulative or fail to involve the sort of laudatory perspective sharing Dewey puts so close to the conceptual heart of "communication." Burke's notion of motive as a linguistic shorthand for a particular *type* of situation and path of response allows us to clear up the role of communication in Dewey's view of situational responsiveness.

Dewey also wants to provide a rich reading of "motive," so this linguistic addition would be a constructive move. For instance, in his portion of the 1932 *Ethics*, Dewey argues that motive is misconstrued when it is taken as an outside force that "moves" an agent to action in a specific situation. Instead he builds on his theme of the "*essential unity of the self and its act*" (288) and argues that the act *expresses* the agent's present character as well as *forms* the agent's future character. "Character" is simply another way of denoting that bundle of habits that forms the core of one's personality or way of reacting to certain situations. While "motive" can mean an object that one is drawn toward, Dewey points out that it is better taken in the form of "interest." As he puts it, "An interest is, in short, the dominant direction of activity, and in this activity desire is united with an object to be furthered in a decisive choice" (290). Like Burke, Dewey is arguing that "motive" is really shorthand for a specific situation involving an agent, his desires, his position, and certain paths of action in relation to certain objects (goals, other people, states of affairs, and so forth). Dewey concludes his point by arguing, "A motive is not then a drive *to* action, or something which moves *to* doing something. It *is* the movement of the self as a whole, a movement in which desire is integrated with an object so completely as to be chosen as a compelling end" (291). "Motive" is simply a reflective way of describing how an agent, with certain formed habits, pursues certain objects in a given situation. Thus, in the example of the suspicious situation, one's motive would be labeled as "suspicion," but this primarily occurs as a way of summing up certain habituated responses to stimuli in that situation (a conversational stranger wanting one's home address, say). The label helps us categorize the specific interaction, which in turn helps us orient our responses to the situation.

Is one justified in the second half of that last claim? Why not say that motive is *merely* a way to capture what happened in a situation *after* all is said and done? What Burke's line of thought forces on Dewey is the explicit recognition that orientation involves developed linguistic concepts that are habitually used not only in reflecting on a situation that has occurred but also in the engagement with that situation. Two things in Dewey's reading of language and ethics should prepare him for this, and yet he does not take this step. A *Deweyan* pragmatist rhetoric could make this move, however. First, Dewey points out that words become habituated in terms of meaning just as other events do. "Meaning" means, in typical pragmatist fashion, certain expectancies in terms of experience. Such meaning also is grounded in our past experience. Thus "fire" means something hot, and we typically learn this through socialization combined with some experience of fire. Once these words (arbitrary in their basic nature) become habituated through acceptance of some sort of group symbol system (*Logic* 55), an individual reacts to them in as immediate a fashion as one does to a naturally occurring phenomenon. As Dewey points out, "When we hear the words, *table, chair, stove, coat,* we do not have to reflect in order to grasp what is meant. The terms convey meaning so directly that no effort at translation is needed" (*How We Think* 294). Thus words that are habituated or incorporated into one's orientation are an important part of how one reacts to situations and the communicative action therein. It is but a short step to the Burkean position that most of our reactions to social situations are 1) toned by the vocabularies we use in making immediate meaning of things and 2) changeable or contingent (namely, no one vocabulary is essential or necessary).

A second way that the Burkean reading of orientation can help us construct a Deweyan pragmatist rhetoric comes in the form of expanding Dewey's reading of moral approbation. Burke's notion of orientation is explicitly rhetorical, as it involves a persuasive use of language in cutting up the world and our reactions to it. In many cases it is *the agent* that is "moved" by his or her terms. In other cases the other participants are moved via identification. In any case, our linguistic ways of cutting up the world and what we expect from certain stimuli lead us to do certain things and refrain from others. The power of these linguistic aspects to our orientation also influences our moral judgment. Moral judgment is a rich topic in Dewey (see Gouinlock), but I can begin to show how it would be altered with these Burkean intuitions. Take Dewey's reading of the moral situation in the 1930s in his *Ethics* and *Three Independent Factors.* There he indicates that the complexity of moral situations comes from three factors: conflicting ends dictated by individual desires; conflicting demands or expectations coming from social relations; and reactions of approbation/disapproval on the actions of others. These turn into the features of the good, the right, and the virtuous, respectively. What commentators such as Gregory Pappas point out is that Dewey is emphasizing that such complex situations demand a "description of them *as they are experienced*" (Pappas 34).

This demand for taking primary experience seriously is what placed Dewey at odds with moral philosophy that strives always to take a neutral "theoretical position." I would argue that upon closer inspection, our reactions to issues of good, right, and virtue are linguistically mediated. Of course, as Richard Shusterman (125) has argued, language can be immediately experienced even though it serves to mediate experience. Linguistic utterances and terms become habitual, but they can always be brought to reflective attention for reconstruction. In terms of our expectancies in the realm of ends, these become systematized in a form of "classification" that allows for the "acts of judgment, of comparison, of reckoning, [that] repeat themselves and develop in proportion to the increase in capacity for foresight and reflection" (Dewey, *Three Independent Factors* 282). Remembering that Dewey indicates that reflection occurs only through the intervention of symbols, we see the Burkean point—matters of ends are conditioned by linguistic screens, a vital part of our orientation.

Issues of right and virtue, when scrutinized, also seem clearly to involve expectancies deriving content from systems of symbols. "Men who live together inevitably make demands on one another," says Dewey (*Three Independent Factors* 285), and one can see how any developed social situation will render these demands as more than issues of mere physical possession. They will reach the level of *social* duty, often the result of position, role, relationship, and so forth. All of these are the same socialized and contingent aspects to social expectations noted by Dewey in his earlier work in ethics (for example, *Outlines*). Say a teacher acts in a partial way toward one of her students. Others react in a fashion expressive of disapproval (thus, in the terms of virtue) *because* the term "teacher" and the supposedly impartial treatment it prescribes for all involved have been violated. Whether or not they consciously *labeled* the teacher as "teacher," their immediate reaction is captured in its detail by the expectancies summed up in the term "teacher." The expectancies that led to that judgment of social disapproval were based on terminological ways of identifying that role, a point noted by Burke in his earlier work (*Permanence and Change*) as well as in later writings (for example, Burke, *Language*"; Stob, "Terministic Screens"). Right is similarly conditioned, as our expectations of others are based on their roles, denoted and individuated by certain terms that specify the sort of relationship and interaction we ought to expect. My point here is simple: a Deweyan pragmatist rhetoric sees orientation as inherently involving linguistic systems of motive describing situations, since they are implicated in the sort of expectancies and purposes we postulate in regard to concrete situations we react to. For Dewey, morality is situational. For Burke, part of this situational character lies in the specific terms we use to delineate situations from each other. A pragmatist rhetoric would extend both of these insights into the ways habitual orientations lead us to act and react.

Pragmatist Rhetoric and the "Art of Living"

Both Dewey and Burke are notable for isolated, enigmatic references to the "art of living." For Dewey, the situational responsiveness he builds into his early ethics never leaves him. He is perpetually concerned with the tight interlinking of agent/situation and character/act. "Habit" serves as a unifying term in his later work, since our habits are formed by doing certain things, and they set up ways of acting/reacting in future situations. In his early work, though, he puts this in a more aesthetic and tantalizing form. In his *Outlines of a Critical Theory of Ethics,* Dewey tightly links the moral projects of life with art: "If the necessary part played in conduct by artistic cultivation is not so plain, it is largely because 'Art' has been made such an unreal Fetich—a sort of superfine and extraneous polish to be acquired only by specially cultivated people. In reality, living is itself the supreme art; it requires fineness of touch; skill and thoroughness of workmanship; susceptible response and delicate adjustment to a situation apart from reflective analysis; instinctive perception of the proper harmonies of act and act, of man and man" (316).

Life is not *like* art; it *is* an art—at least if done with the sort of sensitivity and progressive adjustment that characterize the absorptive, skilled practices we recognize in fine art (Dewey, *Art as Experience*). This is a strong claim, one that is at odds with Steven Fesmire's more analogical reading of the relation between art and morality. Yet one can clearly see what Dewey is driving at—if we disregard our typical ways of envisioning art, we can see an important similarity in both endeavors. Indeed if we quit looking at morality as learning and following a set of rules, we can instead see the goal of morality as the "development of character, a certain spirit and method in all conduct" (Dewey, *Study of Ethics* 307). The sort of character we ought to develop is one that enshrines a heightened sensitivity or engagement with the present situation one finds herself in—whether that is in a museum, a laboratory, or an ethical dilemma.

Burke is similarly concerned with ossification of orientation, or the rendering of it as mechanical, unchanging, and unnoticed. Dewey did not like the mechanism of much of modern life, leading him to oppose aesthetic experience to not only aimlessness but also to overly mechanized ways of experiencing life (*Art as Experience*). Thus both are concerned about a similar problem with modern life, even if they (or their commentators) do not always notice this consonance. Dewey pushes flexibility and openness in orientation, but the question is always *how* to achieve this. Part of Dewey's answer is education—ways of forming individual habits of interaction and problem solving that are democratic in a deep, communal sense (Dewey, *Democracy and Education*). Burke's solution to the hardening of orientation, at least in *Permanence and Change,* was his "perspective by incongruity." While he unfortunately essentialized science (both Marxist and laboratory) as necessarily inflexible (see, for example, *Permanence and Change* 66), one can still extract a general orientational point that is compatible with Dewey's reading of inquiry as potentially flexible. When any orientation becomes so entrenched that breaking free of it may be beneficial, Burke recommends acts of linguistic "impiety." Burke points out that orientations encourage a sort of "piety"—they include a "*sense of what goes with what*" (*Permanence and Change* 74). This is related to how orientations involve expectancy, but it also can be related to how orientation influences our judgment. Certain points are rejected, seemingly in a rational fashion, because they do not cohere with our orientation. Burke's notion of orientation—and its influence of piety—"extends through all the texture of our lives but has been concealed from us because we think we are so thoroughly without religion and think that 'pious process' is confined to the sphere of churchliness" (75). Aspects we tend to connect to militant religious fundamentalism are really aspects to any established orientation.

Perspective by incongruity concerns what Burke calls the "art of living" (*Permanence and Change* 66). What would characterize this art that Dewey also seemed eager to proffer? Like Dewey, Burke places flexibility close to the heart of the concept of the artful person. Going further than Dewey, Burke provides a *way* to encourage this. Perspective by incongruity is not merely a way to describe how Nietzsche, say, wrote but is instead a prescription for how we ought to use rhetoric to recraft our lives artistically. In this way we become *poets* through adjusting our orientation toward our lives. Perspective by incongruity occurs when one "takes a word usually applied to one setting and transfer[s] its use to another setting." This act of reframing a word through misuse is effective in "violating the 'properties' of the word in its previous linkages" (Burke, *Permanence and Change* 90). In other words, such an individual, like the poet, is violating existing expectancies of standard orientations for the sake of orientational change.

This idea of the artful person as poet is similar to Richard Rorty's notion of the ironist. Both seem to prize the creative use of vocabulary to recraft or reconstruct our self-conceptions. The main difference, though, is that Rorty seems to acknowledge that it would not be best if *all* individuals at *all* times acted as the ironist does (87–88). Burke, on the other hand, seems to propose ongoing perspective by incongruity in all individuals. While a Deweyan view would encourage criticism in all individuals (much like the opening pages of Burke's *Permanence and Change*), it would not encourage critical activity *at all times.* Some accounts do lean further toward ongoing and never-ending criticism than Burke's (for example, McKerrow), but what Dewey would add is that criticism should occur when a human faces a *problematic situation.* This is part of the flexibility and appropriateness of response that form the core to Dewey's notion of artful activity, and I would argue that this could temper blanket Burkean pronouncements to act impiously *always* and to confound always one's standing orientation. The artful person notices *when* his orientation has led him into more problems than it solves, and it is at that point that the argumentative strategies of perspective by incongruity would be called upon. Put in Deweyan terms, it is when our present meanings and habits present themselves as more incapacities than as enabling features that critical thought is called for. As Burke puts it, "Progress means increase of present meaning, which involves multiplication of sensed distinctions as well as harmony, unification" (*Human Nature* 196). Combining this with Dewey's reading of the often-immediate experience of habit, we see that the most artfully lived life will be one of gripping immediacy *and* appropriate periods of consciously mediated critical reflection. The addition from Burke, of course, is that this latter phase can often take the rhetorical form of planned incongruity.

Thus Burke can add to a Deweyan pragmatist rhetoric a notion of *orientational persuasion.* He addresses this sort of important, significant change in the way we engage the world through terms such as "conversion," but one can see its general features. It seems to involve 1) bringing to awareness an accepted orientation, 2) showing a new way to construct linkages and expectancies, and 3) demonstrating the desirability of sticking with the new way of orienting oneself. The last stage is the most interesting—and difficult—of the points Burke proclaims. This is especially the case since Burke recognizes that the criterion of success or worth is *internal* to an orientation. How can one change orientations out of concern for the better when "better" is defined by the very orientation one already possesses?

This is a deep problem, and one that cannot be comprehensively addressed here. I can argue that a Deweyan pragmatist rhetoric has the resources to deal clearly with it over time. Why would I think this? Burke hints that while the criterion of success is internal to an orientation, "planned incongruity should be deliberately cultivated for the purpose of *experimentally* wrenching apart all those molecular combinations on adjective and noun, substantive and verb, that remain with us" (*Permanence and Change* 119, emphasis added). What is important here is Burke's subtle appeal to experience in the form of "experimentation." Dewey's thought privileges experience as the source of novelty and provides what can be called an *experiential account* of rhetoric. What does the experience of a certain text *put us through*? I have argued elsewhere that this is what is at stake in Dewey's moral and aesthetic theory—an aesthetic experience *is* a moral experience, as they are both instances of the live, absorptive attention to situational detail that Dewey puts as the end point to moral development (Stroud, "Pragmatism and Orientation"). Others have argued a similar point in highlighting the phenomenological experience that texts put their readers through (for example, Leff and Sachs). Thus a pragmatist rhetoric would pay particular attention to the experiences that rhetorical acts put their auditors through *as those experiences can serve as reasons to change orientations.* Of course, more must be said as to those cases that one rejects that experience on the basis of one's current orientation. But one sees an emergent project for pragmatist rhetoric in combining Burke and Dewey on orientation. Orientations 1) serve as the basis for rhetorical activity, 2) offer a way to change orientations (disorientation through "perspective by incongruity"), and 3) highlight the importance of experience and its bidirectional relation to agential habit. Furthermore, 4) pragmatist rhetorical study can track the variety of ways experience is employed in actual attempts at orientational persuasion.

WORKS CITED

Alexander, Thomas. "John Dewey and the Roots of Democratic Imagination." In *Recovering Pragmatism's Voice: The Classical Tradition, Rorty, and the Philosophy of Communication,* ed. Lenore Langsdorf and Andrew R. Smith, 131–301. Albany: State University of New York Press, 1995.

Bitzer, Lloyd. "The Rhetorical Situation." *Philosophy & Rhetoric* 1.1 (1968): 1–14.

Blakesley, David. "Kenneth Burke's Pragmatism—Old and New." In *Kenneth Burke and the 21st Century,* ed. Bernard L. Brock, 71–95. Albany: State University of New York Press, 1999.

Burke, Kenneth. *Attitudes toward History.* 3rd ed. Berkeley: University of California Press, 1984.

———. *Language as Symbolic Action: Essays on Life, Literature, and Method.* Berkeley: University of California Press, 1966.

———. *Permanence and Change: An Anatomy of Purpose.* 3rd ed. Berkeley: University of California Press, 1984.

Crick, Nathan. *Democracy and Rhetoric: John Dewey on the Arts of Becoming.* Columbia: University of South Carolina Press, 2010.

———. "John Dewey's Aesthetics of Communication." *Southern Communication Journal* 69.4 (2004): 303–19.

Crusius, Timothy W. *Kenneth Burke and the Conversation after Philosophy.* Carbondale: Southern Illinois University Press, 1999.

Dewey, John. *Art as Experience.* In *The Later Works of John Dewey,* vol. 10, ed. Jo Ann Boydston. Carbondale: Southern Illinois University Press, 1989.

———. *Democracy and Education.* In *The Middle Works of John Dewey,* vol. 9, ed. Jo Ann Boydston. Carbondale: Southern Illinois University Press, 1985.

———. *Ethics.* In *The Later Works of John Dewey,* vol. 7, ed. Jo Ann Boydston. Carbondale: Southern Illinois University Press, 1989.

———. *Experience and Nature.* In *The Later Works of John Dewey,* vol. 1, ed. Jo Ann Boydston. Carbondale: Southern Illinois University Press, 1988.

———. *How We Think.* In *The Later Works of John Dewey,* vol. 8, ed. Jo Ann Boydston, 105–352. Carbondale: Southern Illinois University Press, 1989.

———. *Human Nature and Conduct.* In *The Middle Works of John Dewey,* vol. 14, ed. Jo Ann Boydston. Carbondale: Southern Illinois University Press, 1988.

———. "The Interpretation of Savage Mind." In *The Middle Works of John Dewey,* vol. 2, ed. Jo Ann Boydston, 39–52. Carbondale: Southern Illinois University Press, 1976.

———. *Leibniz's Essays Concerning the Human Understanding.* In *The Early Works of John Dewey,* vol. 1, ed. Jo Ann Boydston, 251–435. Carbondale: Southern Illinois University Press, 1969.

———. *Logic: The Theory of Inquiry.* In *The Later Works of John Dewey,* vol. 12, ed. Jo Ann Boydston. Carbondale: Southern Illinois University Press, 1986.

———. *Outlines of a Critical Theory of Ethics.* In *The Early Works of John Dewey,* vol. 3, ed. Jo Ann Boydston, 237–388. Carbondale: Southern Illinois University Press, 1969.

———. *The Public and Its Problems.* In *The Later Works of John Dewey,* vol. 2, ed. Jo Ann Boydston, 235–372. Carbondale: Southern Illinois University Press, 1984.

———. *The Study of Ethics.* In *The Early Works of John Dewey,* vol. 4, ed. Jo Ann Boydston, 219–362. Carbondale: Southern Illinois University Press, 1971.

———. *Three Independent Factors in Morality.* In *The Later Works of John Dewey,* vol. 5, ed. Jo Ann Boydston. Carbondale: Southern Illinois University Press, 1984.

"Education: Dewey at 80." *Time,* October 30, 1939. (accessed June 10, 2013) Available at http://www.time.com/time/ magazine/article/0,,931809,00.html.

Fesmire, Steven. *John Dewey and Moral Imagination: Pragmatism in Ethics.* Bloomington: Indiana University Press, 2003.

George, Ann, and Jack Selzer. *Kenneth Burke in the 1930s.* Columbia: University of South Carolina Press, 2007.

Gouinlock, James. *John Dewey's Philosophy of Value.* New York: Humanities, 1972.

Hawhee, Debra. *Moving Bodies: Kenneth Burke at the Edges of Language.* Columbia: University of South Carolina Press, 2009.

Hildebrand, David. "Was Kenneth Burke a Pragmatist?" *Transactions of the Charles S. Peirce Society* 31 (1995): 632–57.

James, William. *The Principles of Psychology.* 1890. Reprint. Cambridge, Mass..: Harvard University Press, 1983.

Leff, Michael, and Andrew Sachs. "Words the Most Like Things: Iconicity and the Rhetorical Text." *Western Journal of Speech Communication* 54.3 (1990): 252–73.

McKerrow, Raymie E. "Critical Rhetoric: Theory and Praxis." *Communication Monographs* 56.2 (1989): 91–111.

Pappas, Gregory F. *John Dewey's Ethics: Democracy as Experience.* Bloomington: Indiana University Press, 2008.

Rorty, Richard. *Contingency, Irony, and Solidarity.* New York: Cambridge University Press, 1989.

Shusterman, Richard. *Pragmatist Aesthetics: Living Beauty, Rethinking Art.* Cambridge, MA: Blackwell, 1992.

Stob, Paul. "Kenneth Burke, John Dewey, and the Pursuit of the Public." *Philosophy & Rhetoric* 38.3 (2005): 226–47.

———. "'Terministic Screens,' Social Constructionism, and the Language of Experience: Kenneth Burke's Utilization of William James." *Philosophy & Rhetoric* 41 (2008): 130–52.

Stroud, Scott R. "Constructing a Deweyan Theory of Moral Cultivation." *Contemporary Pragmatism* 3 (2006): 99–116.

———. *John Dewey and the Artful Life: Pragmatism, Aesthetics, and Morality.* University Park: Pennsylvania State University Press, 2011.

———. "John Dewey and the Question of Artful Communication." *Philosophy & Rhetoric* 41.2 (2008): 153–83.

———. "John Dewey and the Question of Artful Criticism." *Philosophy & Rhetoric* 44 (2011): 27–51.

———. "Orientational Meliorism, Pragmatist Aesthetics, and the *Bhagavad Gita.*" *Journal of Aesthetic Education* 43 (2009): 1–17.

———. "Pragmatism and Orientation." *Journal of Speculative Philosophy* 20 (2006): 287–307.

Veblen, Thorstein. *The Instinct of Workmanship and the Irksomeness of Labor.* New York: Macmillan, 1914.

Wang, Jessica Ching-Sze. *John Dewey in China: To Teach and to Learn.* Albany: State University of New York Press, 2007.

Wible, Scott. "Professor Burke's 'Bennington Project.'" *Rhetoric Society Quarterly* 38.3 (2008): 259–82.

Minister of Democracy

John Dewey, Religious Rhetoric, and the Great Community

Paul Stob

In October 1921 William Jennings Bryan launched an aggressive campaign against Darwinism—a campaign that would eventually lead him to the witness stand in the Scopes Trial (Larson 41–59). Delivering the James Sprunt Lectures at Union Theological Seminary in Virginia, Bryan took aim at "a menace to fundamental morality." He elaborated: "The hypothesis to which the name of Darwin has been given—the hypothesis that links man to the lower forms of life and makes him a lineal descendant of the brute—is obscuring God and weakening all the virtues that rest upon the religious tie between God and man" (Bryan, *In His Image* 88). Bryan did not stop there, however. He inveighed against a theory that was "shaking the faith of millions" (88), and he called Darwin's work "absurd as well as groundless" (95). He marveled that "any person intelligent enough to teach school would talk such tommyrot to students" (98). He encouraged his listeners to "ridicule these pseudo-scientists who come to you with guesses instead of facts" (100). In addition he condemned a theory that had "destroy[ed] the faith of Christians and [laid] the foundations for the bloodiest war in history" (125). Bryan's lecture was such a success that he renamed it "The Menace of Darwinism" and began delivering it across the country. He also crafted a second anti-Darwin discourse, "The Bible and Its Enemies," which he hoped would raise a chorus of opposition to what he saw as the most wicked and debased set of ideas in hundreds of years.

As Bryan toured the country mustering opposition to evolution, John Dewey felt compelled to respond. His venue for responding was the *New Republic,* a prominent periodical that for two decades served as "his principal *[sic]* medium for the larger task of public education" (Westbrook, *John Dewey* 193). Staring at a blank piece of typewriter paper and contemplating Bryan's ability to spit fire with words and to enlist others in an antievolution crusade, Dewey faced a difficult set of questions—

questions that centered on the role of communication in public culture. Was there room in American society for intolerant invective such as the kind Bryan spouted? How should readers of the *New Republic* understand Bryan's discursive combat with evolutionists? How should John Dewey, the great philosopher of American democracy, address someone who seemed intent on turning the American people against modern science? What about the religious grounding of Bryan's arguments? Did religious rhetoric—particularly the divisive, antagonistic, intolerant religious rhetoric that Bryan practiced—belong in Dewey's much-hoped-for "Great Community" (Dewey, *Later Works* 2:324)?

Given Dewey's thoughts on communication, answering these questions is less than straightforward. After all, communication in the Great Community is not supposed to sound or function like Bryan's religious rhetoric. It is supposed to proceed through "empathy and foresight" (Belman 29). It is supposed to mimic "a sacred ceremony that draws persons together in fellowship and commonality" (Carey 43). It is supposed to function as "a form of art that has the potential to bring about aesthetic experience in its participants and open their eyes to the world of possibilities embodied within each of us" (Crick, "John Dewey's Aesthetics" 314). Operating within "a context of mutual understanding," communication should create "shared experience" (Burks 121). It should involve "the transformation of external events (both the material of experience and the means of communication) into a real participation and sharing of meaning among individual humans" (Stroud 10). At the heart of Dewey's philosophy was "a Great Community in which a new kind of dialogic communication would produce an enlightened democratic public capable of self-governance" (Jansen 238).

What, then, to do about William Jennings Bryan? If, as Dewey famously insisted, communication is the "most wonderful" of "all affairs," enabling "participation" and "sharing" among the citizenry (Dewey, *Later Works* 1:132), what about Bryan's fire spitting? If communication enables meanings to be "deflected from the rapid and roaring stream of events into a calm and traversable canal" (1:132), what are we to do with religious appeals that make water rougher and more treacherous than it was before? Does Dewey provide an answer? "Communication," he insists, "is uniquely instrumental and uniquely final. It is instrumental as liberating us from the otherwise overwhelming pressure of events and enabling us to live in a world of things that have meaning. It is final as a sharing in the objects and arts precious to a community, a sharing whereby meanings are enhanced, deepened and solidified in the sense of communion" (1:159). Liberation, sharing, and communion do not seem to be the best characterizations of Bryan's crusade.

In fact because religious rhetoric has a relatively unique ability to create division, promote separation, and foster antagonism (see, for example, Lewis 1–11), it creates special problems for Dewey's theory of communication. His discussions of language, dialogue, and meaning seem alien to the conflictual and disruptive religious appeals that permeate American society. Nevertheless any hope for the emergence of a Great Community, any chance for an "organized, articulate Public" to come into being (Dewey, *Later Works* 2:350), must in some way grapple with the often divisive function of religious symbols. Dewey's theory of communication seems to evade such grappling, focusing instead on "the mutuality which ought to be at the heart of democratic communication practices" (Keith 103).

However, Dewey's theory of communication is not the only place to turn for answers about grappling with religious symbols in the creation of the Great Community. It is also possible to turn to Dewey's own rhetorical undertakings. To be sure, Dewey said little about rhetoric itself (see, for example, Crick, *Democracy and Rhetoric* 8–10), but he was constantly engaged in rhetorical projects, using his visibility in public culture to help individuals perceive, judge, and act on common problems in specific ways. Dewey was "both a philosopher and a public intellectual who devoted his mental energies to thinking about the social and cultural changes that were impacting his world" (Cochran 2). Time and again he undertook acts of public education—or better, the education of specific publics—regarding the intersection of religion, language, and society. As a result we can approach Dewey's work for its "full rhetoricality," to borrow Cara Finnegan's phrase (162), insofar as he helped general audiences understand the problems and possibilities of religious discourse.

As we shall see, Dewey frequently modeled strategies for handling religious symbols in accord with a stronger democratic community—the result of which was a kind of Deweyan religious rhetoric. At the heart of this rhetoric, I argue, was a process of redirection, in which Dewey seized the power of religious symbols, divorced them from their problematic tendencies, and integrated them into the discursive fabric of a pluralistic, democratic, cooperative culture. Faced with profound communicative tension, he not only entered religious controversies but also showed his listeners and readers how religious symbols were integral to the creation of a Great Community.

Exploring Dewey's religious rhetoric is partly a matter of pointing out that religious language permeates his work, which is something scholars have long known (see, for example, Rockefeller, *John Dewey* 4–5; and Pihlström 212–21). Yet there is a tendency among Dewey scholars to describe his religious terminology as implicitly or explicitly areligious. Dewey, writes Michael Eldridge, articulated a "secular project in religious language" (10). His process of "transforming experience," which was communicated through some religious terminology, is best understood "as intelligence generally or specifically as the secular form of cultural criticism that he understood to be philosophy" (Eldridge 169). Alan Ryan approaches the issue by questioning the authenticity of Dewey's religious language: "To put it unkindly, one might complain that Dewey wants the social value of religious belief without being willing to pay the epistemological price for it. To put it less unkindly, we may wonder whether, in fact, it is possible to have the *use* of religious vocabulary without the accretion of supernaturalist beliefs that Dewey wishes to slough off" (Ryan

274). Hans Joas similarly criticizes Dewey's religious terminology by writing that his "sacralization of democracy" and his proclamation of a "common faith" result in "an empty universalism of the democratic ideal" (Joas 123). Richard Rorty goes furthest in this regard when he argues that Dewey worked to mobilize "Americans as political agents" by redescribing the nation in terms of "thoroughgoing secularism" (Rorty 15).

Such characterizations can be misleading if we place too much emphasis on secularization and areligiosity. The above commentators suggest that Dewey used religious language for political, democratic ends but, in the process, emptied such language of its religious content. This essay tells a different story by focusing on Dewey's own rhetorical practices. Dewey was not, I argue, using religious symbols in a way that emptied them of their religious content. He was not trying to strip religion out of religious rhetoric. Rather, Dewey was trying to infuse public culture with a new religious purpose. His hope, writes Steven Rockefeller, was "to overcome the problematical split in modern culture between religion and science, . . . the split between the sacred and the secular, religious life and everyday life" ("Dewey's Philosophy" 125). Consequently Dewey's religious symbols formed the basis of a very religious project—the project of making democracy *more effectively* religious. By engaging and employing his own religious rhetoric, he became more than "the most important advocate of participatory, deliberative democracy" of the twentieth century (Westbrook, "Making of a Democratic Philosopher" 18); he became America's minister of democracy, preaching a gospel and seeking converts as ardently and hopefully as any traditional minister.

DEWEYAN RELIGIOUS RHETORIC

Perhaps the best way to approach Dewey's handling of religious symbols is to investigate how he did, in fact, discuss Bryan's antievolution invective. "The campaign of William Jennings Bryan against science and in favor of obscurantism and intolerance," Dewey stated in the opening sentence of his article "The American Intellectual Frontier" for the *New Republic,* "is worthy of serious study" (*Middle Works* 13:301). The reason it was worthy of serious study was not because Bryan was a fool or a marginal figure but because his appeals captivated a sizable portion of the American public. "In its success (and it is meeting with success)," Dewey explained of Bryan's campaign, "it raises fundamental questions about the quality of our democracy. It helps us understand the absence of intellectual radicalism in the United States and the present eclipse of social and political liberalism" (13:301).

The article's opening paragraph illustrated Dewey's appreciation of the power of religious symbols. Bryan's campaign needed to be addressed, he insisted, because Bryan had crafted a set of ideas and appeals that captivated audiences in town after town. Simply dismissing his discourse as obscurantism and intolerance—even though it was distinguished by obscurantism and intolerance—dangerously underestimated Bryan's rhetorical prowess. As a "typical democratic figure," continued

Dewey, Bryan "has stood for and with the masses, not radically but 'progressively,'" demonstrating "a genuine and effective connection between the political and doctrinal directions of his activity, and between the popular responses they call out" (*Middle Works* 13:301). Given Bryan's success, Dewey felt compelled to explore the "Great Commoner's" ability to connect with "the masses" and to influence the direction of American society.

In Dewey's mind, Bryan was able to connect with the American people because of his religious appeals—that is, because "the middle classes are for the most part the church-going classes, those who have come under the influence of evangelical Christianity" (*Middle Works* 13:301). Dewey was not prepared to dismiss this evangelical public, however. Instead he recognized the importance of this public for his own sociopolitical project: "These persons form the backbone of philanthropic social interest, of social reform through political actions, of pacifism, of popular education. They embody and express the spirit of kindly goodwill toward classes which are at an economic disadvantage and toward other nations, especially when the latter show any disposition toward a republican form of government" (13:301–2). By celebrating the reformist history of the churchgoing middle class, Dewey oriented readers toward the importance of interacting with the very people who responded favorably to Bryan's appeals. Indeed the religiously minded "'Middle West,' the prairie country, has been the centre of active social philanthropies and political progressivism," and it may, if properly directed, continue to function as the hub of social and political reform. The task, then, was to move its energies away from intolerance and toward more pluralistic, cooperative endeavors. After all, these were the people who "followed Lincoln in the abolition of slavery" and "followed Roosevelt in his denunciation of 'bad' corporations and aggregations of wealth" (13:302).

Despite such praise for the religious reform spirit, Dewey was sober about the problematic tendencies of the churchgoing middle class, which "has never had an interest in ideas as ideas, nor in science and art of what they may do in liberating and elevating the human spirit" (*Middle Works* 13:302). Given the social, political, and religious history of the United States, this public has often embraced "social and political liberalism combined with intellectual illiberality," and Bryan himself is "an outstanding symbol" of this peculiar ideological concoction (13:302). Dewey further explained that after the Second Great Awakening and the populist success of Andrew Jackson—"the man who marks the change of the earlier aristocratic republic into a democratic republic"—religion "was popularized, and thought, especially free-thought which impinged adversely upon popular moral conceptions, became unpopular, too unpopular to consist with political success" (13:303). The result was a reformist democratic public clinging to the strange "intellectual prejudices of the masses" (13:303–4).

Dewey's argumentative strategy in the middle part of the article amounted to a kind of dissociation.[1] In particular, the strategy was to dissociate the possibilities from the drawbacks of the churchgoing middle class, separating what it could do from what it had done in recent memory. In Dewey's eyes, the churchgoing middle class represented tremendous possibilities *because of* its religious impulses, because of its philanthropic, help-the-disadvantaged, follow-Lincoln-and-Roosevelt spirit. But it presently tended toward intellectual intolerance, following people similar to Bryan in fearing and denouncing challenging ideas. If the public's reformist spirit could be disentangled from its intolerant intellectual disposition, then the possibility for truly democratic progress could take root.

To encourage this disentanglement, Dewey highlighted the role of "the churches" in American public life—organizations that "performed an inestimable social function in frontier expansion. They were the rallying points not only of respectability but of decency and order in the midst of a rough and turbulent population. They were the representatives of social neighborliness and all the higher interests of the communities. The tradition persisted after the incoming of better schools, libraries, clubs, musical organizations and other agencies of 'culture'" (*Middle Works* 13:304). As time went by, however, the ability of organized religion to unite members of a community led to "indirect power of the church over thought and expression. . . . As the frontier ceased to be a menace to orderly life, it persisted as a limit beyond which it was dangerous and unrespectable for thought to travel" (13:304).

Dissociating the benefits from the drawbacks of the religious middle class created a logic for the continuation of religious work, so long as religious work could shed its problematic tendencies. Dewey's solution to the Bryan issue, therefore, was not to discard the attitudes and emotions into which Bryan tapped; nor was it to relegate religion—despite its many problems—to the private sphere. The solution was to redirect people's religious aspirations toward forms of life that were more tolerant, democratic, cooperative, and pluralistic. Because the church had been "upon the whole the most democratic institution" in communities across the country, it represented an incredible opportunity to nurture democratic life (*Middle Works* 13:304).

With the pieces of a religious redirection in place, Dewey grappled with Bryan once again in the conclusion of his article. As in the introduction, he highlighted Bryan's rhetorical effectiveness, pointing readers to the success of "his appeals and his endeavors" in "holding down the intellectual level of American life" (*Middle Works* 13:305). For Dewey, redirecting this rhetorical effectiveness meant using religious appeals to elevate, rather than hold down, the intellectual level of American life. "The forces which are embodied in the present crusade," he explained, "would not be so dangerous were they not bound up with so much that is necessary and good. We have been so taught to respect the beliefs of our neighbors that few will respect the beliefs of a neighbor when they depart from forms which have become associated with aspiration of a decent neighborly life. This is the illiberalism which is deep-rooted in our liberalism" (13:305). The way forward, then, was to understand the liberal-illiberal mixture in the American psyche and to urge people toward the liberal end of the spectrum. As Dewey summarized in the conclusion, "No account of the decay of the idealism of the progressive movement in politics or of the failure to develop an intelligent and enduring idealism out of the emotional fervor of the war, is adequate unless it reckons with this fixed limit to thought. No future liberal movement, when active liberalism revives, will be permanent unless it goes deep enough to affect it" (13:305). In other words, the future of Dewey's own sociopolitical project depended on affecting and redirecting America's religious public.

Running throughout Dewey's article was a deep and abiding respect for the power of Bryan's religious rhetoric. Dewey surely wanted to strip the intolerance and obscurantism from the content of Bryan's appeals, but Bryan's decision to engage the religious impulses of the American people was undoubtedly correct, according to Dewey. Moreover, Dewey seemed to recognize the necessity of religious engagement for his own undertakings. Failing to animate the liberal, democratic character of the churchgoing middle class would greatly impede the emergence of a truly liberal, democratic society.

Dewey's article on Bryan was more than a meditation on religious appeals and the churchgoing middle class, however. It was also an enactment of the kind of rhetorical practices needed to move American society forward. By taking to the pages of the *New Republic* to confront Bryan's campaign, Dewey illustrated the necessity of public combat. Part of building a truly liberal, democratic society was confronting the divisive, mean-spirited appeals of people such as Bryan, for only by confronting the good and the bad in public life, and only by affirming the good over the bad, could the American people see their way toward the Great Community. While readers of the *New Republic* may have felt like dismissing Bryan as a charlatan speaking to an ignorant multitude, Dewey demanded that they take Bryan's work seriously and confront his effectiveness, despite the troubling content of his appeals.

However, the most important aspect of Dewey's confrontation with Bryan, at least for the purposes of this essay, is that it was not an isolated case. It was, in fact, part of a larger pattern of confrontation that spanned Dewey's corpus. Whether addressing religious questions directly or arriving at religious considerations from an areligious starting point, Dewey interacted with religious symbols in a strikingly consistent manner. Across his public work on religious issues, three general strategies stood out, forming the core of his rhetorical redirection. First, Dewey readily acknowledged the power and importance of religious symbols in public discourse. Even when he disagreed with the use of these symbols, he did so because they connected with a sizable public. Second, Dewey distinguished the proper from improper, liberal from illiberal, valuable from harmful tendencies of religious appeals. Doing so provided a rationale for the continuation of religious rhetoric, so long as it proceeded according to a truly democratic spirit. Third, Dewey integrated religious symbols with the markers of democratic life, thereby demonstrating how religious ideals, properly deployed, could assist a liberal project. To be sure, not each strategy appeared equally and with the same emphasis in all of Dewey's writings on religious issues. But taken together, the strategies brought his public utterances into a recognizable pattern, illustrating what Steven Rockefeller has termed Dewey's "new spiritual attitude and way of being, . . . a distinctly American democratic form of spirituality" ("Dewey's Philosophy" 4).

The first strategy of Dewey's religious rhetoric involved a direct or indirect acknowledgment that religious symbols contained a special, almost unique power to influence public discourse. When writing on religious fundamentalism for the *New Republic,* for example, Dewey began by insisting that "the right name is half the battle in moral and social disputes. With the fundamentalists, their key-word, whether or no it turn out to be half the battle, is nine-tenths of their case, perhaps ninety-nine one-hundredths. The craving of human beings for something solid and unshakable upon which to rest is ultimate and unappeasable" (*Middle Works* 15:3). Whatever else one might conclude about fundamentalist ideology, the group had tapped into a basic human desire by building their case on supposedly religious, moral foundations. The fundamentalists were, therefore, at least rhetorically adept, providing an answer to "man's cry for security" (15:3).

Dewey made a similar point when commenting on "Religion in the Soviet Union." When Marx insisted that "Religion is the opium of the people," Dewey wrote, he provided the impetus for communists to overthrow traditional religion in Russia (*Later Works* 5:355). However, the overthrow was so thorough that "communism has itself become a religion that can tolerate no rival. . . . It commands in its adherents the depth and intensity of emotional fervor that is usually associated with religion at its height. Moreover, it claims intellectually to cover the whole scope of life. There is nothing in thought and life that is not affected by its claims; it has, one might almost say it *is,* a body of dogmas as fixed and unyielding as that of any church that ever existed" (5:356). By dismantling the authority of the church, Dewey explained, communists turned their own symbols into religious symbols that commanded, inspired, and unified individuals and groups. Indeed communists could not have avoided building their movement religiously, as the overthrow of the church created an intellectual vacuum that needed to be filled. With traditional religion banished, "the creed of dialectical materialism interpreted as scientific truth" became the new catechism (5:356).

In Dewey's discussions of fundamentalism in America and communism in the Soviet Union, religious symbols occupied a privileged position for the movement under consideration. This is not to say that Dewey was endorsing the ends for which the symbols were used. But he was thoroughly cognizant of the role religious appeals played in motivating people to act. Moreover he did not fault either movement for deploying religious symbols. He wanted only that religious discourse be used for the right ends. Such was Dewey's point in an article for the *Christian Century* on the book *Is There a God? A Conversation,* by Henry Nelson Wieman, Douglas Clyde

Macintosh, and Max Carl Otto. "One thing is clear," Dewey insisted in the article. "The existence or non-existence of such a God is something to get excited about. Existence makes a difference to every aspect and phase of life" (*Later Works* 9:215). Yet Dewey was far more interested in the *name* God than in the notion of a supernatural being, for the name was what ultimately commanded adherence and motivated people to act: "In a time of transition and disturbance many persons will find it helpful and consoling to continue to use the *word* 'God' to designate what actually are a collection of forces, unified only in their functional effect: the furtherance of goods in human life" (9:221).

When Dewey acknowledged the power of religious symbols in these and other writings, he created a sense of hope around these symbols.[2] The symbols should not, he maintained, be used in precisely the same ways they had been used, but their connection to fundamental human needs and desires was too strong to dismiss. As a result Dewey's religious rhetoric emerged from the potential of religious symbols to coordinate action and to provide the emotional thrust needed to unify individuals. The project, he summarized in 1910 when offering "Some Thoughts Concerning Religion," was to "discover the types of emotional attitudes that various historic religions have appealed to and nourished" (*Later Works* 17:378).

As in the article on Bryan, however, Dewey recognized the tremendous problems religious discourse (and religion in general) could create. Bringing religious rhetoric into the creation of the Great Community required care and consideration specifically because religious symbols were so powerful. It required, for Dewey, dissociating the good from the bad, a process that served as the second strategy of his religious rhetoric. By separating the potential of religious symbols from their harmful tendencies, by removing perceived incompatibilities between religious discourse and democratic life, Dewey provided a rationale for the continuation of religious appeals.

When discussing the book *Is There a God?*, for example, he distinguished between *a* God and *the* God, which spoke to the difference between inclusive and exclusive senses of religious experience. To speak of *a* God in general is to speak of a supernatural being who dictates "particular attitudes of worship and dependence," leading to "special kinds of experience which are alone regarded by [members of a church] as religious, because alone having to do with the unique objects which can evoke true religious attitudes" (*Later Works* 9:216). *A* God is a reference that members of a particular faith deploy "in accord with the idea of intense jealousy and exclusiveness" (9:217). On the other hand, *the* God refers to the object of "a particular nation, creed, confession, church, or thinker" (9:215). When referring to *the* God of a particular group, one avoids exclusivity and uses the term in accord with the "variety of distributed goods of experience" (9:222). By distinguishing between *a* God and *the* God, we are prepared, wrote Dewey, to depart from "the exclusiveness of the religious tradition" and instead "to derive your conception of religion and of God wholly from the implications of the moral life" (9:218). The God symbol remained, but by dissociating it from exclusive traditions, Dewey enabled it to move toward more pluralistic, naturalistic ends.

A similar dissociation occurred when Dewey penned "What I Believe" for the March 1930 issue of *Forum.* He wanted to make clear to the magazine's readers that he had faith, that he had his own creeds and deeply held beliefs. But his faith was different from a "body of doctrines and dogmas based upon a specific authority" (*Later Works* 5:267). Traditional notions of faith, he wrote, deny "that experience and life can regulate themselves and provide their own means of direction and inspiration," resulting in "dominant moral codes and religious beliefs" that appeal "for support to something above and beyond experience" (5:268). These codes and beliefs then lead to "philosophies of escape" that create separation from the "ills and sufferings of the experienced world" (5:268). Dewey, in contrast, wanted faith to remain—the symbol was a powerful one indeed—but he wanted it to proceed through the idea that "experience itself is the sole ultimate authority" (5:267). The result was not separation from ills and sufferings but a concerted effort to alleviate pain, for "Experience now owns as a part of itself scientific methods of discovery and test; it is marked by ability to create techniques and technologies—that is, arts which arrange and utilize all sorts of conditions and energies, physical and human. These new possessions give experience and its potentialities a radically new meaning" (5:269).

Also consider Dewey's discussion of "Religion and Our Schools," an essay built on the realization that "Education is the modern universal purveyor, and upon the schools shall rest the responsibility for seeing to it that we recover our threatened religious heritage" (*Middle Works* 4:166). Dewey, however, praised the intersection of religion and education with the qualification that "it is the business of those who do not believe that religion is a monopoly or a protected industry to contend, in the interest of both education and of religion, for keeping the schools free from what they must regard as a false bias" (4:166). For Dewey, religion and education had business together, but only if moved away from "dogmatic, catechetical and memoriter methods" (4:172). The goal was to educate about religion so that "it can be considered publicly, openly, and by common tests, even among religious people" (4:172). When shorn of dogmatic, secretive, and exclusive forms of inquiry, religion would have a place in public education. But until that time, schools "serve best the cause of religion in serving the cause of social unification," for "under certain conditions schools are more religious in substance and in promise without any of the conventional badges and machinery of religious instruction than they could be in cultivating these forms at the expense of a state consciousness" (4:175).

Keenly aware of the importance of religion, especially in American history and culture, Dewey had little interest in discarding religious ideals writ large. Rather his goal was to sever religious aspirations from dogmatic legacies and to position newly dissociated ideals as the proper way forward. Put somewhat differently, he hoped to use religious symbols in accord with liberal, pluralistic, intellectually sophisticated ends, and this hope led to the third strategy of his religious rhetoric: demonstrating how religious symbols could merge with the symbols of a truly democratic life. With this third strategy Dewey created a kind of religio-democratic discourse that transferred the energy of religious symbols into cooperative social endeavors.

Some of the best evidence of Dewey's religio-democratic discourse emerged in his address at the centennial celebration of Hollins College on May 18, 1942. For Dewey, World War II was ultimately a question of faith—a question of "whether the faith in which we were brought up and the hopes we learned to cherish are illusory" (*Later Works* 15:170). The history of civilization, he elaborated, has left "an evil heritage" of conflict, as the "brutal persecution of those of other faiths and races" unfortunately stands as "the ultimate sign of national virility" (15:171). In the midst of genocide and evil, Dewey publicly pondered whether the "articles of liberal faith" remained relevant (15:171). His answer, unsurprisingly, was that such articles did remain relevant so long as we collectively remembered that civil liberties were not terms of political and legal expediency but had a "fundamental connection with the moral and the religious values which free societies exist to express and promote" (15:172).

Dewey's faith, the faith he hoped to share with his listeners at Hollins College, was at once moral, religious, liberal, and democratic. Having condemned "evil" and the "persecution" of other faiths and races, he then performed a kind of profession of faith, detailing the tenants of his democratic creed: "faith in freedom of conscience, freedom of worship, freedom to unite voluntarily to pursue common religious, industrial, and educational aims, freedom of thought, of speech and publication" (*Later Works* 15:172). Clinging to these fundamentals—just as fundamentalists might cling to their fundamentals—was especially important in times of bloody conflict: "In carrying the practical struggle in which we are engaged on to its successful conclusion, we also need to make sure of the grounds of our faith in the ideals and methods of a free society, and we need to make sure that these grounds are moral and religious in quality, not matters of external prudence, policy, material gain, ease and comfort" (15:173).

The remainder of the Hollins College speech further wove religious and democratic symbols into a singular textual fabric. He identified "the belief that freedom of intelligence is the central article in the moral creed of a free society" (*Later Works* 15:175). He condemned as evil the "moral absolutism" of the Nazis (15:175). He praised "free inquiry and free communication" as central to the "moral and religious aims" of democratic life (15:178–79). He again identified communication as the "essence and life blood of human society" (15:179). He named "freedom of mind" as that which "justifies faith" in other freedoms, all of which were part of the democratic creed (15:182). He affirmed "the faith of the American people in education" and defended those who have embraced education as "a religion" (15:183). And he concluded by uniting his listeners in a kind of sacred oath to democratic life:

> Search for ever more and more wisdom and insight may become intense enough to have religious quality. And this religious quality is strengthened and deepened by realization that discovery of the truth that governs our relations to one another in the shared struggles, sorrows and joys of life is our common task and winning it our common reward. . . . Amid all differences of religion, we may, I believe, be one in the belief that the religion of a free society includes faith in the possibility of continued development; search for new truth as a condition of growth, and that mutual respect and regard which constitute charity as the inspiration of peace and good will among men. (15:183)

Once religious symbols had been dissociated from their dogmatic, absolutist, illiberal tendencies, they became useful for strengthening the bonds of democratic life. Especially in times of war, conflict, and death, religious rhetoric could inspire hope, could picture deliverance, and could remind people of their reasons for fighting. Dewey's address to Hollins College was, as a result, an address about good and evil, about heaven and hell, about sin and salvation—so long as we understand such terms naturalistically and within the rhythms of human experience.

The ministerial quality of the Hollins College address underscored the rhetorical advantage of redirecting the power of religious symbols. In preaching a new gospel, Dewey was able to celebrate as godly the features of his sociopolitical program, and he was able to condemn as sinful that which violated his program. His rhetorical tools became the same rhetorical tools of the pulpit. Consider his discussion of "The Democratic Faith and Education," published in 1944 in the *Antioch Review.* After acknowledging that the war shook "that old faith" in uninterrupted human progress, and after condemning "powerful totalitarian states with thorough suppression of liberty of belief and expression" (*Later Works* 15:251–52), Dewey argued that people's faith must be redirected toward "deliberate cooperative human effort" (15:253). While many commentators would turn "the scientific attitude" into "the scapegoat for present evils," thereby advocating "the beliefs and practices of a prescientific and pretechnological age" as "the road to our salvation," Dewey had other thoughts on the road to salvation (15:255). By discarding "abstract moral precepts" that divorce "ends from the means by which they must be realized," humanity could "put into practice the means by which science and technology shall be made fundamental" (15:255). In Dewey's hands, cooperative scientific effort became the new fundamentalism. "Scientific method and conclusions," he said, "will not have gained a fundamentally important place in education until they are seen and treated as supreme agencies in giving direction to collective and cooperative human behavior" (15:258). Furthering a "liberal spirit" and a "democratic faith" requires that we "humanize science," making it a servant "of the democratic hope and faith" (15:259–60). Dewey concluded the article with a kind of prayer built on a new trinity: "In this achievement science, education, and the democratic cause meet as one. May we be equal to the occasion. For it is our human problem. If a solution is found it will be through the medium of human desire, human understanding, and human endeavor" (15:260).

Redirected religious rhetoric enabled Dewey to deploy terms of good and evil—perhaps the most powerful and motivating terms in human discourse (see, for example, Burke 7–42)—within a naturalistic frame. With religious symbols shorn of their problematic tendencies, he could range as widely as any religious rhetor, issuing such statements as "When we allow ourselves to be fear-ridden and permit it to dictate how we act, it is because we have lost faith in our fellowmen—and that is the unforgivable sin against the spirit of democracy" (*Later Works* 17:86). He could position "mutual fear, suspicion, and jealousy" as evils that "deflect and impoverish human experience beyond any calculation" (*Later Works* 5:275). He could juxtapose his own beliefs to these evils, committing himself to "types of religious feeling and thought which are consistent with modern democracy and modern science" (*Middle Works* 4:167). With the aid of religious symbols, Dewey could proclaim his "faith in the possibilities of an abundant and significant experience, participated in by all" (*Later Works* 5:274). And he could advocate a religious social order "in which our human relations will be regulated by the principles that have regulated our investigations into nature: belief in truth; belief in reality; belief in the public and in the right of the public to share in whatever is gained by humanity! . . . And that, my friends, is the reason that I see the necessity for a *new kind* of politics, a *new kind* of moral conception in politics, and a new alignment and organization of the power vested in government, to help promote a new and a more humane, a just and more intelligent order in our contacts and intercourse with one another" (*Later Works* 11:281).

Dewey's call for a new politics, like his promotion of science, education, and democracy, was infused with a kind of zeal and righteous reckoning that one might hear from a pulpit. But that was precisely the point of his advocacy. His religious tone was meant to inspire, unify, and strengthen believers in his cause. Before a congregation dispersed throughout American society, Dewey preached of sin and deliverance, of evil and good, of private interest and public righteousness. His eyes were fixed on a spiritual awakening to the possibilities of science, technology, and freshly democratic politics.

CONSEQUENCES OF DEWEYAN RELIGIOUS RHETORIC

Questions about Dewey's religious commitments and religious language have long occupied scholars of his work (see, for example, Rogers 6–23). So what can a consideration of his religious rhetoric add to our understanding of his philosophy, advocacy, and place in public culture? What are the consequences of his efforts to redirect the power of religious symbols? Three primary consequences stand out: the first concerning Dewey's view of religious appeals in public life; the second concerning the complexity of his understanding of communication; and the third concerning the extent of his ministerial persona.

First, as pointed out in the introduction, several scholars have noted Dewey's use of religious terminology, but they have described his religious symbols as areligious, as stripped of religious content. My reading of Dewey's religious rhetoric suggests something different. Recognizing the power of religious symbols, Dewey spoke of social and political affairs in a way that infused them with religious purpose and direction. He was not simply co-opting religious discourse but redirecting and celebrating it. In his publicly oriented rhetoric, Dewey envisioned an America in which religious appeals were not only acceptable but also integral. He did not, as Melvin Rogers has noted, "intend for individuals to abandon . . . specific religious institutions, beliefs, and rituals" (126). Instead he maintained that "religious accommodation and negotiation can have greater currency in political matters" (135). Accommodation and negotiation do not go far enough, however. Dewey worked to construct public life around many of the same markers that defined traditional religions. Notions such as faith, belief, creed, sin, evil, and salvation were meant to structure people's attitudes in a new, pluralistically religious society. For Dewey, religious rhetoric could form the discursive bedrock of democratic life so long as religious appeals were understood within the currents of experience. As Rogers puts it, Dewey "shows us how to be pious without lapsing into blind deference and so threatening democracy. And he shows us how to have faith, without that faith being placed beyond the purview of reflection" (242).

The second consequence of Dewey's religious rhetoric is closely related to the first and concerns his theory of communication. If Dewey's theory of communication is too idealistic, too wedded to notions of sharing, unification, and communion, then it may not be the kind of theory we need, or can realistically use, in a democracy. Many scholars, in fact, have critiqued Dewey on this very ground, arguing that his theory does not properly account for the conflictual, antagonistic, often vicious modes of communication in civil society. Michael Schudson, for example, argues that "democratic talk" is not defined by the rational, problem-solving, cooperative discourse Dewey envisioned. Instead "it is essentially *public,* and if this means that democratic talk is talk among people of different values and different backgrounds, it is also profoundly *uncomfortable*" (Schudson 299). "Conversation," he elaborates, "provides no magic solution to problems of democracy. Democracy has little to do with intimacy and little to do with community. It can be thrilling, it can be boring, it can provoke anxiety, it is often uncomfortable" (307). Ronald Greene approaches Dewey's theory of communication from a different direction but similarly concludes that it is misdirected. He writes, "Due to the changing nature of capitalist production, it becomes necessary to re-think the aesthetic-moral theory that underwrites Dewey's contribution to the eloquent citizen. . . . The problem with [Dewey's moral imperative to remain open to the call of communication] is that it posits communication as a transcendental authority commanding the subject to speak" (Greene 198). Even Robert Asen, who generally lauds Dewey's thoughts on democratic society, worries that Dewey wrongly privileged "face-to-face communication as the primary force that forms local communities" (183). According to Asen, Dewey "promised an unattainable mode of interaction: an ideal of direct, unmediated communication with another" (184).

Schudson, Greene, and Asen all argue, albeit from different perspectives, that Dewey's theory of communication did not properly characterize speech in a democracy and that it was not complex enough to address the dynamics we see and experience in public life. Yet if we broaden our understanding of Dewey's view of communication to include his own rhetorical practices, we can better see his appreciation of the complexity, antagonism, and conflict of democratic speech. Dewey himself worked in and through the battles of the public sphere, especially when dealing with people such as Bryan. Indeed he met Bryan on the field of public discourse because only through rhetorical combat would the energies of Bryan's appeals be directed toward more fruitful ends. He did the same when dealing with issues of politics, war, education, and science. As Cara Finnegan has written of Dewey's call for a third political party, "Rather than the conversational, dialogic approach found in Dewey's theoretical works, in the *New Republic* essays Dewey argues quite forcefully for an *agonistic* approach to communication practice" (169). His religious rhetoric reveals much the same dynamic. Dewey not only recognized the role of conflict in a democracy but also became part of such conflict, redirecting the power of potentially divisive symbols toward the means and ends of the Great Community.[3]

The third consequence of Dewey's religious rhetoric concerns the extent of his persona as minister of democracy, which we can witness clearly in his most famous religiously directed text, *A Common Faith.* Thus far I have purposefully left aside consideration of *A Common Faith* because the book has received substantially more attention than Dewey's other religious works. My hope has been to reveal Dewey's dedication to religious redirection and his consistent pattern of argumentation in broad and various writings relative to broad and various problems. Nevertheless the book deserves mention insofar as it illustrates the upshot of his religious persona. Based on the 1933 and 1934 Terry Lectures at Yale University, *A Common Faith* acknowledged the power of religious symbols to command "obedience and reverence" for "a great variety of powers and spirits" (Dewey, *Later Works* 9:5). Dewey wanted readers to understand the wide applicability and potential of religious symbols, including when "an unseen power controlling our destiny becomes the power of an ideal. All possibilities, as possibilities, are ideal in character. The artist, scientist, citizen, parent, as far as they are actuated by the spirit of their callings, are controlled by the unseen. For all endeavor for the better is moved by faith in what is possible, not by adherence to the actual" (17). On top of this affirmation of religious symbols, Dewey employed the same kind of dissociative argument that appeared in his other religious writings. In *A Common Faith* the dissociation involved "'religion' as a noun substantive and 'religious' as adjectival" (8). Dewey's goal was to direct his readers around the problems of "religion" while embracing "'religious' as a quality of experience" (9). Once we recognize the pervasiveness of the religious, he explained, we can work for the "development of social intelligence . . . with greater hardihood and on a larger scale" (51). We can work for the "transfer of idealizing imagination, thought and emotion to natural human relations" (54).

Having redirected religious symbols away from supernatural dependence, Dewey then presented his democratic view of deliverance: "The continuing life of this comprehensive community of beings includes all the significant achievement of men in science and art and all the kindly offices of intercourse and communication. It holds within its content all the material that gives verifiable intellectual support to our ideal faiths" (*Later Works* 9:56). With "practical faith in ideal ends," with "understanding of our relations to one another," with a sense of "the doings and sufferings of the continuous human community," the minister of democracy ended with a prayer for experience: "Ours is the responsibility of conserving, transmitting, rectifying and expanding the heritage of values we have received that those who come after us may receive it more solid and secure, more widely accessible and more generously shared than we have received it. Here are all the elements for a religious faith that shall not be confined to sect, class, or race. Such a faith has always been implicitly the common faith of mankind. It remains to make it explicit and militant" (57–58).

For Dewey, sharing the democratic gospel was about converting souls and creating soldiers for the Great Community. Of course these were different soldiers than those of other faiths. But they were called forth with many of the same appeals of other faiths. Perhaps we might even say that the fervor and intensity of Dewey's democratic creed positioned him alongside Bryan in terms of rhetorical approach. Dewey's gospel, like Bryan's gospel, relied on judgments of sin and evil, of hope and deliverance, of community and communion. Dewey grappled with opponents to reveal what he believed to be the proper way forward in a given conflict. He built arguments on divisions and dissociations, separating the just from the unjust, the righteous from the unrighteous, hoping to bring people around his conception of the good. Bryan did much the same in his antievolution crusade. This is not to say that Dewey and Bryan sounded exactly the same or that they were working for the same ends. When Dewey shared his democratic gospel and promised deliverance from darkness, he did so apart from a supernatural being. His conception of deliverance, unlike Bryan's, was grounded in concerted, cooperative effort and human experience. Nevertheless, Dewey often spoke of experiential deliverance with the same sense of hope and assurance that a traditional minister spoke of supernatural deliverance. He, Bryan, and countless clergymen recognized the power of religious symbols for their own projects.

Linking John Dewey to William Jennings Bryan is certainly peculiar. Then again, attending to Dewey's own rhetorical practices provides us with a distinctive way of considering his work. Viewing him as a rhetor, even though he said little about the art of rhetoric, allows us to position him "within an interconnected public to whom [he] has responsibilities" (Crick, *Democracy and Rhetoric* 190). How he spoke about religious issues is telling in this regard because he had to work through the divisive tendencies of religious symbols. Moreover, because he was speaking and writing relative to specific controversies, audiences, and ends, he had to attend to the details of his long-hoped-for Great Community. At the center of this imagined community was a democratic church, and behind the church's pulpit was John Dewey, relying on religious appeals to rededicate a body of believers.

NOTES

1. For more on dissociative arguments, see Jasinski 175–82; and Perelman and Olbrechts-Tyteca 411–59. To borrow Perelman and Olbrechts-Tyteca's terminology, when Dewey worked to dissociate religious language from its problematic tendencies, he tried to remove a perceived incompatibility between religious rhetoric and the Great Community.

2. For other examples of Dewey's thoughts on the power of religious discourse in public life, see his writings on the revolution in Turkey during the 1920s: "Secularizing a Theocracy," in *Middle Works* 15:128–33; "Angora, the New," in *Middle Works* 15:134–38; "The Turkish Tragedy," in *Middle Works* 15:139–43; and "Foreign Schools in Turkey," in *Middle Works* 15:144–49.

3. For similar arguments about the role of conflict in Dewey's work, see Langsdorf; Russill; and Rogers, especially 191–235.

WORKS CITED

Asen, Robert. "The Multiple Mr. Dewey: Multiple Publics and Permeable Borders in John Dewey's Theory of the Public Sphere." *Argumentation and Advocacy* 39.3 (2003): 174–88.

Belman, Lary S. "John Dewey's Concept of Communication." *Journal of Communication* 27.1 (1977): 29–37.

Bryan, William Jennings. *The Bible and Its Enemies: An Address Delivered at the Moody Bible Institute of Chicago.* 3rd ed. Chicago: Bible Institute, 1921.

———. *In His Image.* New York: Fleming H. Revell, 1922.

———. *The Menace of Darwinism.* New York: Fleming H. Revell, 1922.

Burke, Kenneth. *The Rhetoric of Religion: Studies in Logology.* Berkeley: University of California Press, 1970.

Burks, Don M. "John Dewey and Rhetorical Theory." *Western Speech* 32.2 (1968): 118–26.

Carey, James W. *Communication as Culture: Essays on Media and Society.* New York: Routledge, 1992.

Cochran, Molly. Introduction. In *The Cambridge Companion to Dewey,* ed. Molly Cochran, 1–12. Cambridge: Cambridge University Press, 2010.

Crick, Nathan. *Democracy and Rhetoric: John Dewey on the Arts of Becoming.* Columbia: University of South Carolina Press, 2010.

———. "John Dewey's Aesthetics of Communication." *Southern Communication Journal* 69.4 (2004): 303–19.

Dewey, John. *The Later Works, 1925–1953, Vol. 1: 1925: Experience and Nature.* Ed. Jo Ann Boydston. Carbondale: Southern Illinois University Press, 1988.

———. *The Later Works, 1925–1953, Vol. 2: 1925–1927: Essays, Reviews, Miscellany, and The Public and Its Problems.* Ed. Jo Ann Boydston. Carbondale: Southern Illinois University Press, 1988.

———. *The Later Works, 1925–1953, Vol. 5: 1929–1930: Essays, The Sources of a Science of Education, Individualism, Old and New, and Construction and Criticism.* Ed. Jo Ann Boydston. Carbondale: Southern Illinois University Press, 2008.

———. *The Later Works, 1925–1953, Vol. 9: 1933–1934: Essays, Reviews, Miscellany, and A Common Faith.* Ed. Jo Ann Boydston. Carbondale: Southern Illinois University Press, 2008.

———. *The Later Works, 1925–1953, Vol. 11: 1935–1937: Essays and Liberalism and Social Action.* Ed. Jo Ann Boydston. Carbondale: Southern Illinois University Press, 1991.

———. *The Later Works, 1925–1953, Vol. 15: 1942–1948: Essays, Reviews, and Miscellany.* Ed. Jo Ann Boydston. Carbondale: Southern Illinois University Press, 1989.

———. *The Later Works, 1925–1953, Vol. 17: 1885–1953: Miscellaneous Writings.* Ed. Jo Ann Boydston. Carbondale: Southern Illinois University Press, 1990.

———. *The Middle Works, 1899–1924, Vol. 4: Essays on Pragmatism and Truth, 1907–1909.* Ed. Jo Ann Boydston. Carbondale: Southern Illinois University Press, 1977.

———. *The Middle Works, 1899–1924, Vol. 13: Essays on Philosophy, Education, and the Orient, 1921–1922.* Ed. Jo Ann Boydston. Carbondale: Southern Illinois University Press, 1988.

———. *The Middle Works, 1899–1924, Vol. 15: Essays on Politics and Society, 1923–1924.* Ed. Jo Ann Boydston. Carbondale: Southern Illinois University Press, 1988.

Eldridge, Michael. *Transforming Experience: John Dewey's Cultural Instrumentalism.* Nashville: Vanderbilt University Press, 1998.

Finnegan, Cara A. "Elastic, Agonist Publics: John Dewey's Call for a Third Party." *Argumentation and Advocacy* 39.3 (2003): 161–73.

Greene, Ronald Walter. "John Dewey's Eloquent Citizen: Communication, Judgment, and Postmodern Capitalism." *Argumentation and Advocacy* 39.3 (2003): 189–200.

Jansen, Sue Curry. "Phantom Conflict: Lippmann, Dewey, and the Fate of the Public in Modern Society." *Communication and Critical/Cultural Studies* 6.3 (2009): 221–45.

Insert Jasinski, James. *Sourcebook on Rhetoric: Key Concepts in Contemporary Rhetorical Studies.* Thousand Oaks, CA: Sage Publications, 2001.

Joas, Hans. *The Genesis of Values.* Trans. Gregory Moore. Chicago: University of Chicago Press, 2000.

Keith, William M. *Democracy as Discussion: Civic Education and the American Forum Movement.* Lanham, Md.: Lexington Books, 2007.

Langsdorf, Lenore. "Argumentation, Conflict, and Teaching Citizens: Remarks on a Theme in Recent Dewey Scholarship." *Argumentation and Advocacy* 39.3 (2003): 214–21.

Larson, Edward J. *Summer for the Gods: The Scopes Trial and America's Continuing Debate over Science and Religion.* Cambridge, Mass.: Harvard University Press, 1997.

Lewis, Camille K. *Romancing the Difference: Kenneth Burke, Bob Jones University, and the Rhetoric of Religious Fundamentalism.* Waco: Baylor University Press, 2007.

Perelman, Chaim, and L. Olbrechts-Tyteca. *The New Rhetoric: A Treatise on Argumentation.* Trans. John Wilkinson and Purcell Weaver. Notre Dame, Ind.: Notre Dame University Press, 1969.

Pihlström, Sami. "Dewey and Pragmatic Religious Naturalism." In *Cambridge Companion to John Dewey,* ed. Molly Cochran, 211–41. Cambridge: Cambridge University Press, 2010.

Rockefeller, Steven C. "Dewey's Philosophy of Religious Experience." In *Reading Dewey: Interpretations for a Postmodern Generation*, ed. Larry A. Hickman, 124–48. Bloomington: Indiana University Press, 1998.

———. *John Dewey: Religious Faith and Democratic Humanism*. New York: Columbia University Press, 1991.

Rogers, Melvin L. *The Undiscovered Dewey: Religion, Morality, and the Ethos of Democracy*. New York: Columbia University Press, 2009.

Rorty, Richard. *Achieving Our Country: Leftist Thought in Twentieth-Century America*. Cambridge, Mass.: Harvard University Press, 1998.

Russill, Chris. "Through a Public Darkly: Reconstructing Pragmatist Perspectives in Communication Theory." *Communication Theory* 18.4 (2008): 478–504.

Ryan, Alan. *John Dewey and the High Tide of American Liberalism*. New York: W. W. Norton, 1995.

Schudson, Michael. "Why Conversation Is Not the Soul of Democracy." *Critical Studies in Mass Communication* 14.4 (1997): 297–309.

Stroud, Scott R. "John Dewey and the Question of Artful Communication." *Philosophy & Rhetoric* 41.2 (2008): 153–83.

Westbrook, Robert B. *John Dewey and American Democracy*. Ithaca, N.Y.: Cornell University Press, 1991.

———. "The Making of a Democratic Philosopher: The Intellectual Development of John Dewey." In *Cambridge Companion to John Dewey*, ed. Molly Cochran, 13–33. Cambridge: Cambridge University Press, 2010.

PART II

Dewey and His Interlocutors— Thomas Jefferson, Jane Addams, W. E. B. Du Bois, Walter Lippmann, James Baldwin

Dewey on Jefferson

Reiterating Democratic Faith in Times of War

Jeremy Engels

As rhetorical theorists, we often conflate the practice of rhetoric with its theorizing. It is one thing to ask how a particular writer practices rhetoric; it is another thing altogether to ask if that writer has a theory of rhetoric—if that author thinks self-reflexively enough about his or her rhetorical practice to articulate principles for guiding its production and interpretation. Clearly, John Dewey practices rhetoric. Yet it is not clear at all that he has a theory of rhetoric—which, for me, must center on identification, division, and their overlapping perfections and perversions as they play out in the political realm of contingency, chance, and fallibility. "Put identification and division ambiguously together, so that you cannot know for certain just where one ends and the other begins," Kenneth Burke writes, "and you have the characteristic invitation to rhetoric" (*Rhetoric* 25). This is also the characteristic invitation to rhetorical theorizing.

This does not mean that Dewey has nothing to say to rhetorical scholars; quite the contrary. William Keith and Robert Danisch argue that Dewey's philosophy creates space for rhetorical practice and solidifies rhetoric's importance to democratic politics. Indeed, Dewey's work is historically significant given a general cultural shift during the late nineteenth century in the importance attributed to rhetoric in the United States, which in academia fell from its perch as the cornerstone civic art for educating citizens and leaders to become just another *techne* for imparting narrow grammatical lessons. Once conceptualized as training for the rough-and-tumble world of democratic deliberation, by the turn of the century rhetoric was reduced to a vehicle for learning *like/as* distinctions (Cmiel 236–57). While it may be a stretch to suggest that Dewey himself articulates a rhetorical theory, nevertheless he acted as a necessary prompt for rhetorical theorizing in the early twentieth century and continues to do so today. "If," Nathan Crick writes, "Dewey outlined a philosophy that makes rhetoric necessary, it falls to rhetoricians to clarify not only why it is necessary but also how it informs a philosophy that often ignores its presence" (78).

In *The American Evasion of Philosophy,* Cornel West begins his genealogy of pragmatism with Ralph Waldo Emerson and then reads John Dewey as the fullest embodiment of certain key Emersonian tendencies in American philosophy. While there is ample evidence for Emerson's importance to the pragmatists, it was to Thomas Jefferson, not Emerson, that Dewey turned at the close of *Freedom and Culture* to bolster his defense of liberalism from the rising horror of totalitarianism. West argues that one of pragmatism's central tenets is a sense of historical relativity; the pragmatists were well aware, in short, that the present is conditioned by the past (6, 69–70). The pragmatists also understood that history is a vital resource for democratic action in the present. Democratic rhetorics, for Dewey, were historical rhetorics, and the "democratic faith" he often spoke of was premised on a reading of the past. To understand how Dewey made rhetoric a tool for achieving democratic culture, we must understand Dewey's historical rhetorics.

In this essay I investigate Dewey's use of Jefferson in *Freedom and Culture* in order to better understand the importance of historical rhetorics to his philosophy. At first blush, it is surprising that Dewey made so much of Jefferson because he spent much of the 1920s and 1930s railing against the mindless reiteration of historical platitudes. In *Individualism Old and New,* written in 1930, for instance, he lamented how Americans mindlessly confronted an uncertain present by repeating historical beatitudes as though old slogans would ward off modern evils. "Being mentally and morally unprepared, our older creeds have become ingrowing; the more we depart from them in fact, the more loudly we proclaim them" (Dewey, *Individualism* 48). "Many American critics of the present scene are engaged in devising modes of escape," he continued; "some flee to Paris or Florence; others take flight in their imagination to India, Athens, the Middle Ages or the American age of Emerson, Thoreau and Melville. Flight is solution by evasion" (101). Repeatedly, Dewey made it clear that escape to the past was no solution to present problems. Yet in the end Dewey invoked Jefferson in *Freedom and Culture* as a solution to democratic crisis in the late 1930s. How can this be?

Freedom and Culture was written in 1939, on the edge of war breaking out in Europe, and Dewey was profoundly concerned about what might happen to American democracy were the United States to enter into the war. After all, the memory of the brutal suppression of democracy during World War I was still fresh in his mind. While Dewey supported Woodrow Wilson's war for democracy in 1917, in 1939 he was firmly opposed to the United States entering another European war because he feared, in no uncertain terms, that war abroad would bring about the destruction of democracy at home. Concerned that many Americans had already judged another war inevitable, Dewey, by my thinking, wrote *Freedom and Culture* as an attempt to provide a historical grounding for democracy so that it might successfully fight its ideological enemies and, equally important, so that democracy in the

United States might be able to weather the storm better than it did in 1917. Democracy, Dewey insisted, was a fighting faith, and *Freedom and Culture* was Dewey's attempt to bolster democracy both against its foreign enemies and against itself. In the end Dewey's use of Jefferson helped to clarify the moral nature of controversy over democracy. For Dewey, the lesson of Jefferson's thought was that democracy could not survive without a democratic faith in the abilities of common folks to act intelligently and govern themselves. Thus, Dewey used Jefferson to affirm this faith and to remind Americans of its importance during a time of crisis when democratic values could so easily be dismissed.

THE PUBLIC AND ITS RHETORICAL PROBLEMS

Woodrow Wilson's campaign slogan in 1916 was "He kept us out of the war." Yet Wilson was never neutral in World War I, and when Germany resumed unrestricted submarine warfare in the Atlantic in the spring of 1917, the president asked Congress for a fight. "The world must be made safe for democracy," Wilson beseeched Americans in his war message of April 2, 1917, and thus, "we shall fight for the things which we have always carried nearest our hearts, for democracy, for the right of those who submit to authority to have a voice in their own governments, for the rights and liberties of small nations, for a universal dominion of right by such a concert of free peoples as shall bring peace and safety to all nations and make the world at last free." Wilson framed war as a progressive instrument for intervening in world politics and achieving noble ends: to make the world safe for democracy and, even more strongly, to ensure the survival of civilization itself. In a theme that has since become all too familiar, perhaps here, for the first time in U.S. history, war was framed as the means of achieving democracy.

For John Dewey, it was no time for wishy-washy, willy-nilly politics. Americans had to take a stand. Thus he supported World War I unequivocally and without a hint of reservation. "Ever since President Wilson asked for a breaking of relations with Germany, and afterwards for war against that country," he revealed in December 1917, "I have been a thorough and complete sympathizer with the part played by this country in this war, and I have wished to see the resources of the country used for its successful prosecution" (Dewey, "Democracy and Loyalty" 158). He continued to prophesize that World War I would represent a second Revolutionary War—it was the United States' coming-out party as a major player in world politics. "The Declaration of Independence is no longer a merely dynastic and political declaration," he pronounced, for "the war has shown that we are no longer a colony of any European nation nor of them all collectively. We are a new body and a new spirit in the world" (Dewey, "In a Time" 258, 259). The old belief that Americans were unique, that they were made of a different clay than Europeans, influenced Dewey's take on the war. The United States was exceptional, and with the creative, intelligent use of war to realign world politics, Americans would make a difference. This was no time for hesitation. Americans were going to war for democracy.

Dewey supported World War I because he was persuaded by President Wilson's words: this was a war to make the world safe for democracy, and this was a war to end all wars. Robert Westbrook suggests that "Dewey's support for American intervention in World War I [was] rooted less in pragmatic reason than in blind hope"—blind hope that President Wilson was correct, and blind hope that the public was rational enough not to be affected by the heated passions often associated with war (202). Dewey openly proclaimed that the old norms of war rhetoric were outdated and ineffective, for "to create a war motivation by resort to 'patriotic' appeal when large numbers of people are convinced that nationalistic patriotism was chiefly responsible for the outbreak of war is to operate against the tide of events and almost to invite failure" ("What America" 273). "Burnt-out ashes cannot be made to glow, no matter how fervid the appeal," he insisted, and he was caught off guard when these smoldering ashes were stoked into a patriotic, jingoistic blaze in the early months of the war.

After war was declared, Dewey was sanguine about the prospects of victory. He believed that the United States was special and that, entering the war without interest or preconception, it was impervious to the emotions that rage in the populace at war—the emotions of fear, hatred, and anger that Americans experienced during past conflicts. Thus Dewey was genuinely surprised at how quickly the tide turned sour. For a brief time the United States became a police state as free speech was curtailed and dissenters including Eugene Debs were thrown in jail. At the street level, the democratic discussion Dewey championed degenerated into the vitriolic abuse of outsiders and political opponents. "The increase of intolerance of discussion to the point of religious bigotry has been so rapid that years might have passed," he reported in November 1917 ("In Explanation" 292). It was only *months.*

Dewey's support for the war promoted his famous disagreement with Randolph Bourne, which Westbrook labels "one of the classic set pieces in American intellectual history" (Westbrook 197). In 1915 Bourne announced admiringly that Dewey "has seen the implications of democracy more clearly than anybody else in the great would-be democratic society about him," and he pleaded with the philosopher to turn his gaze toward public affairs and teach Americans what concrete things they might do to improve their democracy (Bourne 332). Bourne quickly became disillusioned with his teacher, however, for during World War I Dewey's philosophy became just another type of war rhetoric. Bourne criticized Dewey for thinking that war was an instrument that could be controlled by intelligent, well-meaning actors, and he chided progressives such as Wilson and Dewey by comparing them to "the child on the back of a mad elephant"—in other words, they were helpless to control war (316). For Bourne, Dewey's support of war contradicted the principles of his own philosophy. And thus he attempted to turn the ghost of William James against Dewey, asking, "If William James were alive would he be accepting the war-situation so easily and complacently?" (336). Rather than jump on the war bandwagon or attempt to exert progressive control over war, Bourne speculated that James would have stood by his side—not Dewey's—and searched for an "immoral equivalent" of war "which, in swift and periodic saturnalia, would have acted as vaccination against the sure pestilence of war" (338).

In the short term, Bourne lost the debate with Dewey. His opposition cost him many of his friends and his job writing at the *Nation;* he died on December 22, 1918, at the age of thirty-two, penniless and alone. Dewey never formally responded to his criticisms. Yet there is ample evidence to suggest that, in the long run, Bourne won the debate. According to Louis Menand, "Dewey never referred publicly to Bourne or his criticisms again, but after seeing Wilson's vision for a democratic Europe dissolve in the Treaty of Versailles, he became a pacifist, too" (406). Showing the substantial evolution of his opinions, Dewey observed in his 1927 work *The Public and Its Problems* that "reason would teach that oftentimes even the politicians who are most successful in instigating the willingness of the civilian population to support a war are by that very fact incapacitated for the offices of making a just and enduring peace" (284). Dewey's experience during World War I convinced him that war was unmanageable and undemocratic. Accordingly he became an advocate of peace in the 1920s, participating in the "Outlawry of War" movement that sought to make war illegal under international law (Westbrook 260–74).

In the late 1930s, with the rise of fascism in Europe and increasingly aggressive actions by well-armed Germany and Italy, it began to look to many observers in the United States that war was again likely. In opposition to American participation in any coming war, Dewey wrote an essay in the March 1939 issue of *Common Sense* titled "No Matter What Happens—Stay Out," in which he voiced his agreement with Herbert Hoover: "as I read his prediction that if the United States is drawn into the next war we shall have in effect if not in name a fascist government in this country, I believe that he is completely in the right" (364). Participation in the war would likely bring about "a semi-military, semi-financial autocracy," resulting in "the suppression of all the democratic values for the sake of which we professedly went to war" (364). Dewey lamented that many politicians and intellectuals had already made up their minds about the necessity of war, and he encouraged Americans to spurn inevitability and voice their dissent. "If we but make up our minds that it is not inevitable, and if we now set ourselves deliberately to seeing that no matter what happens we stay out, we shall save this country from the greatest social catastrophe that could overtake us, the destruction of all the foundations upon which to erect a socialized democracy" (364). Generally a temperate writer, Dewey used some of his strongest language in this essay to make it clear that war was no small matter—in no uncertain terms, he argued that war would likely be the death of democracy. "Resort to military force is a first sure sign that we are giving up the struggle for the democratic way of life, and that the Old World has conquered morally as well as geographically," he reiterated in October 1939 ("Democratic Ends" 367). "If there is one conclusion to which human experience unmistakably points, it is that democratic ends demand democratic methods for their realization," and war was no such method (367–68).

World War I prompted a general crisis in liberalism that lasted into the 1930s. Dewey's work in rearticulating liberalism to meet the demands of the twentieth century is well known. In works including *Individualism Old and New* and *Liberalism and Social Action,* Dewey argued against an outdated notion of the ready-made, fully formed, solitary individual preceding society and argued instead for a social individual enmeshed in webs of cooperative endeavor and intelligent deliberation. Unlike those philosophers he dubbed "old" liberals, who were more concerned with protecting free individuals from governmental intrusion, Dewey outlined the conditions under which free individuals could be produced and nurtured.

Though he disagreed with many liberal theorists, there is no question that Dewey was a fervent defender of liberalism to the end. "Objections that are brought against liberalism ignore the fact that the only alternatives to dependence upon intelligence are either drift and casual improvisation, or the use of coercive force stimulated by unintelligent emotion and fanatical dogmatism—the latter being intolerant by its very constitution" (Dewey, *Liberalism* 37). In the 1930s Dewey was forced to defend his vision of liberalism not just from old-fashioned liberal theorists but also from liberalism's political opponents: the fascists and totalitarians who doubted the ability of people to govern themselves and who governed with propaganda and nationalistic appeals, or which he called "unintelligent emotion and fanatical dogmatism." As Kenneth Burke noted in 1941, Hitler derided liberalism and blamed democracy for Germany's problems, claiming that following World War I, the once proud German nation had become "a democracy fallen upon evil days" (*Philosophy* 200). Hitler's rhetoric praised violence in place of deliberation, and he spoke in order to achieve the "materialization of a religious pattern"—to constitute a world divided into friends and enemies, angels and demons, the clean and the impure (194). Democracy was not possible in this European world of "ultra-politics," which achieved "the radicalization of politics into the open warfare of Us against Them" (Zizek 35). The trouble for Dewey was that the United States in the 1930s had also fallen upon the tough times of economic depression, and thus the rhetorical potential for totalitarianism existed at home. World War I forced Dewey to recognize that the United States was not exceptional and that democracy was easily susceptible to the types of pressure and propaganda that sustained European totalitarianism—especially during wartime. War generates damaged publics by reducing democratic discussion to Yes or No propositions, by cleaving the political field into friends and enemies, and by turning all the negative, reactive emotions characteristic of democratic modernity loose into fantasies of murder and revenge.

In *The Public and Its Problems,* Dewey argued that a public came into existence when it recognized that there are "evil consequences" of social action that must be controlled (246). For Dewey, the public was a realm of recognized common interests where citizens organized to manage the consequences of social action. The question Dewey left unanswered in this work was an important one: what type of rhetorical strategies must be put into play so that the public recognizes itself as a public? How a public is formed matters as much as the ability of that public to regulate consequences successfully—because the composition of the public will determine the type of individuals produced and the potential for democratic communication. If the public comes together to fear or hate, then this will have an effect on the composition of the demos. Hateful knowledge might be creative, Nietzsche observed in *On the Genealogy of Morals*, but the result is poison. Nevertheless if there is anything that can bring a public together it is talk of a dangerous enemy. This was the first principle of politics for one of liberalism's most influential critics, Carl Schmitt, who hoped to replace the weak liberal politics of post–Weimer Germany with a strongly enchanted, theological politics committed to naming and confronting enemies. For Schmitt, "the *protego ergo obligo* is the *cogito ergo sum* of the state" (52). Here he invoked Thomas Hobbes, who taught one of the central lessons of the rhetoric of "enemyship": "protection therefore obligation, or, to put it slightly differently, the sovereign's ability to provide protection created the obligation to obey" (Engels, *Enemyship* 210). Enemyship, or the bond forged in mutual opposition to an enemy, might produce publics, but it challenges democracy by transforming rhetoric into an instrument of fear and oppression. Under conditions of enemyship, rhetoric is a means of *public* but not *democracy* formation.

Dewey acknowledged that enemyship was one way that publics were formed: "history shows that more than once social unity has been promoted by the presence, real or alleged, of some hostile group. It has long been a part of the technique of politicians who wish to maintain themselves in power to foster the idea that the alternative is the danger of being conquered by the enemy" (*Freedom* 89). During such moments democratic publics were damaged and deliberation was subverted by fear. During World War I, Dewey discovered that war could make the demos crazy with paranoia, xenophobia, and jingoism. As war turned publics into mobs, it reinforced the totalitarian critique of democracy: that self-government was illusion conjured up by liberalism and that the people really needed strong leaders to manage them. Americans put a bad foot forward during World War I. Dewey was afraid that World War II would be the straw that broke democracy's back, paving the way for American totalitarianism.

Dewey closed *Liberalism and Social Action* with a call to action, rousing his fellow liberals against their totalitarian enemies: "It is in organization for action that liberals are weak, and without this organization there is danger that democratic ideals may go by default. Democracy has been a fighting faith. When its ideals are reinforced by those of scientific method and experimental intelligence, it cannot be that it is incapable of evoking discipline, ardor, and organization" (64). Democracy was a fighting faith capable of taking on its enemies, but only when bolstered with intelligence. He continued to rally the troops in the following terms: "To narrow the issue for the future to a struggle between Fascism and Communism is to invite a catastrophe that may carry civilization down in the struggle. Vital and courageous democratic liberalism is the one force that can surely avoid such a disastrous narrowing of the issue" (64). In conclusion he invoked two icons of American history to suggest that, perhaps, Americans could defeat their totalitarian enemies. History thus gave Dewey hope that Americans would not fail in this desperate hour: "I for one do not believe that Americans living in the tradition of Jefferson and Lincoln will weaken and give up without a whole-hearted effort to make democracy a living reality" (64).

Dewey understood democracy to be a fighting faith, and he also understood that democracy needed to fight, and defeat, its enemies. *Just not on the battlefield.* "Resort to military force is a first sure sign that we are giving up the struggle for the democratic way of life," he cautioned (*Freedom* 187). If Americans went to war in Europe, the game was up because democracy could not handle another war. For Dewey, "war under existing conditions compels nations, even those professedly the most democratic, to turn authoritarian and totalitarian as the World War of 1914–18 resulted in Fascist totalitarianism in non-democratic Italy and Germany and Bolshevist totalitarianism in non-democratic Russia, and promoted political, economic and intellectual reaction in this country" (180).

If war was coming, and if the coming war was likely to bring totalitarianism, then the thoughtful democratic theorist was in a bind. I read *Freedom and Culture* as Dewey's response to this conundrum. As war in Europe became more and more likely, Dewey strove to find an intelligent grounding for democracy—an ontological, prepolitical foundation that would keep Americans from straying too far from the democratic cause and that would keep democracy itself from transforming into something else entirely. This foundation was historical; it was Thomas Jefferson.

DEMOCRACY IS A HUMANISM

When he invoked Jefferson, Dewey entered into a conversation that had been occurring, with various degrees of intensity, since the early republic. This conversation pitted Jefferson against Alexander Hamilton as two sides of the American democratic experience, with Jefferson representing the more democratic sides of the American personality and Hamilton the more aristocratic (Peterson). The Jefferson/Hamilton split was central to political discourse from the Jacksonian period, through the Civil War, and into the Progressive Era—with Progressives including Herbert Croly, in *The Promise of American Life,* and Walter Lippmann, in *The Phantom Public,* praising Hamilton's realism about the inadequateness of the demos and his willingness to use state power to improve the lives of citizens at the expense of Jefferson's dreamy optimism. The Jefferson/Hamilton split was given perhaps its fullest statement in Claude G. Bowers's 1925 work *Jefferson and Hamilton: The Struggle for Democracy in America,* which chose Jefferson over Hamilton as the champion of American democracy and denounced the Hamiltonians as closet despots. It was into this rich cultural heritage that Dewey spoke his kind words about Jefferson.

"I make no apology for linking what is said in this chapter with the name of Thomas Jefferson," Dewey wrote in the final, concluding chapter of *Freedom and Culture*, "for he was the first modern to state in human terms the principles of democracy" (173). "Were I to make an apology," he continued, "it would be that in the past I have concerned myself unduly, if a comparison was to be made, with the English writers who have attempted to state the ideals of self-governing communities and the methods appropriate to their realization." The apology, in short, was that Dewey had looked abroad for democratic justifications when there were native sources to be mined that were just as good. Why Jefferson? Not, Dewey maintained, "because of American provincialism," though, he admitted, "I believe that only one who was attached to American soil and who took a consciously alert part in the struggles of the country to attain its independence, could possibly have stated as thoroughly and intimately as did Jefferson the aims embodied in the American tradition." Dewey turned to Jefferson because Jefferson knew America, because Jefferson helped to create a more democratic United States, and because Jefferson's understanding of democracy was first and foremost *moral*. "The chief reason is that Jefferson's formulation is moral through and through: in its foundations, its methods, its ends" (173).

"To say that the issue is a moral one is to say that in the end it comes back to personal choice and action" (Dewey, *Freedom* 170). Democracy, for Dewey, was a form of government that empowered citizens to take control of their destinies in a world in which structural and economic changes made such control seem like a dream. For Dewey, democracy would ideally be a way for citizens to exercise control over their environments. Yet, as he wrote in *Individualism Old and New*, "individuals are groping their way through situations which they do not direct and which do not give them direction. . . . Their conscious ideas and standards are inherited from an age that has passed away; their minds, as far as consciously entertained principles and methods of interpretation are concerned, are at odds with actual conditions. This profound split is the cause of distraction and bewilderment" (75). In *Freedom and Culture* he observed similarly that "individuals at present find themselves in the grip of immense forces whose workings and consequences they have no power of affecting" (176). Increasingly bureaucratized and hierarchal, modern industrial society produced subjects who were outrun by massive technological changes that transcended the individual, who were gripped by social forces that affected them and their families deeply but were beyond their control. The democratic citizen was left feeling weakened and uncertain. Totalitarianism preyed on this weakness by providing simple solutions to complex problems. Democratic morality, in turn, had to answer objective violence by empowering citizens to act.

Apart from adopting the methods of discussion and intelligence, democracy did not provide moral instructions to citizens; it did not tell them to do this or say that.

Democracy, Dewey contended, "is expressed in the attitudes of human beings and is measured by consequences produced in their lives" (*Freedom and Culture* 151). Morality in democracy meant empowering citizens to act, to exercise control over their lives, and to form publics to rectify common harms. This vision of democracy was dependent on a belief in the capacity of citizens for self-governance, and thus democratic theory had to envision the people as though they were capable of intelligent action. "Were I to say that democracy needs a new psychology of human nature, one adequate to heavy demands put upon it by foreign and domestic conditions, I might be taken to utter an academic irrelevance," Dewey suggested (150–51). "But if the remark is understood to mean that democracy has always been allied with humanism, with faith in the potentialities of human nature, and that the present need is a vigorous reassertion of this faith, developed in relevant ideas and manifested in practical attitudes, it but continues the American tradition," he surmised, "for belief in the 'common man' has no significance save as an expression of belief in the intimate and vital connection of democracy and human nature" (151). Thus, "the task of those who retain belief in democracy is to revive and maintain in full vigor the original conviction of the intrinsic moral nature of democracy" (155).

Much of Dewey's later work was invested in developing this new psychology of human nature, one suitable for democratic governance in the modern age. While I do not find a detailed and highly developed rhetorical theory in Dewey's work, here was a moment where Dewey's philosophy called out for rhetorical practice—indeed the democratic psychology meant nothing without rhetoric, without the development of language games in which one of the rules was to speak about the people with fidelity and love. In short, for democracy to be successful, it had to constitute the people in particular ways and then seek to make that rhetorical vision real through civic education.

A democratic axiom: the democratic project is dependent on psychology, rhetoric, and politics, but in the end democracy is ultimately dependent on faith in citizens, however undeserved or misplaced this faith may at times seem. This means that democracy is akin to religion, which is not at all surprising given how profoundly modern visions of democracy have been influenced by Christian doctrines of equality, grace, and self-worth. Democracy might be about intelligence, control, and choice, but if "the people"—however this entity may be imagined and troped—are incapable of making good decisions, if the people are stupid, arrogant, easily manipulated, or short-sighted (as the founders of the United States believed), then democracy is at best nonsensical and at worst a terrible nightmare. Without faith in citizens, democracy does not work. Thus Dewey talked repeatedly in his later works about "democratic faith," understanding that, in the words of William James, "democracy is a kind of religion, and we are not bound to admit its failure" (James 1245). The people are the god of democracy; if they cease to exist or fail to exalt wonder, then democracy withers. Democracy is a humanism.

The founders of the United States lacked faith in the demos, and thus they chided democracy as an idiot notion (Engels, *Enemyship* 12–13, 102–5). Yet as the nineteenth century progressed, democracy quickly came to seem like a transhistorical inevitability, like something preordained by God. "Democracy" became synonymous with "America," and the demophobia of the founders was supplanted by a demophilia that spoke of the people with love rather than hate (Engels, "Demophilia"). During the 1920s and 1930s demophilia was shaken around the world, as the democratic faith was challenged by the new political atheists who were not swayed by loving talk of the people. At the time Dewey wrote *Freedom and Culture,* democratic faith had come under fire. "It used to be said (and the statement has not gone completely out of fashion) that democracy is a by-product of Christianity, since the latter teaches the infinite worth of the individual human soul," Dewey explained, and "we are now told that weakening of the old theological doctrine of the soul is one of the reasons for the eclipse of faith in democracy" (*Freedom* 152). To critics of both democracy and Christianity, Dewey responded by reiterating the democratic faith. He wrote, "Is human nature intrinsically such a poor thing that the idea is absurd? I do not attempt to give any answer, but the word faith is intentionally used. For in the long run democracy will stand or fall with the possibility of maintaining the faith and justifying it by works" (152).

A crucial figure in moving the United States from demophobia to demophilia was Thomas Jefferson. "I am not among those who fear the people. They, and not the rich, are our dependence for continued freedom," Jefferson opined (1400). According to Dewey, Jefferson was one of the first to state the principles upon which modern democracy is based: including democratic faith. In the final chapter of *Freedom and Culture,* Dewey discussed, in some detail, Jefferson's positions on the rights of man, states' rights vs. federal rights, community life, and private property. "I have referred with some particularity to Jefferson's ideas upon special points because of the proof they afford that the source of the American democratic tradition is moral—not technical, abstract, narrowly political or materially utilitarian," he explained (178). "It is moral," he continued, "because based on faith in the ability of human nature to achieve freedom for individuals accompanied with respect and regard for other persons and with social stability built on cohesion instead of coercion." Jefferson thus helped Dewey to clarify the terms in which a defense of democracy from its enemies had to be articulated. "Since the tradition is a moral one," he averred, "attacks upon it, however they are made, wherever they come from, from within or from without, involve moral issues and can be settled only upon moral grounds. In as far as the democratic ideal has undergone eclipse among us, the obscuration is moral in source and effect" (178).

Dewey reiterated these thoughts in 1940, in a long introduction to a collection of Jefferson's writings that he edited, *The Living Thoughts of Thomas Jefferson,* an entry in the popular Living Thoughts Library series. Here Dewey called Jefferson "our first great democrat," in large part because of his stated faith in the capacities of common folks for self-government ("Presenting" 202). "Jefferson's trust in the people was a faith he sometimes called their common sense and sometimes their reason. They might be fooled and misled for a time, but give them light and in the long run their oscillations this way and that will describe what in effect is a straight course ahead," Dewey explained (214). Jefferson's democratic faith made him an idealist, but "his idealism was a moral idealism, not a dreamy utopianism" (215). This moral optimism was central to Dewey's pragmatism, founded as it was on the faith that citizens were capable of acting moral; yet more than this, Dewey suggested that democracy was not possible without this moral idealism, because without this faith in people, then democracy made no more sense than totalitarianism. "It is doubtful, however, whether defense of democracy against the attacks to which it is subjected does not depend upon taking once more the position Jefferson took about its moral basis and purpose, even though we have to find another set of words in which to formulate the moral ideal served by democracy," Dewey asserted. "A renewal of faith in common human nature, in its potentialities in general and in its power in particular to respond to reason and truth, is a surer bulwark against totalitarianism than is demonstration of material success or devout worship of special legal and political forms" (220).

The Jefferson/Hamilton binary was a common motif during the nineteenth and twentieth centuries because it was a way of organizing the metaphorical entailments of democratic practice. From the beginning of the republic, politicians and political theorists were divided about the wisdom of the people. Should American politics seek to empower citizens or restrain them? Should American politics be progressive or conservative? Those who doubted the wisdom of the people turned to Hamilton to historically ground their suspicions; those who believed in the people turned to Jefferson to justify their faith. Hamilton was to demophobia what Jefferson was to demophilia. While the Jefferson/Hamilton dyad helped to clarify certain important tensions in American politics, Dewey's historical rhetoric did not employ the Jefferson/Hamilton split like his progressive peers. Dewey did not choose one thinker and deride the other, as did Croly, Lippmann, and Bowers. Croly advocated "the rejection of a large part of the Jeffersonian creed, and a renewed attempt to establish in its place the popularity of its Hamiltonian rival" (153). Dewey denied such dualistic thinking, insisting that "we should do well to declare a truce in party controversy till we have congratulated ourselves upon our great good fortune in having two extraordinarily able men formulate the fundamental principles upon which men divide" ("Presenting" 203). Dewey recognized that Jefferson and Hamilton represented real historical differences, but instead of pitting these two intellectual giants against each other, he lauded aspects of them both. This makes sense, for Dewey did not have the animus toward the state that many Jeffersonian thinkers possessed; nor did he distrust the people like the Hamiltonians. Yet in the end it was clear on which side of the debate Dewey came down.

Dewey was not a historian; he had little use for history for history's sake. Instead Dewey studied history to make use of it in the present. "The past as past is gone, save for esthetic enjoyment and refreshment, while the present is with us. Knowledge of the past is significant only as it deepens and extends our understanding of the present," he explained (*Liberalism* 52). Paying careful attention to Jefferson helped to shed light on the democratic present, and yet talk of Jefferson did more than just illuminate. In fact Dewey invoked Jefferson in 1939 and 1940 to achieve three crucial rhetorical goals. First, invoking Jefferson helped Dewey to clarify the moral issues at stake in controversy about democracy. Second, invoking Jefferson helped Dewey to provide a philosophical foundation for, and hence to manage rhetorically, the publics that would be damaged by the enemyship of the coming war. Third, invoking Jefferson raised the crucial pragmatic problems of vocabulary and translation—hence charting a course for the direction that Dewey desired democratic theory to take in the coming years.

Dewey was a believer in the power of deliberation, and yet the communication he lauded as democracy's "consummation" was not mindless talk or aimless conversation but intelligent discussion modeled on the scientific method (*Public* 350). Such communication was dependent on the clarification of the issues at stake. Dewey had faith that citizens were capable of doing this, for "the man who wears the shoe knows best that it pinches and where it pinches, even if the expert shoemaker is the best judge of how the trouble is to be remedied" (364). Democracy could facilitate good discussion by empowering the people affected by harms to frame the conversation about those harms, but what if democracy itself was the topic of debate? Invoking Jefferson helped to ensure that the proper stasis was identified as the locus of the controversy over democracy—for according to Dewey, Jefferson stated the moral nature of democracy first and most clearly. "Anything that obscures the fundamentally moral nature of the social problem is harmful, no matter whether it proceeds from the side of physical or psychological theory," Dewey maintained, for any doctrine that obscures the moral nature of democracy "helps create the attitudes that welcome and support the totalitarian state" (*Freedom* 184–85). Invoking Jefferson helped Dewey clarify the terms of controversy concerning democracy; Jefferson also helped Dewey to dictate the terms of an answer. Dewey insisted that democracy was a fighting faith. Quoting Jefferson provided democracy with ammunition for its fight with the totalitarian enemies of liberalism.

For Dewey, democracy could emerge victorious only by providing a moral answer to the question, why democracy? The trouble was that war tarnished the answer by making it seem as if the demos were incapable of self-governance. Remembering World War I, Dewey reversed his earlier opinions about the relationship between war and democracy. No longer could war be the means to achieving, securing, or spreading democracy. Dewey came to agree with Bourne—war was the enemy of democracy. To invoke Jefferson was to argue against American participation in another world war because war would corrupt democracy.

To invoke Jefferson was also to provide a foundation for discussion, public-formation, and political conduct should the United States enter war. Jeffersonian ideals provided a baseline for the regulation of the damaged publics that would be formed by the enemyship of war, because he was a reminder of the centrality of democratic faith to the American experience. Democratic faith might even keep the horrors of war in check. One can kill an enemy only by disregarding the basic humanistic credo to treat others as mistaken, not evil—by, in short, disregarding the democratic faith. If the enemy's capacity for self-government and intelligent action was not forgotten, then he or she could be engaged in talk rather than eradicated. Dewey's historical rhetorics thus provided a standard for democratic conduct. Jefferson's memory symbolized the persistent humanism that should not be compromised even under the exceptional conditions of violence, terror, fear, and invective.

In addition, invoking Jefferson helped Dewey to raise a crucial problem for democratic thinkers—how best to express the democratic faith under modern conditions. Engaging Jefferson broached the rhetorical problem of translation and the question of vocabulary. "With the founders of American democracy, the claims of democracy were inherently one with the demands of a just and equal morality," Dewey professed, and "we cannot now well use their vocabulary. Changes in knowledge have outlawed the significations of the words they commonly used . . . for this very reason, the task of those who retain belief in democracy is to revive and maintain in full vigor the original conviction of the intrinsic moral nature of democracy, now stated in ways congruous with present conditions" (*Freedom* 155). "Nothing is gained," Dewey alleged, "by attempts to minimize the novelty of the democratic order, nor the scope of the change it requires in old and long cherished traditions. We have not even as yet a common and accepted vocabulary in which to set forth the order of moral values involved in realization of democracy" (178).

This observation applied to Jefferson too. "Even if we have an abiding faith in democracy, we are not likely to express it as Jefferson expressed his faith" (Dewey, *Freedom* 179). To make history as useful as possible in the present, it was necessary to translate old ideas into new vocabularies. Dewey began this process by suggesting that Jefferson's use of "natural," as in natural rights, should now be rendered as "moral," and that every time Jefferson talked in grand terms about "Nature," contemporary Americans should replace this word with "culture" (174–75). By raising the question of translation, Dewey moved democratic theory forward—suggesting that no matter what new ideas were expressed about democracy in the future, one of the foremost problems would be for demophiles to rearticulate democratic faith in terms palatable to contemporary audiences. In other words, those fighting for democracy would never escape Thomas Jefferson.

FAITH AND DELIBERATION

When moving forward in their studies of Dewey's philosophy, rhetorical scholars would do well to understand Dewey's work as an expression of a past and as the product of a history. Dewey's work was innovative in many ways, but in other ways he was telling a familiar story with familiar characters and familiar plot points. Dewey should therefore be understood genealogically; he should be placed in context. This genealogy, however, must stretch back past the Civil War to the very beginning, to the Revolutionary War and the Declaration of Independence, to the Constitution and *The Federalist,* to Jackson and Tocqueville. Americans from the founding of our nation have been debating the value of democracy. Indeed debate over democratic faith was as much a part of American history during the nineteenth century as was the Jefferson/Hamilton motif.

In 1831 the famed French aristocrat Alexis de Tocqueville traveled to the United States in search of "an image of democracy itself, of its penchants, its character, its prejudices, its passions" (Tocqueville 13). The anecdotes and observations from his whirlwind tour of the United States were published in 1835 as *Democracy in America.* Though Tocqueville was sympathetic to democracy's dogged insistence on human equality, he found American politics stifling. "I do not know of any country where, in general, less independence of mind and genuine freedom of discussion reign than in America," he observed, a counterintuitive reading of political culture seemingly at odds with the rowdiness of the 1820s as Andrew Jackson battled the Whigs and in the process inaugurated a more democratic era in American politics (244). Even more fundamentally, Tocqueville found himself at odds with James Madison's philosophical insight in *Federalist No. 10* that the best way to deal with factions was to encourage their proliferation across space and set them to battle.

Though Madison and the other founders valued controlled, decorous political deliberation between elites making policy decisions with an eye toward the long-term public good, *Federalist No. 10* forecast a popular politics of clash that forbade permanent majorities by making diversity and debate hallmarks of American politics (Bessette). Yet Tocqueville found no discord in the United States. For him, democratic social space was strangled by the majority that, seen as an authentic expression of the will of the people, took on a special and unprecedented power in democracy. In American democracy, then, there was little tolerance for dissenting positions because the majority restrained dissent, debate, and thought itself. "Chains and executioners are the course instruments that tyranny formerly employed; but in our day civilization has perfected even despotism itself, which seemed, indeed, to have nothing more to learn," Tocqueville concluded, suggesting that American-style democracy was the perfection of despotism because, instead of controlling subjects with crude physical force, it "leaves the body and goes straight for the soul" (244).

Americans did not have to wait long for a response to Tocqueville's harsh appraisal. George Sidney Camp's *Democracy* was published in 1841 in New York. Breaking with past theorists who demeaned humanity's capacity for self-government and lampooned democracy as an idiot notion, Camp claimed to break new theoretical ground by rooting democracy in the Christian gospel, in human nature and conscience, and in transcendental concepts of justice. Ultimately "democracy"—a term

Camp used interchangeably with "republicanism"—was the best form of government because it preserved the individual's right of self-determination and allowed citizens to exercise judgment. "The real foundation of republican government is the truth of the proposition that men have a right to judge for themselves" (Camp 147). Given these opinions, it was only natural that Camp took on Tocqueville's argument about the tyranny of the majority. Dissent was a daily occurrence in the United States, Camp reported, and for him this simple fact rendered Tocqueville's observations absurd. Moreover, Camp claimed that majorities could not "concur in perpetuating a palpable injustice" because "the majority that *is* is responsible to the majority that *is to be.* Let it act with violence or tyranny, and it will inevitably be converted into a minority" (188, 190). Camp pictured democracy differently than did Tocqueville. For Tocqueville, democracy was a vehicle for political majorities to extend and solidify political, military, religious, and cultural control over minorities. For Camp, democracy was a political battlefield of shifting allegiances where minorities were perpetually on the break of becoming majorities. Majorities might overreach, but they would always be put back in their place by vigilant citizens.

For Camp, Tocqueville was empirically and theoretically incorrect. He was also out of step with the emerging cultural faith in democracy in the United States, and thus Camp suggested that he was a heretic. Camp was prescient for he recognized that democracy requires a tremendous degree of faith in people and their ability to government themselves, and thus for him, *Democracy in America* was a profane text that violated political dogma. "Faith is as necessary to the republican as to the Christian, and the fundamental characteristic of both," he wrote (20). Thus, Camp followed Jefferson in acting as an early and eloquent spokesman for a new form of secular religion, democratic faith.

"Democracy is based upon a belief in human decency, even potential for individual and collective goodness, and needs only to achieve the realization of this inherent decency to bring about democracy in its most fully manifested, even ideal form," the political theorist Patrick Deneen concludes, suggesting that democracy is best understood as a kind of religion (2). The problem with democratic faith, Deneen argues, is that it has been cleansed of the elements of religious faith that serve to check its totalizing, utopian urge: democratic theory "lays claim to the most idealistic, even 'religious' transformative impulse, but in so doing jettisons the accompanying traditional religious belief in the ineradicable human sinfulness, self-interest, and self-deception. It regards the prospect of universal reason and democratic deliberation as eminently realizable; it is not viewed as 'utopian' but as a practicable goal" (26). Democratic theorists thus construct "the people" in a way that they are always lacking: "The idealism of the American creed makes it susceptible to profound disillusionment; in keeping with the 'dynamics of democratic faith,' unrealized visions of democratic apotheosis can leave its adherents with the bitterness of lost faith" (60). Though democratic faith sets itself up to be let down, "in light of the individual excellences that democracy calls upon," Deneen continues, "it is not surprising to encounter expressions of the need to promote belief in democracy, and indeed to see such belief as a requisite feature of democracy's fruition" (166). For Camp, faith is foundational to democracy. The same was true for Dewey. For Deneen, this faith perpetuates a cycle of disenchantment.

A debate over democratic faith might well behoove us today. One trouble with democratic faith is that it leads philosophers and politicians to dismiss critics out of hand—much in the way Camp dismissed Tocqueville. Dewey was at times guilty of this, especially when speaking about Karl Marx and Marxism (as opposed to Soviet communism). A hallmark of faith is the question; through questioning, faith achieves grounding. Democratic theorists must therefore listen to their critics who, speaking with different accents and in different idioms, are all too easy to dismiss. Demophiles can and should learn from their critics, from those who philosophize with hammers (to use Nietzsche's pertinent metaphor), for they highlight blind spots and the places where thinking is muddled. Attacking illusions and idols, they point the way forward.

At the same time, we should not be so easy to dismiss old insights. The Jefferson/Hamilton trope persisted for much of American history because it captured something vital about democratic politics. Deneen critiques democratic faith for setting theorists up for failure; he prefers a philosophy such as Plato's or Tocqueville's, which is less upbeat and more realistic about the democratic capabilities of the people. Yet Dewey's reading of Jefferson in *Freedom and Culture* articulates something absolutely essential about democracy: without faith in the people, democracy does not work. This faith might prove misplaced, and it can be modified and tempered, but it cannot be erased.

Here I take issue with Robert Lacey's argument that there are certain preconditions for Dewey's democratic faith, including "democratic epistemology," "democratic psychology," and "democratic metaphysics" (Lacey 18–19). Lacey believes that "should any of the three tenets prove untenable, however, participatory democracy rests on shaky ground" (18–19, 24). I also question Richard Rorty's thesis that Dewey "shows us how liberal democracy can get along without philosophical presuppositions" (Rorty 179). My reading of Dewey in this essay is not antifoundationalist. Instead, when confronted with the crisis of war and exception, Dewey articulated a basic foundation, democratic faith, on which incredibly variable democratic worlds can be built. There are no preconditions for democratic faith. This faith is the precondition, the a priori, the foundation of democracy. Hence the rhetorical problem of translation: of how best to render democratic faith to the jaded ears of a postmodern generation. Dewey argues that democracy without a moral foundation becomes vacuous, an instrument of oppression and war rather than of education and empowerment. And without a foundation in democratic faith, understood as respect for one's interlocutors and opponents based in shared recognition of humanity and the capacity for intelligence, deliberation is likewise impossible. Consequently democratic faith has profound rhetorical consequences.

Democratic faith put into practice can help to prevent what Dewey feared: democracy succumbing to the intolerance of war. Yet we should not let democratic faith blind us to the types of despotism that Madison and Tocqueville outlined—to the tragic, as opposed to the comic, side of democracy. Striking a critical balance, democratic faith, grounded in Jeffersonian optimism, acts as a crucial resource for rhetorical action and rhetorical criticism in times of war.

WORKS CITED

Bessette, Joseph M. *The Mild Voice of Reason: Deliberative Democracy and American National Government.* Chicago: University of Chicago Press, 1994.

Bourne, Randolph. *The Radical Will: Selected Writings 1911–1918.* Ed. Olaf Hansen. Berkeley: University of California Press, 1977.

Bowers, G. *Jefferson and Hamilton: The Struggle for Democracy in America.* Boston: Houghton Mifflin, 1925.

Burke, Kenneth. *The Philosophy of Literary Form.* Baton Rouge: Louisiana State University Press, 1941.

———. *A Rhetoric of Motives.* 1950. Reprint. Berkeley: University of California Press, 1969.

Camp, George Sidney. *Democracy.* New York: Harper, 1841.

Cmiel, Kenneth. *Democratic Eloquence: The Fight over Popular Speech in Nineteenth-Century America.* Berkeley: University of California Press, 1990.

Crick, Nathan. *Democracy and Rhetoric: John Dewey on the Arts of Becoming.* Columbia: University of South Carolina Press, 2010.

Croly, Herbert. *The Promise of American Life.* New York: Macmillan, 1914.

Danisch, Robert. *Pragmatism, Democracy, and the Necessity of Rhetoric.* Columbia: University of South Carolina Press, 2007.

Deneen, Patrick J. *Democratic Faith.* Princeton, N.J.: Princeton University Press, 2005.

Dewey, John. "Democracy and Loyalty in the Schools." In *John Dewey: The Middle Works, 1899–1924,* vol. 10, ed. Jo. Ann Boydston, 158–63. Carbondale: Southern Illinois University Press, 1985.

——— "Democratic Ends Need Democratic Methods for Their Realization." In *John Dewey: The Later Works, 1925–1953,* vol. 14, ed. Jo Ann Boydston, 367–68. Carbondale: Southern Illinois University Press, 1991.

———. *Freedom and Culture.* In *John Dewey: The Later Works, 1925–1953,* vol. 13, ed. Jo Ann Boydston, 63–188. Carbondale: Southern Illinois University Press, 1988.

———. "In a Time of National Hesitation." In *John Dewey: The Middle Works, 1899–1924,* vol. 10, ed. Jo Ann Boydston, 256–59. Carbondale: Southern Illinois University Press, 1985.

———. "In Explanation for Our Lapse." In *John Dewey: The Middle Works, 1899–1924,* vol. 10, ed. Jo. Ann Boydston, 292–95. Carbondale: Southern Illinois University Press, 1985.

———. *Individualism Old and New.* In *John Dewey: The Later Works, 1925–1953,* vol. 5, ed. Jo Ann Boydston, 41–123. Carbondale: Southern Illinois University Press, 1988.

———. *Liberalism and Social Action.* In *John Dewey: The Later Works, 1925–1953,* vol. 11, ed. Jo Ann Boydston, 1–65. Carbondale: Southern Illinois University Press, 1991.

———. "No Matter What Happens—Stay Out." In *John Dewey: The Later Works, 1925–1953,* vol. 14, ed. Jo Ann Boydston, 364. Carbondale: Southern Illinois University Press, 1991.

———. "Presenting Thomas Jefferson." In *John Dewey: The Later Works, 1925–1953*, vol. 14, ed. Jo Ann Boydston, 201–23. Carbondale: Southern Illinois University Press, 1991.

———. *The Public and Its Problems*. In *John Dewey: The Later Works, 1925–1953*, vol. 2, ed. Jo Ann Boydston, 235–372. Carbondale: Southern Illinois University Press, 1988.

———. "What America Will Fight For." In *John Dewey: The Middle Works, 1899–1924*, vol. 10, ed. Jo Ann Boydston, 271–75. Carbondale: Southern Illinois University Press, 1985.

Engels, Jeremy. "Demophilia: A Discursive Counter to Demophobia in the Early Republic." *Quarterly Journal of Speech* 97.2 (2011): 131–54.

———. *Enemyship: Democracy and Counter-Revolution in the Early Republic*. East Lansing: Michigan State University Press, 2010.

James, William. "The Social Value of the College-Bred." In *William James: Writings, 1902–1912*, ed. Bruce Kuklick, 1242–49. New York: Library of America, 1987.

Jefferson, Thomas. *Writings*. Ed. Merrill D. Peterson. New York: Literary Classics of the U.S., 1984.

Keith, William. *Democracy as Discussion: Civic Education and the American Forum Movement*. Lanham, Md.: Lexington Books, 2007.

Lacey, Robert J. *American Pragmatism and Democratic Faith*. De Kalb: Northern Illinois University Press, 2008.

Lippmann, Walter. *The Phantom Public*. Piscataway, NJ: Transaction Publishers, 1993.

Menand, Louis. *The Metaphysical Club: A Story of Ideas in America*. New York: Farrar, Straus and Giroux, 2001.

Nietzsche, Friedrich. *On the Genealogy of Morals*. Trans. Walter Kauffman and R. J. Hollingdale. 1967. Reprint. New York: Vintage, 1989.

Peterson, Merrill D. *The Jefferson Image in the American Mind*. 1960. Reprint. Charlottesville: Thomas Jefferson Memorial Foundation and the University Press of Virginia, 1998.

Rorty, Richard. "The Priority of Democracy to Philosophy." In *Objectivism, Relativism, and Truth: Philosophical Papers*, vol. 1, 175–96. Cambridge: Cambridge University Press, 1991.

Schmitt, Carl. *The Concept of the Political*. Trans. George Schwab. 1932. Reprint. Chicago: University of Chicago Press, 1996.

Tocqueville, Alexis de. *Democracy in America*. Trans. Harvey C. Mansfield and Delba Winthrop. 1835. Reprint. Chicago: University of Chicago Press, 2000.

West, Cornel. *The American Evasion of Philosophy: A Genealogy of Pragmatism*. Madison: University of Wisconsin Press, 1989.

Westbrook, Robert B. *John Dewey and American Democracy*. Ithaca, N.Y.: Cornell University Press, 1991.

Wilson, Woodrow. War Message, April 2, 1917. www.AmericanRhetoric.com. (accessed March 21, 2011).

Zizek, Slavoj. "Carl Schmitt in the Age of Post-Politics." In *The Challenge of Carl Schmitt*, ed. Chantal Mouffe, 18–37. London: Verso, 1999.

John Dewey and Jane Addams Debate War

Louise W. Knight

In the introduction to this collection the editors observe that John Dewey's work as a professional philosopher has served as "a well that rhetorical scholars draw from when they study rhetoric as the constitutive democratic practice." More specifically, his theory that democracy is a way of life suggests that the performance of rhetoric is a key expression of one's citizenship. What then, the editors ask, of Dewey's own rhetorical practices? How did he enact and embody the particular values, attitudes, habits, and behaviors that constitute . . . a democratic culture? This essay offers a partial answer by examining a moment in Dewey's life—World War I—when, in debating his old friend Jane Addams, he found the practice of rhetoric in a democracy to be fraught with perplexities.

This essay also touches on the broader topic of the development of Dewey's pragmatism. Charlene Haddock Seigfried, a philosopher and leading scholar of the pragmatism of Dewey and Addams, has written about Dewey's view that pragmatism required the "constant and effective interaction of knowledge and practice" (Introduction 6). She argues that he practiced what he preached, noting that Dewey's positions "evolve[d] as conditions change[d]" (Introduction 10). She adds, "Dewey has been called the last of the great public intellectuals because his own practice informed his theory and his theory was carried out in practice" (Introduction 17). Although this essay is not focused on the way his pragmatic thought developed per se, its evolution is part of the story of the Dewey-Addams debates. This essay thus provides further evidence for the interesting corollary, one that Seigfried has also argued, that, in her words, Jane Addams was a "pragmatically-oriented philosopher . . . at an earlier stage [than Dewey], particularly . . . . [when one considers] their views on democracy" (Seigfried, "Democracy" 1).

Dewey supported the U.S. government when it declared war on Germany in April 1917, but his old and good friend Jane Addams, the political activist who would later become the first American woman to receive the Nobel Peace Prize, did not.

When two months later she defended herself and other pacifists as "patriots" in a speech that received national attention, John Dewey took up his rhetorical cudgels in the *New Republic* to attack her position. At its heart their dispute was whether and how antagonism in the form of war could be morally justified, but beneath that discussion lay another dispute: whether it was a good thing in wartime for citizens in a democracy to debate openly the value of war and to disagree with the majority view if that was what their consciences required.

In the spring of 1917 Dewey was fifty-eight years old, an age at which some philosophers had already written their best work, but that was not true for him. Although he was a prominent philosophy professor at Columbia University, he had not yet produced his most important work. This was particularly true of his writings about democracy.

To be sure, the ideas that he published before the war were substantial. In four books about education as well as in other writings, he embraced a participatory democratic society as the ideal, argued that nurturing democracy in schools and in industry was the best way to help create it, and stressed the benefits to society of individual self-development. "If democracy has a moral and ideal meaning," he wrote, "it is that a social return be demanded of all and that opportunity for development of distinctive capacities be afforded all. The separation of the two aims is fatal to democracy" (Dewey, *Democracy* 142–43). Dewey was an activist within the field of education, having formed a successful laboratory school at the University of Chicago, lectured often to educators, and cofounded the American Association of University Professors.

Still, as Benson, Harkavy, and Puckett have noted, it was only after the war that he began to "spell out much more clearly what a participatory democracy entailed" (52). Thus to examine his disagreement with Addams in 1917 is to examine a moment when Dewey was not yet the profound democratic theorist he would become.

He faced a challenging rhetorical situation. Drawn for the first time into a heated national political debate, he boldly deployed his armament of philosophers' weapons to support the war and criticize its opponents, the pacifists. In the process he demonstrated how he thought rhetoric should be practiced in a democracy in wartime. But he did more than that. He also revealed something about how he perceived his own responsibilities as a citizen. The German philosopher Hans Blumenberg writes that "rhetoric is a system not only of soliciting mandates for action but also of putting into effect . . . a self-conception that is in the process of formation or has been formed" (quoted in Hyde 103). The point is illustrated by Dewey's, as well as Jane Addams's, wartime experience.

Jane Addams was fifty-six in the spring of 1917. Active as a social reformer, author, lecturer, and political leader since the 1890s, she had become one of the most admired and influential women in the United States by 1912, when she seconded Theodore Roosevelt's nomination as the presidential candidate for the Progressive Party. By then she had also written two books about democracy, *Democracy and*

Social Ethics and *Newer Ideals of Peace,* as well as four other books, including her best-selling, partial memoir *Twenty Years at Hull-House,* about life in the Chicago settlement house she had cofounded in 1889. Her ideas about democracy, like Dewey's, stressed its social essence. In her first book, she urged her readers to "give truth complete social expression" by "identif[ying] with the common lot," such identification being "the essential idea of Democracy" (Addams, *Democracy* 11; Fischer 281–82). Having converted to Tolstoyism in the 1880s, she was committed to nonresistance in all human relations and since 1900 had been an opponent of war as a method to resolve international disputes (Knight, *Citizen*).

Like Dewey, Addams was an educational philosopher and an activist. Hull House was a social and educational institution in a working-class neighborhood. Also like Dewey, she believed in the benefits of self-development for a democracy. Indeed she thought that self-development was democracy's whole purpose. In 1897 she wrote that education and democracy are only the means "to the ultimate end, . . . the development of human nature in scope and power and happiness, in a word, of life and enjoyment" (Addams, "Growth" 41).

Dewey and Addams were both famous by 1917, but Addams was the more prominent. As Addams was a popular and well-traveled lecturer; a writer whose pieces appeared in a wide variety of national publications, from religious, to labor, to ladies' magazines; an author of six widely read books; a longtime advocate for woman suffrage; and a leader for progressive reforms on behalf of African Americans, women and children of all classes, and peace, hers was a household name. She also had more experience than Dewey in engaging in public debate over national political questions (Knight, *Jane Addams*).

They came to their 1917 debate as old friends. They had met in early 1892, when Dewey spent a week at Hull House on a visit from Ann Arbor, Michigan. After he moved to Chicago in 1894, his ties with the settlement house and with Addams became close. He taught there, served on the board of trustees, and named his daughter Jane after Addams. Addams sought his advice, including on her writing, invited him to dinner at Hull House often, dined at his house, and worked with him on his educational reform projects (Knight, *Citizen* 237, 238–40, 360; Ryan 151–52). They also came to their 1917 debate having already argued about war earlier, but in an abstract way. By a strange coincidence, in the fall of 1894, as they were just getting to know each other better, they debated for the first time the issue that they would debate again twenty-three years later: What is the value of antagonism? Is it morally justified, and on what grounds?

THE 1894 DEBATE

In the summer of 1894, when Chicago, and then the nation, was in an uproar regarding the Pullman Strike, John Dewey moved to the city to serve as the first chair of the Department of Philosophy at the University of Chicago. Coming from bucolic Ann Arbor, where he had been teaching at the University of Michigan, he observed the strike as a new urban citizen, fascinated though uninvolved. Jane Addams, in her fifth year of living in Chicago as head of Hull House, was in the thick of events. In the beginning she tried, as a member of the Civic Federation of Chicago's Conciliation Board, to bring the two sides to the negotiating table. Though this effort failed, she remained in contact with the strikers, spending hours talking with them about their reasons for striking, which were that their employer George Pullman refused to negotiate regarding his severe wage cuts and his high rents for their mandated company housing and that they desperately needed money to support their families. To her dismay, the strike ended with shocking scenes of riots in the railroad yards and troops patrolling Chicago.

That fall, after the crisis was over, Dewey and Addams talked about the strike. History rarely records the content of most conversations, but remarkably this conversation was documented and—here was even more good fortune—by a skilled observer of argument. Dewey's wife Alice was still in Europe that fall, and he wrote her a letter describing what he and Addams had discussed.

Being of philosophical mind, Addams and Dewey easily turned to an abstract question raised by the strike: might conflict, or "antagonism," as they called it, ever be good or useful? Dewey, at this time strongly influenced by Hegel, told Addams that conflict was both inevitable and possibly a good thing. Addams's firm reply, reflecting her belief in nonresistance, was that "historically only evil had come from antagonisms." (John Dewey to Alice Chipman Dewey, October 10, 1894, Collection). She "had always believed and still believed," Dewey wrote, that "antagonism was . . . useless, . . . harmful, [and] entirely unnecessary." She explained that antagonisms were caused by, as Dewey summed up her point, a person's assumption that antagonism was going to happen and that such assumptions arose because of "a person's mixing in his own personal reactions." Personal reactions, she elaborated, were such things as someone taking pleasure in opposing others, or wishing not to be a moral coward, or feeling hurt or insulted. In other words, antagonism was caused by personal attitudes. The source of antagonism, in Addams's view, "never lay in objective differences," which, in any case, would "always grow into unity if left alone." To sum up, antagonism was always useless, pointless, and a bad thing.

She "kept asking me what I thought," Dewey wrote. He told her he doubted her claims, so Addams elaborated. When Jesus angrily drove the money changers out of the temple for desecrating the house of God, she said, his anger was personal and avoidable. He had "lost his faith," she said, "and reacted." Or consider the bad result of the antagonism of the Civil War. Northerners freed the slaves, but the former slaves were still not really free as individuals because of racism, and in addition northerners had to "pay the costs of war and reckon with the added bitterness of the [white] southerner besides."

But, Dewey countered, what about conflicts between ideas and institutions? Those did not arise because of personal reactions, did they? And did not these broader conflicts—for example between Christianity and Judaism or between "labor and capital" or "the church and democracy"—help society progress via struggle and adaptation? Was not the "realization of . . . antagonism necessary to an appreciation of the truth and a consciousness of growth?" She replied no, Dewey told Alice. Jane Addams thought that the "antagonisms of institutions were always [due to] the injection of the personal attitude and reaction."

The next day Dewey struggled to restore his belief in Hegelian principles and his faith in reason. "My pride of intellect," he confessed to Alice, "revolts at thinking" that "all this conflict and warring of history [are] . . . all merely negative" and "meaningless." At the same time what struck him the most was the depth of Addams's conviction. Her statement seemed to him "the most magnificent exhibition of intellectual & moral faith" he had ever seen. "When you think," he wrote Alice, "that Miss Addams does not think this as a philosophy, but believes it in all her senses & muscles—Great God." The force of her certainty stunned him. "I never had anything take hold of me so" (John Dewey to Alice Chipman Dewey, October 10, 1894, Collection).

The encounter showed him something else as well. He wrote that he realized he had always stressed how unity resulted from the reconciliation of opposites and now saw that Addams stressed how opposites were the spur for growth into unity (John Dewey to Alice Chipman Dewey, October 10, 1894, Collection). To say the same thing differently, Dewey saw for the first time that he was more focused on the ultimate goal while Addams was more focused on the process of getting there.

Dewey could not forget the conversation. Philosopher that he was, he continued to ponder it even after he mailed the letter to Alice. A few days after he and Addams talked, he decided that he agreed with her and sent her a short note saying he now believed that antagonism always began with personal feelings and, as such, was bad (John Dewey to Jane Addams, October 12, 1894, Collection).

Addams thought more about the conversation too, but it was not just Dewey's arguments she was pondering. After living in a working-class district full of underpaid, frequently striking workers for five years and having just spent the summer witnessing George Pullman's defiant refusal to negotiate with his employees, she could feel life prodding her to recognize Dewey's point that antagonism could arise from the realities of impersonal conflicts. In the fall of 1894 her strong mind was still resisting that truth, but before long she came to agree with Dewey. In her early 1896 speech "A Modern Lear," while she focused on the contrasting moralities of George Pullman and his striking workers, she also endorsed the workers' call for justice (Addams, "Modern Lear" 173–74).[1]

By 1896, then, it appears that each had persuaded the other. Their thoughtful, respectful debate had led to mutual learning to such a degree that they had both reversed their positions. But their 1894 conversation still held a seed of contention. When Dewey had argued for the usefulness of large-scale antagonism, he was making the case that antagonism was acceptable as a means for society to reach a distant, useful goal—the appreciation of truth; he was focused on the long term. The debate in 1917 would reveal that he had not really abandoned that belief, his 1894 note to Addams notwithstanding. For Addams, as her example of the Civil War illustrated, the immediate consequences were what mattered. If antagonism led to more antagonism, then it was the wrong means. She wrote in 1892 that "the spirit of opposition . . . thrusts men apart" (Addams, "Subjective Necessity" 24).

Another way to frame the same distinction is to say that Dewey and Addams disagreed about which values, or ethics, should provide the warrant for the argument. As Dewey noted, Addams's beliefs about antagonism arose from her personal conviction. To borrow a concept from the German sociologist Max Weber, their contemporary, she held to "the ethic of individual responsibility." Dewey believed, in Weberian terms, in "the ethic of ultimate ends." Weber would write in his 1919 essay "Politics as a Vocation" that these two ethics were tragically opposed. In 1917 Dewey and Addams would discover the truth of that observation before Weber had even made it.

WHEN A DEMOCRACY GOES TO WAR

When Addams and Dewey debated the morality of antagonism in 1894, their conversation was private and theoretical. But the next time they took up the question, in 1917, serious consequences were at stake, and they conducted their debate in public as intellectuals whose opinions carried weight. Furthermore they were no longer considering many types of antagonism but only one kind—that of war.

By then they both had given the topic of war a good deal of thought, having both been pacifists since the early years of the twentieth century. Addams spoke at the First National Peace Congress in 1907 and helped to host the Second National Peace Congress in Chicago in 1909 (Knight, *Jane Addams* 156). She agreed with the ideas stressed in these gatherings—that the world needed to create new international laws and bodies, including a world court and a league of nations—but thought that the place to start was not with changing laws but with changing the hearts of citizens. "In the progress of society," she wrote in 1907, "[changing] sentiments and opinions have to come first, then habits of action and lastly moral codes and institutions" (Addams, *Newer Ideals* 8). When she spoke of citizens, she meant people around the world. She was not a nationalist but an internationalist.

Dewey's pacifism was more amorphous and contained some potential contradictions. On the one hand, influenced by his faith in using social intelligence as a force in the world, an idea that appeared often in his prewar writings, he was drawn to the reforms in international law that were much discussed between 1900 and 1914. On the other hand, as his 1894 conversation with Addams made clear, he thought that large-scale antagonism useful and, as his biographer Alan Ryan notes, he was a mild nationalist (Cywar 580–81; Ryan 153). In all these contradictions, Dewey was more typical of pacifists of his day than Addams was.

Like most Americans, Dewey and Addams supported the U.S. government's position of neutrality when the European nations declared war on each other in the summer of 1914. Dewey laid out his views between 1915 and 1916 in a series of short essays in the brand new political opinion magazine the *New Republic.* These magazine pieces were his first attempts to write philosophically about current political issues, and they marked his emergence as a multifaceted public intellectual.

To Dewey, as to many, the eruption of war among the European monarchs and czars perfectly illustrated the dangers of one-man rule, with its militaristic, nationalistic traditions and its hunger for territory. But if Dewey disapproved of the war's short-term goals, he did not disapprove of the use of force per se. He based his argument, presented in his 1916 essay "Force, Violence, and the Law," on the distinction between "force," which he defined as power, and "violence." This allowed him somewhat remarkably to conclude that not all wars were "violent." "Violent" wars, he said, were only those wars that led to "excessive . . . undesirable results" and involved too much "waste and loss." The key question, he wrote, "concerns the most effective use of force in gaining ends in specific situations." He declined to say whether the current war was using "force," that is, was pursuing desirable results efficiently, or "violence" (Dewey, "Force" 213, 215).

He was ready, however, to make some sweeping assertions about the pacifists, with whom he no longer identified. In "Force, Violence, and the Law" he charged them (mentioning no names) as being opposed to "all force" and "unable to conceive the task of organizing the existing forces so they may achieve their greatest efficiency." That is, they disagreed with his view that there could be such a thing as a good, efficient war that did not involve "violence" (213–14). Thus, with some fancy philosophical footwork, he laid down the gauntlet to the pacifists, of whom the most prominent in the nation was his old friend Jane Addams.

Addams too faced the challenge of applying her pacifism to war-time conditions. Though she supported U.S. neutrality in August 1914, in the months and years that followed she did not think that President Woodrow Wilson was doing enough to use that position to help end the war. She wanted him to experiment, to be more proactive. In 1914 and 1915 Addams was elected president of four new war-time peace organizations: one local; two national; and one international, the Women's International League for Peace and Freedom. The platforms of all four called for a war-time conference as well as for postwar reforms such as a League of Nations, international arbitration treaties, international courts, and arms control. Throughout 1915 and 1916 she and her pacifist colleagues pressed Wilson in letters and in meetings to convene a conference of representatives from the neutral nations to try to resolve the disputes that had launched the war. In April 1915 Addams attended a women's international peace meeting in battle-torn Europe, and ready to try anything to shorten the war, she served on a delegation that subsequently met with foreign ministers of the belligerent and neutral European nations to urge them to endorse a neutrals conference. It was a long shot and certainly experimental, but she felt it worth the risk. Her pacifist activities received a great deal of publicity, some of it favorable and some hostile. By early 1917 she was one of the most admired as well as notorious pacifists in the United States (Knight, *Jane Addams* 189–214).

Addams knew about Dewey's attacks on pacifists, and Dewey knew that when he criticized pacifists, he was criticizing her. Their disagreement should have led to a conversation, and surely it would have if Dewey still lived in Chicago. But he was gone. In 1904 he had accepted a position in the philosophy department at Columbia University and moved to New York City, and they had fallen out of touch. In 1911, when they happened to sit next to each other at a formal dinner in Manhattan, they enjoyed the chance to talk (Addams to Mary Rozet Smith). But that was before the war.

THE 1917 DEBATE

In April 1917, at the president's urging and in response to recent events, the U.S. Congress declared war on Germany. Woodrow Wilson's stated goal was for the United States to make the world safe for democracy. Quickly he and Congress put in place the nation's first massive government propaganda machine, the U.S. Office of Public Information, to persuade Americans that every citizen had a moral responsibility to support his government in wartime. He asked all American citizens to give their "undivided and willing support" to the war's prosecution. In May, Congress passed and the president signed the Espionage Act, which gave the U.S. government the power to outlaw seditious speech. Wilson asked for that power because he believed that any expression of dissent during wartime was like "stab[bing] our soldiers in the back" (Knight, *Jane Addams* 214–15). Soon thereafter a draft law was passed, and thousands of young American men enthusiastically reported to their draft boards. John Dewey's oldest son, Frederick, was commissioned as an officer in the U.S. Army. Others who believed war to be against their consciences felt caught in a moral crisis. Some became conscientious objectors; some fled to Canada to avoid imprisonment. Abruptly the pacifists were condemned as traitors, first by the president and then by a freshly aroused, passionately anti-German public.

Addams too faced a choice. Between 1914 and 1916 she had withheld her fire against Dewey and the *New Republic.* She had long believed that counterattacks were not constructive. But she also believed in freedom of speech. In 1905 she said in a talk, "If democracy is to advance along with events, we must have absolutely free speech and insist that people who are dissatisfied with the existing state of affairs be allowed to express their minds" (Addams, "Address" 364–65). Now, with freedom of speech under siege, she stepped forward. In May and June in a talk titled "Patriotism and Pacifists in Wartime," which she gave in Chicago twice and again in nearby Evanston, she enacted her right to free speech by defending pacifists and justified her position by invoking her conscience.

It is clear from her speech that she intended it, at least in part, as a direct response to the criticisms of pacifists that Dewey and others had made in the *New Republic.*

Near the beginning she addressed herself to one of the magazine's 1914 editorials, "Pacifism vs. Passivism." In it the editors had warned that if people agreed with the pacifists that "peace and war are irreconcilably antagonistic terms," then that would allow the militarists to take over the world and make peace an "unattainable ideal." "Force cannot be eliminated from life," they argued. The "sin" was not fighting but failing "to fight for a good cause." Borrowing the title of Addams's book *Newer Ideals of Peace* (1907), the editors used the words to mean the opposite of what she meant. To her, the newer ideals of peace were about cooperation and respect for all human beings that would make war impossible. According to the editors of the *New Republic,* "the newer ideal of peace, whether in domestic or foreign policy," meant that nations were ready to go to war for the right reasons ("Pacifism vs. Passivism" 6, 7).

In response, Addams turned the rhetorical tables on the editors. She incorporated words from *their* essay's title into a sentence of her own and, for good measure, cited another piece the magazine had recently published by a British pacifist, H. N. Brailsford, to support her case. She wrote, "The similarity of sound between the words 'passive' and 'pacifism' is often misleading, for most pacifists agree with such statements as that made by Mr. Brailsford in *The New Republic* of March 17th." Pacifists, she explained, shared his support for new international institutions and his view that the war was a response, in her words, to "hampered conditions and unsolved problems." She added that "far from passively wishing nothing to be done, . . . we pacifists" believe that "this world crisis" should be used to create an "international government" with an "international charter . . . of international rights" that could make the political and economic changes needed (Addams, "Patriotism" 354–55). She even allowed herself a bit of sarcasm, calling the *New Republic* "that wonderful journal . . . from which so many preachers are now taking their texts in preference to the New Testament" (353).

Addams went on in her speech to rebut Dewey's and the editors' assertion that pacifists rejected the use of American influence in international relations. After noting that pacifists sometimes despaired "over our inability to make our position clear," she explained that they believed "this country should lead the nations of the world into a wider life of coordinated political activity." She remained doubtful, however, about war as the means. Pacifists had hoped that such changes "might have been obtained without our participation in the war." She added, "It is very easy to go to war for a well-defined aim which changes imperceptibly as the war progresses, and to continue the war or even end it on quite other grounds. Shifting aims is one of the inherent characteristics of war as an institution" ("Patriotism" 358–59). Her claim was her usual one: immediate consequences should shape decisions.

In addition, without mentioning his name, she addressed Dewey's advocacy for force as a justification for war. Instead of engaging with his argument, however, she called for respect for those who disagreed. "Many of the pacifists . . . have long striven for social and political justice with a fervor perhaps equal to those employed by the advocates of force," she wrote (364). Between the lines she was asking her old friend to respect her position rather than categorically dismiss it. Addams further laid out the pacifists' case. Their claim was pragmatic; it was about what worked and what did not work. Pacifists have developed "a conviction," she added, that "justice between men or between nations can be achieved only through understanding and fellowship" and that justice "cannot be secured in the storm and stress of war." Focused on the immediate results of war, she noted that it "arouses the more primitive antagonisms" and that "the spirit of fighting burns away all of those impulses, certainly towards the enemy, which foster the will to justice" (364). Addams also challenged the assumption that the pacifist, in disagreeing with her government or the majority of citizens, harmed society in some way. Rather, she said, society benefited when an individual acted according to his conscience.

In standing by her conscience, Addams was committing an act of antagonism, of course. In 1917 she was willing to do so, having concluded that *that* kind of antagonism was grounded in objective conditions and essential in a democracy. In her "Patriotism" speech she praised as courageous "that man . . . who, seeing that which is invisible to the majority of his fellow countrymen, still asserts his conviction and is ready to vindicate its spiritual value over and against the world" (363). Society would benefit. "Each advance in the zigzag line of human progress," she said, "has traditionally been embodied in small groups of individuals who have ceased to be in harmony with the status quo and have demanded modifications." Her choice of the word "harmony" was a direct rebuttal of Dewey's belief that a harmonious society was the ultimate goal. Sometimes, Addams was saying, a desire to avoid disharmony should be secondary to a commitment to the higher value of justice.

Dewey was not persuaded. He promptly penned his rebuttal, "The Future of Pacifism," which the editors of the *New Republic* published in July. His essay makes clear that he had read her speech, which had been published in June in the *City Club of Chicago Bulletin* (Addams, "Patriotism") after she addressed the club in May. In addition, when she gave the speech in June in the Chicago suburb of Evanston, newspapers around the country, including some in New York City, drawing on an Associated Press wire story, had carried short items about it and many had also run editorials that called her pro-German and un-American (Knight, *Jane Addams* 216).

For whatever reasons, most likely those of friendship, Dewey tried to avoid appearing to attack Jane Addams personally in his essay. Crediting her by name as having made "the best statement" of the pacifist position he had seen, he carefully drew a distinction he had failed to make earlier between "intelligent" pacifists such as Addams and the "professional pacifists" he was criticizing. Quoting her speech, he acknowledged that in her view pacifism stood for the creation of an international agency and a "strenuous endeavor to lead all nations of the earth into an organized international life" (Dewey, "Future" 266–67).

But he was not done with Addams. He disputed whether she was right to claim that most pacifists agreed with her and then criticized the pacifists for being focused on "momentary methods" (by which he meant the method of war) instead of "permanent results," by which he meant the creation of an international organization and peace. He called this failure a "stupidity." Clearly they lacked leadership, he said. The implicit message was clear. If he thought that the pacifists lacked leadership, whose fault could that be but Jane Addams's, their undisputed leader? He closed by acknowledging that while war did not guarantee that an international organization would be created, it at least made such a development possible and also went a long way to deal frankly with "the controlling forces of the modern world" (268). His position, he concluded, was grounded in facts, while the pacifists, including "too many influential personages," were "pure romanticists" (270). In other words, he thought that Addams was simply being naive and sentimental. In these decades men often made this charge of women who had entered the political realm; it was a standard way to avoid having to take their ideas seriously.

As to the subject of individual conscience, Dewey ignored it in his "Future of Pacifism" essay, but he took it up in an earlier essay published in the *New Republic* that same month. In that piece, "Conscience and Compulsion," he claimed that issues of conscience were irrelevant to a person deciding to go to war. The pacifist young men who were now having a crisis of conscience, he explained, were victims of a misguided moral education. He wrote, "The evangelical Protestant tradition has fostered the tendency to locate morals in personal feelings instead of in the control of social situations" (Dewey, "Conscience and Compulsion" 262). The question of whether to fight should have nothing to do "with the inhibitions of inner consciousness" (263). Such an inhibition, he said, was morally futile, given that the world was at a "critical juncture" (264). In the light of these "objective facts," such young men should "connect conscience with the forces that are moving" (264). His was a startling claim; indeed in making it he had revised the meaning of the word "conscience" by arguing that it should be guided by social requirements, not individual conviction.

Addams and Dewey had locked horns. Beyond the substance of their disagreements, other differences were apparent. One was in the way they made their respective cases. Dewey, distrustful of emotions, repeatedly sought to make logical distinctions, often by redefining the meanings of words and by setting up absolute, opposite choices. In addition he emphasized the need to focus on "objective facts" (although his essays contained few). Addams accepted that emotions and feelings were powerful motivators, whether for good or ill. And she endorsed personal experience and conviction as the right bases for decisions.

Another difference was the relative moral weight each gave to ends vs. means. Dewey thought that a war was justified (and not "violent") if it used force efficiently toward a desirable end. He made this clear in "Conscience and Compulsion" when he rejected the conscientious objectors' argument that war was the wrong means to achieve peace. These men, he said dismissively, should cease "separating ends from means and then identifying morals with ends [only]" ("Conscience and Compulsion" 262). By this he meant that if one's ultimate aims were moral, then the means one used to achieve them were moral too, that is, the ends justified the means. As in 1894 he believed in, in Weber's terms, "the ethic of ultimate ends." Addams still stressed the immediate consequences of the means. She would later write about the pacifists, "Some of us had suspected that social advance depends as much upon the process through which it is secured as upon the result itself" (Addams, *Peace* 133). In Weber's phrase, she still believed in "the ethic of individual responsibility," which contained within it the ethic of immediate consequences. Again hers was the more pragmatist ethic.

One is tempted to agree with Weber and call this disagreement tragic, for several reasons: because of its magnitude; because of the fact that it arose during a period of national crisis; and because it was between old friends. Given the profound respect they had for each other, they could only have been pained to disagree so thoroughly about the war. Whether they felt personal hostility is hard to say. Addams tended to turn her anger at others inward. Recalling later how she was persecuted for her convictions during World War I, she noted that the pacifist in wartime "finds it possible to travel from the mire of self-pity straight to the barren hills of self-righteousness and to hate himself equally in both places" (Knight, *Jane Addams* 208). Dewey, in contrast, had a tendency toward vindictiveness. When his brilliant former student Randolph Bourne attacked him incisively in print for betraying pragmatism and supporting the war, Dewey made sure that the struggling journalist never wrote again for the *New Republic* and was removed from the editorial board of the *Dial* (Ryan 203).

To be sure, there is a gentle hint in Addams's speech that she thought Dewey needed to be more tolerant of diverse views. She said, "We must occasionally remind ourselves of Emerson's saying, that the test of a real reformer is his ability to put up with the other reformers" (Addams, "Patriotism" 353). She had a point. Although Dewey never called the pacifists traitors for speaking out in wartime, his feelings were veering in that direction. In another essay, published in the *New Republic* in September 1917, he called for more debate about the war's aims and peace policies, that is, its ultimate ends; but he also wrote, "As with the soldier, so with the civil population, there is demand for closed ranks [in wartime]. . . . The needed cohesion in action is best attained along with intellectual and emotional unity. . . . Some abandonment of the liberties of peace time are inevitable" (Dewey, "Conscription" 277). For all his devotion to the ideal of democratic debate, for much of 1917 Dewey was disturbed by the pacifists' refusal to unify with the rest of the nation behind the war.

Addams left no record of how she felt about Dewey's support for the war and his criticism of her pacifist position. But something she said in a speech in 1905 suggests that she would have interpreted his prowar stance compassionately. "The man of affairs who takes a wrong road [needs] a chance to think," she wrote. When he has that chance, then "his blunder becomes his great educator. . . . People are bound to blunder" (Addams, "Address" 364–65).

She also chose not to raise the question in print of whether the fact that Dewey was a man made him more likely to identify with the prowar invocations of manliness that Woodrow Wilson, Theodore Roosevelt, and many other men were making in 1916 and 1917.[2] Still the point can be raised. Perhaps Dewey's sex did make it harder for him to consider objectively the reasons to reject war. This essay argues, however, that long-held ideas were the main factor shaping his position.

LESSONS LEARNED

World War I is famously the war that disillusioned the world. Millions died. It was particularly bloody for soldiers because they shot each other using new, devastating technologies—the small bore rifle, the machine gun, and rapid-fire artillery. Civilians also died in huge numbers, often of starvation. The war was especially tragic for two other reasons as well: the widespread belief among the educated citizens of Europe and North America before the war that they were "too civilized" ever to be willing to slaughter their fellow human beings again; and the contrast between the high ideals that belligerent governments, including the United States, used to justify it and the tawdry reality of territorial greed that was its cause and its consequence. The brutal vindictiveness of the Peace Treaty of 1919 was the final, painful disillusionment.

As for so many others, World War I was a transformative experience for Jane Addams. As early as 1896 she had come to agree with Dewey's point that reality could create legitimate antagonisms, but the war drove that lesson home to her much more profoundly and personally. Until World War I she had not stood against the views of the majority of American people in a sustained and public way. Later, remembering how she struggled with that decision, she wrote, "In the hours of self-doubt and distrust, the question again and again arises, has the individual, or a very small group, the right to stand out against millions of his countrymen?" (Knight, *Jane Addams* 219). Unwilling to deny the objective conditions that aroused her conscience, she was compelled to be antagonistic herself.

World War I was also a transformative experience for John Dewey. He changed his mind about some things, as many have noted (Caspary 3, 6; Howlett, *Troubled* 40–42; Ryan 203; Westbrook 231). His doubts began before the war was over. By November 1917 he had grown increasingly concerned about the government's repression of freedom of speech and published an essay about it in the *New Republic* (Dewey, "In Explanation" 292–95). And although he had not been interested in the war's immediate consequences while it was being fought, once it ended in late 1918 he was freshly concerned. In an essay titled "The Post-War Mind," published in the *New Republic* in December of that year, he wrote of "the uglier reactions of war—fear and its twin[,] hate" (115). He now judged them to be "unhappily . . . more enduring" than the positive emotions felt during a war, such as an "exaltation of mood" and a "preoccupation with the future" (113–116). In addition he now agreed with Addams's point about the nasty aftereffects of the Civil War (did he recall the conversation?). Writing of that war, he echoed the point she had made, observing that Americans should have learned from "the consequences of 'reconstruction' imposed by distrust and hate[,]" which persisted "long after the inevitable emotional reconciliation" (116). In 1920, shocked and disappointed by the failure of the war to save democracy, he sounded a new note of caution about being swept away by high ideals: "We must guard ourselves against the idealizations with which we customarily protect ourselves from seeing the realities of an unpleasant situation" (Dewey, "Our National Dilemma" 5). Clearly he understood that *he* had been swept up in war enthusiasm.

More broadly and most significantly, at some point after the war he abandoned his belief that the ends justified the means. In 1937 he wrote, "The fundamental principle of democracy is that the ends of freedom and individuality for all can be attained only by means that accord with those ends" (Dewey, "Democracy Is Radical" 298–99). In a 1945 essay that he wrote about Jane Addams, he quoted approvingly her statement that social advance "depends as much upon the process through which it is secured as upon the result itself" and called it, correctly, a statement of her "philosophy" and "the key to understanding her" (Dewey, "Democratic versus Coercive" 195). This was possibly the most important moral lesson Dewey drew from the war and from Addams.

After World War I, most notably in the 1930s, Dewey began to emphasize the contribution that the exercise of individual conscience made to a democracy. In *Liberalism and Social Action* in 1935, he explained that there is "a right of private conscience" and that it needs to be recognized as a "public function" (Dewey, *Liberalism* 92). "The individual inquirer," he continued, "has not only the right but the duty to criticize the ideas, theories and 'laws' of science" (67). In Dewey's lexicon, "science" referred to systematic methods of inquiry in any field, including ethics (Campbell 101, 110). Perhaps most significantly, he now was willing to put more emphasis on self-development as the goal. "Liberalism is committed to an end that is enduring," he wrote, "the liberation of individuals to realize . . . their capacities" (Dewey, *Liberalism* 56). Dewey dedicated *Liberalism and Social Action* to Jane Addams.

Their friendship survived the war. When Dewey's wife Alice died in 1927, Jane Addams sent him her "affectionate sympathy" and invited him to seek solace by visiting her at her summer home in Maine (Addams to Dewey). In May 1930 he represented former Hull House trustees at the settlement's fortieth anniversary reunion (Addams to Grace Abbott). Addams was one of only two people chosen—the other was the historian and former Columbia University professor James Harvey Robinson—to speak in October 1929 at a luncheon in New York City attended by twenty-three hundred people honoring Dewey on his seventieth birthday. At the banquet Addams credited Dewey with teaching her many things and noted in passing that their disagreement about World War I had "almost threatened" her "confidence in the . . . road" she had chosen. She added, perhaps with a touch of irony, that her experiences during the war "often confirmed John Dewey's contention that unless truth vindicates itself in practice it easily slips into futile dogma" (Addams, "John Dewey" 148).

Dogmatism was indeed dangerously present during World War I. Dewey had clearly thought Addams was dogmatic. In fact she had only urged experimentation to find alternative ways to resolve international disputes and took a position that was based on her conscience. Dewey, in contrast, *had* been dogmatic. He had made sweeping truth claims about the categorical, ultimate benefits of force when pursued efficiently in war. After the war, however, he viewed dogma's applications more skeptically. In 1935 in *Liberalism and Social Action* he addressed the dangers of dogma when invoked to justify "the use of violent force," a phrase clearly meant to include war. (By then Dewey had dropped his earlier sophistry that violence occurred only in bad wars, not in good ones.) He explained, "Insistence that the use of violent force is inevitable limits the use of available [social] intelligence. . . . [C] ommitment to inevitability is always the fruit of dogma." By contrast, "intelligence does not pretend to know *save* as a result of experimentation." He concluded, "The method of democracy is to bring [conflicting claims] out into the open" (Dewey, *Liberalism* 78–79). It was a full endorsement of Jane Addams's stance during the war.

Dewey's new view was already in evidence six years before, at his seventieth birthday banquet. In his remarks following the two toast speeches, he challenged Addams's claim that *he* had taught *her* the truth untested by experience slipped into dogma. "Indeed," he said, with true graciousness, this was something *she* had taught *him*. "One of the things that I have learned from her," he said, "is the enormous value of mental non-resistance, of tearing away the armor-plate of prejudice, of convention . . . that keeps one from sharing to the full in the larger . . . ranges of human . . . experience" (Dewey, "In Response" 179). Toward the end of his remarks he added, "We need to revive a faith in individuality and what belongs to the internal springs and sources of individuality" (181).

In rejecting dogma, that is, absolutist truth claims, and in endorsing the individual's responsibility to counter conventional ideas with those arising from their own individuality, Dewey was stating his views as a mature pragmatist. Although he had long endorsed experience as a way to appreciate truth and the need for education to reflect that insight, it was only after the war that he understood what it meant personally to enact these beliefs fully. In 1917 his rhetorical practices, as distinct from his philosophy, relied on absolutist rationality and, when necessary, sophistry, but the John Dewey toasted in 1929 by Jane Addams was more open-minded and experimental, as well as grateful to his patient interlocutor for her example and wisdom.

That Dewey found he had much to learn from Jane Addams is not surprising given that she had spent many years drawing her philosophical lessons from her richly lived life. Robert Danisch hints at some of this when he observes, "What makes Addams remarkable as a pragmatist and a rhetorician is her ability to develop a distinct perspective on the complexity of deliberation in a modern, large-scale democracy and her ability to practice pragmatism successfully given her own circumstances" (Danisch 66). Most of all, Addams had long made a great effort to put her beliefs into action and insure that her actions reflected her beliefs. She did this quite self-consciously. She wrote, "It is so easy to commit irreparable blunders because we fail to correct our theories by our changing experience" (Addams, *Newer Ideals* 186–87). Dewey had avoided that fate after the war by correcting his theories, and Addams surely admired him for it, knowing that this was no small thing for anyone but especially for a professional philosopher. The consequences for Dewey would be huge. In realizing the need to abandon dogma, to appreciate the value of extended debate and individual conscience in a democracy, even, or possibly especially, in time of war, and to embrace an enacted experimental pragmatism, Dewey made a crucial turn in his thinking that would bear magnificent results in his future writings.

As for how much credit Addams should receive for Dewey's change of mind, it is safe to say that she should receive more than she has. The war-time debate between Randolph Bourne and John Dewey over many of these same issues has been given a good deal of scholarly attention, perhaps understandably, since Bourne attacked Dewey directly, cogently, and with pointed language that was eminently quotable (Schlissel). Opinion has been expressed that it was Bourne's arguments that Dewey eventually adopted (Howlett, *Troubled* 102, 89–90, 140, 146; Westbrook 231). But given Dewey's long friendship and deep respect for Jane Addams, the ways that he changed his mind, and the credit he gave her for what he learned, she was clearly the most important influence.

Addams had learned from Dewey and experience, and Dewey had learned from Addams and experience. Their debate over World War I thus perfectly illustrates how they applied their ideas of pragmatism to their own lives as well as a point made often in this book: that when, over time, debate turns into shared inquiry, there is mutual learning on both sides.

NOTES

1. Because dating this speech accurately is complicated, it is often misdated. See Knight, *Citizen* 502n74, 507n60.

2. Addams believed, however, that of the two sexes, it was men who found war more appealing. See Knight, *Jane Addams* 167.

WORKS CITED

Addams, Jane. "Address at the Dedication of the Abraham Lincoln Center, Chicago, 1905." *Unity* 55 (July 27, 1905): 364–65.

———. *Democracy and Social Ethics.* New York: Macmillan, 1902.

———. "Growth of Corporate Consciousness." In *Illinois State Conference of Charities and Correction Proceedings,* vol. 2, 40–42. Springfield: Illinois State Conference of Charities, 1897.

———. "John Dewey and Social Welfare." In *John Dewey, the Man and His Philosophy: Addresses Delivered in New York in Celebration of His Seventieth Birthday,* 140–51. Cambridge, Mass.: Harvard University Press, 1930.

———. Letter to Grace Abbott. April 25, 1920. Excerpt. In *The Correspondence of John Dewey, 1871–1952,* vol. 2, ed. Larry A. Hickman, Barbara Levine, Anne Sharpe, and Harriet Furst Simon. Electronic ed. Charlottesville, Va.: InteLex Corporation, 2001. Web (accessed August 2, 2011) http://www.nlx.com/collections/132

———. Letter to John Dewey. July 20, 1927. In *The Correspondence of John Dewey, 1871–1952,* vol. 2, ed. Larry A. Hickman, Barbara Levine, Anne Sharpe, and Harriet Furst Simon. Electronic ed. Charlottesville, Va.: InteLex Corporation, 2001. Web (accessed August 2, 2011).

———. Letter to Mary Rozet Smith. February 1911. Excerpt. In *The Correspondence of John Dewey, 1871–1952,* vol. 1, ed. Larry A. Hickman, Barbara Levine, Anne Sharpe, and Harriet Furst Simon. Electronic ed. Charlottesville, Va.: InteLex Corporation, 1999. Web (accessed August 4, 2011).

———. "A Modern Lear." In *The Jane Addams Reader,* ed. Jean Bethke Elshtain, 163–176. New York: Basic Books, 2002.

———. *Newer Ideals of Peace.* Urbana: University of Illinois Press, 2007.

———. "Patriotism and Pacifists in Wartime." In *The Jane Addams Reader,* ed. Jean Bethke Elshtain, 352–64. New York: Basic Books, 2002. First published in *City Club of Chicago Bulletin* 10 (June 1917): 184–90.

———. *Peace and Bread in Time of War.* New York: Macmillan, 1922.

———. "The Subjective Necessity for Social Settlements." In *The Jane Addams Reader,* ed. Jean Bethke Elshtain, 14–28. New York: Basic Books, 2002.

———. *Twenty Years at Hull-House with Autobiographical Notes.* New York: Macmillan, 1910.

Benson, Lee, Ira Harkavy, and John Puckett. *Dewey's Dream: Universities and Democracies in an Age of Education Reform.* Philadelphia: Temple University Press, 2007.

Bourne, Randolph. *The World of Randolph Bourne: An Anthology of Essays and Letters.* Ed. Lillian Schlissel. New York: Dutton, 1965.

Campbell, James. *Understanding John Dewey: Nature and Cooperative Intelligence.* Chicago: Open Court, 1995.

Caspary, William R. *Dewey on Democracy.* Ithaca, N.Y.: Cornell University Press, 2000. John Dewey Collection. Special Collections Research Center, Carbondale: Southern Illinois University Carbondale, 1915–2005.

Crick, Nathan. *Democracy & Rhetoric: John Dewey and the Arts of Becoming.* Columbia: University of South Carolina Press, 2010.

Cywar, Alan. "John Dewey in World War I: Patriotism and International Progressivism." *American Quarterly* 21.3 (Autumn 1969): 578–94.

Danisch, Robert. *Pragmatism, Democracy, and the Necessity of Rhetoric.* Columbia: University of South Carolina Press, 2007.

Dewey, John. "Conscience and Compulsion." In *John Dewey: The Middle Works, 1899–1924,* vol. 10, ed. Jo Ann Boydston, 260–64. Carbondale: Southern Illinois University Press, 1980. Print.

———. "Conscription of Thought." In *John Dewey: The Middle Works, 1899–1924,* vol. 10, ed. Jo Ann Boydston, 276–80. Carbondale: Southern Illinois University Press, 1980. Print.

———. *The Correspondence of John Dewey, 1871–1952,* 4 vols., ed. Larry A. Hickman, Barbara Levine, Anne Sharpe, and Harriet Furst Simon. Electronic ed. Charlottesville, Va.: InteLex Corporation, 1999–?. Web (accessed August 4, 2011) http://www.nlx.com/collections/132

———. *Democracy and Education.* New York: Macmillan, 1916.

———. "Democracy Is Radical." In *John Dewey: The Later Works,* 1925–1953. vol. 11, ed. Jo Ann Boydston, 298–99. Carbondale: Southern Illinois University Press, 1987. Print.

———. "Democratic versus Coercive International Organization: The Realism of Jane Addams." In *John Dewey: The Later Works, 1925–1953,* vol. 15, ed. Jo Ann Boydston, 112–98. Carbondale: Southern Illinois University Press, 1989. Print. First published in the Anniversary Edition of Jane Addams, *Peace and Bread in Time of War.* New York: King's Crown Press, 1945.

———. "Force, Violence, and the Law." In *John Dewey: The Middle Works, 1899–1924,* vol. 10, ed. Jo Ann Boydston, 211–15. Carbondale: Southern Illinois University Press, 1980. Print.

———. "Future of Pacifism." In *John Dewey: The Middle Works, 1899–1924,* vol. 10, ed. Jo Ann Boydston, 265–75. Carbondale: Southern Illinois University Press, 1980. Print.

———. "If War Were Outlawed." In *John Dewey: The Middle Works, 1899–1924,* vol. 14, ed. Jo Ann Boydston, 110–14. Carbondale: Southern Illinois University Press, 1983. Print.

———. "In Explanation of Our Lapse." In *John Dewey: The Middle Works, 1899–1924,* vol. 10, ed. Jo Ann Boydston, 292–95. Carbondale: Southern Illinois University Press, 1980. Print.

———. "In Response." In *John Dewey, the Man and His Philosophy: Addresses Delivered in New York in Celebration of His Seventieth Birthday,* 173–81. Cambridge, Mass.: Harvard University Press, 1930.

———. *The Later Works, 1924–1953.* 17 vols. Ed. Jo Ann Boydston. Carbondale: Southern Illinois University Press, 1969–72.

———. *Liberalism and Social Action.* New York: Putnam, 1935.

———. *The Middle Works, 1899–1924.* 15 vols. Ed. Jo Ann Boydston. Carbondale: Southern Illinois University Press, 1976–91.

———. "Our National Dilemma." In *John Dewey: The Middle Works, 1899–1924,* vol. 12, ed. Jo Ann Boydston, 3–7. Carbondale: Southern Illinois University Press, 1982. Print.

———. "The Post-War Mind." In *John Dewey: The Middle Works, 1899–1924,* vol. 11, ed. Jo Ann Boydston, 112–16. Carbondale: Southern Illinois University Press, 1982. Print.

———. *The School and Society and The Child and the Curriculum.* Introduction by Philip W. Jackson. Chicago: University of Chicago Press, 1990.

———. "What Outlawry of War Is Not." In *John Dewey: The Middle Works, 1899–1924,* vol. 15, ed. Jo Ann Boydston, 115–21. Carbondale: Southern Illinois University Press, 1983.

Fischer, Marilyn. "Jane Addams Critique of Capitalism as Patriarchal." In *Feminist Interpretations of John Dewey,* ed. Charlene Haddock Seigfried, 278–96. University Park: Pennsylvania State University Press, 2002.

Howlett, Charles F. "John Dewey and Peace Education." In *Encyclopedia of Peace Education,* ed. Monisha Bajaj. http://www.tc.edu/centers/epe/entries.html (accessed August 16, 2011).

———. *Troubled Philosopher: John Dewey and the Struggle for World Peace.* Port Washington, N.Y.: National University Publications, 1977.

Hyde, Michael J. *Conscience and Rhetoric: Heidegger and Levinas, Rhetoric and the Euthanasia Debate.* Columbia: University of South Carolina Press, 2001.

John Dewey, the Man and His Philosophy: Addresses Delivered in New York in Celebration of His Seventieth Birthday. Cambridge, Mass.: Harvard University Press, 1930.

Knight, Louise W. *Citizen: Jane Addams and the Struggle for Democracy.* Chicago: University of Chicago Press, 2005.

———. *Jane Addams: Spirit in Action.* New York: W. W. Norton, 2010.

"Pacifism vs. Passivism." Editorial. *New Republic* 1.6 (December 12, 1914): 6–7.

Ryan, Alan. *John Dewey and American Democracy.* Ithaca, N.Y.: Cornell University Press, 1991.

Schlissel, Lillian. Introduction. In *The World of Randolph Bourne: An Anthology of Essays and Letters,* ed. Lillian Schlissel, xv–xxxiv. New York: Dutton, 1965.

Seigfried, Charlene Haddock. "Democracy as a Way of Life: Addams' Pragmatist Influence on Dewey." Paper presented at the Society for the Advancement of American Philosophy, Spokane, Wash., March 10–12, 2011. Unpublished manuscript in the author's possession.

———. Introduction. In *Feminist Interpretations of John Dewey,* ed. Charlene Haddock Seigfried, 1–22. University Park: Pennsylvania State University Press, 2002.

Weber, Max. "Politics as a Vocation." In *Dead Sociologists' Index.* Pfeiffer University. http://media.pfeiffer.edu/lridener/dss/Weber/polvoc.html (accessed August 20, 2011).

Westbrook, Robert. *John Dewey and the High Tide of American Liberalism.* New York: W. W. Norton, 1995.

John Dewey, W. E. B. Du Bois, and a Rhetoric of Education

Keith Gilyard

John Dewey's conception of democratic culture and of the attendant traits of fair play, dialogic deliberation, and social equality floated above his underlying sense of the productive possibilities of rhetoric. Of course rhetorical practice of some kind will obtain in any instance and help to instantiate any number of ends, some profoundly undemocratic. But Dewey rode boundless hope, as he expressed most clearly over the closing pages of *The Public and Its Problems,* on the exercise of critical intelligence—that is, the careful forwarding and evaluating of propositions by an informed and educated citizenry (204–19). A consultative, negotiating, debate-ready, artfully expressive *human articulate* functioned as the linchpin in his imagined network of amiable reconciliations.[1] Moreover, in Dewey's view, the necessary habits of mind would best be inculcated through formal education; thus, though he never stated it quite in these terms, he considered education to be a form of rhetorical preparation. Furthermore, I maintain, his educational philosophy, especially as detailed in "My Pedagogic Creed," functions as rhetorical theory, particularly with respect to invention given that proposals can be derived from and weighed against a taxonomy that can be constructed from Dewey's precepts.

One especially intriguing set of proposals belongs to W. E. B. Du Bois, the most distinguished African American educator-activist in American history, who, in the words of Arsene O. Boykin, emerged as Dewey's envisioned "wise parent," meaning that Du Bois became an exemplary proponent of Deweyan pedagogical ideals and thereby developed an explicit Deweyan strand inside the African American discourse on education (Boykin). He was the foremost advocate for directing African American critical intelligence toward the solution of social problems. This is not to imply that Du Bois's educational views were merely derivative of Dewey's or that the two were always akin ideologically. Du Bois, as indicated by some of his earliest writings, did not wait on Dewey to assume the lead. In addition he chanced a public engagement with formal leftist thought that Dewey never dared.[2] And we must remember, as Derrick Alridge points out, that Du Bois was steeped in a black intellectual tradition that included the educators Alexander Crummell, Booker T. Washington, Anna Julia Cooper, Kelly Miller, Nannie Helen Burroughs, Alain Locke, Carter G. Woodson, Mary McLeod Bethune, Charles H. Thompson, and Horace Mann Bond (Alridge). Nonetheless, because of Dewey's eventual prominence and the fact that Du Bois reached out to him on occasion, it is indeed fair to characterize Dewey as not necessarily a straightforward influence on Du Bois—they both could have arrived at an insistence on the development of human powers directly through Emerson—but an unmistakable one while Du Bois authored over the decades, in works such as *The Souls of Black Folk, The Education of Black People,* his *Crisis* editorials, and the novel *Mansart Builds a School,* an extensive program of study for African Americans keyed to notions of democratic possibility.[3] To discuss the essential parameters of what can be regarded, therefore, as a Dewey-Du Bois cocrafted rhetoric of education, one with pressing implications for all of current American culture, is the overriding purpose of this essay.

Dewey first published his creed in *School Journal* at the outset of 1897. To tease out his basic suggestions and cast them in the affirmative, education must

1) stress the social welfare of the groups to which students belong,
2) be informed by psychological insight,
3) reflect sensitivity to social conditions,
4) allow for development of every student's full capacities,
5) assume as a process the character of democratic communities,
6) foster an active mode for students,
7) position teachers as guides to expose students to and help them respond to influences,
8) include study of language, science, and art at every grade level,
9) emphasize the students' power of imagery,
10) reconcile individualistic and institutional ideals ("My Pedagogic Creed" 442–54).

Dewey thus laid a rational and ethical foundation upon which to construct more elaborate pedagogical arguments and appeals, including some of his own. For example, in *The Public and Its Problems* he asserted, following Tocqueville, that popular government is peculiarly educative in that it "forces a recognition that there are common interests, even though the recognition of *what* they are is confused; and the need it enforces of discussion and publicity brings about some clarification of what they are" (207).[4] *The* problem of the public, he continued, "is the improvement of the methods and conditions of debate, discussion and persuasion" (208). Read against the educational framework of "My Pedagogic Creed," the desired communication is a logical outgrowth rooted, at the very least, in ideas about developing student capacities (point 4), exercising community practices (point 5), encouraging active participation by students (point 6), and facilitating student response to influences (point 7).

Moreover, Dewey asked in *Experience and Education,* "Is it not the reason of our preference [for democratic social arrangements, individual freedom, and kind social relations] that we believe that mutual consultation and convictions reached through persuasion make possible a better quality of experience than can otherwise be provided on any wide scale?" (*Experience* 34). By promoting varied experiences over a push for uniformity and championing dialogue over coercion, Dewey remained attentive to the stipulations of his education framework relative to social welfare (point 1), astuteness pertaining to psychology (point 2), and concern about overall social conditions (point 3). As Jay Martin points out, "Dewey assumed that if the schools organized modern intelligence effectively, democracy would be the inevitable result. And if democratic citizens emerged, they would organize education, and in turn education would become more democratic" (Martin 245). Whatever the case, to enact Dewey's major propositions involved, as Dewey understood, "the art of full and moving communication" (Dewey, *Public* 184).

Given his embrace, influenced heavily by William James, of philosophical pragmatism, testing and creating provisional truths were always essential for Dewey and would become so for Du Bois, who began his academic studies as a confirmed idealist convinced that the most germane philosophical quest was for transcendent truth. Although he recalled late in life, "I became a devoted follower of James at the time he was developing his pragmatic philosophy" (Du Bois, *Autobiography* 133), he stopped well short of declaring that as a student at Harvard University he was devoted to *James's philosophy.* The likely situation, as the biographer David Levering Lewis indicates, is that Du Bois valued most the intellectualism of James and his pluralistic, antiracist, and antiimperialist sentiments—along with his personal encouragement of Du Bois. On the other hand, with fondness for the ideas of Kant and Hegel, Du Bois would have resisted a shift in emphasis from truth to knowledge (Lewis, *Biography of a Race* 88, 96). Such conversion would come when Du Bois turned to the social sciences, but he preferred neither pragmatism's nor rhetoric's persuasion. He imagined that his scholarly contribution would be to collect data rigorously and present it with detachment. He once surmised, "The ultimate evil was stupidity. The cure for it was knowledge based on scientific investigation" (Du Bois, *Dusk of Dawn* 58). This was a prophet's appeal, privileging exposure (the light) over argument, though without the prophet's passion. Interestingly Du Bois did voice quite early an appreciation for the democratizing potential of rhetoric, at least along the dimensions of style and delivery, writing "Public Rhetoricals" as a twenty-year-old undergraduate in 1888. He argued, "When Fred Douglass appealed to the Caesar of the American people on behalf of a race despised, spit upon and trodden under the feet of men, he had to be eloquent and thank God he was!" (Du Bois, "Public

Rhetoricals" 21). Despite his later social-scientific persona, Du Bois knew preveniently that it would take more than historical and sociological data to effect racial uplift.

Du Bois began teaching in 1886, when he accepted a job in rural Tennessee during a summer away from Fisk, his first undergraduate institution. From the outset he pondered the contribution that schooling could make to racial equality and thus American democracy. His thinking furthermore anticipated, however tentatively, many of the *topoi* that Dewey, then starting out on the faculty of the University of Michigan after a stint as a high school teacher in Pennsylvania, would publish eleven years later. The firm alignment of their ideas noted by Alridge (39–42) and Ross Posnock (127–41) would occur after that point when Du Bois more deeply theorized the potential of popular education as part of a program of civil rights. His nascent inclinations as an instructor were probably more prescriptive and less democratic than Dewey would have approved (phrased alternately, fairly weak on points 5 and 6 above).

Du Bois stressed liberal education, as did Dewey. In 1891, while still a student at Harvard University, he delivered an address before the National Colored League in Boston titled "Does Education Pay?" He cleverly addressed the popular notion that practical or manual training was the most suitable course for black students by providing numerous examples of the practical benefits of liberal thinking. He even credited the spread of Platonic ideals about justice, right, freedom, and love with ending slavery. In his chain of reasoning, those formulations "destroyed feudalism, leveled serfdom, scorched aristocracy, melted crowns, took hold of the heart of William Wilberforce and burned into the soul of William Lloyd Garrison and the slave went forth a man" (Du Bois, "Does Education Pay" 5). Du Bois clinched that particular argument by asserting that "in this case certainly liberal education was a mighty practical thing" (5). Du Bois did not oppose the sort of vocational training predominant at Hampton and Tuskegee; he opined that black students should learn trades and learn them well (7). But he offered that they should also avail themselves of a broader education by which they could learn the "best method for the end in view" as well as learn to determine the "best end to have in view" (7).

Although sharing with Dewey a sense of the value of liberal education, with his pronouncement that "Truth, Beauty and Virtue" are ends worth attaining, Du Bois still differed significantly at that stage from the pragmatist philosopher, who was interested in multiple forms of lower-case truth, beauty, and virtue ("Does Education Pay?" 4). Du Bois also differed from Dewey, a gap later narrowed, given his focus on higher education. He was intrigued by the idea of developing a black leadership cadre, eventually conceived of as the much-discussed "Talented Tenth."[5] He perhaps possessed a stronger notion of great men than of vibrant democratic culture, evident in his praise of Thomas Carlyle's ideas about heroic leadership (Du Bois, "Carlyle" 1–6). Of the proslavery Carlyle, Dewey later remarked that the Scottish writer was "no admirer of democracy" (Dewey, *Public* 110).[6]

By the turn of the century, after having embraced philosophical idealism and then the methods of the social sciences, Du Bois adopted yet another perspective. Although always enormously proud of the systematic historical and sociological study concerning African Americans that he and his colleagues undertook at Atlanta University, he nonetheless revealed that in 1899 his faith in knowledge as the primary solution to the "Negro problem" became greatly diminished. Du Bois pointed to the pursuit and lynching that year of Sam Hose and the public display of Hose's fingers and toes in an Atlanta meat market.[7] Du Bois had written a letter about the Hose situation to Joel Chandler Harris, who served on the staff of the *Atlanta Constitution,* and he was en route from the university to hand-deliver the message when he learned of the capture-and-lynch phase of the incident. He remarked, "Well, I didn't deliver the letter. I went back to Atlanta University. And then I made up my mind that knowledge wasn't enough, that even if people were ignorant of essential matters which they had to know, they wouldn't correct their actions without more realization of just what the difficulties were. They had not only to know, but they had to act" (Du Bois, "Atlanta Years").

In placing the emphasis on action rather than on the application of an existing knowledge base, Du Bois was warming up to his major role as an activist, public intellectual, and self-described propagandist, a process that led to his pivotal role in the Niagara Movement and in the 1909 founding of the National Association for the Advancement of Colored People (NAACP).[8] By the time the historic civil rights organization was established, he had published additional views on education, most notably in his classic 1903 text *The Souls of Black Folk,* and had delivered several addresses on education, including "The Hampton Idea" and "Galileo Galilei," which were later printed in *The Education of Black People.*

Throughout *Souls* he continued to sketch his vision of the liberally educated African Americans whom he felt schools should be attempting to produce, emphasizing the powers—capacities—of African Americans to be coworkers in the kingdom of culture (5); the education of youth according to ability (45); the potential of African Americans to inject new points of view into American, particularly southern, discourse and thus serve as valuable social capital with regard to constructing a just America, rather than focusing on revenge and revolt (88–90); the flourishing of individuality (90); the development of civic virtue (142); the necessity of a functional public school system (146); and the acknowledgment of a common humanity and destiny (150). Du Bois also reaffirmed his belief in the primacy of liberal higher education, stating, "The roots of the tree, rather than the leaves, are the sources of its life; and from the dawn of history, from Academus to Cambridge, the culture of the University has been the broad foundation-stone on which is built the kindergarten's ABC" (69–70).

In 1906 he spoke at a major center of industrial education for blacks, Hampton Institute, and once again argued for the development of human capacity, meaning, to the consternation of Hampton officials, that a trade curriculum should be seen as worthwhile only when linked to broad liberal concerns and movement toward a politically progressive society (*Education of Black People* 9–10). Two years later he visited Fisk, twenty years after his graduation, and exhorted administrators to invest sufficiently in liberal education lest they compromise the true emancipation of African Americans (*Education of Black People* 29).

Du Bois had not commented much, as Dewey had, about the actual unfolding of pedagogical practices. However, by the time of his return to Fisk, he had abundantly affirmed the social and psychological goals that Dewey set as tasks for public schools. His specific revisions of or additions to Dewey's rhetoric of education would, as suggested, include appeals for

1) higher liberal arts education for African Americans to foster the advance of a Talented Tenth,
2) a platform of adequate funding for African American education at all levels,
3) promotion of precise advocacy for racial justice,
4) explicit expression of the common humanity of American ethnic groups,
5) the stressing of civic virtue over material gain, and
6) development of the trait of forthright criticism.

Du Bois pushed the critical engagement that he considered "the soul of democracy and the safeguard of modern society" (*Souls* 40).

In the spring of 1909 Dewey and Du Bois figured prominently in the first meeting of the National Negro Conference, the organization that evolved into the NAACP. Both addressed the audience of three hundred or so liberals and progressives. Striking the balance that would characterize their relationship as they circled each other in political groups and in the public sphere over the ensuing decades, Dewey made an understated, utilitarian presentation about racism, decrying the loss of social capital it entailed, a point that Du Bois had made in *The Souls of Black Folk*. To be fair to Dewey, he expressed a key statement against still-influential theories of biological determinism. Yet his remarks were more about the potential for social opportunity than about forceful advocacy for it. To the contrary, Du Bois bluntly called for aggressive antiracist action (Lewis, *Biography of a Race* 391–96). Indeed Du Bois would become increasingly frustrated with Dewey's expressions of ethical-democratic vision given its decoupling from the sort of spirited confrontation with white supremacy that he favored. At one point in his biography, Lewis characterizes Du Bois as "sounding like an angry John Dewey" (*Fight for Equality* 147).[9] Du Bois wished that had been true of Dewey on matters of racism.

This particular difference between them was still evident during the four-year existence of the League for Independent Political Action (LIPA), which was founded in 1929 by several dozen academics, literary figures, and activists, including Reinhold Niebuhr and Norman Thomas, to pursue a third-party route to political and economic reform. Dewey, seventy years old at that point, served as national chairperson; Du Bois, sixty-one, began a tenure as one of several vice chairpersons. But Du Bois, although remaining mostly supportive of Dewey and the league—he invited Dewey to speak on behalf of LIPA at the 1932 annual convention of the NAACP—soon scaled back his own involvement because of the group's unwillingness to place aggressive antiracism on its action agenda (Lewis, *Fight for Equality* 252–53).

During the period of the closest contact and cooperation between Dewey and Du Bois, their elaborations and refinements relative to what I am referring to as their joint education platform naturally reflected their ideological positions and temperaments. Dewey, for example, presented the most expansive and deeply reflective treatment of his social vision and his liberal pedagogic approach in the hefty *Democracy and Education.* Published in 1916 and stretching to more than four hundred pages, the volume carefully fleshed out the propositions of "My Pedagogic Creed."

Dewey began by revealing that his basic purpose was to discern and characterize the principles of democratic society and make specific application to education (*Democracy* v). Then, addressing the rhetorical nature of all societies, he developed the concept, while highlighting the semantic relationships among "common," "community," and "communication," that societies are perpetuated through and in verbal exchange (5). Dewey postulated that all social environments educate those who participate in them, and he imagined the impact of such education to be directly related to the degree of the subject's involvement or immersion. Schools have no privileged place in such dynamics until, Dewey reasoned, a society becomes complex and needs to designate special social environments—schools—to induce the society's most valued dispositions in the young (26–27). The achievement of this guiding function, best realized in Dewey's conception through emotional and intellectual as opposed to direct control, thereby becoming intrinsic and not extrinsic, relies on the "identity of interest and understanding" (48), a process Kenneth Burke, in *A Rhetoric of Motives,* more succinctly would term "identification" (Burke 19–29).

However, not all identifications are democratic, as Dewey well knew. He thus proceeded to posit the importance of a democratic ideal to education, issuing perhaps, as indicated elsewhere (Gilyard 73–74), the superordinate statement in his educational and political thought:

> A democracy is more than a form of government; it is primarily a mode of associated living, of conjoint communicated experience. The extension in space of the number of individuals who participate in an interest so that each has to refer his own action to that of others, and to consider the action of others to give point and direction to his own, is equivalent to the breaking down of those barriers of class, race, and national territory which kept men from perceiving the full import of their activity. These more numerous and more varied points of contact denote a greater diversity of stimuli to which an individual has

> to respond; they consequently put a premium on variation in his action. They secure a liberation of powers which remain suppressed as long as the incitations to action are partial, as they must be in a group which in its exclusiveness shuts out many interests. (Dewey, *Democracy* 101)

Dewey clearly explicated the transactional quality, to which language is vital, of what he considered to be the most desirable social arrangement, and he continued throughout the remainder of the text to detail laboriously his trademark ideas about grounding instruction in student experience, exposing students to culture as a means to expand conceptual range and to sharpen perception, promoting intellectual freedom, and embracing diversity.

But similar to his activist pronouncements, *Democracy and Education* failed to advance beyond the social-capital argument to incorporate a vigorous antiracist line, particularly with regard to antiblack racism. The implicit consequence was to weaken Dewey's proposals given that the American society he contemplated as he espoused his ideals had in large part been racially constructed. To posit a series of external referrals as the solution to racism and to remain silent, in his most widely circulating words, about particular needs of African American students had the practical effect of not addressing the education of African Americans at all. His works read, therefore, as a canon of educational theory that is exclusionary in the same manner as have been canons of American literature or American history. Of course one could argue that he was addressing the situation of African American students because of his habitual insistence on grounding instruction in student experience, which perforce means African American student experience at times. But that constitutes a roundabout way of getting at a matter that begged for a head-on approach. As the philosopher and social critic Cornel West indicates, racism both as discrimination and as the "racing" of America through the role played by blacks in the evolution of American economics, politics, and culture should always be a component of serious social analysis (West 147). West suggests grappling with at least two questions: "To what degree have the demands of blacks fostered and expanded American democracy? In which way is democracy dependent on these demands, given their spin-off effects in demands made by larger ethnic groups, women, gays, lesbians, and the elderly?" (West 147). In a similar fashion, Susan Searls Giroux contends, "Specifically, our task as educators is to open up dialogue by resurrecting the public memory of racial oppression and exclusion in the interests of exploring more democratic arrangements for government, the economy, and civil society, as well as those changes in consciousness, culture, and education needed to sustain such reforms" (Giroux 242). However, even Dewey's concise reworking of his views in the 1938 *Education and Experience*, his last major statement on education, does not—several years after inattention to racism was a point of contention in the League for Independent Political Action—overtly address racial injustice. Dewey, however, could always thank Du Bois for such forthrightness.

Echoes of Dewey, always traceable in Du Bois, are never clearer than in the following passage from a 1929 editorial, "Pechstein and Pecksniff":

> Yet the United States, Germany, France, and most civilized countries have urged the public school and democracy in education for all. And they have done this because of the fact that whatever may be lost in this group education, the human contact which comes through democratic education of all the youth of a great country infinitely overbalances it. They realize that if peace, good will and industrial democracy are going to triumph in the world, they can only triumph by increase in the intelligence of individuals and the increase of direct knowledge and sympathetic human relationship among men. Any step backward from this, any building up of artificial barriers or overemphasizing of natural barriers, is a blow in the face of civilization and human advance. (140–41)

An intertextual link was forged strongly by Du Bois's discussion of "human contact," a smoother equivalent to Dewey's "conjoint communicated experience," and Du Bois's cautioning against "building up of artificial barriers or overemphasizing of natural barriers," which virtually reprises Dewey's concern with "breaking down of those barriers of class, race, and national territory." Similarly Lewis notes that in "The Immortal Child" perhaps Du Bois's most extended statement about the education of precollege students, the crusader's language about the full development of all children ("Immortal Child" 101) and about the fostering of critical intelligence ("Immortal Child" 102) and about democracy ("Immortal Child" 102) fervently and lyrically evokes the arguments of both Deweys—John and Alice (Lewis *Fight for Equality* 17). In the same essay, though, Du Bois displays a strident tone about racial matters that neither Dewey would exhibit on the page: "We know in America how to discourage, choke, and murder ability when it so far forgets itself as to choose a dark skin" ("Immortal Child" 97). Similarly in an editorial titled "Education," he wrote that "they are tired of democracy; they want caste: a place for everybody and everybody in his father's place, with themselves on top and 'niggers' at the bottom where they belong" (Du Bois, "Education" [1912] 121). In a second piece also titled "Education," Du Bois tethered the issue of African American education with American schooling writ large as he railed against those who sought to restrict education for African Americans, arguing that "their attack on real education for Negroes is in reality one with their attack on education for workingmen in general, and this is part of the great modern attack on democracy for the working class which is an attack upon democracy" (Du Bois, "Education" [1915] 123).

Du Bois turned increasingly toward Afrocentric conceptions of education. As early as 1919 he presented the case for *rapprochement panafricain* and advised African Americans to learn to speak French and Spanish because those were languages spoken by many educated people of African descent who resided outside of the United States (Du Bois, "French and Spanish" 127). Focusing on black pride, he was especially dismayed that a poll conducted among 127 juniors and seniors at Lincoln University, one of the Historically Black Colleges and Universities (HBCU), revealed that 81 of the students (64 percent) opposed having African American professors (Du Bois, "Students of Lincoln" 139). Understanding the result as a manifestation of society's undervaluing of African American achievement, he eventually recommended black-centered, separatist if necessary, programs. This was a striking turn because no one had fought harder against segregation. Nonetheless, Du Bois avowed, "You are teaching Negroes. There is no use pretending that you are teaching Chinese or that you are teaching white Americans or that you are teaching citizens of the world" (Du Bois, *Education of Black People* 92).

Henry Lee Moon, who interacted with Du Bois on several occasions and who became the editor of the *Crisis* in the 1960s, attributed the latter's "certain ambivalence" to an incurable liberalism that allowed him to see more than one side of an issue and to shifts of attitude and perspective (14). But liberalism alone accounts for no shifts. That Du Bois was by then operating as more of an experimentalist, a pragmatist, does. Viewing a Eurocentric orientation as the logical outcome—the default result—of an educational process that was inattentive to African American experience, Du Bois proffered an Afrocentric framework as the best hope to develop the full critical capacities of African American students. He later reflected, "I was fighting segregation but simultaneously advocating such segregation as would prepare my people for the struggle they were making" (*Autobiography* 297). His Afrocentric posturing did not convey explicit rejection of Dewey's theories. Because Dewey privileged local experience over so-called universal experience in education programs, he would have had to concede, on grounds of consistency, that local experience for black students, to be authentic, had to be "black." It would have been a problematic concession, to be sure. Dewey was not overly provincial. Nor was, at heart, Du Bois. In fact his lifelong advocacy of liberal education relied on the notion that such education made the best of accumulated human experience available to every child. As Du Bois wrestled with the authenticity dilemma, he provisionally resolved it in favor of Afro-particularity. It was a position justifiable by Dewey's theorizing, but one doubts that Dewey could have endorsed it.

In May 1931 Du Bois wrote to ask Dewey for a statement on African American education for publication in the annual college education issue of the *Crisis:* "It seems to me that the Booker T. Washington idea has broken down because of great economic changes, and that a re-statement of educational philosophy for the Negro is needed. I do not expect, of course, anything long or comprehensive, but if you could make a short statement of 500 or 1,000 words, I would very greatly appreciate it."[10] Du Bois had been a fierce critic of Washington's viewpoints for many years and a producer of voluminous work about education for American Americans. He obviously was seeking amplification of his own ideas, the heavy testimonial weight that he felt Dewey could provide. But for whatever reason (was the *Crisis* too radical by then?), Dewey never delivered.

Perhaps Du Bois was hoping that Dewey would expound on the idea of a people's college for African Americans, an idea that Du Bois eventually helped to implement in 1942 when he was back at Atlanta University. However, partly inspired by Dewey, he had been seriously considering some form of the idea since the mid-1920s.[11] In January 1930 Du Bois mentioned a people's college in a letter to Lillian A. Alexander, who worked with him on the *Crisis,* explaining, "Its object would be to realize democracy in the United States by the education of human beings in liberal lines" ("To Lillian" 415). Du Bois proposed to do the educating with whatever help he could enlist. Although he doubted that many whites would apply for admission or offer to teach, he explained that the school would be open to white students and to white faculty who possessed what he considered the appropriate viewpoint. About a year later, his nationalist approach beginning to solidify, he envisioned such a school to be expressly for African Americans. He solicited feedback from Soren A. Mathiasen, a noted practitioner in the field of adult education. Mathiasen founded Pocono People's College near Henryville, Pennsylvania, in 1923 and directed the school until it ceased operations in 1930 due to financial difficulties. He subsequently directed the American People's College in Europe—Dewey served on the advisory committee—and founded the American People's School in the Bronx, New York, in 1934. He managed to keep that institution running until 1945. When Mathiasen heard from Du Bois in 1931, he responded encouragingly and pledged to assist if needed. He also informed Du Bois that Dewey had formed a group that planned to establish a series of colleges. He promised to send under separate cover the group's document, "Presentation for a Chain of People's Colleges," and a brochure about the school that had existed in the Poconos. Du Bois never did attract much funding. When Atlanta University began to operate a people's college in 1942, the open-admissions program featured volunteer teachers from the campus and the surrounding community (Cooper 308).

Ultimately Du Bois worked out his ideas about schooling in the 1959 historical novel *Mansart Builds a School,* the middle book of *The Black Flame* trilogy. Dewey, the late John Dewey by then, whose role in the founding of the NAACP is mentioned in the text (Du Bois, *Mansart* 43), would have appreciated Du Bois's artistic achievement. As the literary scholar Mark Sanders notes in his afterword to the 2007 edition, "As per John Dewey, it is through the aesthetic—that is, through subjective experience re-presented by art—that the individual communicates with the group, and that different groups communicate with one another" (270).[12] Through the vehicle of Manuel Mansart, superintendent of the colored public schools in Atlanta and later president of the Georgia State A&M School, Du Bois reanalyzes connections among a rapidly industrializing society, vocational training, the uplift ambitions of African Americans, liberal education, equitable labor opportunities, racialized funding inequality for education programs, and social democracy. In addition, informed significantly by Marxism, as he had been in his master historical treatise *Black Reconstruction,* he describes the issues pertaining to the actual operation of schools within American and worldwide environments of racism and economic exploitation (Du Bois, *Mansart* 62–75, 89–100).

Du Bois never said much about specific rhetorical training. Dewey said even less. Yet in their impressive assembling of a rhetoric of education, they indisputably made the case for rhetoric *in* education—Dewey by his conception of the Great Community and Du Bois by his similar vision of democracy, the force of his own writing and speaking career, and his celebration of eloquence. Dewey's hope for rhetorical training would be that it might find its best expression in astoundingly productive town hall meetings. He imagined that "free social inquiry" and deep, artful communication should be "indissolubly wedded," thereby bringing democracy to its "consummation" (Dewey, *Public* 184). Du Bois would love to prep students to produce the great agitational speech or muckraking article in service of a world community that "tries to get good and does get better" (Du Bois, *ABC of Color* 70). "Good" is ultimately unreachable, as Du Bois comprehended, but "better" is a quality for which we can fight.

An updated, recombined, Dewey-Du Bois, cocrafted rhetoric of education may thus be expressed:

1) Stress the social welfare of the groups to which students belong and promote racial justice, adopting Afrocentric perspectives when necessary as part of a process that reflects sensitivity to social conditions and is informed by psychological and cultural insights.
2) Allow for development of every student's full capacities and place liberal arts education, including higher education, within reach of all.
3) Assume as a process the character of democratic communities, which involves expression of the common humanity of American ethnic groups and at least consideration of an emphasis on civic virtue over material gain.
4) Foster an active mode for students, including development of the trait of forthright criticism.
5) Position teachers as guides to expose students to and help them respond to influences such as national and world economic arrangements as students attempt to reconcile individualistic and institutional ideals.
6) Include study of language, science, and art at every grade level, accentuating the students' power of imagery and blending in at appropriate points the teaching of foreign languages and specific training in rhetoric.
7) Provide adequate funding for education at all levels.

Most assuredly this model does not indicate the full range of thinking required to address all of today's challenges and problems in education and the broader world. Gender, for example, would need more extensive and intensive treatment. Further, it is not my assertion that the convictions advanced are not derivable from other thinkers. Jane Addams, with whom Dewey and Du Bois consulted, influenced both.[13] However, the rubric, admittedly somewhat contrived, represents Dewey, who so valued dialogue, in "conversation" with one of his most important interlocutors.

As we ponder the troubled state of American culture and wonder about the extent to which formal education can improve our democracy in an era of extreme partisanship—*no compromise* has become a badge of honor in some quarters—and as we strive, along with our students, to confront intelligently new situations—to, as Giroux frames it, "reverse the desperate experience of fear, anxiety, uncertainty, and alienation that accompanies the painful erosion of individual and social agency" (242)—we would do well to revisit and attempt to extend and revise fruitfully our liberal, progressive, and radical education traditions. In other words, a useful move would be to reconsider Dewey and Du Bois.

NOTES

1. As Cornel West expresses, Dewey's conception of philosophical pragmatism, his basic orientation, suggests, "first, that reconciliation is possible between two extremes; second, that this reconciliation can be arrived at in an amiable manner; and third, that this amiable reconciliation will be better than either extreme" (*American Evasion* 57).

2. Although West has celebrated Dewey, he criticizes what he sees as the latter's gradualism, failure to articulate concrete plans for large-scale social reform, insufficient race and class analyses, and too much of a restriction of his practical politics to schooling (*American Evasion* 101–11).

3. For Emerson's view of power(s), see West, *American Evasion* 11–25; for the influence of Emerson on Dewey, see 69–70; for the same on Du Bois, see 142–43.

4. Although he does not specify so, Dewey is drawing from Tocqueville's *Democracy in America*, vol. 1, pt.2, chaps. 5 and 6, "Government by Democracy in America," 181–212, and "The Real Advantages Derived by American Society from Democratic Government," 213–26, respectively.

5. Du Bois popularized the notion of the "Talented Tenth," that is, the belief that cultivating the gifted and capable "Tenth" was the quickest way to advance African Americans as a whole. He revised his thinking when he realized that the Talented Tenth often lacked social commitment. His 1903 essay "The Talented Tenth" and his 1948 revision, "The Talented Tenth Memorial Address," are reprinted back-to-back in Henry Louis Gates Jr. and Cornel West's *Future of the Race*, 133–77. In the second essay Du Bois writes, "My Talented Tenth must be more than Talented, and work not simply as individuals. Its passport to leadership was not alone learning, but expert knowledge of modern economics as it affected American Negroes; and in addition to this and fundamental, would be its willingness to sacrifice and plan for such economic revolution in industry and just distribution of wealth, as would make the rise of our group possible" (163).

6. In 1840 Carlyle presented six lectures on heroism, reconstructed in *On Heroes* as "The Hero as Divinity," "The Hero as Prophet," "The Hero as Poet," "The Hero as Priest," "The Hero as a Man of Letters," and "The Hero as King." He forwarded his racial views most pointedly in his 1849 discourse "The Nigger Question."

7. On April 12, 1899, during a heated argument between employer Alfred Cranford and employee Sam Hose, Cranford apparently took aim at Hose with a gun, which prompted

Hose, who was at work with an ax in hand, to throw the tool at Cranford, killing him. Hose fled but was captured and lynched eleven days later. In the interim, mob-inciting rumors circulated that he had assaulted Cranford's wife and child.

8. Du Bois labeled himself a propagandist in *The Education of Black People* (40). He used the word often; it never had the sinister connotations for him that it had for some, particularly after the onset of the cold war.

9. Lewis, in *W. E. B. Du Bois: The Fight for Equality in the American Century, 1919–1963*, refers to the 1927 student strike at Hampton Institute about which Du Bois, sympathetic to the students, remarked, "Students are not sent to school to learn to obey. They are sent there to learn to do, to think, to execute, to be men and women" (147).

10. Du Bois wrote to Dewey on at least five other occasions, four times related to the *Crisis* (June 22, 1931; August 2, 1931; January 12, 1932; January 22, 1932) and once to introduce Dewey to John Hope, president of Atlanta University (April 2, 1930). Dewey wrote a letter to Du Bois dated January 20, 1932, but apparently it has been lost.

11. On November 21, 1925, Abram Harris, executive secretary of the Minneapolis Urban League and later head of the economics department at Howard University, wrote to Du Bois about the need to preserve the "liberal view" in education for African Americans. Harris was pessimistic about changing the "superstitions and orthodoxies" of HBCUs; therefore he proposed the creation of an institution similar to the New School for Social Research, what Harris termed Newer Spirit College. Of course he sought Du Bois's opinion of the idea. On December 15, 1925, Du Bois wrote back expressing enthusiasm and volunteering to help. However, unlike Harris, he exuded no optimism about receiving funding from philanthropies.

12. Sanders provides no citation for Dewey's thought; perhaps he had in mind Dewey's ruminations about art and civilization near the close of *Art as Experience*. In that work Dewey writes, for example, that "it is by way of communication that art becomes the incomparable organ of instruction" (347) and "it is more or less a commonplace to say that a person's ideas and treatment of his fellows are dependent upon his power to put himself imaginatively in their place" (348).

13. For an example of Addams's well-known influence on Dewey, see Jay Martin, *Education of John Dewey*, 164–68. Lewis, in *Biography of a Race*, reports instances of Addams's connection to Du Bois and of her imprint on his work (223, 370, 377–78, 416).

WORKS CITED

Alridge, Derrick P. *The Educational Thought of W. E. B. Du Bois: An Intellectual History.* New York: Teachers College Press, 2008.

Aptheker, Herbert, ed. *The Correspondence of W. E. B. Du Bois: Selections 1877–1934.* Vol. 1. N.p.: University of Massachusetts Press, 1973.

Boykin, Arsene O. "Du Bois as Dewey's Wise Parent." *Educational Forum* 42.3 (1978): 337–44.

Burke, Kenneth. *A Rhetoric of Motives.* 1950. Reprint. Berkeley: University of California Press, 1969.

Carlyle, Thomas. "The Nigger Question: Occasional Discourse on the Nigger Question." 1849. In *The Works of Thomas Carlyle in Thirty Volumes*, vol. 29, *Critical and Miscellaneous Essays*, ed. H. D. Traill, 348–83. London: Chapman and Hall, 1907.

———. *On Heroes, Hero-Worship, and the Heroic in History.* 1841. Ed. Michael K. Goldberg, Joel J. Brattin, and Mark Engel. Norman and Charlotte Strouse Edition of the Writings of Thomas Carlyle. Berkeley: University of California Press, 1993.

Cooper, William M. "Adult Education Programs of Negro Colleges and Universities." *Journal of Negro Education* 14.3 (Summer 1945): 307–11.

Dewey, John. "Address to National Negro Conference." 1909. In *The Collected Works of John Dewey*, ed. Jo Ann Boydston, vol. 4, *John Dewey: The Middle Works, 1899–1924*, 156–57. Carbondale: Southern Illinois University Press, 1977.

———. *Art as Experience*. New York: Minton, Balch, 1934.

———. *Democracy and Education*. 1916. New York: Macmillan, 1940.

———. *Experience and Education*. 1938. Kappa Delta Pi Lecture Series. New York: Simon & Schuster, 1997.

———. "My Pedagogic Creed." In *The Philosophy of John Dewey*, ed. John J. McDermott, 442–54. Chicago: University of Chicago Press, 1981.

———. *The Public and Its Problems*. 1927. Athens: Swallow Press; Ohio University Press, 1954.

Du Bois, W. E. B. *An ABC of Color*. 1963. Reprint. New York: International Publishers, 2001.

———. "Atlanta Years (excerpt)." In *Our Souls Have Grown Deep Like the Rivers: Black Poets Read Their Works*. Rhino, 2000. CD.

———. *The Autobiography of W. E. B. Du Bois: A Soliloquy on Viewing My Life from the Last Decade of Its First Century*. Ed. Herbert Aptheker. New York: International Publishers, 1968.

———. *Black Reconstruction: An Essay toward a History of the Part Which Black Folk Played in the Attempt to Reconstruct Democracy in America, 1860–1880*. New York: Harcourt, Brace, 1935.

———. "Carlyle." W. E. B. Du Bois Papers (Miss. 312). Special Collections and University Archives, W. E. B. Du Bois Library, University of Massachusetts, Amherst.

———. *Darkwater: Voices from within the Veil*. 1920. Oxford W. E. B. Du Bois. New York: Oxford University Press, 2007.

———. "Does Education Pay?" In *Writings by W. E. B. Du Bois in Periodicals Edited by Others*, vol. 1, comp. and ed. Herbert Aptheker, 1–18. *Complete Published Works of W. E. B. Du Bois*. Millwood, N.Y.: Kraus-Thomson Organization, 1982.

———. *Dusk of Dawn: An Essay toward an Autobiography of a Race Concept*. 1940. Oxford W. E. B. Du Bois. New York: Oxford University Press, 2007.

———. "Education." June 1912. In Henry Lee Moon, *The Emerging Thought of W. E. B. Du Bois: Essays and Editorials from the Crisis with an Introduction, Commentaries and a Personal Memoir*, 119–21. New York: Simon and Schuster, 1972.

———. "Education." July 1915. In Henry Lee Moon, *The Emerging Thought of W. E. B. Du Bois: Essays and Editorials from the Crisis with an Introduction, Commentaries and a Personal Memoir*, 122–24. New York: Simon and Schuster, 1972.

———. *The Education of Black People: Ten Critiques, 1906–1960*. Ed. Herbert Aptheker. Amherst: University of Massachusetts, 1973.

———. "French and Spanish." April 1919. In Henry Lee Moon, *The Emerging 4 Thought of W. E. B. Du Bois: Essays and Editorials from the Crisis with an Introduction, 5 Commentaries and a Personal Memoir*, 127–128. New York: Simon and Schuster, 1972.

———. "The Immortal Child." In Du Bois, *Darkwater: Voices from within the Veil*, 95–106. New York: Oxford University Press, 2007.

———. Letter to John Dewey. June 22, 1931. W. E. B. Du Bois Papers (Miss. 312). Special Collections and University Archives, W. E. B. Du Bois Library, University of Massachusetts, Amherst.

———. Letter to John Dewey. August 2, 1931. W. E. B. Du Bois Papers (Miss. 312). Special Collections and University Archives, W. E. B. Du Bois Library, University of Massachusetts, Amherst.

———. Letter to John Dewey. January 12, 1932. W. E. B. Du Bois Papers (Miss. 312). Special Collections and University Archives, W. E. B. Du Bois Library, University of Massachusetts, Amherst.

———. Letter to John Dewey. January 22, 1932. W. E. B. Du Bois Papers (Miss. 312). Special Collections and University Archives, W. E. B. Du Bois Library, University of Massachusetts, Amherst.

———. *Mansart Builds a School.* 1959. Oxford W. E. B. Du Bois. New York: Oxford University Press, 2007.

———. "Pechstein and Pecksniff." September 1929. In Henry Lee Moon, *The Emerging Thought of W. E. B. Du Bois: Essays and Editorials from the Crisis with an Introduction, Commentaries and a Personal Memoir,* 140–44. New York: Simon and Schuster, 1972.

———. "Public Rhetoricals." W. E. B. Du Bois Papers (Miss. 312). Special Collections and University Archives, W. E. B. Du Bois Library, University of Massachusetts, Amherst.

———. *The Souls of Black Folk.* New York: Oxford University Press, 2007.

———. "Students of Lincoln." June 1929. In Henry Lee Moon, *The Emerging 4 Thought of W. E. B. Du Bois: Essays and Editorials from the Crisis with an Introduction, 5 Commentaries and a Personal Memoir,* 138–140. New York: Simon and Schuster, 1972.

———. "The Talented Tenth." 1903. In Henry Louis Gates Jr. and Cornel West, *The Future of the Race,* 133–57. New York: Knopf, 1996.

———. "The Talented Tenth Memorial Address." 1948. In Henry Louis Gates Jr. and Cornel West, *The Future of the Race,* 159–77. New York: Knopf, 1996.

———. "To Abram Harris." November 21, 1925. In *The Correspondence of W. E. B. Du Bois: Selections 1877–1934,* vol. 1, ed. Herbert Aptheker, 328. N.p.: University of Massachusetts Press, 1973.

———. "To Lillian A. Alexander." January 1930. In *The Correspondence of W. E. B. Du Bois: Selections 1877–1934,* vol. 1, ed. Herbert Aptheker, 415. N.p.: University of Massachusetts Press, 1973.

Fallace, Thomas D. *Dewey and the Dilemma of Race: An Intellectual History, 1895–1922.* New York: Teachers College Press, 2011.

Gates, Henry Louis Jr., and Cornel West. *The Future of the Race.* New York: Knopf, 1996.

Gilyard, Keith. *Let's Flip the Script: An African American Discourse on Language, Literature, and Learning.* Detroit: Wayne State University Press, 1996.

Giroux, Susan Searls. *Between Race and Reason: Violence, Intellectual Responsibility, and the University to Come.* Stanford, Calif.: Stanford University Press, 2010.

Harris, Abram L. "To W. E. B. Du Bois." In *The Correspondence of W. E. B. Du Bois: Selections 1877–1934,* vol. 1, ed. Herbert Aptheker, 327–28. N.p.: University of Massachusetts Press, 1973.

Lewis, David Levering. *W. E. B. Du Bois: Biography of a Race, 1868–1919.* New York: Holt, 1993.

———. *W. E. B. Du Bois: The Fight for Equality and the American Century, 1919–1963.* New York: Holt, 2000.

Martin, Jay. *The Education of John Dewey.* New York: Columbia University Press, 2002.

Mathiasen, Soren A. "To Du Bois." January 6, 1931. In *The Correspondence of W. E. B. Du Bois: Selections 1877–1934*, vol. 1, ed. Herbert Aptheker, 433–34. N.p.: University of Massachusetts Press, 1973.

———. Introduction. In Moon, *The Emerging Thought of W. E. B. Du Bois: Essays and Editorials from the Crisis with an Introduction, Commentaries and a Personal Memoir*, 11–44. New York: Simon and Schuster, 1972.

Posnock, Ross. *Color and Culture: Black Writers and the Making of the Modern Intellectual.* Cambridge, Mass.: Harvard University Press, 1998.

Sanders, Mark. Afterword. In Du Bois, *Mansart Builds a School*, 267–282. 1959. Oxford W. E. B. Du Bois. New York: Oxford University Press, 2007.

Tocqueville, Alexis de. *Democracy in America.* 1835. Ed. J. P. Meyer and Max Lerner. Trans. George Lawrence. New York: Harper and Row, 1966.

West, Cornel. *The American Evasion of Philosophy: A Genealogy of Pragmatism.* Madison: University of Wisconsin Press, 1989.

Zamir, Shamoon. *Dark Voices: W. E. B. Du Bois and American Thought, 1888–1903.* Chicago: University of Chicago Press, 1995.

Walter Lippmann, the Indispensable Opposition

Jean Goodwin

> The opposition is indispensable. A good statesman, like any other sensible human being, always learns more from his opponents than from his fervent supporters.
>
> WALTER LIPPMANN, "The Indispensable Opposition" (1939)

Every hero must have his antagonist, and for John Dewey, theorist of democratic communication, that role has long been played by Walter Lippmann of the Lippmann-Dewey debate. Pessimistic, where Dewey was optimistic; concerned to remove decision-making from a feeble public to a technocratic elite, where Dewey would solve the problems of democracy with more democracy; invested in value-free scientific rationality, where Dewey embraced reasoning joined with aesthetic, emotional, and ethical responsiveness; interested in communication mostly as a tool for manufacturing consent, where Dewey understood it as the conversational process through which citizens could mutually form each other: this Lippmann's errors provide the dark background against which Dewey's virtues shine.

But recent scholarship—as scholarship will—has revised this received view (Crick; Jansen, "Straw Man"; Jansen, "Phantom Conflict"; Russill; Schudson). The familiar Lippmann created to be Dewey's foil appears to be a phantom. "Lippmann never advocated propaganda as a tool for domestic politics," Nathan Crick states bluntly (489). Nor did the actual Lippmann depart from the pragmatist's commitment to uniting reason and interest, nor did he defend technocratic rule, and his pessimism at the end became so thoroughgoing that (as we shall see) it turned into a sort of hope. Both men were trying to reconstruct democratic practices to meet the exigencies of a new age. Their exchange resembled more a call and response than a debate. In the years after the Great War, Lippmann wrote a series of books, trying to absorb the lessons it had taught on the impotence of journalists, citizens, officials, and even experts to think their way out of its "brutality and hysteria" (Lippmann, *Public Opinion* 262). *Public Opinion* (1922) and *The Phantom Public* (1925) were the final two works in the series, laying out Lippmann's most comprehensive views. Dewey responded to both in laudatory reviews in the *New Republic* ("Public Opinion" and "Practical Democracy," respectively) and was spurred to extend his remarks in lectures delivered in 1926 at Kenyon College, published the following year as *The Public and Its Problems.* In one of that book's few explicit mentions of others' works, Dewey acknowledges "his indebtedness" to Lippmann "for ideas involved in my entire discussion even when it reaches conclusions diverging from his" (116–17n1). In public at least, Lippmann did not respond.

"There is something of a tragic irony to the narrative often used to recount the Dewey/ Lippmann debate," Crick comments. "In their original works, each thinker attempted to move beyond the binary oppositions that polarize complex issues and paralyze public discussion" (Crick 483). Sue Curry Jansen notes the same distortions and remarks that "clearly there is something about the exchange that resonates closely with our own collective anxieties about the viability of participatory democracy" ("Phantom Conflict" 222). We will learn more, however, if we refrain from projecting onto Dewey and Lippmann our need for drama.

In this essay I propose putting aside the phantom Lippmann in order to recover two aspects of the real Lippmann's thinking that help throw light on Dewey's. First, I examine Lippmann's critique of contemporary democratic practice, in which Dewey joined; second, I consider Lippmann's proposed communicative solution, from which Dewey departed. By examining their shared problematic and their common conceptions, we can construct a more nuanced reading of their works, one which throws into relief their diverging views on the roles communication can play in democratic life. Dewey's influence on communication theory and pedagogy may be familiar; Lippmann's less well-known alternative, as it turns out, is equally democratic and allows us to renew our appreciation of vital but not always valued aspects of the traditions of communication theory and pedagogy. In the end we will see that Lippmann indeed provided Dewey his indispensable opposition.

LIPPMANN, DEWEY'S ALLY ON THE CHALLENGES FACING CONTEMPORARY DEMOCRACY

We can start from the common ground: Dewey's diagnosis of the problem of democracy, drawn from Lippmann, who had built in turn on the work of the early social psychologist Graham Wallas. Wallas was a Fabian socialist, an education reformer, and a faculty member at the inaugurations of both the London School of Economics and the New School for Social Research. On a visiting appointment at Harvard, he had formed a close relationship with the undergraduate Lippmann, joining an oddly assorted fan club that also included William James and George Santayana. In his 1914 book dedicated to Lippmann, Wallas coined the phrase "the Great Society" to capture his sense of the emerging crisis (Weiner). Contemporary society was

"Great" not as the superlative of "good" (as with Lyndon Baines Johnson's social program) but as the superlative of "big." Changes in communication, transportation, and energy technologies over the previous century had dramatically increased the scale of social relations, creating "an environment which, both in its world-wide extension and its intimate connection with all sides of human existence, is without precedent in the history of the world" (Wallas, *Great Society* 1). "A sudden decision by some financier whose name he has never heard," Wallas continued, "may, at any moment, close the office or mine or factory in which [the worker] is employed. . . . The widow who takes in washing fails or succeeds according to her skill in choosing starch or soda or a wringing-machine under the influence of half-a-dozen competing world-schemes of advertisement" (*Great Society* 4). But the scale and complexity of society had not been matched by any new growth in human endowments. So Wallas found himself "sometimes doubting, not only as to the future happiness of individuals in the Great Society, but as to the permanence of the Great Society itself. Why should we expect a social organisation to endure, which has been formed in a moment of time by human beings, whose bodies and minds are the result of age-long selection under far different conditions" (*Great Society* 8).

Lippmann and, after him, Dewey shared these doubts. Modes of democratic political organization originally imagined as suited for "remote, unspoiled country villages" (Lippmann, *Public Opinion* 169) were inadequate to deal with the problems that arose as "local communities without intent or forecast found their affairs conditioned by remote and invisible organizations" (Dewey, *Public and Problems* 98). The media, even where not corrupted by censorship and propaganda, were subject to inevitable "distortion arising because events have to be compressed into very small messages" (Lippmann, *Public Opinion* 18) and because journalists were themselves unable to determine the "meaning" of events, to place "the new. . . in relation to the old" (Dewey, *Public and Problems* 180). In addition individual citizens encountering a now-enlarged world found themselves adrift, at the mercy of "unseen environment" (Lippmann, *Public Opinion* 40), "hapless subjects of overwhelming operations with which they were hardly acquainted and over which they had no more control than over the vicissitudes of climate" (Dewey, *Public and Problems* 130). The Great War had demonstrated as much.

It is this last problem that most occupied both Lippmann and Dewey. Human cognitive capacities evolved to manage social interactions in small communities were not sufficient to enable the citizen to judge, or even understand, or even perceive a society grown "Great." "The world that we have to deal with politically is out of reach, out of sight, out of mind," Lippmann explains (*Public Opinion* 18); "modern society is not visible to anybody, nor intelligible continuously and as a whole" (Lippmann, *Phantom Public* 32). But while "the environment is complex, man's political capacity is simple"[1] (*Phantom Public* 68); "we are not equipped to deal with so much subtlety, so much variety, so many permutations and combinations" (Lippmann, *Public Opinion* 11). The citizen "cannot know all about everything all the time, and while he is watching one thing a thousand others undergo great changes" (*Public Opinion* 15). In an argument prescient of recent thinking about the "attention economy," Lippmann asks, "how, while he is earning a living, rearing children and enjoying his life, [the citizen] is to keep himself informed about the progress of this swarming confusion of problems" (*Phantom Public* 14). Citizens do not possess "an unlimited quantity of public spirit, interest, curiosity and effort" (*Phantom Public* 14); their attention is limited, and thus their knowledge as well. So no citizen could hope to be "omnicompetent" in the way that would be necessary in order for him or her to have a sound opinion on all matters of public business.

"Mr. Lippmann has thrown into clearer relief than any other writer the fundamental difficulty of democracy," Dewey wrote in his "Public Opinion" (288). As he explained in his own book, "the problem of a democratically organized public is primarily and essentially an intellectual problem" (Dewey, *Public and Problems* 126). Referring repeatedly to the "Great Society," Dewey endorses Wallas's conclusion that we have entered "a new age of human relations" (for example, Dewey, *Public and Problems* 96–98, 141). There is "too much of public concern for our existing resources to cope with," he concludes (*Public and Problems* 126). "The local face-to-face community has been invaded by forces so vast, so remote in initiation, so far-reaching in scope and so complexly indirect in operation, that they are, from the standpoint of the members of local social units, unknown" (*Public and Problems* 131). But how are citizens supposed to make good decisions about "unknowns"?

Both Lippmann and Dewey confessed the "intellectual" restrictions of most citizens—of most but not all. Both also recognized two more epistemically privileged groups. The insiders to any particular affair were interested enough to invest their time in it, had taken opportunities to gain experience in it, and thus had the knowledge to form sound decisions concerning it. Of course the success of these insiders made more noticeable how everyone else—lacking interest, opportunities, and knowledge—remained outsiders to that affair, not positioned to understand it. Both Lippmann and Dewey also held fast to the progressive hope that contributions from experts of various kinds could improve the management of public affairs. In particular both looked to the new social sciences to take the Great Society itself as an object of inquiry. Such experts could cultivate methodically the comprehensive view of the vast and interconnected world that ordinary citizens were not positioned to develop.

This diagnosis of the diseases of democracy still rings true. Consider some examples. What should be the U.S. policy toward Laos? How if it all should the rules of various sports be modified to reduce the number and severity of concussions? What should be the buffer zone separating genetically modified from unmodified crops—five yards, fifty yards, five hundred? Likely the limit should be different for different crops and possibly for different local environmental conditions, but how? I am confident that farmers, conventional and organic, have views on this subject worthy of respect. My colleagues over in the agronomy department can report their scientific findings. It is an important public issue in many areas of the country. But it is not one on which even I would give much credit to my own "public opinion." I am sure I could learn enough about the subject if I wanted to—I was not born to outsider status. But I have other things to do.

As one of Dewey's biographers has remarked, "Dewey accepted most of Lippmann's complaints against the existing order of things" (Ryan 217). Jansen's retracing of the immediate reception of *The Public and Its Problems* has documented that contemporary readers took the book in the same way, "as an affirmation and amplification of Lippmann's diagnosis of the eclipse of the public" (Jansen, "Phantom Conflict" 226). For both men, the central problem facing democracy in the Great Society was epistemic: the inability of ordinary citizens to know the world in which they had to act.

DEWEY ON DEMOCRACY AND COMMUNICATION

It is at this point that Dewey and Lippmann finally begin to diverge. Before reconstructing the nonphantom Lippmann's proposals for making democracy work in a Great Society, a brief examination of Dewey's proposals, expressed in a series of provocative, often-quoted—and maddeningly brief—passages in *The Public and Its Problems*, is in order.

Dewey's insiders are those directly involved in some joint action (a "private transaction"); they are positioned to perceive some of the consequences of what they are doing and to take those consequences into account in making decisions. The actual consequences of many transactions spill over, however, to affect others. These outsiders constitute the public. They share an interest in managing the broader "extensive and enduring indirect consequences" (Dewey, *Public and Problems* 47) of local transactions, although they do not have the means to perceive those consequences clearly as they ripple outward through the vast reaches of the Great Society. But the public's ignorance is not irremediable. Knowledge for Dewey is not an individual accomplishment but a social one; through participating in any of the forms of activity made available through the organization of society, each person gains the accumulated knowledge "embodied" in it. As Dewey puts it, "many a man who has tinkered with radios can judge of things which Faraday did not dream of" (*Public and Problems* 210). For public affairs, this principle suggests that if the public's activities were better organized, even outsiders could share in existing knowledge and indeed begin to create new knowledge.

Dewey hints at this solution in "Practical Democracy," his review of *The Phantom Public*, endorsing Lippmann's discussion "of the inherent problems and dangers the Great Society has brought with it" but also calling for "further analysis" of the "organization of society itself" as providing "the only sure road out" ("Practical Democracy" 54). *The Public and Its Problems* provides that analysis. "The prime condition of a democratically organized public is a kind of knowledge and insight which does not yet exist," Dewey says (*Public and Problems* 166). To bring it into existence, the public's affairs need to be reconceptualized and eventually reinstitutionalized as a vast "social inquiry" into the problems of the Great Society. Adopting a suitably pragmatist "experimental" method, policy proposals will "be treated as working hypotheses, . . . subject to constant and well-equipped observation of the consequences they entail when acted upon, and subject to ready and flexible revision in the light of observed consequences" (202–3). The inquiry must detect "the energies which are at work and trac[e] them through an intricate network of interactions to their consequences" (177). Experts can aid the public by "recording and interpreting (organizing)" (203) the results of the inquiry. The public, however, retains responsibility for coming to recognize its own interests in the course of figuring out what to do. In Dewey's analogy, "the man who wears the shoe knows best that it pinches and where it pinches, even if the expert shoemaker is the best judge of how the trouble is to be remedied" (207).

"Popular government," Dewey concludes, "is educative as other modes of political regulation are not" (Dewey, *Public and Problems* 207); it changes citizens, forming them to be competent for public affairs. To make democracy as social inquiry work, "the essential need . . . is the improvement of the methods and conditions of debate, discussion and persuasion. That is *the* problem of the public" (Dewey, *Public and Problems* 208). The results of the social inquiry must be communicated among the public, so that citizens can share the knowledge being created, articulate their interests, and come to recognize themselves as a public. While the technologies to accomplish this already exist—"telegraph, telephone, and now the radio, cheap and quick mails, the print press, capable of swift reduplication of material at low cost" (*Public and Problems* 179)—the practices for using these media are in need of overhaul. In both his reviews of Lippmann's works Dewey calls for a journalism that will "sensationalize" social inquiry, making the "thrill" of seeing the "underlying forces moving in and through events" accessible through a "union of social science, access to facts, and the art of literary presentation" (Dewey, "Public Opinion" 288; see also Dewey, "Practical Democracy" 54). In *The Public and Its Problems,* Dewey elaborates this call through a discussion of the need for artistry in communicating public affairs. "Artists have always been the real purveyors of news," he explains, "for it is not the outward happening in itself which is new, but the kindling by it of emotion, perception and appreciation" (Dewey, *Public and Problems* 184). So the renewal of democracy awaits a new movement of artist-journalists who will take advantage of the powers the new media afford.[2] Dewey sums up with the following prophetic announcement: "till the Great Society is converted into a Great Community, the Public will remain in eclipse. Communication can alone create a great community" (Dewey, *Public and Problems* 142).

DEWEY'S IMPACT ON COMMUNICATION PEDAGOGY AND THEORY

Scholars and teachers of communication responded enthusiastically to Dewey's gestures of friendship for their subject. The immense impact of Dewey's political/

epistemological views on communication pedagogy has been documented by William Keith in his excellent *Democracy as Discussion* and is the focus of other contributions to this volume. Equipping students to deliberate with each other has long been a central preoccupation of rhetoricians in the traditions of English and communication courses (Jackson). The Dewey-inspired "discussion method," with its coconstruction of knowledge through collaborative, open, face-to-face communication, has leaped beyond the confines of the communication fields to become in the form of "group work" one of the mainstays of contemporary instruction. Dewey's pragmatism has also emerged as a main current in communication theory (Craig). Every approach stressing the cooperative nature of argumentation shows the direct or indirect effects of Dewey's ideas (for example, Walton). Dewey's greatest impact on theory, however, has been in provoking a tradition of work on public deliberation that preceded and in significant ways differed from the Habermas-inspired scholarship on the public sphere. In his classic essay "The Rhetorical Situation," Lloyd Bitzer filled in the outlines Dewey had sketched, establishing what rhetoric must be if it is to serve as the public's instrument for social inquiry in a pragmatist mode. In later works Bitzer, joined by his students Thomas Farrell and Gerard Hauser—and eventually by their students—went on to examine further how rhetoric takes up and creates public knowledge (Bitzer, "Rhetoric and Public Knowledge"; Farrell; Hauser). This tradition continues to place at the center of theoretical attention the communicative processes through which the public comes to *know*—know itself and its world.

LIPPMANN, DEWEY'S ADVERSARY ON DEMOCRATIC COMMUNICATION

Dewey's response to the epistemic challenges of the Great Society may be familiar, as are some of these responses to his work by communication scholars and teachers. Lippmann's response is less so, in part because of the distorting influence of the scholarly tradition that has needed him to be Dewey's antagonist (Schudson; Jansen, "Straw Man"; Jansen, "Phantom Conflict"; Crick) and in part because of his own changes of mind. As has been frequently pointed out, Lippmann took full advantage of the columnist's privilege of having opinions four times a week. At one time or another he experimented with a democracy that institutionalized virtually every possible arrangement of the available roles. In the early *Liberty and the News* he foreshadows Dewey's position, proposing the creation of a bureau of social science experts to aid journalists in providing a full account of events to the public. In *Public Opinion* he tosses this view aside, arguing that at best the news media can report on what has become public; it has no power to "bring to light the hidden facts, to set them into relation with each other, and make a picture of reality on which men can act" (Lippmann, *Public Opinion* 226). Instead he proposes now that the experts should work with the officials charged with the public's business, to "represent the unseen" in their deliberations (*Public Opinion* 241). But by 1925, when he wrote *The*

Phantom Public, his pessimism had deepened. No one—not journalists, not experts, not officials, and certainly not ordinary citizens—could develop the breadth of knowledge that would render them capable of the intelligent management of public affairs. No one was omnicompetent, not even Lippmann himself, "for, although public business is my main interest and I give most of my time to watching it, I cannot find time to do what is expected of me in the theory of democracy; that is, to know what is going on and to have an opinion worth expressing on every question which confronts a self-governing community" (Lippmann, *Phantom Public* 10). To open a reconstruction of Lippmann's view, we can start by noting that in *The Phantom Public* he managed to work his way so deeply into pessimism as to come out the other side. If none of us is *omni*competent, everyone is *competent;* each of us has the capacity to mind our own business.

The work of the world is carried on by men in their executive capacity, by an infinite number of concrete acts, plowing and planting and reaping, building, and destroying, fitting this to that, going from here to there, transforming A into B and moving B from X to Y. The relationships between the individuals doing these specific things are balanced by a most intricate mechanism of exchange, of contract, of custom, and of implied promises. Where men are performing their work they must learn to understand the process and the substance of these obligations if they are to do it at all (Lippmann, *Phantom Public* 41–42).

All knowledge, in short, is local knowledge. Everyone is an insider—in some matters. Everyone is an expert, credentialed or not—about the activities that have engaged his or her interests. Beyond that, as an outsider to other transactions, he or she is "necessarily ignorant, usually irrelevant and often meddlesome: (Lippmann, *Phantom Public* 140).

But if there is no one who is omnicompetent—if there is no solution to the epistemic problems created by a Great Society—what is left of democracy? Why publics at all? Lippmann points out that while insiders to a transaction know enough to get along, the insiders do not always agree; as in the extended example he had given in *Public Opinion,* workers and capitalists at a steel mill do not always agree about appropriate wages (*Public Opinion* 253–54). Sometimes these conflicts can be managed by recourse to government officials: adjudications in courts; rule making in executive agencies; or even the back-room dealings of ordinary politics (Lippmann, *Phantom Public* 62–63). But sometimes the conflict spills over these established means. At this point the insiders have only two choices. They can resort to force or they can appeal to outsiders to intervene. It is these conspicuous, irresolvable disagreements among insiders—Lippmann calls them "crises" (for example, in *Phantom Public* 54, 56)—that bring a public into being.

It is worth pausing to contrast Lippmann's account of the birth of publics with that of Dewey. For Dewey, a public emerges when the consequences of some local activity are perceived by outsiders, understood, and recognized as ill. For Lippmann, a public emerges when a local dispute is perceived by outsiders, understood, and recognized as disturbing the peace. Although our authors do not use this terminology consistently, we might say that a Deweyan public confronts *problems,* while a Lippmannian public faces *issues.*[3] To diagnose a problem correctly requires specialized knowledge about the way that aspect of the world works. But to notice that people are fighting about something or other requires only a commonsense understanding of ordinary social relations. To return to the previous example, while it is hard to say exactly how big the buffer zone between genetically modified and organic corn ought to be, it is easy to notice that a lot of people have a lot of diverging views on this issue and are arguing with each other vigorously. To understand the appropriate buffer zone might require a doctorate in agronomy or long experience in farming—although we notice that even the PhDs and farmers are disputing; to notice diverging views might require a "degree" achieved on the kindergarten playground.

It is not surprising that outsiders called in to defuse an issue are unable to figure out the right course of action, since the insiders themselves cannot agree. In Lippmann's view, the issues that the public must judge are precisely "the hardest controversies to disentangle. . . . Where the facts are most obscure, where precedents are lacking, where novelty and confusion pervade everything, the public in all its unfitness is compelled to make its most important decisions. The hardest problems are those which institutions cannot handle. They are the public's problems" (Lippmann, *Phantom Public* 121).

In such disputes, the outsiders, mere "spectators of the action, cannot successfully intervene in a controversy on the merits of the case. They must judge externally." They have access only to "the overt, external forms of behavior" (Lippmann, *Phantom Public* 134) being exhibited by the parties in the dispute. Their only job "is to locate by clear and coarse objective tests the actor in a controversy who is most worthy of public support" (120). They conclude the debate not by deciding the issue but by deciding only which insider they would throw their weight behind, should the dispute come to blows. When a majority is mobilized and aligns itself with one side of the dispute, the insiders directly concerned are by the threat of the majority's force "driven to make terms" (64) and compose their controversy. The process is less one of deliberative decision-making than of "sublimated" (50) civil war.

Lippmann offers us what he calls a "wholly tentative" (Lippmann, *Phantom Public* 133) list of some of the "overt, external forms of behavior," aka "clear and coarse objective tests," aka "coarse signs" (54) that the outsider member of the public can use to figure out which insider to back. In most of these Lippmann directs the outsider to examine the conspicuous communicative conduct of the insiders who are disputing with each other, taking that conduct as an indicator of the insiders' trustworthiness. Consider the following list of behaviors, or tests, or signs, arranged from the first arising of an issue to its final resolution.

The willingness of some insiders to call for outside intervention in their business demonstrates the significance of the dispute, since the insiders would risk the unpredictable outcome of public interference only if they were seriously disturbed by the status quo. Gambling on a call for intervention thus suggests that the dispute is indeed worth the outsider's attention. As Lippmann says, "their argument may be wrong, the remedy may be foolish, but the fact that they openly criticize at some personal risk is a sign that the [established] rule [for the transaction] is not working well" (*Phantom Public* 113).

Once the public has been called in, another "test" it "can apply . . . is to note which party to the dispute is least willing to submit its whole claim to inquiry and to abide by the result" (Lippmann, *Phantom Public* 122). (Note that "inquiry" here does not mean a joint, experimental investigation; it means an "ordeal" [*Phantom Public* 122], a trial of strength held before a tribunal of some sort.) The failure to accept full public exposure of his or her reasoning suggests that the insider may be putting forward reasons less to identify some mutual accommodation of the dispute and more to achieve some purely individual goal—what Lippmann terms the insider's "own unaccountable will" (*Phantom Public* 59) or "arbitrary desires" (*Phantom Public* 134). For instance, in the dispute at the steel mill mentioned above, if the capitalist claims "for reasons that he refuses to state" that higher wages for workers would bankrupt him (Lippmann, *Public Opinion* 254), then the outsider can take his refusal to proffer evidence as a sign that he has no publicly admissible reasons to offer. By contrast, conspicuous readiness to endure "the test of public inquiry is the surest clue to the sincerity of the claimant, to his confidence in his ability to stand the ordeal of examination, to his willingness to accept risks for the sake of his faith in the possibility of rational human adjustments" (Lippmann, *Phantom Public* 122).

Once the debate has started, the outsider "will not be able, we may assume, to judge the merits of the arguments." Still, observing the interaction may prove useful. "The advocates are very likely to expose one another. Open debate may lead to no conclusion and throw no light whatever on the problem or its answer, but it will tend to betray the partisan and the advocate" (Lippmann, *Phantom Public* 104).

The outsider may occasionally be able to "judge who has won the dialectical victory" (Lippmann, *Public Opinion* 143) in the debate. For example, the outsider can observe when one side failed to respond to another's argument at all and can then declare that argument won, even without understanding it. In general the conspicuous fact that the winner was able to muster more arguments on a particular occasion is a coarse sign that his or her position is indeed more reasonable. (Lippmann hastens to add that "we are virtually defenseless against a false premise that none of the debaters has challenged, or a neglected aspect that none of them has brought into the argument.")

Finally, the outsider may make a "cumulative judgment" about the apparent consequences of past decisions by the insiders (Lippmann, *Phantom Public* 119). "To support the Ins when things are going well; to support the Outs when they seem to be going badly, this . . . is the essence of popular government," Lippmann explains (116). Here Lippmann foreshadows Dewey's emphasis on consequences. But instead of deliberating together about the future consequences of a decision to be made, the outsider is invited to adjudicate a forensic controversy over the past consequences of one already taken.

All but the last of these coarse signs direct outsiders to "select a few samples of behavior"[4] (Lippmann, *Phantom Public* 133)—in specific to perceive, understand, and judge how the insiders are *communicating* in the controversy about some affair. Lippmann is thus the equal of Dewey in putting communication at the center of democratic life, although communication of a very different sort. Lippmann's desired talk is not cooperative but conflict-ridden. It is aimed not to reach a decision that everyone can agree is right but to declare a winner. It takes place not among open-minded inquirers but between advocates set in preexisting positions. In addition it does not allow active participation by all but is presented before spectators whose only job is to judge the performance. Lippmann, in short, is advising us to debate.

LIPPMANN'S POTENTIAL IMPACT ON COMMUNICATION PEDAGOGY AND THEORY

Debate, of course, raises interesting challenges for communication theory and pedagogy. Some have even claimed that it "fail[s] to embody democratic ideas" (Keith 96). Despite its enormous success as an extracurricular activity for undergraduates, debate remains somewhat of a curricular stepchild. At least that is what is suggested by the apologies that argumentation textbooks seem required to make in their opening chapters (reviewed in Goodwin, "Theoretical Pieties"), minimizing the adversarial aspects of the activity they are about to teach and generally trying to reframe it in a more cooperative, Deweyan mode. Lippmann is unapologetic. He offers us a democratic rationale for the dignity of debate.

Recognizing the dignity of debate gives us permission to acknowledge that most of us, most of the time, are only spectators of others' arguments. This insight cannot be prominent within a Deweyan frame, with its emphasis on the active collaboration of all citizens in the construction of social knowledge. But it provides a motivation for our long-standing curricular emphasis on the skills of the citizen-spectator. Although Lippmann's *Public Opinion* does not live up to its reputation as the groundbreaking work on the art of propaganda, it was a central text in the development of propaganda analysis (Sproule), an approach to critical-thinking instruction native to the communication fields. Even Lippmann's pessimism about citizens' small abilities to deal with the Great Society can play an important role in justifying our critical-thinking pedagogy. As he comments:

> It is often very illuminating . . . to ask yourself how you got at the facts on which you base your opinion. Who actually saw, heard, felt, counted, named the thing, about which you have an opinion? Was it the man who told you, or the man who told him, or someone still further removed? And how much was he permitted to

> see? When he informs you that France thinks this and that, what part of France did he watch? How was he able to watch it? Where was he when he watched it? What Frenchmen was he permitted to talk to, what newspapers did he read, and where did they learn what they say? You can ask yourself these questions, but you can rarely answer them. They will remind you, however, of the distance which often separates your public opinion from the event with which it deals. And the reminder is itself a protection. (Lippmann, *Public Opinion* 29)

Critical thinking is not only warranted on the somewhat cynical assumption that everyone else is out to fool us; accepting our own vulnerability to being fooled, and even to fooling ourselves, can also be a ground for a moderate skepticism.

Lippmann's defense of the dignity of debate also directs us to a central challenge for theory: how critical thinking can proceed at all in the face of deep asymmetries in knowledge. Lippmann's response to this question is paralleled in several respects by recent work in the "Studies of Expertise & Experience" ("SEE"—for example, Collins and Evans). Like Lippmann, "SEE" does not limit expertise to those with official credentials. Rather, anyone with long experience in a given practice is qualified to speak as an expert. Still, those of us who lack relevant experience in some practice remain in a difficult position. When a purported expert harangues us, we cannot tell whether he or she is spouting pretentious nonsense or is offering important insights beyond our ken. What can we do? Like Lippmann, "SEE" proposes that outsiders proceed by "making *social* judgments about *who* ought to be agreed with, not *scientific*"—or more generally, *epistemic*—"judgments about *what* ought to be believed" (Collins and Evans 47). The expertise required to make such social judgments is ubiquitous, arising from our long experience in making "judgments about friends, acquaintances, neighbors, relations, politicians, salespersons, and strangers" (Collins and Evans 45). As Lippmann comments, "we do well enough with doctors, though we are ignorant of medicine; . . . why not, then, with a Senator, though we cannot pass an examination on the merits of an agricultural bill?" (Lippmann, *Phantom Public* 150). But only recently have "SEE" scholars begun to examine exactly how these social judgments are to be made (for example, Collins and Weinel). Communication instructors have inherited a standard doctrine for assessing expertise, generally expressed as a protocol for analyzing appeals to expert authority. We would do well to heed the calls from Lippmann and "SEE" and reexamine the theory behind our pedagogy (Goodwin, "Force"): under what conditions is an outsider indeed justified in trusting what an insider says?

Where Dewey sets out his ideals in ringing phrases but necessarily leaves the details to be worked out in the future, through the experimental process of social inquiry into democratic institutions (MacGilvray), Lippmann in the second half of *The Phantom Public* reads more like a how-to manual for citizens called in to observe and adjudicate controversies. The coarse signs and objective tests he identifies are largely constituted through the communication activities of the disputing insiders.

So Lippmann's work invites us, finally, to shift our attention from outsiders back to insiders and ask what debaters can do to put spectators in a better position to judge their performances. For example, to get a Lippmannian debate off the ground, the first step must be to create the "crisis" that creates a public—in other words, to make an issue of some affair. Exactly how do issues get made? Noortje Marres, drawing in part from Lippmann, has recently called for expanded attention to the specific rhetorical "affordances" that "facilitate a distinctive articulation of issues, as matters of public concern"; this is a question that theorists should pursue (Marres; see also Goodwin, "Designing Issues"; Craig and Tracy). Or again, Lippmannian debaters need to demonstrate their willingness to undergo the "ordeal" of debate. What strategies can debaters use to conspicuously undertake an obligation to defend their claims (Kauffeld, "Presumptions"; Kauffeld, "Probative Obligations")? How can debaters make clear to spectators when they have won a "dialectical victory"? What can they do to demonstrate the partisanship of the other side? And so on. Lippmann depends on outsiders to make a vital judgment. Even if it is not an epistemic judgment of the merits, it is still one that communication can support or impede, and communication theorists are called to explain how.

CONCLUDING THOUGHTS

This sketch of Lippmann's theories has shown him indeed to be Dewey's adversary in his conception of communication. But it also has shown him to be no adversary of democracy and neither an elitist nor an advocate of technocracy. Dewey, always a good reader of Lippmann, pointed out that Lippmann's theories could support radically democratic conclusions. "To avoid misconception," Dewey explains, "Mr. Lippmann means by 'insiders' something more than *political* insiders; more than governmental administrators and more than managers of machines." Considering both workers and capitalists as *insiders* to the enterprise of running a steel mill, for example, might suggest a "decentralization in governmental affairs," something like a "guild" or even a "soviet" form of organization (Dewey, "Practical Democracy" 53–54).

In some sense we do not need to decide between these competing conceptions of democratic communication. As Patricia Roberts-Miller has argued, we have always maintained diverse pedagogical traditions, each focusing on a particular set of problems and practices and each grounded in its own democratic theory; there is no single, "perfect model" (223). If society is great, then communication can be great too, I suppose, with room for a variety of local ways.

Still, as good pragmatists, both Dewey and Lippmann would know that getting theory straight matters. Critique of democracy is too important to leave to the foes of democracy; as Graham Wallas said, "if democracy is to succeed [its difficulties] must be frankly considered by the democrats themselves" (Wallas, *Human Nature* 253). Theory is lived out in practice. A true ideal will "express the true possibilities" of democracy to the citizens trying to measure up to it, Lippmann says; a "false ideal" being impossible, will mislead them, and the "failure to achieve it" will eventually produce "disenchantment" (Lippmann, *Phantom Public* 29). It remains easy to prefer "Dewey's hopeful offerings of communication, community, and communion to Lippmann's austere menu of method, asceticism, and skeptical realism" (Jansen, "Phantom Conflict" 236). So I will close with two reasons for thinking that the nonphantom Lippmann I have sketched here remains at least a live alternative to Dewey—that he continues to provide the indispensable opposition.

Parts of *The Phantom Public* can be read as backing democracy only as a relatively efficient method for keeping the peace, convenient because it manages disagreements without resorting to violence. It is this Lippmann that Dewey may be gesturing at in his initial review of theories of the state: "just one of many social institutions, having a narrow but important function, that of arbiter in the conflict of other social units" (Dewey, *Public and Problems* 4). "The principle that all controversies are soluble by peaceable agreement" (Lippmann, *Phantom Public* 124), however, is indeed a principle and one worthy of respect. Lippmann's debates may not produce reasoned decisions. But they remain spectacles of reason, expressing the public's "demand" for the "method and spirit of reason, . . . even if the material for a reasoned conclusion is lacking" (Lippmann, *Phantom Public* 124). Perhaps the "ordeal" of debate will do no more than force the disputing insiders to produce rationalizations for the positions they hold on other, less publicly admissible grounds. If so, the obligation to rationalize may at least prod the insiders to think a bit about what positions they are willing to risk defending. Further, in putting forward a specific rationalization, the insider will often make explicit the future that his or her preferred outcome is predicted to achieve. The outsiders can use this commitment to measure whether things are going the way they are supposed to. If the consequences turn out conspicuously otherwise, they can, as Lippmann says, vote the other guys in. Rationalizations, in other words, lay the groundwork for accountability. Finally, "by insisting in all disputes upon the spirit of reason, we shall tend in the long run to confirm the habit of reason" and perhaps even "extend the frontiers of reason" (Lippmann, *Phantom Public* 124–25). This may be "a pruned and temperate democratic theory," as Dewey remarked, but it is still "a reasonable conception of democracy" that "can be made to work, not absolutely, but at least better than democracy works under an exaggerated and undisciplined notion of the public and its powers" (Dewey, "Practical Democracy" 52).

One of the embarrassments Dewey occasions for his friends is his unabashedly organic view of society (for example, Bohman). Although he occasionally mentions the existence of diverse views, it is not by mistake that he tends to speak of *the* Public, recognizing *its* interest in the process making *an* inquiry into the consequences of some choice. By contrast, Lippmann not only recognizes the existence of diversity and disagreement among the "random publics" (Lippmann, *Phantom Public* 67) that inhabit his democracy but also makes it the basis of his theory of democratic communication. "Men do not agree as to their aims, and it is precisely the lack of agreement which creates the problems that excite public attention" (*Phantom Public* 56). In playing out their disagreements in public, insiders create for their fellow citizens the coarse signs they need to render sound social judgments. Continuing to listen to Lippmann's indispensable opposition to Dewey may thus help us cherish even our most heated, contentious, partisan, and divisive civic discourse, understanding its "true possibilities" in making public issues, rendering reasonableness apparent, and allowing public opinion to become a manifest force in our Great Society.

NOTES

1. For aesthetic reasons I will refrain from inserting *sic* next to every one of Lippmann's frequent references to citizens as exclusively male.

2. It is Dewey, not Lippmann, who is skirting close to advocating propaganda here "by suggesting that artists use their skills to evoke emotions and rally the public to action" (Westhoff 43).

3. In an otherwise insightful article, Marres argues that Lippmann and Dewey share a focus on issues. Although the pair use the terminology of "issues" and "problems" somewhat indiscriminately, their conceptions of what calls a public into being are different in ways her argument elides.

4. It should be noted that Lippmann also proposes a third set of coarse signs. Outsiders can make an "external" examination of the insiders' specific policy proposals to see how they are designed. For example, Lippmann advises that a policy is to be preferred if it is so "organized that experience will clearly reveal its defects" (Lippmann, *Phantom Public* 125). On the face of it, this foreshadows Dewey's later conception of policy as an experiment. But again, Lippmann's rationale is different. Instead of relying on the policy experiments to produce social knowledge, Lippmann reasons that a self-testing, self-modifying policy will provide a settlement of the controversy that is more likely to endure.

WORKS CITED

Bitzer, Lloyd F. "Rhetoric and Public Knowledge." In *Rhetoric, Philosophy, and Literature: An Exploration,* ed. Don M. Burks, 67–93. West Lafayette, Ind.: Purdue University Press, 1978.

———. "The Rhetorical Situation." *Philosophy & Rhetoric* 1.1 (1968): 1–14.

Bohman, J. "Participation through Publics: Did Dewey Answer Lippmann?" *Contemporary Pragmatism* 7.1 (2010): 49–68.

Collins, Harry, and Robert Evans. *Rethinking Expertise.* Chicago: University of Chicago Press, 2007.

Collins, Harry, and Martin Weinel. "Transmuted Expertise: How Technical Non-Experts Can Assess Experts and Expertise." *Argumentation* 25.3 (2011): 401–13.

Craig, Robert T. "Pragmatism in the Field of Communication Theory." *Communication Theory* 17.2 (2007): 125–45.

Craig, Robert T., and Karen Tracy. "'The Issue' in Argumentation Practice and Theory." In *Argumentation in Practice,* ed. Frans H. van Eemeren and Peter Houtlosser, 11–28. Amsterdam: John Benjamins, 2005.

Crick, Nathan. "The Search for a Purveyor of News: The Dewey/Lippmann Debate in an Internet Age." *Critical Studies in Media Communication* 26.5 (2009): 480–97.

Dewey, John. "Practical Democracy." *New Republic* (December 2, 1925): 52–54.

———. *The Public and Its Problems: An Essay in Political Inquiry.* New York: Henry Holt, 1927.

———. "Public Opinion." *New Republic* (May 3, 1922): 286–88.

Farrell, Thomas B. "Knowledge, Consensus, and Rhetorical Theory." *Quarterly Journal of Speech* 62.1 (1976): 1–14.

Goodwin, Jean. "Accounting for the Force of the Appeal to Authority." In *Argument Cultures: Proceedings of the 8th International Conference of the Ontario Society for the Study of Argumentation,* ed. Frank Zenker, 1–9. 2011. CD-ROM.

———. "Designing Issues." In *Dialectic and Rhetoric: The Warp and Woof of Argumentation Analysis,* ed. Frans H. van Eemeren and Peter Houtlosser, 81–96. Dordrecht: Kluwer, 2002.

———. "Theoretical Pieties, Johnstone's Impiety, and Ordinary Views of Argumentation." *Philosophy & Rhetoric* 40.1 (2007): 36–50.

Hauser, Gerard A. *Vernacular Voices: The Rhetoric of Publics and Public Spheres.* Columbia: University of South Carolina Press, 1999.

Jackson, Brian. "Cultivating Paideweyan Pedagogy: Rhetoric Education in English and Communication Studies." *Rhetoric Society Quarterly* 37.2 (2008): 181–201.

Jansen, Sue Curry. "Phantom Conflict: Lippmann, Dewey, and the Fate of the Public in Modern Society." *Communication and Critical/Cultural Studies* 6.3 (2009): 221–45.

———. "Walter Lippmann, Straw Man of Communication Research." In *The History of Media and Communication Research: Contested Memories,* ed. David W. Park and Jefferson Pooley, 1–23. New York: Peter Lang, 2008.

Kauffeld, Fred J. "Presumptions and the Distribution of Argumentative Burdens in Acts of Proposing and Accusing." *Argumentation* 12.2 (1998): 245–66.

———. "What Are We Learning about the Arguers' Probative Obligations." In *Concerning Argument,* ed. Scott Jacobs, 1–31. Washington, D.C.: National Communication Association, 2009.

Keith, William. *Democracy as Discussion: Civic Education and the American Forum Movement.* Lanham, Md.: Lexington Books, 2007.

Lippmann, Walter. "The Indispensable Opposition." *Atlantic Monthly* (August 1939): 186–89.

———. *Liberty and the News.* New York: Harcourt, Brace and Howe, 1920.

———. *The Phantom Public.* 1925. Reprint. New Brunswick, N.J.: Transaction, 1993.

———. *Public Opinion.* 1922. Reprint. New York: Free Press Paperbacks, 1997.

MacGilvray, Eric. "Dewey's Public." *Contemporary Pragmatism* 7.1 (2010): 31–47.

Marres, Noortje. "The Issues Deserve More Credit: Pragmatist Contributions to the Study of Public Involvement in Controversy." *Social Studies of Science* 37.5 (2007): 759–80.

Roberts-Miller, Patricia. *Deliberate Conflict: Argument, Political Theory, and Composition Classes.* Carbondale: Southern Illinois University Press, 2004.

Russill, Chris. "Through a Public Darkly: Reconstructing Pragmatist Perspectives in Communication Theory." *Communication Theory* 18.4 (2008): 478–504.

Ryan, Alan. *John Dewey and the High Tide of American Liberalism.* New York: W. W. Norton, 1995.

Schudson, M. "The 'Lippmann-Dewey Debate' and the Invention of Walter Lippmann as an Anti-Democrat 1986–1996." *International Journal of Communication* 2.1 (2008): 1031–42.

Sproule, J. Michael. *Propaganda and Democracy: The American Experience of Media and Mass Persuasion.* Cambridge: Cambridge University Press, 1997.

Wallas, Graham. *The Great Society.* New York: Macmillan, 1914.

———. *Human Nature in Politics.* 3rd ed. New York: Alfred A. Knopf, 1921.

Walton, Douglas. *The New Dialectic: Conversational Contexts of Argument.* Mahwah, N.J.: Lawrence Erlbaum Associates, 1998.

Weiner, Martin. *Between Two Worlds: The Political Thought of Graham Wallas.* Oxford: Clarendon, 1971.

Westhoff, L. M. "The Popularization of Knowledge: John Dewey on Experts and American Democracy." *History of Education Quarterly* 35.1 (1995): 27–47.

"All Safety Is an Illusion"

John Dewey, James Baldwin, and the Democratic Practice of Public Critique

Walton Muyumba

At the beginning of the bicentennial year 1976, though his cultural stardom had cooled, James Baldwin still practiced an intense, daring public intellectualism. In a *Los Angeles Times* op-ed entitled "A Challenge to Bicentennial Candidates," Baldwin urges the potential Republican and Democratic candidates to face the nation's "chaos, and help the country to face itself, and, for the sake of all our children, to change it" (*Cross* 106). But Baldwin prefaces this call with his critique of the insipid discourse on American freedom then percolating in the election campaign cycle.

What each candidate pretends to offer voters on the nation's two hundredth birthday, Baldwin explains, is "freedom from the discontented, freedom from the criminals who roam our streets; he is to offer, out of such a dangerous history, at so dangerous a time, nothing less than freedom from danger . . . the final banishment of the beast in the American playground" (*Cross* 104). American history and poverty, Baldwin tells us, form a two-headed beast. Candidates present freedom from the poor as a "stunning gift" for a people "whose originality resides entirely and precisely in the poverty which drove them to these shores." Even more, this kind of campaign promise actually suggests a freedom from "the past and freedom from any responsibility for the present: for the poor are always with us; and they can also be against us" (*Cross* 104). In order for American political institutions to change, thus changing American life, the national political rhetoric must confront historical realities rather than elide or erase them.

When Baldwin discusses freedom, he is most often discussing its rarity. "Baldwin maintains," writes Lawrie Balfour, "that freedom requires the exercise of moral agency in the face of disagreeable truths" (130). During the 1960s Baldwin forwarded this insight as part of his discourse on African American citizenship and American democracy. In 1976 Baldwin's focus included all ethnic Americans, democracy, and economic justice. As Balfour suggests, Baldwin's ideal form of freedom demands personal responsibility, not freedom from it. Baldwin's definition of American freedom requires a personally responsible, "honest appraisal of the historical roots, as well as the current conditions, of one's situation" (Balfour 131).

I argue in *The Shadow and the Act* (2009) that Baldwin's interrogation of American freedom and democracy is attached to his attempt to construct an American public arranged radically. However, neither a radical public nor a radical democracy can emerge until American political arrangements shift from forming a great society to what John Dewey calls a "great community." As he argues in *The Public and Its Problems,* American "society" is born of the nation-state's political arrangements, while "community" is an unrestricted, diverse array of associated groups. Dewey's form of American democratic community is woven from human solidarity.

Like Dewey, Baldwin believes in democracy as solidarity. But Baldwin, attuned to the realities of American racial history, claims in various essays that American democratic solidarity has been inhibited by Americans' refusal to confront their racial history. Baldwin asserts over and again that American democratic solidarity cannot be achieved until African Americans are full participants in the great community. And the community cannot form until white Americans understand that their own freedom is attached to African American freedom. Baldwin's radical critical connection creates rhetorically a public sphere in which "[African Americans], with love, shall force our [white] brothers to see themselves as they are, to cease fleeing from reality, and begin to change it . . . we can make America what America must become" (Muyumba 123). In other words, in Baldwin's essays the country is forced to "face itself" so as to make itself.

Baldwin's cultural critical writing is intellectually related to John Dewey's call for the radicalization of American democracy. In his essay "Democracy Is Radical" (1937), Dewey argues that democracy cannot be realized unless citizens forgo the illusory safety encoded in the sociopolitical status quo: "*The end of democracy is a radical end. For it is an end that has not been adequately realized in any country at any time.* It is radical because it requires great change in existing social institutions, economic, legal and cultural. A democratic liberalism that does not recognize these things in thought and action is not awake to its own meaning and to what that meaning demands [author's emphasis]" (*Essential* 338). Writing in the midst of the Great Depression, Dewey understood that American political rhetoric encouraged citizens to maintain their loyalties to institutions that regularly failed them. Though Dewey is often seated at American liberalism's philosophical center, his proposition of a radical democracy, even after the tumult of the 1960s, has never been realized in American life.

My thinking about the relationship between Dewey and Baldwin's rhetorical practices is aimed at considering the ways in which American democratic hopes are subverted by our failures to address American racial history piously. My claim here is that when instituting changes in our social institutions, say toward radical democracy, for instance, we need cultural critics who, through their own "inventions and arrangements," persuade individuals to invent and arrange their experiences expansively. If one definition of "rhetoric" is "the power of persuasive discourse to constitute audiences out of individuals, to transform singularities into collectivities, to fashion a 'we' out of a plurality of 'I's,' and to move them to collective action," then accordingly arts and cultural critics are primary rhetorical architects (Biesecker 1).

Baldwin and Dewey are central figures in the twentieth-century American intellectual tradition. Though they never had direct interaction, since the late 1990s scholars working in literary criticism, pragmatist cultural criticism, and educational philosophy have connected Dewey and Baldwin through critical genealogies. My approach is informed literary and cultural criticism, pragmatist philosophy, and rhetorical studies, placing them in conversation in order to illustrate the intellectual links between their ideals of radical democracy. I initiate their discourse by first tracing Robert Danisch's analysis of Dewey's pragmatism as a means to performance in rhetorical situations. Danisch's reading will provide a springboard to dive into a discussion of communication as the focal point of Dewey's radical democratic ideal. Paying specific attention to Dewey's *Art as Experience* (1934) and his discussion of critics and arts criticism therein, I argue that the pragmatist-inspired arts or cultural critic performs a crucial role in generating communication and knowledge, and in forming the public spheres in which radical democracy is engineered. In Deweyan criticism "art" is a rough synonym for "rhetoric." Finally, returning to Baldwin's essays and memoirs, I analyze several passages, detailing how his cultural criticism offers a strong example of Deweyan critical inclinations promulgated to construct public spheres expressly meant to achieve radical democracy. Baldwin's critical practice creates rhetorical situations that confront American racial amnesia and thus reject "intellectual segregation and blindnesses in democratic theory" (Margonis 297). Ultimately Baldwin's critical practice argues for a conception of democratic love that is linguistically artful and historically responsible.[1]

DEWEYAN PRAGMATISM, RHETORICAL SITUATIONS, AND THE ROUTE TO RADICALITY

At the end of "Democracy Is Radical," Dewey maintains that American democracy cannot reach radicality unless our pursuit of it "springs from a living faith in our common human nature and in the power of voluntary action based upon public collective intelligence" (*Collected Essays* 339). Alternatively twenty-six years later, in *The Fire Next Time* (1963), Baldwin argues that radical democracy will lie stillborn unless Americans willingly embrace the national racial history as central to any social hope for more freedom (*Collected Essays* 287–347). The first step toward democracy's radical end, Baldwin argues, is acknowledging African American humanity and citizenship as integral to achieving American democracy.[2] He argues consistently for a deeper democracy, as Judith Green suggests, by proposing "a new kind of cooperative, mutually transformative, cross-difference" citizenship, a public committed to mutual human recognition and to democracy as a critical practice of communicating our mutual responsibility to American history (Green 41). Dewey's and Baldwin's thoughts on radicality converge around the notion that public spheres must be formed through discourse, communication that develops collective knowledge and intelligence and produces sociopolitical changes.

The route to achieving this radicalism is through the connection between Dewey's liberalism and his sense of intellectual experimentalism: radical democracy is a product of liberalism's continual reinvention. As the literary historian Lawrence P. Jackson suggests, Deweyan liberalism means that citizens will be liberated from "material insecurity and from the coercions and repressions that prevent multitudes from participating in the vast cultural resources that are at hand" (Jackson 5). Dewey is interested in a political theory that helps citizens generate knowledge about how their social and political institutions function and might be changed rather than ones that obfuscate about institutional practices. Liberalism is a theoretical practice meant to spur "public intelligence in opposition to even a coercion that claims to be exercised in behalf of the ultimate freedom of all individuals" (Dewey, *Essential* 338). At the core of Dewey's sense of radical democracy is an argument against the status quo: those who might defend temporary dictatorships at democracy's expense; who might subvert the Constitution in the name of freedom; or who may support market arrangements that concretize wealth for the few while claiming falsely that freedom and opportunity exist for the American mass.

Dewey's form of regenerated liberalism suggests that citizens relinquish the rationalizations of "protective fantasies" (the status quo's enabling narratives we hold fast to in the face of vast sociopolitical and technological changes) in favor of "intelligence" as a social asset, and a "function as public as is its origin, in the concrete, in the social cooperative" (Dewey, *Political Writings* 142). Dewey's renascent liberalism initiates radical democracy only after "thought" is understood as the beginning action in changing social and political institutions. As Robert Danisch suggests, Dewey's conception of radical democracy communicates both his pragmatist philosophy and his rhetorical theory.

Danisch suggests that Deweyan pragmatism illustrates the necessity of "the practice of rhetoric for democratic affairs," replacing "rhetoric" with the word "communication" (Danisch 15). Though Dewey never wrote specifically about rhetorical theory, his philosophical sensibility is framed by an awareness of rhetorical situations. Danisch's theoretical claim is that pragmatism's intellectual commitments parallel those of classical rhetoric. If one of pragmatism's central tenets "is that the value of an action is judged by the consequences that result from that action," then Dewey considers that ideal a production of "the rhetorical situation and *phronesis*" (Danisch 54). *Phronesis*—focused, sagacious speech and action—is like Deweyan pragmatist utility in practice: thoughts, focused by knowledge and experience, are tools for acting upon or changing sociopolitical problems. If the rhetorical situation is about advancing American democracy to its radical end, then thoughtful analysis (or recognition) is the initial active mode for delivering radical change. "When Dewey asserts that practical activity must be made more intelligent," writes Danisch, "he implies that cultivating *phronesis* is the best means by which philosophers can act within a given rhetorical situation" (54). Dewey's effort to urge democracy to its end begins when he communicates the possibility of an alternative to the sociopolitical status quo. When he announces that liberalism instigates intelligent action, Dewey must subsequently model the kind of active, sagacious analysis that he is suggesting will lead to radical ends.

In "Renascent Liberalism," for instance, Dewey consistently argues for the experimental development of knowledge, emphasizing scientific methodology as the best way of developing intelligent solutions for social and political problems. When the individual citizen tests beliefs against experience, experiments with ideas, questions existing theories, or criticizes the establishment, he is working from "a socially generated body of knowledge and by means of methods that are not of private origin and possession. He uses a method that retains public validity even when innovations are introduced in its use and application" (Dewey, *Political Writings* 142). In other words, the individual works within a discourse community that builds upon communicated ideas in order to establish and revise modes of practice and social arrangements. As Danisch explains, the significance of Dewey's argument is that thoughts are modes of pragmatic action that direct us in our natural interactions. Dewey's point about "the experimental method" is that it offers ways of grasping and organizing our experiences so that we "can 'control' those 'things' and 'direct their changes as we desire'" (Danisch 56). Rather than adhering to the political and economic elite's edicts, liberal political philosophy, according to Dewey, incites us to produce thoughts and discourse experimentally. As individuals exchange their ideas, public communities are formed. These publics, awakened in thought and action, may begin theorizing or experimenting with concepts that will change "existing social institutions, economic, legal and cultural," radically.

Dewey's most cogent claims about what we recognize as rhetoric suggest that artful experimentation or artistic experimentation for the purpose of practical action inspires two critical aspects of rhetorical theory: invention and arrangement. Invention, one of the five canons of classical rhetoric, is about developing methods for persuading audiences, about inventing narratives that shift indeterminate matters or questions into finite ideas in the minds of a specific audience (see Hauser 14–24). Arrangement, Danisch writes, "points to the aesthetic and logical dimensions of rhetoric and the necessity of shaping discourse into a form for maximum effect" (Danisch 57). Experiment, invention, and arrangement are important facets of rhetorical practice because they target the ways social problems are defined, how arguments for problem solving are constructed, and how messages are arranged for the greatest persuasive punch.

Again, the rhetorical situation is about radical democracy. In order to transition toward radicalism, we must experiment and invent methods of illustrating how American democracy has been limited in practice; we must arrange persuasive narratives that communicate the benefits of Americans investing in regenerated liberalism. The relationship among experiment, intelligence, and radical democracy is about communication. As Dewey details in *Art as Experience,* "communication is the process of creating participation, of making common what had been isolated and singular" (*Art* 244). Dewey places communication as central to democratic practices because he understands that "socially radical ends" can be gained only through "liberal democratic means" (*Essential* 338). As Danisch suggests, we ought to read "communication" as Dewey's word for "rhetoric." When we do, as I suggest above and as we will see with Baldwin, liberal democratic practice can be understood as a set of contingent practices: *phronesis*—active sagacity, thoughtful action; intellectual experimentation and invention; and rhetoric—the artful arrangement of concepts so as to create exchange and participation among the members of a public community, thus inspiring them to make their individual, personal ideas into shared concerns and solutions.

The liberal experimental process is radical because it is about "the coordination of social action" (Danisch 59). Communication organizes experiences into participation and association and gives birth to knowledge. Knowledge is determined socially because it "depends upon tradition, upon tools and methods socially transmitted, developed and sanctioned" (Dewey, *Essential* 298). But what social actors experiment methodically, invent and arrange persuasive arguments for social change or transition, and initiate participatory, communicative associations, thus creating knowledge? Though Danisch argues that philosophers and scientists are at the center of Dewey's reading of rhetorical situation and *phronesis,* I argue that key intermediaries offering illustrations of the interactions of our public intelligence and our social desires in the processes of achieving those desires are cultural critics.

THE DEWEYAN CULTURAL CRITIC AS RADICAL DEMOCRATIC COMMUNICATOR

Though criticism is about judgment, Dewey claims that legalistic or judicial criticism actually distracts from realizing art as an experience. Since art objects "are expressive, they communicate" (Dewey, *Art* 104). That is, an artwork expresses experience publicly, communicating not the artist's intention specifically but rather "the nature he shares with others" (270). Ultimately, Dewey argues, art works are the only "media of complete and unhindered communication" able to create communities of experience. Art, accordingly, communicates in such a way as to initiate experiences that form or frame public spheres as those experiences are expressed and exchanged among individuals. Any attempt to foment radical democratic changes will demand artfully invented and arranged concepts that initiate shared experiences publically and instigate communication within communities of experience.

An aesthetic sort of cultural criticism—"aesthetic" in the sense of initiating shared experiences and instigating discussion about the object of the criticism—is required as well. Indeed critics are crucial to this enterprise because they often begin communication about human experiences by inventing ideas and arranging knowledge artfully. But this is not true of legalistic critics. A legalistic critic begins with "subconscious self-distrust and a consequent appeal to authority for protection" (Dewey, *Art* 299). Thus that sort of critic will hem her appraisal of an object with the threads of "influential rules" and the claims of earlier, prestigious critiques rather than with her own "direct experience" of the art. The critic sounds, finally, as though she were an advocate general for the "unquestionable sovereignty" of said rules and prestigious analyses. In appraising what the object of critique communicates, the Deweyan critic (and James Baldwin may well be a grand exemplar) will avoid the certainties of sovereign critical traditions, turning instead to interrogate closely her own responses in order to arrange her own judgment beautifully.

Critics who rely on the "work of outstanding personalities," on other writers' governing critical principles, produce only weakened versions of those previous efforts. Dewey is more interested in the critic who produces responses derived from experiencing the art object as individual (Dewey, *Art* 301). Rather than leaning on previous legalistic critical judgments, named erroneously as "eternal," Dewey favors a critical approach that draws sustenance from the techniques and forms that artists use to create specific pieces. Paying close attention to the technical and formal aspects of an art object will aid the critic's ability to "cope with the emergence of new modes of life—of experiences that demand new modes of expression" (303). Dewey explains:

> The very meaning of an important new movement in any art is that it expresses new in human experience, some new mode of interaction of the live creature with his surroundings, and hence the release of powers previously cramped or inert. . . . Unless the critic is sensitive first of all to "meaning and life" as the matter which requires its own form, he is helpless in the presence of the emergence of experience that has a distinctively new character. Every professional person is subject to the influence of custom and inertia, and has to protect himself from its influences by a deliberate openness to life itself. The judicial critic erects the very things that are the dangers of his calling into a principle and norm. (*Art* 304)

Rather than cling to "custom and inertia," the critic must give herself over to the sensitive or impressionistic appraisal of "meaning and life" within the piece under consideration. "To define an impression," Dewey writes, "is to analyze it, and analysis can proceed only by going beyond impression, by referring it to the grounds on which it rests and the consequences which it entails" (305). This is the very process of developing a judgment. Critical impression is not about unfiltered response; it is just the opposite, in fact.

This analytical process is crucial because it challenges the critic to read her impressions in relation to her own moment in time and the artwork's moment of arrival. Without that self-awareness the critic's vision is no better than the "gush of the immature enthusiast" (Dewey, *Art* 305). In its primary phase, the analytical process "is a search for the properties of the object that may justify [the critic's] direct reaction" (308). In the secondary phase, that process is advanced by the critic's sense of the criteria of judgment. Taking into account form and matter, meaning and medium, the nature of the expressive object, the critic is trying to "find out what a work of art is as an experience: the kind of experience which constitutes it" (309).

If she is able to move through this challenge and then make a claim about the value of such an experience, then the critic's insights will be more intelligent because her "perceptive appreciation is now more instructed" (Dewey, *Art* 308). Even more, since her criticism "issues as a social document," others who have access to the object under appraisal can interrogate her essay. Dewey suggests that even with value judgments included, the critic ought to place more emphasis on "the objective traits" of a piece in order for her perspectives to assist the direct experiences of others.

This is how Dewey puts the matter: "The question for the critic is the adequacy of form to matter, and that of the presence or absence of any particular form. The value of experience is not only in the ideals it reveals, but in its power to disclose many ideals, a power more germinal and more significant than any revealed ideal, since it includes them in its stride, shatters and remakes them. One may even reverse the statement and say the value of ideals lies in the experiences to which they lead" (*Art* 322). Ultimately "the moral office of criticism is performed indirectly"; in an individual's experience of art the critic's role is supplementary. While the art's moral function is to "remove prejudice" from the eyes of the beholders, "the critic's office is to further this work, performed by the object of art" (325). The critic helps the individual's already-inspired art experience expand, and she helps perfect his powers of perception.

Though Dewey's discussion of criticism is set in relation to the plastic arts, it is possible to imagine that his conception could be productively expanded to also include criticism of social or political constructs. The critic's ability to aid the expansion and perfection of individuals' perceptive powers suggests an ability to organize audiences around her social documents, at the very least. Expanding on Danisch's suggestion of connection between Deweyan pragmatism and rhetoric, we ought to see these Deweyan critical practices as integral to James Baldwin's practice of cultural criticism.

JAMES BALDWIN AS DEWEYAN RADICAL DEMOCRATIC CRITIC

Colin Koopman argues that "melioristic cultural criticism" is pragmatism's best legacy for contemporary philosophy. Pragmatist critics should see their "commission as that of articulating, problematizing, and reconstructing the plural publics and cultures in which we find ourselves. According to this view, the best work in philosophy is public thought or cultural critique" (Koopman 28). In this sense I think that one of the most provocative ways of understanding Dewey's *Art as Experience* is to read it as a manifesto for the pragmatist as cultural critic, a practice that includes criticism of the arts.

It is worth a reminder that Dewey believes that on the path to knowledge, the experimental method offers ways of grasping and organizing our experiences in order to change our social conditions. As well, the critic serves a crucial role in this process because her social documents, her criticism of objects and arrangements, encourage others to evaluate or reevaluate their own experiences with art. For Dewey, critics and criticism in general can guide us through the labyrinths of art, aesthetic theories and practices, and our experiences with them. The best critics force us to ask of our encounters with the aesthetic, "what element, in the formation of experience, each system has taken as central and characteristic. If we start from this point, we find that theories fall of themselves into certain types, and that the particular strand of experience that is offered reveals, when it is placed in contrast with esthetic experience itself, the weakness of the theory. For it is shown that the system in question has superimposed some preconceived idea upon experience instead of encouraging or even allowing esthetic experience to tell its own tale" (Dewey, *Art* 275). The critic's social role is to help individuals forgo arts and performance theories in favor of telling the tales of their own "esthetic" experiences. I want to push this point and argue that critics, in their abilities to help individuals recognize and articulate their responses to esthetic experiences, are also in the business of helping generate the communication necessary for creating associations and knowledge regarding shared cultural or community experiences: they help build public spheres.

This brings me back to "A Challenge to Bicentennial Candidates" and Baldwin's effort to illustrate how American political rhetoric, working to cross out our "plural publics and cultures," has stalled our achieving a radical democracy. Emphasizing his right to critique American political spectacles, Baldwin frames his deconstruction of bicentennial "freedom" narratives with his own family history and the landmarks of his birthplace, Harlem, New York City. As in his famous essay "Notes of a Native Son," Baldwin's analysis begins with his stepfather, David Baldwin. An African American lay preacher and day laborer, David Baldwin was limited triply: black, undereducated, and poor, he was "the last to be hired and the first to be fired" (Baldwin, *Cross* 103). The irony of the American "freedom" story, as Baldwin interprets it, is that his father, who worked himself onto welfare and into madness and death in the process, "died in an American asylum—and at the expense, needless to say, of the so-victimized American taxpayer. (My father was also an American taxpayer, and he paid at an astronomical rate)" (*Cross* 104). Introducing his stepfather as genesis of his critique, Baldwin ought to be seen as naming, in Deweyan rhetorical fashion, the "central and characteristic" element shaping emphatically his experience of the American democratic "system." This is the critic's initial step toward building what Gerard Hauser calls a "reticulate public sphere." Hauser's term connotes a "*well-ordered*" sphere made up of diverse, interbreeding public arenas related contingently to each other; this veined network is porous, allowing public and private matters to comingle in our rhetorical exchanges as "we learn and also contribute themes that inculcate shared motives" (Hauser 65).

The quality of a given public sphere depends on the commitment of its participants to "language and thought," including their limits and contingencies, that aid in resolving issues and making civic judgments. The public sphere's rhetorical features should "encourage open consideration of a question from a variety of perspectives, making the quality of our public life a rhetorical achievement" (Hauser 77). If the Deweyan critic articulates a reflective experience of art, cultural, and political forms (systems), she is also rendering artfully or rhetorically the public sphere where others can speak of their experiencing of those forms.

For instance, when Baldwin centralizes David Baldwin's suffering during the Depression as an illustration of a geographical, communal death happening in Harlem in 1976, he is generating "contextualizing" language or narrative to draw his diverse readers into a position where they might comprehend themselves as part of a believable collective. Contextualized language and believable appearance are two pillars of Hauser's five rhetorical criteria for achieving a public sphere. Baldwin understands that in order to communicate his experiencing of American democracy's failures, he must establish a rhetorical norm of contextualized language that public participants can subsequently accept and use in order to "render their respective experiences intelligible to one another" (Hauser 78). Baldwin's argument is about the disconnection of contemporary political speech from American economic history, American racial history, and radical democracy. His framing of this problem must contextualize that speech in such a way as to "foster clear apprehension" of the issue while also demonstrating rhetorically how his narrative "contains the struggle between dominant and dissident society to appropriate historicity" (Hauser 78).

Baldwin spent his writing career articulating the historical struggle between the dominant and dissident parts of American life. One clear antecedent to "A Challenge to Bicentennial Candidates" is *The Fire Next Time,* in which Baldwin arranges the struggle between dominants and dissidents as a chronic collective psychological and political crisis that stymies our ability to "achieve our country" (Baldwin, *Collected Essays* 347). The crisis is American racism, of course. Baldwin reads American racial history and racialized social arrangements as one large penitentiary wherein the white jailers and black inmates are tightly bound and incarcerated: "[Negroes] cannot be free until [whites] are free" (295). Baldwin's vision of white American freedom is itself *radical:* his claim suggests that without African American *participation* in our deepest political *arrangements* American *democracy* does not function and cannot reach its radical end.

Baldwin arrives at this realization through his close readings and celebrations of African American life. The art object he is communicating about, you might say, is African American experience—which is itself a composition in the Deweyan sense—and its various expressions. Baldwin's attention to the consequences of his father's experience in "A Challenge" is an example of this. But in *The Fire Next Time,* Baldwin critiques through a wider optic. Though the African American past is made up of "rope, fire, torture, castration, infanticide, rape; death and humiliation; fear by day and night, fear as deep as the marrow of the bone; doubt that he was worthy of life, since everyone around him denied it . . . this past, this endless struggle to achieve and reveal and confirm a human identity, human authority, yet contains, for all its horror, something very beautiful" (*Collected Essays* 342–43). While not sentimentalizing suffering, Baldwin does argue that black Americans, by force of their experiences, have earned an unshakable human authority: they have learned to "look beneath appearances, to take nothing for granted, to hear the meaning behind the words" (343). That is, African Americans, according to Baldwin's "grasping and organizing" of them here, constitute a reticulate public sphere wherein analyses of impressions and their subsequent expression generate knowledge. Interestingly, we might view Baldwin's criticism as an extension of Deweyan critical communication and as a representative model of the kind of critical practice that is at the center of black experience.

Instead of invention and arrangement, we might see Baldwin as improvising and arranging. As Dewey might suggest, the value of African American experience is in its germinal power to disclose many ideals, shatter those ideals, and then remake them. This is what African American improvisers in the blues idiom musical tradition have done rather famously. It is through improvisational music, Baldwin claims, that black people have been able to rejoice in "life itself," to assert their human identities sensually. For Baldwin, "sensuality" is about asserting one's earthly *presence* in every human action.

Baldwin's idea contains an echo of Dewey: "Of all affairs, communication is the most wonderful. That things should be able to pass from the plane of external pushing and pulling to that of revealing themselves to man, and thereby to themselves; and the fruit of communication should be participation, sharing, is a wonder by the side of which transubstantiation pales" (Dewey, *Experience* 166). Jazz musicians improvise expressions, the "fruit of communication," which inspire participation and sharing among their listeners. Yet one must be *present,* sensual, in order to catch those musical ideas that "pass from the plane of external pushing and pulling," in order to participate or share in, as Baldwin has it, the "effort of loving to the breaking of bread" (Baldwin, *Collected Essays* 311).

Baldwin's radicality springs from his notion that in African American public spheres, in the beauty and struggle of black life, American democracy can be realized. As Eddie Glaude Jr. argues, Baldwin's attention to black life and struggle forces the nation to "encounter the grim realities of suffering and thus undermine the belief that America is an example of democracy realized" (Glaude 11). While Dewey yearns for citizens to relinquish their attachments to the sociopolitical status quo so that new public spheres might form and urge their democratic institutions through radical change, Baldwin's critique of African American trauma and expression suggests that black folks represent democracy's radical realization. Black Americans have had the great advantage, Baldwin writes, "of having never believed that collection of myths to which white Americans cling: that their ancestors were all freedom-loving heroes, that they were born in the greatest country the world has ever seen, or that Americans are invincible in battle and wise in peace, that Americans have always dealt honorably with Mexicans and Indians and all other neighbors or inferiors, that American men are the world's most direct and virile, that American women are pure. Negroes know far more about white Americans than that" (Baldwin, *Collected Essays* 344).

Baldwin again presents African Americans as a discreet and knowledgeable public. Note that Baldwin representing both the Deweyan critical line and the African American critical discourse is able to derive a critique that does not rely on or uphold the "sovereign," "legalistic," traditional theories about American life. His reading illustrates a point that he makes in another essay, "The Artist's Struggle for Integrity" (1963). There Baldwin declares, as if channeling Dewey, that "art is here to prove, and to help one bear, the fact that all safety is an illusion" (Baldwin, *Cross* 42). African American life read as art communicates that Americans cannot rely on the sociopolitical status quo for safeguarding or sustenance if they claim any desire for democracy. Rather it reminds them of the fundamental lesson of democracy: if democracy is to hold together, its citizens must hold it themselves.

Baldwin knows, however, that "real Americans" would rather maintain the hollow mythology than accept the Other as the promise of radical democracy. As he declares mockingly in "A Challenge," "real Americans know that the American taxpayer is being ruined by the Indian/Chicano/Mexican/Puerto Rican/black. These dominate the welfare rolls, and the prison populations, and roam, and make unlivable, the streets of the American cities" (Baldwin, *Cross* 104). This is the narrative, he argues, that American candidates purposefully promote albeit shielded by the "niceties of rhetoric" that keep them from speaking about any groups specifically. This is an aesthetic experience too; however, it is one that maintains the status quo and the white heroic mythology at the expense of intelligent discourse and democracy. Still, it is a narrative that persists powerfully in American political rhetoric today.

As Baldwin's determined examination illustrates, it is the sort of work of art that demands critical response.

Baldwin speaks disagreeable truths. It may seem, in fact, that Baldwin's inspired speech about American racial history's disquieting consequences stands in the way of the possibility of human solidarity and the realization of a Deweyan democratic community. One could go so far as to suggest that Baldwin might not love America enough or, worse, that he hates America. When he eviscerates white American mythology, what does he leave us with to fashion our democratic narrative? Can we actually achieve a "we" out of a plurality of "I's" and act collectively without confronting American racial history? Or put another way, as Baldwin might, can an African American public sphere communicate its knowledge in such a way as to inspire other Americans (seeing common human nature expressed there) to voluntarily collect into other public spheres, act intelligently, and engineer social change? Can the conversation of the one sphere enter the pores of another, thus reshaping the conversation there?

Baldwin always leaves us with exclamations and damning prophecies. At the end of *The Fire Next Time* he argues that "if we do not dare everything," that is, if we do not face our history and change our society and politics radically, God's wrath will be upon us: "*No more water, the fire next time*" (Baldwin, *Collected Essays* 347). At the end of his enraged, trenchant, improvisational, and beautiful memoir of the civil rights movement, *No Name in the Street* (1972), Baldwin argues that African Americans, standing adjacent to the mainstream status quo, can see "spinning above the thoughtless American head, the shape of the wrath to come" (*Collected Essays* 474).

However, that damnation, Baldwin believes, can be halted through love. Dewey has a similar idea at the end of *Art as Experience* where he offers a quotation from Shelley's "Defense of Poetry": "the great secret of morals is love . . . and the identification of ourselves with the beautiful which exists in thought, action, or person not our own" (*Art* 349). Dewey takes up this line as he argues that recognition or identification of self through the reflections found in beautiful art is not enough. Just as the critic cannot rely on her immediate impressions as critique itself, after the moment of perception one must extend that recognition through the "remaking of impulsion and thought" into a form and expression of critique (349). Art charges and changes our imaginations, our conceptions of the actual and the possible forcing us to analyze, revise, and express—and so share—our experiences. In addition it can insinuate "possibilities of human relations not to be found in rule and precept, admonition and administration" (349). Such love requires not just recognition of ourselves through art or in another; it requires accepting the responsibility for the possibility of uncharted human relations.

Baldwin's conception of democratic love is artful and responsible. Examining the beauty and trauma of African American life, Baldwin finds love at its core: "To be an Afro-American, or an American black, is to be in the situation, intolerably exaggerated, of all those who have ever found themselves part of a civilization which they could in no wise honorably defend—which they were compelled, indeed, endlessly to attack and condemn—and who yet spoke out of the most passionate love, hoping to make the kingdom new, to make it honorable and worthy of life" (Baldwin, *Collected Essays* 474). African American life is artful and radical because other Americans see themselves and the possibility for new social and political arrangements through the black experience. In order to get there, however, they must develop active, sagacious, and public thought that does the work of discussing critically within that community the implications inherent in the narratives of dominant American public discourse, and they must do so in ways that the public spheres (in the Hauser sense of that concept) that encompass other Americans can include. Such a project, one that Baldwin tried to practice, could do the essential civic work that democracy requires. Baldwin shifts to citizens the ongoing responsibility of ensuring that the promise of democratic culture's safety is, after all, *not* illusory. That responsibility requires, as Dewey insisted, a civic practice of love, a love of country that reaches "to the entire extent of love," as Shelley described it. As Baldwin insisted, this kind of love requires citizens to face together our traumatic racial history. Confronting that history, we will change our institutions radically and ensure that our past realities and errors propel us toward a broader, stronger democratic community.

NOTES

1. In separate essays Frank Margonis and Howard McGary offer both Dewey and Baldwin as key thinkers in their considerations of rhetoric, pragmatism, democracy, and equality. Other scholars working similar lines of inquiry include Robert Genter (*Late Modernism: Art, Culture, and Politics in Cold War America* [2010]); Judith Green (*Deep Democracy: Community, Diversity, and Transformation* [1999]); Ross Posnock (*Black Writers and the Making of the Modern Intellectual* [2000]); Richard Rorty (*Achieving Our Country: Leftist Thought in Twentieth-Century America* [1999]); and Ivy Wilson (*Specters of Democracy: Blackness and the Aesthetics of Politics in the Antebellum U.S.* [2008]).

2. Though Dewey does not cite any specific economic category or racial/ethnic groups, he anticipates Baldwin's (and Malcolm X's) arguments when he claims to understand why those in close contact with the "inequities and tragedies of life" of the Depression-era political status quo are "impatient and long for the overthrow of the existing system by any means whatever" (Dewey, *Essential* 338).

WORKS CITED

Baldwin, James. *Collected Essays.* New York: Library of America, 1998.

———. *The Cross of Redemption: Uncollected Writings.* New York: Pantheon, 2010.

Balfour, Lawrie. *The Evidence of Things Not Said.* Ithaca, N.Y.: Cornell University Press, 2000.

Biesecker, Barbara. *Addressing Postmodernity: Kenneth Burke, Rhetoric, and a Theory of Social Change.* Tuscaloosa: University of Alabama Press, 1997.

Danisch, Robert. *Pragmatism, Democracy, and the Necessity of Rhetoric.* Columbia: University of South Carolina Press, 2007.

Dewey, John. *Art as Experience.* New York: Perigree, 1934.

———. *The Essential Dewey.* Bloomington: Indiana University Press, 1998.

———. *Experience and Nature.* Mineola, N.Y.: Dover, 1958.

———. *The Political Writings.* Indianapolis: Hackett, 1993. Print.

Glaude, Eddie, Jr. *In a Shade of Blue: Pragmatism and the Politics of Black America.* Chicago: University of Chicago Press, 2007.

Green, Judith. *Pragmatism and Social Hope: Deepening Democracy in Global Contexts.* New York: Columbia University Press, 2008.

Hauser, Gerard A. *Vernacular Voices.* Columbia: University of South Carolina Press, 1999.

Jackson, Lawrence P. *The Indignant Generation: A Narrative History of African American Writers and Critics, 1934–1960.* Princeton, N.J.: Princeton University Press, 2011.

Koopman, Colin. *Pragmatism as Transition: Historicity and Hope in James, Dewey, and Rorty.* New York: Columbia University Press, 2009.

Margonis, Frank. "The Path of Social Amnesia and Dewey's Democratic Commitments." In *Philosophy of Education* (2003), 296–304. PDF. Web (accessed October 2012) http://ojs.ed.uiuc.edu/index.php/pes/article/view/1749

McGary, Howard. "Achieving Democratic Equality: Forgiveness, Reconciliation, and Reparations." *Journal of Ethics* 7.1, Race, Racism, and Reparations (2003): 93–113.

Muyumba, Walton. *The Shadow and the Act: Black Intellectual Practice, Jazz Improvisation, and Philosophical Pragmatism.* Chicago: University of Chicago Press, 2009.

PART III

Dewey as Teacher of Rhetoric

Rhetoric and Dewey's Experimental Pedagogy

Nathan Crick

In John Dewey's reading of Greek history, the Greek Sophists emerge as the first practitioners of democratic experimental pedagogy. Referring to them as "the first body of professional educators in Europe," he treats the Sophists as "symptoms of the change from the regime of custom to the regime of analysis and reflective thought" who embodied "a certain opposition between social customs organized in institutions, and the procedure of critical, analytical intelligence" (Dewey, *Democracy* 330). In other words, for Dewey, the Sophists represented the tension between *nomos* and *logos*—that is, between tradition and invention, between culture and criticism, and between habits and language—that emerged in Greece during the fifth century B.C.E. when democracy became not only the dominant form of social life but also the highest manifestation of political power. The Sophists exploited these tensions by providing paying students the means to become successful in the new democratic order. By providing "skilled excellence in the arts, especially the political arts," the Sophists gave citizens "power to command the attention of others which would assure civic preeminence" (Dewey, "Logic" 4). They also, if indirectly, provided them the capacity to reason, at least insofar as the training "to speak in private groups and in the public forum" formed the basis of "the beginnings of a kind of practical logic" ("Logic" 4). In sum, Dewey understood the Sophists as employing experimental methods of education not for their own sake but as the most adequate technique for cultivating a critical, competent, and participatory citizenry necessary to sustain a democracy.

Unique about Dewey's reading of the Sophists is less the fact that he associates sophistical education and democracy than that he locates in their practice the origins of logic, which for him is the basis of the modern sciences. The Sophists thus represented for Dewey the beginnings of a form of education in which rhetoric has an important function in the training not just of logic but also of other more content-centered disciplines such as history, sociology, geography, and physics, as well as the practical arts. Although Dewey's overall philosophy and character were far more Aristotelian then sophistical, the Sophists nonetheless embodied something that Aristotle did not—an attitude consistent with contemporary movements in democratic pedagogy. As I have defined elsewhere, the sophistical attitude represents "an experimental approach to things, people, events, and ideas that brings intellectual resources to bear on the means and ends of artistic production in order to generate new methods of invention necessary to master the contingencies of life and guide the flux of nature" (Crick, "Sophistical Attitude" 28). In other words, they viewed knowledge as an active, ongoing form of inquiry whose origin was found in problematic situations and whose end was found in its satisfactory resolution. For Dewey, then, the Sophists provided him with historical evidence that our interest in "theory" almost always grows out of an initial interest in "practice." In short, they showed not that we became democratic by first becoming intelligent but that we became more intelligent by learning how to act democratically, and that we first learned how to reason through engaging in rhetoric and only afterward learned to improve our rhetoric by having become more reasonable.

I use the Sophists to introduce an essay on the relationship between rhetoric and John Dewey's experimental pedagogy in order to ground his theories in a long tradition of teaching the language arts in a democracy. As Susan Jarratt has pointed out, the Sophists have come to represent a starting point for progressive education. Thus she argues that for "teachers who wish to participate in the revitalization of our own democracy, the voice of sophistical rhetoric speaks out in playful, persuasive, and promising tones" (Jarratt 117). This essay follows this insight by showing how a more explicit sophistical attitude toward rhetoric might be incorporated into Dewey's model of experimental education. Such an attitude would view communication primarily as a tool for generating ideas that serve as practical means for overcoming shared problems and obstacles, and it would view the creation, advocacy, criticism, and defense of theories and hypotheses as vital activities within this cycle of inquiry. In short, this essay shows not only how sophistical rhetoric can contribute to the maintenance of civic life in the way already expressed by contemporary critical pedagogy, but also how it plays an integral role in the teaching of experimental habits of mind within a laboratory classroom. Rhetoric can thus be made to serve the purposes not just of criticism and dialogue but also of invention, encouraging what I have called a "rhetorical consciousness necessary to create new ideas and persuade others within the public sphere that such ideas are worthy of test" (Crick, "Capital" 342). In this way integrating sophistical rhetoric into Dewey's experimental pedagogy brings us close to the original spirit of unity between theory and practice that was the driving force behind the sophistical movement that made them the first true democratic educators in the Western world.

DIALOGUE, CRITICISM, AND RHETORIC IN CRITICAL PEDAGOGY

Before investigating the potential relationship between rhetoric and inquiry in the experimental classroom, it is important to observe the degree to which elements of a sophistical attitude have already become integrated into the methods of critical pedagogy. As Jarratt has argued, "in their attempts at reinstating the public intellectual, conceiving of schools in Deweyan terms as laboratories for democracy, and empowering students by giving them a voice, critical pedagogues revive the goals of the first Sophists" (Jarratt 107). Expressed in the works of such authors as Paulo Freire, Henry Giroux, bell hooks, Ira Shor, and Stanley Aronowitz, among others, critical pedagogy has a directly sophistical character to the degree that it focuses on stimulating adult learners to call into question common assumptions, identify and criticize institutional forms of power, and embrace identities as engaged citizens actively involved in transforming global political culture. According to Henry Giroux, "critical pedagogy forges critique and agency through a language of skepticism and possibility" (Giroux 186). As a consequence, the classroom portrayed by critical pedagogy often resembles a rhetorical forum in which students engage in argumentation, analysis, and criticism, which produce predictable tensions. Ira Shor writes that "critical pedagogy invites students to re-perceive, to examine what they know and how they learn it, to question existing conditions, all of which can arouse anxiety and resistance." (Shor 260).

In contrast with Dewey, who largely spoke of students as "children" engaging in various stages of playful inquiry, critical pedagogy assumes an adult learner who has already been considerably socialized and disciplined, whose curiosity has been stunted, and whose formal knowledge is largely a hegemonic by-product. The arts of *logos* thus become necessary means of disrupting conventional assumptions and hierarchies while simultaneously empowering students to develop their own unique voices. In this way the student as "child" is replaced by the student as adult learner who draws on his or her unique life experience to criticize and question elements of the dominant nexus of power and knowledge in a way that exposes that familiar opposition between traditional culture and institutions and the procedure of critical, analytical intelligence.

Specifically, critical pedagogy and sophistical education share five basic principles. First, they both reject what Freire calls the "banking" concept of education in which education "become[s] an act of depositing, in which the students are the depositories and the teacher is the depositor" (Freire, *Pedagogy* 72). Instead of viewing knowledge as something that can be exchanged through words, knowledge is seen to emerge only through "invention and reinvention, through the restless, impatient, continuing, hopeful inquiry human beings pursue in the world, with the world, and with each other" (Freire, *Pedagogy* 72). Second, these methods integrate a "problem-posing" approach to education that begins with something to be interrogated and investigated rather than something merely to be absorbed and memorized. Reminiscent of Protagoras, Shor recommends even "presenting science as debates and controversies and competing interpretations [in which] the critical teacher would pose the subject matter as a problem for students to think through rather than a bland official consensus for them to memorize" (Shor 41). Third, the teacher stresses how the subject matter of the classroom relates to ongoing social conditions, such that "knowledge will be offered in a context that is functional to student life and work that reveals critical problems in society" (Shor 36). Fourth, the critical classroom actively encourages students to participate and express themselves on the assumption that their life experiences are valuable sources of knowledge. For instance, rejecting the common assumption that teachers "have nothing to learn from their students," hooks walked into the classroom positioning herself partly as a learner and the classroom as "a community of learners *together*" (hooks 153). Last, both critical and sophistical pedagogy aspire to what Jarratt sees as the same goal: to promote "the democratic process of group decision-making on which our democracy still rests" (Jarratt 107). Rather than just instilling knowledge, critical and sophistical pedagogy aim to create good, capable citizens with the skills to constitute a good society.

Of the two tendencies of the Sophists, critical pedagogy tends to emphasize the practical, focusing as it does on themes that grow directly out of students' experiences with issues of social justice and injustice. Freire, in his work teaching literacy to landless Brazilian peasants, is the most explicit in this goal. He writes that "the central problem is this: how can the oppressed, as divided, unauthentic beings, participate in developing the pedagogy of their liberation?" and that "the pedagogy of the oppressed is an instrument for their critical discovery that both they and their oppressors are manifestations of dehumanization" (Freire, *Pedagogy* 48). Translated into U.S. classrooms, in which university students do not easily fit the category of "oppressed," the critical eye usually turns outward. Shor, in his discussion on "problem-posing," consistently emphasizes how any subject matter can become a problem if it is brought into the sphere of political economy. In an extensive list of topics that could serve as problems, he includes the following: "urban housing policies that help reduce homelessness"; "hunger and its roots in various corporate-government policies"; "unemployment resulting from corporations moving jobs to cheap labor areas in the South or to antiunion countries abroad in search of lower wages and taxes"; "the big business of militarism"; "secret United States government aid to right-wing guerrillas around the world"; and "government surveillance of dissident groups and censorship of war coverage" (Shor 56). These examples are consistent with what Giroux sees as a central assumption of critical pedagogy: "that knowledge and power should always be subject to debate, held accountable, and critically engaged" (Giroux 185).

Of the arts of *logos* available to accomplish this aim, critical pedagogy tends to focus on the relationship between dialogue, criticism, and rhetoric. In the first case, Freire identifies dialogue as a fundamentally emancipatory exercise in which people come together as equals to name and transform the world according to their shared needs and desires. It exists as "the encounter in which the united reflection and action of the dialoguers are addressed to the world which is to be transformed and humanized" and whose success requires "an intense faith in humankind, faith in their power to make and remake, to create and re-create, faith and their vocation to be more fully human" (Freire, *Pedagogy* 88, 90). In simpler terms Shor describes dialogue as a "horizontal" form of communication in which "people talk mutually, instead of the teacher talking at students or down to them" (Shor 86). Represented by the circle rather than the pyramid, dialogue collapses the distance between teacher and learner by making both coproducers of knowledge in which multiple perspectives are shared on issues of common concern. By treating students as if they have something to contribute that is unique and valuable to class discussion, dialogue activates their interest in the subject matter and turns passivity from a virtue to a vice.

However, dialogue alone does not allow students to be able to emerge fully from what Freire calls various forms of "oppression," by which he means a consciousness that defines itself in terms of the words of a dominating class. Also required are the tools of criticism by which individuals can decode the various forms of propaganda, management, and manipulation that are designed to reduce people to the status of objects. Thus, "true dialogue cannot exist unless the dialoguers engage in critical thinking," a kind of "thinking which does not separate itself from action, but constantly immerses itself in temporality without fear of the risks involved" (Freire, *Pedagogy* 92). Giroux applies this principle in what he calls a "border pedagogy" that "not only incorporates the postmodern emphasis on criticizing official texts and using alternative modes of representation" but "also incorporates popular culture as a serious object of politics and analysis and makes central to its project the recovery of those forms of knowledge and history that characterize alternative and oppositional Others" (Giroux 51). In practical terms, criticism often takes the form of bringing in cultural artifacts to analyze and critique in order to understand their relation to various forms of power, whether as vehicles of domination or of resistance.

In each of these aims, rhetoric becomes an art by which student-citizens are able to develop their own voices as means of engaging in public affairs. Giroux thus calls on educators, particularly in the composition classroom, to "reinvigorate democracy by assuming the pedagogical project of prioritizing debate, deliberation, dissent, dialogue, and public spaces as central to any viable notion of global citizenship" (Giroux 184). Taken together, these methods of dialogue, criticism, and rhetoric contribute to a goal of producing a community of citizens based in mutual self-respect who have mastered the tools of critical reason to decode the messages of their political culture and articulate their own perspectives with eloquence and power. Aronowitz sums up the game as follows: the education of an "individual who is able to discern knowledge from propaganda, is competent to choose among conflicting claims and programs, and is capable of actively participating in the affairs of the polity" (Aronowitz 17). This language clearly resonates with that of the Sophist Protagoras as preserved by Plato, who defines his goal as an educator teaching "sound deliberation, both in domestic matters—how best to manage one's household and in public affairs—how to realize one's maximum potential for success in political debate and action" (Plato 319a). To accomplish this task, Protagoras taught his students how to master the methods of argumentation, critical thought, and creative imagination to be able to argue both sides of a question while at the same time instilling the virtues of temperance and respect, cultivated through dialogue, which are necessary to hold a community together. In this way the Sophists have already been incorporated into the college composition classroom.

EXPERIMENTAL METHOD IN EDUCATION

Although critical pedagogy has in many ways successfully carried forward the sophistical emphasis on praxis, it has had less success articulating methods by which rhetoric can play constitutive roles in the teaching of specialized discourses and the production of experimental knowledge and attitudes. It is one thing to draw parallels between the Sophists and the teaching of expressive composition; it is quite another to demonstrate their relevance to the teaching of what Shor calls "academic themes" that are often associated with a technical jargon "remote from the discourse and knowledge of daily life" (Shor 73–74). Freire, speaking of his own experience teaching peasants, sums up the criticism that it "is always said that it is impossible to dialogue with peasants about agricultural techniques, just as it is impossible in the primary school to dialogue, for example, about the fact that 4 x 4 cannot be 15" (Freire, *Education* 110). Freire's response is that "everything can be presented problematically," and he suggests that "instead of mechanically memorizing 4 x 4, the people ought to discover its relation to something in human life," such as "making four bricks four times" (Freire, *Education* 111–12). But this example merely proves the criticism valid insofar as the teaching of mathematics becomes a vehicle for a discussion of cultural history or political economy rather than the learning of multiplication tables, not to mention the sheer labor-intensive act of having to make bricks to teach math.

Of the theorists of critical pedagogy, Shor comes the closest to articulating a vision that follows the experimental trajectory of the Sophists and that brings him in closest proximity to Dewey's educational philosophy. Addressing the elementary science classroom, he suggests developing activities in which students become interested in the subject matter and answer questions by the manipulation of material and the application of hypotheses. For instance, by implementing "hands-on experiments to make the curriculum active" and asking questions related to student experience, such as why apple cider is bubbly and apple juice is not, the teacher attempts to get them interested in subject matter through engaged inquiry into familiar but unexplained processes and phenomena (Shor 78–79). He goes on:

> To include students in decision-making, the science teacher could also present them with a choice of laboratory experiments demonstrating a material, a reaction, an element, or a process. Working on different experiments, the students would report their findings to the class as a whole. Science should be an adventurous field project, especially for younger students, taking trips, exploring the environment, observing whether in stars, growing plants, grains, and flowers. Such projects would require visits to gardening stores as well as reading about what to grow. Each of these activities could be written up in the science journal, so that writing became a method for learning. (79)

Here we see a complete form of communication being employed. Students are neither engaging in criticism of a text to be decoded and deconstructed nor dialoguing with each other about their experiences concerning a matter of shared concern. They are instead manipulating and investigating objects and events while communicating with each other about observations and interpretations in order to produce a coherent explanatory account.

What we see reflected here is Dewey's method of the "laboratory" at work. For Dewey, the "method of the laboratory is an experimental one. It is a method of discovering through search, through inquiry, through testing, through observation and reflection—all processes requiring activity of mind rather than merely powers of absorption and reproduction" (Dewey, "Education as Politics" 109). But by the phrase "activity of mind" Dewey also meant the "activity of body." Indeed here lies the core radicalism of Dewey's philosophy—the idea that genuine learning occurs only in situations in which bodies and minds act together within shared creative environments that offer both challenge and reward. The metaphor of the laboratory conveys this attitude insofar as the "first great characteristic of the laboratory is that in it there is carried on an activity, an activity which involves contact with technical equipment, as tools, instruments and other apparatus, and machinery which require the use of the hands and the body" (Dewey, "Monastery" 107). Experimentalism and education thus collapse traditional binaries by focusing on how embodied minds learn to cooperate through symbolic action.

In practical terms, implementing an experimental method requires more than just skill in the art of *logos;* it often literally means equipping schools with physical laboratory spaces, in which "laboratory" is taken broadly to mean any sphere in which students are physically involved with the manipulation of things in order to develop, test, and verify ideas. Consequently Dewey believed that "where schools are equipped with laboratories, shops, and gardens, where dramatizations, plays, and games are freely used, opportunities exist for reproducing situations of life, and for acquiring and applying information and ideas in the carrying forward of progressive experiences" (Dewey, *Democracy* 161–62). For Dewey, then, "laboratory" had an expansive definition and included a variety of spaces dealing with diverse subject matter. "Any subject, from Greek cooking, and from drawing to mathematics, is intellectual, if intellectual at all, not in its fixed inner structure, but in its function—in its power to start indirect significant inquiry and reflection. What geometry does for one, the manipulation of laboratory apparatus, the mastery of a musical composition, or the conduct of the business affair, may do for another" (Dewey, *How We Think* 39). What is important about the laboratory is not the specific equipment it houses but rather the fact that it provides a space for physical experimentation with things that inspire the mind and imagination.

Equally necessary in transforming mere equipment arranged in a space into a "laboratory" is the application of the experimental method. To ensure that the laboratory setting featured more than "simply trying," or what he called "the bare fact of the omnipresent uncertainty of trial in all action," Dewey consistently emphasized the need for applying the five stages of experimental method in the classroom (Dewey, "Underlying" 94). These stages, which Dewey believed reflected the process of thinking in general, can be represented by the following five activities, each done in succession: 1) *arousing interest,* such that "people have a genuine situation of experience—that there be a continuous activity in which he is interested for its own sake"; 2) *engaging a problem,* such that "a genuine problem develops within the situation of the stimulus to thought"; 3) *acquiring data,* so that students possess "the information and make the observation needed to deal with it"; 4) *suggesting solutions* that students "shall be responsible for developing in an orderly way"; and 5) *testing ideas* "by application, to make their meaning clear and to discover . . . their validity" (Dewey, *Democracy* 163). In short, the most lasting lesson learned in the experimental classroom is not the "content" of the lesson—how plants grow, the density of water, the probability of dice games, or the proper musical score for a school play—but the intelligent habits of thought and action by which students acquire this content.

What distinguishes Dewey's experimental method from the spirit of critical pedagogy is that the former focuses less directly on matters of social praxis and more on cultivating experimental attitudes by investigating a carefully constructed problem-situation in a laboratory setting. The ideal problem-situation must therefore both arouse interest as well as suggest an attainable aim. By "interest," Dewey means a psychological state in which "one is identified with the objects which define the activity and which furnish the means and obstacles to its realization" (Dewey, *Democracy* 102); by "aim," he means "to foresee a future possibility," to "have a plan for its accomplishment," and "to note the means which make the plan capable of execution and the obstructions in the way" (137). A carefully constructed problem-situation will thus bring about a state of mind and body analogous to a person considering jumping across a ditch:

> If he were sure we could or could not make it, definitive activity in some direction would occur. But if he considers, he is in doubt; he hesitates. During the time in which a single overt line of action is in suspense, his activities are

> confined to such redistributions of energy within the organism as will prepare a determinate course of action. He measures the ditch with his eyes; he brings himself taut to get a feel of the energy at his disposal; he looks about for other ways across, he reflects upon the importance of getting across. All this means an accentuation of consciousness; it means a turning in upon the individual's own attitudes, powers, wishes, etc. (347)

Whether one's "ditch" is a mechanical, artistic, economic, personal, or scientific problem is irrelevant; what matters is that problem-situations bring about similar feelings of doubt, curiosity, hesitation, suspense, measurement, preparation, reflection, and expectation. Without these feelings a ditch is not a problem but merely a hole in the ground.

Experimental education is so demanding because it begins with a problem-situation that simultaneously challenges and entices students with a clearly articulated aim. Consequently, observes Dewey, "a large part of the art of instruction lies in making the difficulty of new problems large enough to challenge thought, and small enough so that, in addition to the confusion naturally attending the novel elements, there shall be luminous familiar spots from which helpful suggestions may spring" (Dewey, *Democracy* 157). The goal, then, is to begin with the familiar but problematic situations that naturally call out for inquiry into more complex subject matter with which to construct the solution, ideally producing interest in the subject matter along the way as students discover how it is relevant to their lives. In *The School and Society*, Dewey gives as examples the challenges of growing plants in a school garden, of using raw materials of flax, wool, and cotton to spin thread to make clothes, and of designing a clay smelter large enough to heat iron. By starting with physical and practical challenges that inspire activity and imagination, a teacher allows the situations naturally to call out for inquiry into more complex subject matter with which to construct the solution, ideally producing interest in the subject matter itself along the way as its relevance to students' life experiences is disclosed.

The centrality of communication to Dewey's pedagogical method, often left implicit, becomes clear as soon as one is situated in the lively, oral atmosphere of an experimental classroom in which students excitedly exchange ideas and feelings with the teacher as well as each other in a playful but also structured environment. An interest in communication, or what he calls "social conversation leading to exchange and enrichment of experiences," is one of the three core interests of the student (along with the construction of things and the expression of the creative imagination) that Dewey identifies as being central to justifying his educational philosophy (Dewey, *Lectures* 232). Indeed Dewey explains that a student often values inquiry simply because it is "one way of keeping up his interest in communication" (232). A child will thus ask questions as a way of keeping "up the feeling of social relationship," meaning that the child likes to "find out things just as he likes to tell stories, or call attention to what he has done, or as he likes to play with the object that he finds around him; it makes simply an enlargement of his experience to ask questions primarily as a way of keeping a conversation going" (232). The challenge to experimental education is to transcend the purely social function of inquiry and to "convert the interest in communication into an interest in inquiry" as an end in itself (232).

Approached as a means to inquiry, communication facilitates the creative and cooperative construction of shared meanings that deepens and broadens the significance of events and objects while disclosing new potentialities in action. "When communication occurs," writes Dewey, "all natural events are subject to reconsideration and revisions; they are re-adapted to meet the requirements of conversation, whether it be public discourse or that preliminary discourse term thinking" (Dewey, *Experience* 166). With communication, "natural events become messages to be enjoyed and administered, precisely as our song, fiction, oratory, the giving of advice and instruction. The events come to possess characters; they are demarcated and noted" (174). In experimental education, communication represents a social process whereby symbolic meanings are applied, invented, rearranged, discarded, and transformed, through interaction with events and objects, as means of bringing a shared problem-situation to satisfactory conclusion.

Taken as a whole, the "democratic" character of this pedagogical model is found in the attitude it cultivates rather than in any explicit content it teaches. For Dewey, education for a democracy was not synonymous with the traditional class in "civics" whereby one learned about the three branches of government and the mechanisms of voting and representation; rather its goal was to cultivate democratic attitudes capable of adjusting the great problem of any pluralistic society: "to combine a maximum of different values, achieved by giving free play to individual taste and capacity, with a minimum of friction and conflict" (Dewey, *Democracy* 137). By teaching students how to address shared problems through communicative exchange of diverse ideas and perspectives, the experimental method, according to Dewey, solves this problem as no other method can. He writes, "The experimental method is the only one compatible with the democratic way of life, as we understand it. Every extension of intelligence as the method of action enlarges the area of common understanding. Understanding may not ensure complete agreement, but it gives the only sound basis for enduring agreement" (137). The experimental attitude, in other words, is not merely one facet of democracy; its cultivation within a public is the culmination of democratic social life itself.

RHETORIC AND EXPERIMENTALISM

Rhetoric appears in the experimental classroom through the sophistical method of *dissoi logoi,* or "double argument." First expressed by Protagoras in his dictum that on every issue there are two competing claims, *dissoi logoi* represents the notion "that in order to understand an issue, one must be prepared to listen to at least two contrary sides; and in order to decide how to act, one must espouse one of the two sides or come up with a third" (Poulakos 58). *Dissoi logoi* is not simply a statement that people disagree; it emphasizes that productive action must be *preceded* by thoughtful debate, criticism, and advocacy that draw on the wealth of available knowledge to produce warranted assertions. This experimental interpretation of *dissoi logoi* was expressed most explicitly in the classical world by Aristotle, who argued that "one should be able to argue persuasively on either side of the question . . . not that we may actually do both, but in order that it may not escape our notice what the real state of the case is and that we ourselves may be able to refute it if another person uses speech unjustly" (Aristotle 1354b). In other words, Aristotle defined rhetoric as a means of constituting practical judgment through the invention and clash of persuasive arguments in an open forum in order that the truth could be articulated. Aristotle's contribution to rhetoric was thus to make explicit how the sophistical spirit of *dissoi logoi* was a necessary component to any genuine inquiry in which participants used the power of language to disclose heretofore unrecognized aspects of the world in order to bring clarity to the confused and order to the chaotic.

The most familiar application of rhetoric that one can introduce into such a classroom is the debate. In this model, a scientific controversy is imported into the classroom and examined as if it were a rhetorical agon between competing sides, with the students often being assigned advocacy roles pro and con. Shor explains this rationale:

> Contending thought in any field can be presented to students as a problem for their deliberation. Anthropology classes can examine the debate over the disappearance of the Neanderthals. Economics classes can debate the market system, to puzzle out whether profit driven production is more just or efficient than an industrial system based on producing for social needs. Biology classes can debate whether gradual or catastrophic evolution most influenced the development of flora, fauna, and terrain. In science classes students can read debates on the impact of human exposure to toxic wastes and nuclear radiation. Which view makes most sense to students? (Shor 191)

In many ways this method is reminiscent of Gorgias's recommendation to learn the art of rhetoric by studying the words of astronomers and imitating them. To use the language of Bruno Latour, it teaches students that there "are many ways to win over a jury, to end a controversy, to cross examine a witness or a brain extract" and that "rhetoric is the name of the discipline that has, for millennia, studied how people are made to believe and behave and taught people how to persuade others" (Latour 30). The purpose of this classroom exercise is therefore not only to relate academic themes to consequences in real life, directly or indirectly, but also to develop skills in argumentation and analysis and to see them at work in "real" science.

However, Dewey's experimental method suggests a stronger integration of rhetoric into the laboratory classroom. If we return to the understanding of *dissoi logoi* as a method of invention by which original hypotheses emerge from the clash of competing propositions, we can see how rhetoric might play a constitutive role at each of the stages of inquiry. Rhetoric is not just about trying to manipulate other people to serve personal self-interests; it is about the conscious construction of symbols intended to move others to new beliefs and attitudes by overcoming recalcitrance and stimulating intelligent desire. Consequently rhetoric clearly can address any of these questions raised during each of the stages of inquiry: While arousing interest, "What type of activity promises the most interesting and challenging experience?" In engaging a problem, "What aspect of this situation calls out for an answer?" During the acquisition of data, "What shall we look for and how shall we find it?" While suggesting solutions, "What is the most promising idea that is original and accounts for the facts?" In the testing of ideas, "Does what we have witnessed bolster our case or weaken it?" Clearly each of these questions can simply be answered without recourse to rhetorical debate. But introduce conflict between members of a research team, or between research teams, and rhetoric suddenly becomes inescapable and necessary.

In other words, to make rhetoric a constituent element of the experimental classroom requires a formal delineation between researchers and/or research teams who at various points in the inquiry process must argue for their specific perspectives before a moderating "panel" of other students whose decision will decide the future course of classroom research. Rhetoric becomes a formal instrument by which competing interests are negotiated and complex ideas are framed and defended against competing ideas. To make this exercise effective, however, the teacher cannot dictate ahead of time what is to be the "correct" answer; to do so is to strip rhetoric of its constitutive power and equate it with a merely decorative but useless style. The panel tasked with determining the most persuasive proposal must therefore be free to make an autonomous decision, and the teacher must be prepared to follow through on this decision as long as it is within the resources ready at hand. Consequently, returning to an earlier point, the problem-situation must be carefully constructed beforehand so as not to be too small as to be trivial but not too big so as to be impossible for realistic investigation. Properly done, this method gives the teacher the ability to set limit-conditions while simultaneously allowing the students the freedom to control the course of inquiry within those limits.

For instance, say that elementary students are tasked with designing an inquiry involving anything on the school grounds. During this stage of arousing interest, students would propose various objects or environments to investigate, such as the school garden, the cafeteria kitchen, musical instruments, or athletic shoes. Each student would then argue his or her case in front of the class, members of which would vote on a course of inquiry. Following a designation of a shared interest, such as the garden, students would then advocate a particular problem they wish to be answered about that interest, such as how to keep pests away without fertilizers or to understand the role of earthworms in keeping the soil healthy. After agreeing about what problem to investigate, perhaps the deterrence of pests, students would then be broken into research teams and charged with acquiring data (about which they debate among themselves) and then suggesting solutions to the class in terms of a hypothesis. The panel of nonparticipating students would then decide which solution seems most promising, perhaps between picking off pests, using spiders, or covering the plants with a net, and that solution would either be pursued over others or that team together would be given more time and resources than the competing teams to pursue their investigation. Each team would then pursue testing their suggested solutions and would report back on their findings after a designated time to the moderating panel, who would then determine the most persuasive account for what occurred and would award a "grant," defined in whatever way the teacher finds appropriate. Of course the nature of the problem and the sophistication of the exercise will change as students mature.

The "real life" justification for this model is that it mirrors the sort of rhetorical spirit at play in the way actual scientific research occurs, particularly through the proposal and rewarding of corporate or government resources. As John Ziman observes, "project proposals and research reports are rhetorical documents. They are designed to win favor from highly critical colleagues and/or potential competitors. Thus, they try to present themselves as if they were almost unquestionable, and were already part of the archive" (Ziman 187). Furthermore, much in the way that Latour discusses rhetoric in terms of a method of recruiting allies to one's position, it shows how decisions about the future course of scientific research often rely on factors that have little to do with epistemology as such. In what Ziman calls "post-academic science," science is just as much a means to attain disinterested truth as it is "an instrument for the construction of knowledge in accord with the commercial, political or other social interests of the bodies that underwrite its production" (173). Understood as a form of practice, then, science has rhetoric at its core; for without the ability to convince funding agencies (or the publics that support them) of the value in a particular line of research, no "truth" ever comes from that research. In this way the classroom procedure of persuading a "panel" rather than simply checking the pregiven better reflects the way actual science is carried out and engages the creative imagination and reason of the students who feel they are producing something original.

Last, placing the research proposal in the hands of the students and allowing them (at least in the upper grades and at the university level) to justify their research in part through its social significance accomplish one of the core goals that Dewey set forth for education: the application of scientific knowledge to lived conditions. In *Democracy and Education*, Dewey writes that "isolation of subject matter from a social context is the chief obstruction in current practice to securing a general training of mind" (67). Yet in everyday life it is clear that our entire social environment is interpenetrated with scientific and technological matters that directly impact human welfare. Dewey observes,

> Advanced methods of dealing with such perplexing problems as insanity, intemperance, poverty, public sanitation, city planning, conservation of natural resources, the constructive use of governmental agencies for furthering the public good without weakening personal initiative, all illustrate the direct dependence of our important social concerns upon the methods and results of natural science. With respect then to both humanistic and naturalistic studies, education should take its departure from this close interdependence. It should aim not at keeping science as a study of nature apart from literature as a record of human interest, but a cross fertilizing both the natural sciences and the very human discipline such as history, literature, economics, and politics. (285)

The integration of rhetoric within the experimental classroom accomplishes this almost effortlessly, particularly as students graduate from questions of what material makes the best clothing to questions of what forms of industry increase both productivity and worker well-being or what methods of textile production produce the least environmental waste. When presented with an open-ended problem, students will naturally seek to recruit as many external allies as possible to make their research proposal attractive. Rhetoric thus becomes the vehicle by which the creative mind threads together a multiplicity of arguments into a complex web while simultaneously presenting them in a simplified and eloquent form.

CONCLUSION

To incorporate rhetoric into the experimental classroom is to incorporate passionate intelligence and rational persuasion into the structured activity of cooperative inquiry. For rhetoric is not simply about a clash of opinions or crass efforts to sway audiences through a hodgepodge of appeals; it is the situated act of resolving problematic situations by bringing multiple resources to bear on a matter of collective judgment. But that activity stands at the core of democratic social life. Democracy cannot be achieved through force, whether it be a force of arms or the force of propaganda; "it can be won only by extending the application of democratic methods, methods of consultation, persuasion, negotiation, communication, cooperative intelligence, in the task of making our own politics, industry, education, our culture generally, a servant and an evolving manifestation of democratic ideas" (Dewey, *Freedom* 175). To incorporate rhetoric within the experimental classroom is therefore to bring it that much closer to its democratic ideal, which is the intelligent management of social affairs through communication and persuasion at all levels of life.

Dewey could take this position because he believed that the concern for teaching "content," whether that content be a specialized jargon or an acquaintance with specific practical affairs, was secondary to teaching the habits of mind by which citizens approached problematic situations and came to collective judgments. For him, facts and affairs would take care of themselves as long as citizens knew how to think by having cultivated habits of "suspended judgment, of scepticism, of desire for evidence, of appeal to observation rather than sentiment, discussion rather than bias, inquiry rather than conventional idealizations" (Dewey, "Public Opinion" 335). What matters is not the *what* but the *how* of education, the *what* representing the very "content" of learning and the *how* representing the method by which learning occurs. Dewey realized that the problem of education was never about an information deficit, even if that information seemed directly relevant to matters of social justice. The problem of education was a thinking deficit. He makes this quite clear in his early writings: "I do not wish to make a plea for ignorance, but the amount of information that a person requires in an existing society is comparatively a small thing. The necessary amount of training, of control of his powers, of judgment observation, and action, is very great, but any person who has that control can, with the facilities of getting information to the libraries, magazines, and the possibility of utilizing the experiences of other people when desired, get on with a comparatively small amount of actual information" (Dewey, *Lectures* 57).

In today's mass-mediated environment, this is truer than it ever was. Indeed the problem for most people is not the lack of "facts" but the deluge of them in the form of propaganda that comes from all sides. Passive schooling, even when done with the best intentions, only facilitates this inability to think. Dewey writes,

> The result is that many young people leave school with the attitude of wanting and expecting to be told, rather than with the attitude of realizing that they must look into things, must inquire and examine. There is complaint, and rightly, that the population is too amenable, on the whole, to the influence of propaganda. But why is it? Why are so many people so ready to swallow what is persistently told them, or told them with an air of authority? Why is there so much gullibility? I do not believe that it is mainly from lack of native intelligence. It is because they have acquired the habit of listening and accepting, instead of that of inquiry, and, if you please, intelligent skepticism. (Dewey, "Education for Changing" 159–60)

Producing this kind of intelligent skepticism requires more than introducing debates in class, connecting technical issues to political and ethical inequities, or challenging the prevailing norms and attitudes of students, essential as those things are. It also requires providing them an opportunity to pursue their own interests, to generate their own aims and research agendas, and to posit their own solutions and explanations in competition with rival claims. It requires, in short, the development and application of rhetorical consciousness within a coordinated process of inquiry into a problematic situation that arouses both interest and aim; for only this way will it finally be shown "how the rhetorical tradition can work in conjunction with contemporary science education toward the end of cultivating an intelligent, creative, and critical public" (Crick, "Capital" 340). At that point the Sophists will be seen no longer as critics of empirical knowledge but as the forerunners of experimental method in the arts and sciences.

WORKS CITED

Aristotle. *Aristotle on Rhetoric: A Theory of Civic Discourse.* 2nd ed. Trans. George Kennedy. Oxford: Oxford University Press, 2007.

Aronowitz, Stanley. *Against Schooling: For an Education That Matters.* Boulder, Colo.: Paradigm, 2008.

Crick, Nathan. "'A Capital and Novel Argument': Charles Darwin's Notebooks and the Productivity of Rhetorical Consciousness." *Quarterly Journal of Speech* 91.4 (2005): 337–64.

———. "The Sophistical Attitude and the Invention of Rhetoric." *Quarterly Journal of Speech* 96.1 (2010): 25–45.

Dewey, John. *Democracy and Education.* New York: Free Press, 1944.

———. "Education as Politics." In *John Dewey: The Middle Works,* vol. 13, ed. Jo Ann Boydston, 329–34. Carbondale: Southern Illinois University Press, 1983.

———. "Education for a Changing Social Order." In *John Dewey: The Later Works,* vol. 9, ed. Jo Ann Boydston, 1–60. Carbondale: Southern Illinois University Press, 1986.

———. *Experience and Nature.* 2nd ed. New York: Dover, 1929.

———. *Freedom and Culture.* New York: Putnam, 1939.

———. *How We Think.* New York: Dover, 1997.

———. *Lectures in the Philosophy of Education: 1899.* New York: Random House, 1966.

———. "Logic." In *John Dewey: The Later Works,* vol. 8, ed. Jo Ann Boydston, 3–12. Carbondale: Southern Illinois University Press, 1986.

———. "Monastery, Bargain Counter, or Laboratory in Education?" In *John Dewey: The Later Works,* vol. 6, ed. Jo Ann Boydston, 99–111. Carbondale: Southern Illinois University Press, 1985.

———. "Review of Walter Lippmann's *Public Opinion.*" In *John Dewey: The Middle Works,* vol. 13, ed. Jo Ann Boydston, 337–44. Carbondale: Southern Illinois University Press, 1983.

———. *The School and Society and The Child and the Curriculum.* Chicago: University of Chicago Press, 1990.

———. "The Underlying Philosophy of Education." In *John Dewey: The Later Works,* vol. 8, ed. Jo Ann Boydston, 77–103. Carbondale: Southern Illinois University Press, 1986.

Freire, Paulo. *Education for Critical Consciousness.* New York: Continuum, 1974.

———. *Pedagogy of the Oppressed.* New York: Continuum, 1993.

Giroux, Henry. *The Giroux Reader.* Ed. Christopher G. Robbins. Boulder, Colo.: Paradigm, 2006.

Hooks, bell. *Teaching to Transgress: Education as the Practice of Freedom.* New York: Routledge, 1994.

Jarratt, Susan. *Rereading the Sophists: Classical Rhetoric Refigured.* Carbondale: Southern Illinois University Press, 1991.

Latour, Bruno. *Science in Action.* Cambridge, Mass.: Harvard University Press, 1987.

Plato. *Protagoras.* Trans. Stanley Lombardo and Karen Bell. In *Plato: Complete Works,* ed. John M. Cooper, 746–790. Indianapolis: Hackett, 1997.

Poulakos, John. *Sophistical Rhetoric in Classical Greece.* Columbia: University of South Carolina Press, 1995.

Shor, Ira. *Empowering Education: Critical Teaching for Social Change.* Chicago: University of Chicago Press, 1992.

Ziman, John. *Real Science: What It Is, and What It Means.* Cambridge: Cambridge University Press, 2000.

The Art of the Inartistic, in Publics Digital or Otherwise

Brian Jackson, Meridith Reed, and Jeff Swift

> Facts are stupid things—stubborn things, I should say.
>
> RONALD REAGAN, Republican National Convention, 1988

> Evidence is always construed.
>
> MARILYNNE ROBINSON, *The Death of Adam*

FACTS IN THE RASHOMON WORLD

As we write this essay, the various digital publics are buzzing over a birth certificate. On April 27, 2011, in response to continual accusations that he was born in Kenya rather than Hawaii, President Barack Obama posted his "long-form birth certificate," *a tout le monde,* on the White House's official Web site ("President Obama's"). Three years earlier, while running for president, Obama had felt obliged to provide to news organizations his short-form birth certificate, the one Hawaiians use to get drivers licenses and other official documents. Apparently this was not convincing enough for the "birthers," the right-wing political activists who had been demanding, on bumper stickers and billboards and talk radio, that Obama prove he was born in the United States and therefore eligible to keep his job as president. With potential Republican presidential candidates—specifically Mike Huckabee, Sarah Palin, Newt Gingrich, and Donald Trump—joining in to fan the flames of irrational conspiracy, Obama felt he needed to put the matter to rest. In a press conference to address what should not have needed addressing, Obama argued that political leaders would not be able to solve the serious problems facing the nation if they were distracted by egregious fictions and "if we just make stuff up and pretend that facts are not facts." In the tone of frustrated-parent-in-chief, he concluded that "we do not have time for this kind of silliness" ("President Obama's").

The *Slate* columnist Farhad Manjoo has suggested that we live in a "Rashomon world" where "the very idea of objective reality is under attack" (25). (*Rashomon,* the 1950 film by the Japanese filmmaker Akira Kurosawa, plays on the idea that reality is fragmented by the various points of view of its participants.) In the Rashomon world we hear just as many arguments about *what is* as we do about *what ought.* In rhetorical terms, in the Rashomon world we encounter an inordinate amount of stasis arguments about existence (what exists? what is real?), sometimes at the expense of arguments about quality (what is good/bad?) or policy (what should we do?). Manjoo provides compelling anecdotes that serve as dispatches from the Rashomon public sphere: disagreements about Senator John Kerry's war record, Saddam Hussein's involvement in the 9/11 attacks, climate-change science, the health of the economy, and other public issues. Manjoo is not the only journalist concerned about the health of the republic when Rashomon discourse takes over. In February 2011 the veteran PBS journalist Bill Moyers gave a speech to the History Makers, an organization of broadcasters, titled "Facts Still Matter." Moyers called on his fellow broadcasters to fight for the fragile fortunes of "factual broadcasting," the kind that cares enough to get the story straight. He concluded by arguing that "the web may be the last stand of independent factual broadcasters like you" (Moyers).

Even in postmodern times, and in spite of our healthy suspicions about facts and their broadcasters, we put incredible weight on load-bearing verities that make the world around us more structurally sound. These facts, however obviously or necessarily contested, circulate in public discourse as products of human inquiry meant to assist us in our decision-making. We concede in a post-postmodern world that we cannot know the way things "really are"; in our humility we resort to "reasoning without knowledge," as Paul Woodruff teaches us, trusting that adversarial debate will promote "good judgment" by somehow revealing the better argument, the more dependable cluster of facts (Woodruff 181). Yet it may be fair to say that the classical citizens Woodruff writes about in *First Democracy* were not as obsessed with existence stasis as we moderns are. As far as we know, Pericles never had to produce his long-form birth certificate for his enemies in order to prove he was a Greek citizen.

Facts may be stupid things, as Ronald Reagan accidentally put it, but they work collectively to constitute the world we know, or think we know, and we make important decisions based on the world we know. Thomas Jefferson believed so passionately in the free press because he thought that citizens would better safe-keep the republic if they were in possession of accurate information. However, in spite of the proverb, facts do not speak for themselves. Facts may be stubborn, but they are not arguments. They may *invite* arguments, but they do not argue by themselves. With hands folded, they stand against the wall in the gymnasium, waiting for a claim to ask them to dance. For example, the National Center for Children in Poverty tells us that fifteen million children in the United States live under the poverty level (roughly twenty-two thousand dollars a year for a family of four). This sad fact is not an argument, and therefore does not take on rhetorical importance, until someone deploys it as evidence for a claim, as Diane Ravitch does when trying to account for why Finnish students outperform American students on math tests (Ravitch). Facts get interesting to us only as they are deployed in arguments. Only then are they no longer trivia.

In this essay we explore the relationship between facts and rhetorical appeals in public discourse—a relationship we believe has been insufficiently explored, possibly because Aristotle places facts (laws, witnesses, contracts, and so forth) outside the realm of rhetorical invention. (We acknowledge here the excellent work on the rhetoricality of scientific facts by Ceccarelli, Daston, Fahnestock, Gross, Poovey, and others.) It is our contention that what Aristotle calls "inartistic proofs" (*atechnoi pisteis*) are essential components of contemporary democratic practice and a constitutive element of the "dynamic social organism" that Jackson and Clark write about in the introduction of this collection. A healthy democratic practice, then, depends on what Bruno Latour calls the imbroglio of "the real, and collective, and discursive," a working combination of science, nature, collaboration, and rhetoric (Latour 6). This is something we believe John Dewey understood very well, and we rely heavily on Dewey's *The Public and Its Problems* to articulate how facts *should* circulate in deliberative spheres as the products of shared inquiry. Dewey argued that "the power of physical facts to coerce belief does not reside in the bare phenomena" of the facts themselves (*Later Works* 2:238). Inartistic proof must be made artistic—must, in fact, be given "the potency of art" (349)—or remain trivially unhelpful. In the Rashomon world, transforming facts into useful arguments is an incredible challenge.

In the process of making this argument, we hope to contribute to a rhetoric of inartistic proof that helps us not only understand how facts circulate in publics but also how we can better prepare students to deploy inartistic proofs artistically in their own rhetoric. We are provoked by Bill Moyers's claim that the Web somehow facilitates "independent factual" news reporting, a claim that may be an article of faith for some and a sick joke for others. Web sites such as factcheck.org and politifact.com (a Pulitzer winner in 2009), not to mention the millions of political blogs that make up what blogger Scott Rosenberg believes is "our culture's indispensable public square" (Rosenberg 300), hold out at least the prospect that the Web facilitates, perhaps better than traditional media, the effective rhetoricality of facts, even if, as Manjoo has reported, there is also evidence to the contrary. To get a better sense of the ecology of inartistic proof online, we have selected ten of the top political bloggers in the United States, roughly five from each side of the political fence, and analyzed about a week of their posts. Our analysis is not meant to be quantitative; we are not interested in counting links or calculating comment averages, since this has been done already (Adamic; Benkler and Shaw; Lawrence, Sides, and Farrell; Leccese). Rather we are interested in the rhetorical moves these writers make when presenting or deploying inartistic proof. We hope our collaborative rhetorical criticism gives us a working snapshot of one corner of the ever-expanding digital pluripublic. Furthermore, since Dewey's work so richly informs our own teaching philosophies, we hope that our critical snapshot offers implications for teaching students to deploy inartistic proofs effectively as they engage in online publics. If blogs indeed constitute our culture's "indispensable public square," then *the* problem of that public, to paraphrase Dewey, is the "essential need" to improve the "methods and conditions" of digital "debate, discussion, and persuasion" (Dewey, *Later Works* 2:365).

MAKING A CASE FOR THE ART OF THE INARTISTIC

We begin with a problem that Aristotle has bestowed on us: inartistic proof, from the classical perspective we have inherited, may seem to lie outside the art of rhetoric. In terms of validity and demonstration (*apodeixis*) there are *atechnic pisteis* (nonartistic or inartistic proofs) and *entechnic pisteis* (artistic proofs), and the latter constitute the art of rhetoric, specifically the three popular proofs *ethos, pathos,* and *logos,* which are invented by the speaker (see Kennedy in Aristotle 38). Inartistic proofs, on the other hand, are "preexisting" in the world—"witnesses, testimony from torture, contracts, and such like"—and are used or deployed rather than invented. Nevertheless, after this semantic framework and his discussion of the three species or genres of rhetoric, Aristotle feels it necessary to cycle back to the *entechnic pisteis* for further comment in chapter 15 of book 1 as a capstone to the section on judicial rhetoric. Here he teaches us how to use documentary evidence such as witness, written laws, contracts, evidence, and oaths to amplify our own cases or diminish from the strength of someone else's. If rhetoric is the art of discovering the available means of persuasion, then inartistic proofs are "on hand for the speaker (or writer) independently of the art" (Grimaldi 38).

Roman rhetoricians followed Aristotle's lead in distinguishing between the persuasive strategies speakers come up with themselves (emotional appeals, for example) and the ostensibly artless task of gathering the evidence lying around for use. "For the purpose of proving," says Antonius in Cicero's dialogue, "the orator has two kinds of material at his disposal": "One consists of the things that are not thought out by the orator, but, inherent in the circumstances of the case, are treated methodically by him, such as documents, testimonies, agreements, evidence extracted by torture, laws, decrees of the Senate, judicial precedents, magistrates' rulings, legal opinions, and whatever else that is not discovered by the orator, but is presented to him by the case and the parties involved. The other kind is that which entirely depends on the reasoning and argumentation of the orator" (Cicero 154). This approach, however, elides the art required in using facts such as documents or agreements when making a case—an art that, though technically "inartistic," must be "treated methodically." Writing over 130 years later, Quintilian stuck with the "almost universal acceptance of Aristotle's primary classification" of *atechnoi* and *entechnoi,* and yet he was compelled to admit that "it generally takes high powers of eloquence" to use inartistic proof, even "though these things themselves involve no art" (Quintilian 325).

Whether *atechnoi* involve art or not, Quintilian takes great care to explain to his students how to use them effectively, thereby calling into question their seeming subordination to those strategies directly invented by the speaker. Quintilian is particularly concerned to teach would-be judicial rhetors how to support or destroy witnesses, a process he believes is the most stressful part of being in court (Quintilian 337). Considered synonymous with "evidence," witnesses do not speak for themselves: their credibility must be teased out, emphasized, contextualized, or savaged through a process that must, in the end, be considered an art, or something very much like an art.

Quintilian's approach to witnesses brings to mind a phrase we often hear when we talk about arguments: *making a case.* It is not coincidental that Stephen Toulmin, in his influential *Uses of Argument,* leans on the "jurisprudential analogy" (8) when describing the everyday "habits of inference" (4) we use to reason with each other: "Arguments can be compared with law-suits, and the claims we make and argue for in extra-legal contexts with claims made in the courts" (7). Like Aristotle, Toulmin uses the Greek word *apodeixis* to denote "the way in which conclusions are to be established" in an argument (2), and conclusions are established when arguers draw attention to "the grounds (backing, data, facts, evidence, considerations, features) on which the merits of the assertion are to depend" (12). These grounds act as witnesses in the court of argument; from here on out, it will make sense to call inartistic proofs *witnesses.* In keeping with the jurisprudential analogy, Toulmin then gives us his famous layout of arguments as an analytic for understanding how an argument marshals its witnesses, including data or "the facts we appeal to as a foundation for the claim" (90). Both the data and the backing in an argument are, in Toulmin's words, "straightforward matters-of-fact" (98), while the claims, warrants, and the relationships among the various parts are the contested stuff of argument—the values, common principles, and informal logic that make reasoning possible, and tricky (98).

Our point is that an artful rhetoric requires the artful use of what Aristotle considered artless: facts, witnesses, laws, statistics, scientific findings, and so forth. Toulmin goes even further to say that there is "no argument" without the kind of supporting data that carry a special rhetorical strength (Toulmin 98). It is a mistake, then, to perpetuate Aristotle's original *atechnic/entechnic* binary and assume that throwing data into an argument is an act as brainless as picking up a rock and throwing it. Coincidentally, Isaac Newton compared his scientific discoveries to "playing on the sea-shore," scooping up pebbles and shells while "the great ocean of truth lay all undiscovered" before him. It is a humble concession from a great thinker who certainly did more than pick up fallen apples or seashells. By contrast, Lorraine Daston, executive director of the Max Planck Institute for the History of

Science, deconstructs this unfortunate rock metaphor by pointing out that the etymology of *fact* leads us to *manufacture,* to making. The "folklore of modern facts" sees them as rocks, as unforgiving "mercenar[ies] of proof," as "the thugs of epistemology," when—in fact!—facts are "made" and should be considered "artifacts in the best sense of the word" (Daston 680).

To use so-called "inartistic" proof effectively, a speaker or writer must understand the relative strength of the witness (again, the inartistic proof) in the context of the rhetorical situation and how best to use that witness in relation to other witnesses, claims, values, narratives, assumptions, and appeals. This is the art of the inartistic.

Even in a Rashomon world, we want to ascribe a unique convincing power to witnesses, while at the same time we know we must be on guard for falsehoods and deception. As mentioned before, witnesses, like their flesh-and-blood analogs in court cases, have a special kind of rhetorical strength. The argument scholars Perelman and Olbrechts-Tyteca make their own case for this in *The New Rhetoric* by distinguishing between "the *real,* comprising facts, truths, and presumptions," and "the *preferable,* comprising values, hierarchies, and lines of argument relating to the preferable" (66). Though facts, like all elements of rhetoric, are contingent on the audience's adherence (on the legitimacy of a type of birth certificate, for example), when we use them we assume that "no further strengthening" is required (67), especially when we can agree on "conditions of verification" (such as presenting a digital copy of a birth certificate, for example) (68). Persuasive strategies that incorporate the real are meant to convince any or every reasonable person; when we address such a universal audience, we imagine that anyone who understands and accepts the witness will accept the conclusions (31). Otherwise we run the risk of looking like we are sharing a baseless opinion or just making up stuff.

This issue of rhetoric and reality is far more complicated than we have presented it. However stupid they may be, facts are not like seashells, scattered along the beach by the hand of nature and nature's God (see Poovey's *History of the Modern Fact* for the full treatment of this epistemological context). The earth may be ninety-three million miles from the sun, but a human, using the instruments of human reasoning, had to reveal that fact through the imperfect channels of human inquiry. Our investment in witnesses is contingent on our adherence to a dynamic cluster of propositions about how we know things, such as direct observation or randomized matched-pairs experiments or intuition, and how effectively we share what we know. Often the epistemological methods are just as controversial as their conclusions, as is evident in the debate on climate-change science. But even in the climate-change debate, the opponents of the anthropomorphic view—that is, the point of view that human activity causes global warming—do not question the general epistemology of science itself or scientific expertise but rather present their own list of scientists and scientific findings as counterargument. (They do, however, reject the authority of scientific consensus. See Ceccarelli.)

These debates are not necessarily alarming, since we expect to see Kuhnian paradigm changes in the way we come to conclusions about life, the world, and everything. Furthermore recent metastudies of scientific findings, particularly in the field of medicine, suggest that publication bias, selective reporting, and regression toward the mean tend to cloud even the most certain of conclusions, and we are left, even after the experiments have been conducted and their findings published, still having "to choose what to believe," in the words of the science writer Jonah Lehrer (Lehrer; see also Freedman). With apologies to Hamlet's mother, it seems that more matter requires not less art but more.

Additionally all discourse has bogs of hokum, double-talk, factoids, newspeak, flapdoodle, twaddle, hooey, baloney, balderdash, bunk, truthiness, and "wikiality" to wade through. (The last two terms were coined by the comedian Stephen Colbert.) These words are often considered synonyms for lies, but according to the philosopher Harry Frankfurt, a word such as "bullshit" is meant to describe more than simple mistruth but rather a cavalier "indifference to how things really are" and to the authority of the facts (Frankfurt 34). Such words evoke powerful emotions because in using them we assume their opposites. It is assumed that for every factoid there is a fact, for every statement of truthiness there is a truth. The Menckenesque litany of words to describe a "meh" attitude about truth simply reinforces our desperate desire to get down to the bottom of things, even if in some cases it turns out it is turtles all the way down.

What is most important to us, in the context of John Dewey's contribution to democratic culture and inquiry, is the idea that we use witnesses in argument because witnesses afford a particular strength that other appeals do not have; we assume, as Perelman and Olbrechts-Tyteca do, that witnesses—and again, we mean to evoke by that word anything categorized classically as inartistic proof—provide an aggressive *groundedness* to an argument that could, in certain situations, settle disputes, or you would hope they could. In a post-Enlightenment, technically advanced society, we depend on expert witness to help us make decisions concerning the public good. Though the epistemological value of such witnesses is open for debate, in practice we depend on them to give strength to public arguments, and we teach our students that public intellectuals are adept not only at making emotional or ethical appeals but also at gathering, analyzing, and deploying extrinsic witness as support for their arguments. And there are compelling public reasons for doing so.

DEWEY AND THE CIRCULATION OF WITNESS

As Jackson and Clark explain in the introduction to this book, John Dewey published *The Public and Its Problems* in 1927 as a response to the challenge of Walter Lippmann, a prominent democratic realist in the United States and a colleague of Dewey's at the *New Republic.* (For more rhetorical perspectives on this debate, see Hauser's *Vernacular Voices* and Jean Goodwin's essay in this volume. Goodwin effectively dispels the perception that Lippmann and Dewey were austere adversaries.)

Lippmann saw democracy as a "swarming confusion of problems" that demand of citizens a degree of intelligent reflection beyond their capacities (*Phantom Public* 24). Many public issues are complicated, in fact far too complicated to form an opinion about, especially for those citizens just trying to keep a job, raise a family, and go on vacation each year. And yet the American people are called to form opinions about these issues all the time—*literally* called, right in the middle of dinner, by opinion pollsters looking to aggregate the nation's ignorance.

In his 1922 book *Public Opinion,* Lippmann called U.S. citizens "congenital amateurs," always dependent on experts to tell them what to think and how to act (*Public Opinion* 224). Lippmann turned up the volume of his critique in 1925 with *The Phantom Public* by smashing the ideal of "the omnicompetent, sovereign citizen" with his customarily forceful prose (*Phantom Public* 39). One problem (among many) for Lippmann was that the rhetorical glut of witnesses amassed in public discourse bewilders the average voter, who is condemned to "have one's mind made the receptacle for a hullabaloo of speeches, arguments and unrelated episodes" (*Phantom Public* 44). Despite their best efforts, citizens cannot sit intelligently in judgment of expert testimony on dozens of complicated topics while simultaneously trying to live their lives. The best the public can do is use their critical thinking skills to vote in and out of office those professionals ostensibly suited to handle the complexities of governance and analyze expert opinion free from the meddling of distracted amateurs.

In his response, originally given as a series of lectures at Kenyon College, Ohio, Dewey acknowledged the fantasy of the omnicompetent citizen and other commonly noted problems of the public such as the size of the country, its heterogeneity, citizen indifference, powerful corporations, special interests, party factions, technological complexity, and distracting entertainment. Dewey made these concessions to Lippmann's realism on his way to making a bigger, more theoretically rich argument about the way a public works. The philosopher James Guinlock calls *The Public and Its Problems* Dewey's "proposal for the actual realization of intelligent conduct in practical life" as it emerges from the consequences of conjoint, or social, action (in Dewey, *Later Works* 2:xxiv). Social action has consequences, and those consequences need to be studied, monitored, and regulated for the public good. Dewey imagines "the state" as the administrative body tasked with representing the needs of experimental, reticulate, aggregated communities of interest that he calls "publics," and while his theory of plural publics is not articulated clearly here, it is obvious that he wants to situate intelligent conduct in these self-constitutive collectives.

Dewey's work is an excellent source for imagining ecologies of witness—that is, of inartistic proof—because he ties the health of democracy to our ability to inquire into the nature of things and communicate our findings to each other. As Robert Westbrook writes, *The Public and Its Problems* champions the "union of social science, effective news gathering, and skillful literary presentation of the fruits of social inquiry" (Westbrook 311). Democratic practice is an intellectual endeavor through and through. Publics form and become self-aware through "intellectual instrumentalities" that are circulated with the "tools of communication," by which he means *media* (Dewey, *Later Works* 2:323). These tools, however advanced, cannot by themselves make politicians more responsive to the needs of their constituents. Rather a public manifests its interests "more authoritatively" by learning to "define and express" those interests through rhetorical strategies meant to voice community need and represent the results of "conjoint experience" (*Later Works* 2:327). Rhetoricians appreciate Dewey's stance on this point because he argues, quite emphatically, that the primary challenge of democracy is not voter ignorance, as Lippmann argued, but the interminable need for "the improvements"—in another place he says "the perfecting" (*Later Works* 2:332)—"of the methods and conditions of debate, discussion and persuasion" (*Later Works* 2:365). These improvements include learning to communicate with "the potency of art," which is the only way public *rhetors* can evoke motivating emotions in fellow citizens (Dewey, *Later Works* 2:349; see also Crick, *Democracy* 132–35).

This perspective on rhetorical aesthetics is only half the story. Dewey is not calling for an increase in uninformed opinions, no matter how rhetorically powerful. The public square is already up to its armpits in groundless, albeit artful, emoting. Rather Dewey wants to see the marriage of aesthetic public expression with verifiable witnessing: "genuinely public policy cannot be generated unless it be informed by knowledge, and this knowledge does not exist except when there is systematic, thorough, and well-equipped search and record" (Dewey, *Later Works* 2:346). Social inquiry, by which he means something like professional exploratory research, constitutes "the intellectual wealth of the community" made public through the "flow of social intelligence" in public discourse (371). In Lippmann's realist democracy, technocratic experts act as advisers to the political elite who govern in wisdom, while citizens exercise an imperfect practical judgment to decide who, rather than what, should be believed (see Goodwin, this volume). In Dewey's idealist democracy, experts make their expertise rhetorically palatable so that they may be "absorbed and distributed" among a "genuine and effective public" (344). "Communication of the results of social inquiry," he declared, "is the same thing as the formation of public opinion," which is a more opaque way of saying that effective public judgment comes from rhetorically salient results of our best thinking, experimenting, observing, collecting, crunching, interviewing, and analyzing (345). A healthy public has a healthy ecology of witnessing.

Dewey's pragmatic approach to social inquiry and public deliberation is particularly well suited to thrive in the Rashomon world because it avoids taking a strong stand on the ontological issue of truth. As a pragmatist, Dewey adopted an instrumentalist view of truth: for the pragmatist, truth "works." In other words, "it clears up difficulties, removes obscurities, puts individuals into more experimental, less dogmatic, and less arbitrarily sceptical relations to life" (Dewey, *Middle Works* 6:9). The *true* is essentially the *dependable*, or the *warrant-able*, and it is fully realized when humans engage with their environment through experience and through "making and doing" (Dewey, *Later Works* 4:5). "The office of knowledge," Dewey wrote in *The Quest for Certainty,* is not to "uncover the antecedently real," as it has been in the Western traditions of faith and reason, but to aid "our practical judgments, to gain the kind of understanding which is necessary to deal with problems as they arise" (*Later Works* 4:14). As Danisch clarifies, this argument is central to the "invention" of a distinctly pragmatic brand of "contemporary American rhetorics" (Danisch 63).

What we are calling witnesses (that is, scientific findings, data, observation, expert testimony) have strength rhetorically, for Dewey, because they have been "shaped and tested as tools of inquiry" through public deliberation (*Later Works* 2:362). As rhetors and rhetoricians in the Rashomon world, we may have to give up our quest for certainty and absolute knowledge, but if the tools of social inquiry are sharp and if what Hauser calls "vernacular talk" helps to constitute self-aware publics (Hauser 103), we can at least expect that opinions "formed and held in the absence of evidence" will decline (Dewey, *Later Works* 2:362). At least that is the hope we cling to as students of rhetoric as democratic practice.

DIGITAL WITNESSING AS PRACTICE AND PEDAGOGY

What role, then, do blogs play in circulating witnesses in pubic deliberation as a mode of democratic practice? Before answering this question, and we think it is an important question, we need to admit the obvious, that it is difficult to guess what John Dewey, who died in 1952, would think about blogs and blogging (see Crick, "Search" for a noble attempt). On the one hand, Dewey would be enthusiastic about the prospect of ordinary citizens engaged in contributing their arguments to our collective wisdom. (Inspired now by Dewey's effulgence, we will call it collective wisdom without irony.) *The Public and Its Problems* is a plea for the kind of happy confluence of mass distribution, mass participation, and artful communication made possible by new media through blogging, microblogging, and crowdsourcing. We imagine he would have been pleased with the experimental nature of the Web, which is perhaps the most collectively generated human tool in history, providing, at least ostensibly, the "intellectual means of making discoveries of phenomena having social import" (Dewey, *Later Works* 2:362).

On the other hand, Dewey's political theory seems quaintly tied to a kind of idealized community talk that requires "face-to-face intercourse" among close-quarter equals in a "neighborly community" (Dewey, *Later Works* 2:367, 368). Coupled with Dewey's vague and incomplete notions of democratic machinery, this quaintness, as Robert Westbrook writes, turns out to be a "less than effective counter to democratic realism" (Westbrook 318). The point is that blogs have by and large taken local geography, and certainly face-to-face public engagement, out of the equation. While they maintain a semblance of dialogue through their comments and linking practices, blogs do not generally imitate the neighborhood conversations that Dewey imagined as the process by which publics constitute themselves. We say "generally" because there are likely hundreds of thousands of limited-scope blogs that serve local communities in ways that are difficult to quantify or analyze and that may, in fact, approximate what Dewey had in mind. Other forms of social media such as Facebook may be even more promising in terms of local engagement.

What blogs do promise, unequivocally, is information—information about politics and public problems. Since the invention of Web browsers, reverse-chronology posting, and user-generated Web content we have experienced a remarkable transformation in the way so-called inartistic proof is generated and circulated within and across publics. The pioneers of the medium—for example, Justin Hall, Dave Winer, and Jorn Barger—rode a dramatic, narcissistic learning curve of bold, self-motivated experimentation on the Web by creating the first blogs whose purpose was to link to cool and crazy stuff, invent a digital ethos, and aggregate everything out there (see Rosenberg). There were no editors and hardly any self-editing. The point was mass, uninhibited circulation of Digital Self with an open invitation to an often unknown audience to join each blogger by commenting and linking back. The political implications of blogging, especially its *kairotic* power, were not fully realized until after the September 11, 2001, terrorist attacks on the World Trade Center in New York City, when the "nascent political-blogging scene" took off in a "frenzy of posting and linking" (Rosenberg 137).

Political blogs created a ground-up ecology of witness that spanned the political spectrum, with leaders in the new field such as Josh Marshall of Talking Points Memo setting standards for aggregating stories and facts and then adding "judicious commentary to them" in an attempt to get at something like the truth coupled with argument (Rosenberg 144). Frothy editorializing was of course central to the new medium, but so was fact-checking and truth-telling. In 2002 Senate Majority Leader Trent Lott made remarks at Strom Thurmond's one-hundredth birthday party that seemed a bit too nostalgic for the days of segregation. Using his own reporting, other news sources, and contributions from readers, Josh Marshall forced the story back into the mainstream media by demonstrating that Lott, who eventually resigned his Senate seat, had made similar comments throughout his career. Other Internet scalps have followed as hundreds of thousands, if not millions, of people—most of them amateurs—have taken to blogging as citizen journalists and self-proclaimed political watchdogs, trying to drum up audiences by creating stylistically captivating content that recycles and repurposes the inartistic proofs created by scientists and other academics, the mainstream media, and other social observers. Of course bloggers also create their own witnessing strategies when they do original reporting from their own experiences and investigations.

Political blogs seem to offer a rhetorical atmosphere that closely resembles what John Dewey had in mind when he longed for a better deliberative system to aggregate the results of inquiry and combine them with the back and forth of public opinion (Freelon). Again, it is important to note that Dewey was not interested in the circulation of opinion *merely* but in the interrelationship between opinion and inquiry, by which he meant the results of research studies that produce findings that can be depended on. These findings become the backing, in Toulmin's sense, or in other words "the foundation" for our claims (Toulmin 90). In their textbook on argumentative writing, Ramage, Bean, and Johnson call this the "rhetorical use of evidence," and it is a political blog's specialty (Ramage, Bean, and Johnson 89). In addition to the various rhetorical affordances of the genre—networked credibility, openness to audience participation, a compelling voice, professional Web design, and *kairotic* updating—a blogger's stream of reliable (credible, verifiable, more true than truthy) content is the tool by which a persuasive public ethos is constructed (Warnick 46–50; see also Johnson and Kaye "Choosing"; Perlmutter and Schoen). In recent studies viewers have found political blogs to be more credible than mainstream media sources (Johnson and Kaye "Wag the Blog"; Rettberg 92). This credibility is due in no small part to the artful circulation of witness, aided by the Web's openness to user-generated content and collaborations through which the wisdom of crowds manifests itself.

Surely political blogs also have troubling rhetorical challenges built into the affordances and constraints of the medium. The political theorist Cass Sunstein, for example, has argued using early data on link traffic that political blogs create "echo chambers" and "information cocoons" in which members of digital publics "talk and listen mostly to one another," thereby crippling the free flow of inquiry and argument necessary for publics to develop practical wisdom (Sunstein 44). Some blogs become popular simply by cannibalizing from mainstream news sources, which evokes questions of ethics in journalism (Phillips). The medium favors the hot current story so steroidally that it has a tough time developing, investigating, or percolating; it favors "nanostories" that contribute to "nanopolitics" (Wasik 151, 158). Anonymity is also a problem. When individuals are neither inclined nor forced to reveal who they are in posts and comments, participants more easily fall into flame wars, ad hominem attacks, and other extremes that work to ratchet up hostility without contributing to the public good. The Web, in the words of Evgeny Morozov, is "an unruly tool" that "in the hands of overconfident people" can work against the goals of democracy in various ways (Morozov 284). At the very least, the blogosphere's salutary benefits on public life may have been overstated here and there by its enthusiasts. In the spirit of Dewey's work, we may need yet more inquiry into our tools of inquiry.

In spite of the challenges, educators have seen blogs as a potential site for helping students develop the "trained capacities" that Dewey wrote about in his early work. In "Ethical Principles Underlying Education," a tract he wrote in 1897 while he was developing his Laboratory School at the University of Chicago, Dewey argued that the ultimate end of education is the growth of the learner in her power—"trained capacities of control"—to act in her social environment to serve personal and social ends (Dewey, *Early Works* 5:75). Individual growth in rhetorical capacities finds its ultimate purpose as students learn to engage with others on issues that matter most to them, and this engagement has been generously advanced by user-generated Web programs. In the twenty-first century, learning to be a rhetor in personal, professional, and public life means learning to use digital tools most effectively to establish a networked ethos, providing the kind of artistic witnessing that creates traffic and conversation. Blogs have become a serviceable tool for supporting this kind of rhetorical education (Brooke; Fernheimer and Nelson; Lowe and Williams; Penrod; Rice; Tryon). Furthermore they have the potential to help us reimagine creatively one of the most popular (at least among teachers) witnessing assignments: the research paper.

The researched argument has been central to the undergraduate rhetoric curriculum for more than a century. In public speaking textbooks such as Stephen Lucas's *The Art of Public Speaking,* students are admonished to practice "the skillful use of supporting materials" to avoid the "unfounded assertions" that make oral arguments unconvincing (Lucas 140). In the writing curriculum, where the idea of inartistic proof is more central than it is in the speech curriculum, the "documented essay" became a popular assignment as English professors in the nineteenth century returned to the United States from their studies in Germany with new notions of specialized discourse that used notes and bibliographies as backing (Russell 78). By the 1960s over 80 percent of all writing courses required a research paper or something similarly supported by witness, and that number has not changed much since then, even if, as Carra Hood notes, the assignment has its critics (Hood). Richard Larson, to take one popular example, calls it a "non-form of writing," and others have dismissed it as an irrelevant schoolish exercise (Larson; Smit). Even the *New York Times* recently held an online debate titled "Are Research Papers a Waste of Time?" Nevertheless every writing handbook on the market has several sections reserved to instruct students how to find, evaluate, and incorporate witness into academic arguments. It is an enduring part of rhetoric pedagogy.

The medium of the blog threatens to stir things up a bit. For over a century instructors have taught research writing as a process of producing rows and rows of double-spaced prose with in-text citations as evidence, backed by a works-cited page that slavishly follows the arbitrary minutiae of an often arbitrarily selected style guide to keep students on the level. Even the casual blog reader knows how different the digital medium is from the traditional school exercise, and we will have more to say on this point after sharing the results of our study. As teachers of writing, we wanted to know how inartistic proofs circulate in these venues and how—or whether—rhetoric teachers should respond as digital rhetoric becomes more of a fixture in the undergraduate curriculum.

To get a sense of things, we decided to analyze political blogs to account for the new ecology of witnessing that the medium affords. Though not nearly as formal or scientific, our study complements journalism professor Mark Leccese's 2009 study of how political bloggers link to various kinds of evidence to support their arguments. Using data from his own and previous studies, Leccese reports that political bloggers link to mainstream media sources about 50 percent of the time; use original reporting in 12 percent of their posts; link to themselves in 15 percent of their links, other blogs in 23 percent (and 90 percent of those links go to sources that share the political ideology of the blogger), and primary sources in 15 percent (Leccese 580, 585). He concludes that "political blogs are like a newspaper comprised of only op-ed pages featuring opinion columnists who gather most of their information from secondary sources" (587). Because of their derivative witnessing, Leccese feels that political blogs have dubious value for public deliberation, as long as they continue to recycle mainstream jetsam rather than find more credible, convincing inartistic proofs as support.

Our informal study confirms this hunch but also complicates it in ways we believe are instructive for understanding the affordances and constraints of witness ecology and what it implies for teaching students to use witnesses in digital spaces. To that end we selected ten bloggers from the Web site Technorati's top one hundred political bloggers list and analyzed their witnessing (that is, linking) for a week. We soon found that the Technorati list is so dynamic that no single blogger stays in the same ranking for long. The most popular blogs are news aggregators such as Huffington Post or CNN Political Ticker. Nevertheless these ten bloggers have a robust audience, and they cycle in and out of the list of the top fifty political bloggers on the Web. To get some balance, we selected five blogs with conservative leanings, four with liberal leanings, and one that is difficult to pin down ideologically (Andrew Sullivan), and he probably prefers it that way. We followed previous studies by tracking how many links bloggers use per post (the average was 2.8), where those links lead, and how the links function as evidence intended to add more-than-mere-opinion ballast to the posts.

So how do inartistic proofs circulate in the political blogosphere? It is hard to say. We notice that our informal study seems to support Leccese's claim that blogs use mostly secondary witnessing—in other words, over 60 percent of the links we studied sent us to other blogs or the mainstream media. Three of the bloggers we analyzed linked to themselves in about 30 percent of their posts, suggesting that narcissism complements parasitism. However, we believe that Leccese's academic journalism frame of reference leads him to dismiss much of what these bloggers are doing by considering their linking practices mostly derivative. He assumes that if a blogger does not write or cite (via hyperlink) direct primary reporting, he or she has not contributed much to the circulation of public facts, when in fact much of what a blogger does is aggregate evidence and present it artistically through the often fiery language of blogging. In a very real way the hyperlink itself functions as a witness, an inartistic proof in its own right no matter where it takes us, much like a quote functions in an academic research paper. Here again Aristotle's conception of inartistic proof proves to be unhelpful. Each link in effect delivers us to material the writer did not technically "invent." The problem is trying to separate argument from evidence enough so that the latter can be analyzed. A few examples of this kind of analysis from our group may demonstrate our point.

Matthew Yglesias, a once-prolific blogger for the Center for American Progress who joined the journalism team at *Slate* in November 2011, seems to us to be doing far more useful things than cannibalizing content. When Yglesias incorporates a source—another blog, say—he generally takes two or three paragraphs from the linked-to source and posts them verbatim into his own post, marking the relevant sentences in bold to draw attention to the most salient points. This simple act of witnessing creates salience by repurposing material for a new audience. While Yglesias does not often link to primary sources directly, he demonstrates Dewey's vision for public deliberation by circulating arguments that lead us, eventually, to compelling evidence. He regularly directs us to other bloggers who have access to primary material—research studies, academic papers, scientific evidence, investigative reporting, and so forth. For example, in one post on monetary policy, Yglesias provides a link to the Board of Governors of the Federal Reserve System, a block quote from Fed chairman Ben Bernanke, a few bolded lines from that quote, his own commentary on why Bernanke's argument is weak, and then a link to an Associated Press story that, in addition to embedding statistics from stock indexes, quotes a counterstatement by the Federal Reserve Bank of Dallas president. Obviously as a progressive, Yglesias had a political agenda for amassing these witnesses, but he works to create a smooth ecology of witnessing by giving the reader direct hyperlinked access to the facts and authority on which his argument depends. As Dewey knew well, our practical wisdom develops as we move critically from claims to reasons to data to assumptions, and this process is aided—if not completely made easier—by digital rhetoric.

On the other side of the political spectrum, Michelle Malkin, who blogs at her own Web site for an audience of conservative readers, follows a different style. She also will occasionally use primary sources as the basis for her argument and interprets these facts for her audience. For example, she links the 2011 Annual Report to Congress on White House staff salaries to provide evidence for her claim that Obama's staff in the Office of Public Engagement are overpaid. Most frequently, however, Malkin depends on linking to mainstream media sources and her own blog entries to support her arguments and claims. For example, in a post titled "Beware of Dr. Jihad," Malkin links to four mainstream news sources in the first two paragraphs to establish the threat of bombs that have been surgically implanted into the body to avoid detection. The use of the mainstream news sources here establishes context for Malkin, who can then spend the rest of the post developing her claim that well-educated terrorists pose a major threat. In another post Malkin links to news story after news story of "Obamacare fables," stories of individuals who were used as witnesses for the perils of life without health insurance. The articles to which Malkin links explain how the stories of these individuals were exaggerated to benefit the Obama campaign's push for the health-care bill. In these types of posts, Malkin lets the news stories pile up until they have told the story for her. If she comments on these individually, it is minimal.

Ben Smith, blogging at Politico for both liberal and conservative readers, provides interesting fodder for analysis of the way inartistic proofs circulate in the blogosphere. Smith is a highly prolific blogger, writing around ten posts a day. His posts typically take one of three different forms: the link dump; the brief post featuring one or two links and some minimal commentary; and the longer post featuring a few more links and more extensive analysis and commentary. Most of his posts are of the second kind. In these types of posts, he will quote a paragraph or several paragraphs from a link and include a sentence or two either introducing and contextualizing the quote or explaining briefly why it is noteworthy or how it fits into the current political discussion. For example, in a post entitled "Writing Off Pawlenty," Smith quotes briefly from two news articles that point out some of the weaknesses of Governor Tim Pawlenty's campaign for president. Then Smith ends the post with three sentences suggesting what these commentaries might mean for Pawlenty's chances for success. This is the most typical format for a Ben Smith blog post. Smith ends each day with "link dump" posts, a collection of what he calls "remainders": links to interesting tidbits and news items, all summarized in a sentence each with no commentary.

The longer posts from Smith demonstrate another, more involved method of utilizing inartistic proofs. In these posts Smith spends more time analyzing his sources and interpreting facts. A post entitled "No exodus?" about Jewish support of President Obama provides an interesting example. Smith begins this post with a graphic showing the results for U.S. Jews of a Gallup poll concerning the May 2011 job approval of President Obama. He also links to and quotes from a Lydia Saad article on Gallup.com about the poll. The paragraph of Saad's article that Smith quotes challenges Smith's earlier assertion in a Politico article that Jewish support of President Obama was waning. Saad uses the Gallup poll as rhetorical witness to counter Smith's conclusions drawn from interviews with American Jews. Smith in turn counters Saad's conclusions and says that the poll, as witness, really is not a valid basis for commentary since the sample size is so small. Having discounted this inartistic proof, Smith then clarifies and reasserts the claims of his argument and supports his claim with several unpublished paragraphs from Smith's original Politico article (including quotes from interviews Smith conducted with politically active Jewish Americans) and with a blog post from Greg Sargeant about how the Obama campaign plans to counter conservative criticism of Obama's stance on Israel. Essentially, Smith concludes, if the Obama campaign is planning to make countering this conservative criticism a priority, then there must be a fear that Jewish support may be in decline. This example is interesting because it demonstrates the kinds of discussions happening in the blogosphere about the use of inartistic proof and what it can and cannot support. Participants in online political debate must be able to artfully deploy witnesses and analyze the way others are deploying and interpreting witnesses as well.

Often, as in Malkin's case, the relationship between commentary/argument and witnessing/supporting is complicated by the nature of the medium. Bloggers build a political ethos over time by delivering content—both commentary and witnessing—consistently and constructing a public persona by the way they write, post, share, and link. Sometimes bloggers, like Smith, circulate witnesses without any commentary in link dumps—posts with anywhere from five to twenty-five links embedded in sentences that reveal little or nothing about the blogger's opinion on the subject. The reader needs to be familiar with the ethos of the blogger in order to parse the rhetorical purpose of the witnessing. If you isolate one post, you may get nothing more than a time-lapse video of a sunset or a link to the outcome of a reality TV show. True, these blogs often function as repositories for bloggers' idiosyncratic interests. But most of the time our bloggers were on message, and they were bringing the resources of the Web to bear on the political issues they wanted to establish as rhetorically salient.

What we saw in our informal analysis is a variety of ways to participate in the ecology of witnessing—some rhetorically successful, some weak and irresponsible. Though it is difficult for us to make conclusive, quantitative judgments about link behavior, a clear picture of the affordances and constraints of digital witnessing began to unfold. As teachers we see how digital rhetoric challenges us to rethink the way we teach students how to use evidence effectively in their arguments. As mentioned earlier, the genre most often used to teach students the rhetorical use of evidence is the research paper—a nineteenth-century inheritance from the German model of expertise assigned to introduce students to the normative standards of the academy (that is, writing disciplined, reasoned, supported arguments across the disciplines; see Thaiss and Zawacki). The standard research paper is an argument supported by sources that the student finds compelling—or simply finds. Handbooks teach students how to integrate sources rhetorically by using quotations "appropriately," "setting off long quotations," and using "signal phrases" to provide context and authority for sources (Hacker and Sommers 469, 471, 473). Generally a student gets one shot to make her/his case in one paper with perhaps a dozen or fewer sources. While this model perhaps serves the institution's need for students prepared to write research papers, it does not introduce students to the rich rhetorical world of witnessing that is available online.

When we engage in online rhetoric, we participate in the unscripted aggregation of generous meaning-making that Clay Shirky calls "cognitive surplus." The Web releases the creative capacities of congenital amateurs who throw their stuff out there for other amateurs and also professionals to read, critique, add to, or borrow. While Shirky acknowledges that cognitive surplus often leads to massively popular Web sites devoted to videos of cats falling into toilets—and let us not pooh-pooh the small pleasures we enjoy on an interminable academic afternoon—he also explains how civic value is created through the digital pooling of resources, including the circulation of rhetorical evidence (Shirky 174–75). Individuals who used to be passive media watchers now become continuous volunteer content sharers across multiple platforms that invite, even demand, content sharing. Call it cannibalism if you will, but these bloggers serve as "gatewatchers" who monitor the output of the media and the academy and help us economize our already-fractured attention (Rettberg 103). This practice can be productively cross-referenced with Michael Schudson's argument that in an information glut, the best kind of citizens are "monitorial citizens" who "scan (rather than read) the informational environment in a way so that they may be alerted on a very wide variety of issues for a very wide variety of ends and may be mobilized around those issues in a large variety of ways" (Schudson 310). Schudson argues that this kind of monitoring is more sophisticated than mere "information-gathering" (311). It requires research acumen and rhetorical literacy.

But Schudson wrote *The Good Citizen* before the networking potential of the Web was realized, so he did not imagine citizens monitoring for each other by actually producing content that anyone could see. If we are willing to think ourselves out of research-paper pedagogy, we can help our students see themselves as Deweyan participants in the back-and-forthness of publics, aggregating witnesses through the linking and sharing practices used by popular political bloggers. Our informal analysis suggests that bloggers gain power by delivering content consistently so that over time they develop an ethos for the kind of witnessing they provide. Students should learn to use blogs, for example, as a commonplace book for dumping sources and thoughts as their arguments develop. They must learn how to direct readers to salient witnesses whose authority is tacitly accepted, and then they need to put those witnesses to work rhetorically in their arguments. They should also learn to engage in online dialogue with other students attempting to do the same so that digital *dissoi logoi* can be constituted in critical engagement with others (see Crick in this volume). In sum, digital witnessing offers rhetorical amateurs the chance to participate in "the flow of social intelligence" by sharing their inquiry with other citizens (Dewey, *Later Works* 2:371).

CLOSING THE BOOK ON "INARTISTIC PROOF"

We have argued that Aristotle's enduring distinction between artistic and inartistic proof is not helpful for understanding the way facts and other evidence circulate in real use. Far from speaking for themselves, facts and other collaboratively validated forms of evidence remain trivia until they are deployed in arguments as reasons, warrants, and/or backing. Though we must not be naive about the facts that circulate in public discourse, affixed as they are with various seals of specialized authority, we must recognize that without load-bearing verities we are often left with "says you!" rhetoric. We used the word "witnessing" to describe the rhetorical strategy of bringing in additional evidence or aggressive groundedness to support claims, even though that groundedness, like everything else, is subject to rhetorical inquiry and assent. We look to John Dewey's *The Public and Its Problems* as the primary articulation of how practical wisdom is constituted not only through artful communication but also through the grounded artifacts of social inquiry. Witnesses circulate even more aggressively in digital spaces, and we took a brief look at the way professional and amateur political bloggers circulate rhetorical evidence in their linking practices. These practices suggest a new way of teaching students how to incorporate salient witnesses into a digital platform over time, thus developing an ethos of witnessing.

We end with optimistic caution about the merits of rhetorical evidence in the Rashomon world. Going digital will not solve the serious rhetorical challenges that come from using facts. Recently on the *Opinionator* blog of the *New York Times*, the Notre Dame philosopher Gary Gutting described an online debate about President Barack Obama's budget proposal. A Stanford economist said one thing, a Nobel-laureate economist said another, and they went back and forth online, presenting what seemed to be at the time conclusive facts to support each side of the debate. Gutting pointed out that fact-based rhetoric depends on inductive reasoning from evidence that makes a conclusion probable but not inevitable. He writes, "Even a strong argument from purely factual premises is open to refutation unless we are assured that it has taken account of *all relevant facts*. Realistically, of course, we can never be sure that we have taken account of all relevant facts, especially with an issue as complex as a national budget. But a good inductive argument requires getting as close as we can to this ideal" (Gutting). It is difficult to argue that undergraduates in a first-year writing or speaking class can even begin to approach the ideal of "a good inductive argument," but we want them to try anyway. With a little help from digital platforms, our students can aggregate and situate compelling evidence to make public arguments about issues that matter to everyone. Dewey's democratic faith encourages us to trust that as we refine our communication practices, we will be more fit to govern ourselves. That refining process must include our best efforts to teach students how to use inartistic proofs artistically as they learn to contribute to the social flow of intelligence that makes democratic culture healthy.

WORKS CITED

Adamic, Lada. "The Political Blogosphere and the 2004 U.S. Election: Divided They Blog." In *Workshop on the Weblogging Ecosystem*. Chiba, Japan, 2005.

Aristotle. *On Rhetoric.* 2nd ed. Trans. George A. Kennedy. New York: Oxford University Press, 2007.

Benkler, Yochai, and Aaron Shaw. *A Tale of Two Blogospheres: Discursive Practices on the Left and Right.* Cambridge, Mass. : Berkman Center for Internet and Society at Harvard, 2010. PDF. Web. (accessed 9 Mar 2011). Print.

Brooke, Collin. "Weblogs as Deictic Systems: Centripetal, Centrifugal, and Small-World Blogging." In *Computers and Composition* (2005). Web (accessed November 16, 2011) http://www.bgsu.edu/departments/english/cconline/brooke/brooke.htm

Ceccarelli, Leah. "Manufactured Scientific Controversy: Science, Rhetoric, and Public Debate." *Rhetoric & Public Affairs* 14.2 (2011): 195–228.

Cicero. *On the Ideal Orator.* Trans. James L. May and Jakob Wisse. New York: Oxford University Press, 2001.

Crick, Nathan. *Democracy and Rhetoric: John Dewey on the Arts of Becoming.* Columbia: University of South Carolina Press, 2010.

———. "The Search for a Purveyor of News: The Dewey/Lippmann Debate in an Internet Age." *Critical Studies in Media Communication* 26.5 (2009): 480–97. ComAbstracts Database. Web (accessed June 15, 2011) http://www.cios.org/www/opnab.htm

Daston, Lorraine. "Hard Facts." In *Making Things Public: Atmospheres of Democracy,* ed. Bruno Latour and Peter Weibel, 680–85. Cambridge, Mass.: MIT Press, 2005.

Dewey, John. *The Early Works, 1882–1898.* 5 vols. Ed. Jo Ann Boydston. Carbondale: Southern Illinois University Press, 1967–72.

———. *The Later Works, 1925–1953.* 17 vols. Ed. Jo Ann Boydston. Carbondale: Southern Illinois University Press, 1981–90.

———. *The Middle Works, 1899–1924.* 15 vols. Ed. Jo Ann Boydston. Carbondale: Southern Illinois University Press, 1976–83.

Fahnestock, Jeanne. "Accommodating Science: The Rhetorical Life of Scientific Facts." *Written Communication* 3.3 (1986): 275–96.

Fernheimer, Janice Wendi, and Thomas J. Nelson. "Bridging the Composition Divide: Blog Pedagogy and the Potential for Agonistic Classrooms." *Currents in Electronic Literacy* 9 (Fall 2005): n.pag. Web (accessed November 16, 2011) http://currents.cwrl.utexas.edu/fall05/fernheimernelson.html

Frankfurt, Harry G. *On Bullshit.* Princeton, N.J.: Princeton University Press, 2005.

Freedman, David H. "Lies, Damned Lies, and Medical Science." *Atlantic* (November 2010): 76–86.

Freelon, Deen. "Analyzing Online Political Discussion Using Three Models of Democratic Communication." *New Media & Society* 12.7 (2010): 1172–90. Sage Publications. Web (accessed June 15, 2011) http://nms.sagepub.com/content/12/7.toc

Grimaldi, William M. A. *Aristotle,* Rhetoric *I: A Commentary.* New York: Fordham University Press, 1980.

Gross, Alan G. *The Rhetoric of Science.* Cambridge, MA: Harvard UP, 1990. Print.

Gutting, Gary. "Arguing from the Facts." *Opinionator,* July 6, 2011. Web (accessed November 1, 2011) http://opinionator.blogs.nytimes.com/2011/07/06/arguing-from-the-facts/

Hacker, Diana, and Nancy Sommers. *Rules for Writers.* 7th ed. Boston: Bedford/St. Martin's, 2012.

Hauser, Gerard. *Vernacular Voices.* Columbia: University of South Carolina Press, 1999.

Hood, Carra Leah. "Ways of Research: The Status of the Traditional Research Paper Assignment in First-Year Writing/Composition Courses." *Composition Forum* 22 (Summer 2010): n.pag. Web (accessed February 15, 2011) http://compositionforum.com/issue/22/

Johnson, Thomas, and Barbara Kaye. "Choosing Is Believing? How Web Gratifications and Reliance Affect Internet Credibility among Politically Interested Users." *Atlantic Journal of Communication* 18 (January 2010): 1–21. ComAbstracts Web (accessed June 15, 2011) http://www.cios.org/www/abstract.htm

———. "Wag the Blog: How Reliance on Traditional Media and the Internet Influence Credibility Perceptions of Weblogs among Blog Users." *Journalism and Mass*

Communication Quarterly 81.3 (2004): 622–42. Academic Search Premiere. Web (accessed June 15, 2011) http://www.ebscohost.com/academic/academic-search-premier

Larson, Richard. "The 'Research Paper' in the Writing Course: A Non-Form of Writing." *College English* 44.8 (1982): 811–16.

Latour, Bruno. *We Have Never Been Modern.* Trans. Catherine Porter. Cambridge, Mass.: Harvard University Press, 1993.

Lawrence, Eric, John Sides, and Henry Farrell. "Self-Segregation or Deliberation? Blog Readership, Participation, and Polarization in American Politics." *Perspectives on Politics* 8.1 (2009): 141–157.

Leccese, Mark. "Online Information Sources of Political Blogs." *Journalism and Mass Communication Quarterly* 86.3 (Autumn 2009): 578–93.

Lehrer, Jonah. "The Truth Wears Off." *New Yorker,* December 13, 2010. Web (accessed June 27, 2011) http://www.newyorker.com/reporting/2010/12/13/101213fa_fact_lehrer

Lippmann, Walter. *The Phantom Public.* New York: Macmillan, 1925.

———. *Public Opinion.* New York: Macmillan, 1961.

Lowe, Charles, and Terra Williams. "Moving to the Public: Weblogs in the Writing Classroom." In *Into the Blogosphere: Rhetoric, Community, and Culture of Weblogs,* ed. Laura Gurak et al. 2004. Web (accessed November 16, 2011) http://blog.lib.umn.edu/blogosphere/moving_to_the_public.html

Lucas, Stephen E. *The Art of Public Speaking.* 3rd ed. New York: Random House, 1989.

Manjoo, Farhad. *True Enough.* New York: Wiley, 2008.

Morozov, Evgeny. *The Net Delusion.* New York: PublicAffairs, 2011.

Moyers, Bill. "Facts Still Matter." Speech. February 14, 2011. *Truthout.org* (accessed May 23, 2011).

Penrod, Diane. *Using Blogs to Enhance Literacy: The Next Powerful Step in 21st-Century Learning.* Lanham, Md.: Rowman & Littlefield, 2007.

Perelman, Chaim, and L. Olbrechts-Tyteca. *The New Rhetoric.* Trans. John Wilkinson and Purcell Weaver. Notre Dame, Ind.: University of Notre Dame Press, 1969.

Perlmutter, David D., and Mary Schoen. "'If I Break a Rule, What Do I Do, Fire Myself': Ethics Codes of Independent Bloggers." *Journal of Mass Media Ethics* 22.1 (2007): 37–48. ComAbstracts Database. Web (accessed June 15, 2011) http://www.cios.org/www/abstract.htm

Phillips, Angela. "Transparency and the New Ethics of Journalism." *Journalism Practice* 4 (August 2010): 373–82. ComAbstracts Database. Web (accessed April 7, 2011) http://www.cios.org/www/abstract.htm

Poovey, Mary. *A History of the Modern Fact.* Chicago: University of Chicago Press, 1998.

"President Obama's Long Form Birth Certificate." White House Blog, April 27, 2011. Web (accessed April 29, 2011).

Quintilian. *The Orator's Education.* Bks. 3–5. Ed. and trans. Donald A. Russell. Cambridge, Mass.: Harvard University Press, 2001.

Ramage, John D., John C. Bean, and June Johnson. *Writing Arguments: A Rhetoric with Readings.* 8th ed. New York: Longman, 2010.

Ravitch, Diane. "The Myth of Charter Schools." *New York Review of Books,* November 11, 2010. Web (accessed May 23, 2011) http://www.nybooks.com/articles/archives/2010/nov/11/myth-charter-schools/

Rettberg, Jill Walker. *Blogging.* Cambridge: Polity, 2008.

Rice, Jeff. *The Rhetoric of Cool: Composition and New Media.* Carbondale: Southern Illinois University Press, 2007.

Rosenberg, Scott. *Say Everything.* New York: Three Rivers, 2009.

Russell, David R. *Writing in the Academic Disciplines.* 2nd ed. Carbondale: Southern Illinois University Press, 2002.

Schudson, Michael. *The Good Citizen.* New York: Free Press, 1998.

Shirky, Clay. *Cognitive Surplus.* New York: Penguin, 2010.

Smit, David W. *The End of Composition Studies.* Carbondale: Southern Illinois University Press, 2007.

Sunstein, Cass. *Republic.com 2.0.* Princeton, N.J.: Princeton University Press, 2009.

Thaiss, Chris, and Terry Myers Zawacki. *Engaged Writers and Dynamic Disciplines.* Portsmouth, N.H.: Boynton/Cook, 2006.

Toulmin, Stephen. *The Uses of Argument.* Updated ed. Cambridge: Cambridge University Press, 2003.

Tryon, Charles. "Writing and Citizenship: Using Blogs to Teach First-Year Composition." *Pedagogy* 6.1 (2006): 128–32.

Warnick, Barbara. *Rhetoric Online.* New York: Peter Lang, 2007.

Wasik, Bill. *And Then There's This.* New York: Viking, 2009.

Westbrook, Robert. *John Dewey and American Democracy.* Ithaca, N.Y.: Cornell University Press, 1991.

Woodruff, Paul. *First Democracy.* Oxford: Oxford University Press, 2005.

Dewey's Progressive Pedagogy for Rhetorical Instruction

Teaching Argument in a Nonfoundational Framework

Donald C. Jones

I first read *Experience and Education* while I was an undergraduate student, and I found that Dewey explained many of the frustrations I had felt back in high school. I was one of those students who loved to read, but I was completely turned off, for instance, when I was told that we would be reading Shakespeare because he had "stood the test of time." I was expected to read and revere the immortal bard just as generations of students had before me. As I read *Experience and Education,* I realized that Dewey was offering an alternative to the traditional education that had frustrated me. He provided more engaging methods as well as more compelling reasons for education. For example, canonical literature such as Shakespeare's plays could be read for an interpretation that enriched my own life. When I first read Dewey on education, I wrote "brilliant" in the margins, and now on the best days of my own teaching I like to think I still can feel some of that brilliance.

On these days I am able to pose questions, elicit comments, build a discussion, and help students reach important insights and genuine understanding. Yet on other days, I must admit, as Dewey cautions, progressive education that seems "simple" enough in theory is not so "easy" to practice (*Experience and Education* 30). On these lesser days I may be able to lead students to recognize, say, a particular fallacy in an argument, but their understanding ends there, and I will find myself presenting—or worse yet, repeating—the rest of the logical fallacies. Such repetition of fixed knowledge, which Dewey dismisses as "dictation," rarely fosters true learning and genuine understanding (72).

After one of these mediocre lessons, I find little solace in the fact that others too find progressive education to be, as Dewey predicts, a "harder business" to sustain (*Experience and Education* 76). For example, many argument textbooks employ a progressive approach at least as they begin. These textbooks often appeal to the experiences of their undergraduate audience by highlighting our daily arguments over familiar issues. For instance, the opening of *The Well-Crafted Argument* by Fred White and Simone Billings begins by asserting, "All of us find occasions to argue every day" and offering such examples as arguing over restaurant choices, favorite movies, and educational reform (2). In *Everything's an Argument,* Andrea Lunsford and John Ruszkiewicz extend this experiential approach to such nonverbal disputes as "the clothes you wear" and "the foods you eat" (4). These familiar examples appeal to students, making rhetorical theory seem less daunting.

Yet these textbooks abandon Dewey's pedagogy as readily as they have employed it, and let me specify that I am using these two textbooks because they strike me as typical of most argument textbooks today. After their engaging openings, most argument textbooks abruptly shift to a much more traditional approach. Textbooks such as Lunsford and Ruszkiewicz's *Everything's an Argument* and White and Billings's *The Well-Crafted Argument* present chapter upon chapter of *this* then *that* rhetorical term, which students are expected to memorize, recognize, and employ. After appealing to student experiences with argumentation, *Everything's an Argument,* for instance, continues by presenting seven purposes, three occasions, four kinds of arguments, the rhetorical appeals, and the rhetorical triangle in the next thirty pages of the first chapter (Lunsford and Ruszkiewicz 5–35). With this abrupt shift to content-centered instruction, learning consists of the "acquisition of what already is incorporated in books," as Dewey warns, and there is little "participation of [students] . . . in what is taught" (*Experience and Education* 19). This acquisition is shown as subsequent chapters of *Everything's an Argument* and *The Well-Crafted Argument* elaborate on several kinds of arguments. Chapters 3 to 5 of the latter work present the classical, Toulmin, and Rogerian models of argumentation. The third chapter begins with an outline of a classical argument and a sample essay for students to evaluate (White and Billings 83–88). The rest of the chapter elaborates on the model's use of the rhetorical appeals and ends with two exemplary published essays (White and Billings 88–110). Through this traditional emphasis on the subject matter, "the past [is presented as the] end in itself," and the progressive approach of the introduction has been abandoned (Dewey, *Experience and Education* 72).

In this essay I present a much more thorough implementation of Dewey's progressive pedagogy to teach argument to undergraduate students, and yet I also explore why it is so difficult to do so. A progressive teacher must fulfill two principles that Dewey presents in *Experience and Education:* interaction and continuity. These two principles preclude the permissiveness of 1920s progressivism as well as the traditionalism of today's argument textbooks. I also connect the progressive pedagogy of *Experience and Education* to Dewey's critique of foundationalism in such works as *Experience and Nature* and *The Quest for Certainty.* When we revert to traditionalism in argument pedagogy and enact the "banking concept," as Paulo

Freire explained decades after Dewey, we are lapsing into a foundational epistemology. We are teaching as though knowledge, as Dewey liked to say, is a "brick" that can be passed ready-made from teacher to student. I therefore place this progressive pedagogy for teaching argument in a nonfoundational framework and explain that student experiences are only the first step in this pedagogy. As indicated by the headings in this essay, this progressive approach also will teach students to construct knowledge, examine language, and achieve agency. Yet as "simple" as this pedagogy seems in theory, it is not always "easy" to enact.

STARTING WITH STUDENT EXPERIENCES

Another book on argumentation demonstrates what I believe is an even more effective appeal to student experiences. *Thank You for Arguing* by Jay Heinrichs is a best-selling trade book on rhetorical theory. Heinrichs's book has been lauded as an "entertaining . . . romp through the rules of rhetoric" (Klimpton), and since its publication in 2007, *Thank You for Arguing* has sold more than one hundred thousand copies.

Like most traditional textbooks, *Thank You for Arguing* opens with the ubiquity of arguments and familiar examples for its audience. Heinrichs begins with a first-person account of a mundane argument over, of all things, a tube of toothpaste. The author depicts himself as stepping out of the shower only to find an empty container. He asks his son to fetch him a new tube, but this request turns into an argument over how he can most persuasively seek this assistance. In the end Heinrichs concedes a point to his son, and by doing so he gets the desired toothpaste. Only after this anecdote does Heinrichs announce his aim to "awake [his readers] to the argument[s] all around" (6). This apparently minor difference in order, however, masks a significant difference in pedagogy. This is one of those cases where what seems to be the straightest path, presenting knowledge to students, is not the best one.

Traditional textbooks such as *The Well-Crafted Argument* and *Everything's an Argument* present general concepts first and then provide a specific example or two (for instance, a classical argument consists of . . .). Heinrichs, in contrast, first immerses readers in a specific situation, such as the toothpaste squabble. He leads them from the particulars of a familiar situation to the conclusion that, for instance, arguments suffuse our lives. Only as Heinrichs brings this tale and many others to a close does he explain its significance by naming the rhetorical concepts that have been illustrated. As Heinrichs proceeds inductively instead of deductively, this appeal to familiar experiences engages student interest and encourages them to participate more actively in their learning. As readers follow this inductive path of reasoning, they wonder where it is taking them and often anticipate its outcome.

A professor can take this progressive approach further by asking students to recall some of their own recent arguments before they are asked to read Heinrichs's examples and his conclusions in *Thank You for Arguing*. After students have shared instances of their quarrels with friends, parents, teachers, and employers, a progressive teacher can ask them to consider, "How often do we encounter arguments?" Then a professor can continue this active role and inductive reasoning of students by asking them, "What exactly is an argument? How would you define 'argument'?" Many textbooks include definitions of argument in their introductions. In *The Well-Crafted Argument,* White and Billings offer "A Formal Definition of Argument" that reads, "An argument is *a form of discourse in which the writer or speaker tries to persuade an audience to accept, reject, or think a certain way about a problem that cannot be solved by scientific or mathematical reasoning alone*" (3). Then they "amplify [their] definition" by elaborating on such phrases as "a pattern of reasoning" and "tries to persuade an audience" (4). This definition is to be received and repeated by students; they are expected to acquire "what already is incorporated in books" as quoted above.

When my own argument course is scheduled in a computer classroom, I often ask the students to add images to their definitions of "argument." When one student included the image of a well-known coach named Bobby Knight throwing a chair across a basketball court, this angry example allowed me to raise the issue of whether "argument" should be defined as a dispute between two sides trying to defeat each other or can "argument" mean a less agonistic attempt to alter opinions and build a consensus? The image of the angry coach also created a meaningful context for the introduction of the rhetorical triangle when I asked students whether they thought Knight had made an effective argument. This query led to comments such as "Knight knew the call was wrong, but throwing the chair only upset the ref" and "He may have been right, but he didn't consider the effect of his anger." I think this was when I asked, "The effect of his anger on whom?" Once a student answered, I could elaborate that "Yes, the *speaker* Knight had a clear *message,* but he didn't consider the effect on his *audience.* Long ago the Greeks characterized these three factors as the rhetorical triangle."

Now as I look back on this example, it strikes me that it may have been even better if I had asked students to diagram this rhetorical situation before presenting Aristotle's triangle. Some probably would have struggled with this task, but at least one student likely would have drawn some sort of a triad. I then could have elaborated upon the student's suggestion and introduced the rhetorical triangle (which will be the subject of further discussion below). Asking students to define "argument," to add images, and possibly to diagram the situation may seem like a rather convoluted way to introduce a basic concept. It certainly seems much simpler to declare, as Lunsford and Ruszkiewicz do at the end their first chapter, "The rhetorical situation . . . can be depicted as a simple triangle" and provide the requisite illustration (35). Yet they present the rhetorical triangle without any example, application, or analysis. Lunsford and Ruszkiewicz "withhold" from students "occasions . . . [for] understanding" their experiences (Dewey, *Experience and Education* 38). In contrast, the progressive appeal to experiences and the active role of students make learning more enjoyable and relevant, as the example of Heinrichs's *Thank You for Arguing* demonstrates, but pleasure is not the goal of progressive education. Instead Dewey's pedagogy seeks the construction of knowledge from experience and the achievement of agency through language. Yet for these goals to be understood, progressive education must be placed in the philosophical framework of Dewey's nonfoundational epistemology.

REJECTING FOUNDATIONALISM

Dewey makes a clean break with the foundational epistemology of Western philosophy since ancient Greece. In *The Quest for Certainty* he explains the desire for immutable knowledge in a world of vicissitudes. Since ancient times humans have sought "absolute and unshakeable" certainty, so ancient Greeks such as Plato posited the existence of an absolute reality beyond the immediate world of "catastrophes" and other "unforeseeable conditions" (Dewey, *Quest* 6, 7). For Plato, the fixed "foundation" for knowledge was the ideal forms, such as Truth, Beauty, and Goodness. Then, rather than be trapped in a shadowy cave of ever-changing appearances, it seemed as though a philosopher could possess certainty through the direct perception of this reality by discerning what is presumed to be "the antecedently real" (Dewey, *Quest* 17).

When students and teachers are assumed to stand on the same fixed foundation, the result is traditional education. Certain knowledge is conveyed through textbooks and lectures, using language that assumed to be a clear channel of communication. Yet as knowledge is imposed on "docil[e]" and "receptiv[e]" students in this traditional pedagogy, the experiences of students are ignored and active learning is impossible (Dewey, *Experience and Education* 18).

Since Plato the absolute reality assumed has changed several times. Medieval Christians, such as Augustine and Aquinas, replaced the classical forms with an eternal divinity, and Enlightenment empiricists, such as Bacon and Newton, substituted mathematical quantities for divine traits. Yet they still sought an "ultimate reality" that was presumed to provide a "certainty of knowledge," and with this continuing quest, the central problems of foundationalism were perpetuated (Dewey, *Quest* 29). As these absolute realities were separated from transitory appearances, these divisions created the classic conundrums of mind vs. matter, spirit vs. body, and theory vs. practice. Philosophers from Spinoza to Kant have struggled to put these binaries back together again, but all of their efforts have been in vain. Dewey refers to these problems as the "false dualisms" of foundationalism, and rather than pursue them, he rejects "not merely the old solutions, but the old problems" of philosophy as well (Dewey, "Need" 20–21). His alternative is to place philosophy in a different, nonfoundational framework. In contrast to foundationalists, Dewey does not equate experience with the transitory appearances that obscure an absolute reality. Instead experience provides the "starting point for philosophic thought" and for "all . . . learning" (Dewey, *Experience and Nature* 10; Dewey, *Experience and*

Education 74). Dewey defines experience as an individual's transactions with the physical and social environment. Like William James, he considers these transactions to be "double-barreled" because they are undergone first and known later (quoted in Dewey, *Experience and Nature* 10). Once an experience is undergone, an individual can engage in a deliberate development of knowledge. An experience does not have to be dumbly endured or randomly enjoyed. Nor does an individual have to escape from an allegorical cave for some absolute Truth to be known. An individual instead can construct knowledge from experience. Thus, for a progressive teacher, "finding the material for learning within experience is only the first step" (Dewey, *Experience and Education* 73). According to this nonfoundational epistemology, the next step is to construct knowledge.

CONSTRUCTING KNOWLEDGE

To explain the construction of knowledge, I return to the example of asking students to define "argument" on the first day of class. Students usually will offer various definitions, such as "an attempt to persuade" and "trying to defeat your opponent in a debate." From these responses an instructor can—or better yet, a student will—pose a provocative question such as "So is persuasion the same as argumentation?" This query epitomizes what Dewey terms a "felt difficulty," which is experienced as a physical need, an emotional tension, and/or an intellectual problem (Dewey, *How* 107).

To resolve this difficulty, students can learn to engage in a process of inquiry that begins with defining the problem, such as by confronting the multiple meanings of "argument" and questioning the relationship between persuasion and argument. With a problem defined, students next form a hypothesis, as did one of my students who once ventured that every argument includes persuasion but every persuasion does not include an argument trying to defeat an opponent. Then to validate this belief, students can return to experience in order to test it. For example, the students' own examples of disputes could be used to test whether every argument involves persuasion and the converse. They would not simply be told to equate argument with persuasion, such as by the definition of "argument" in *The Well-Crafted Argument* ("a discourse that . . . tries to persuade"). Instead the students would be pursuing a felt difficulty and constructing knowledge.

In another class a student might define "argument" as "using reason to convince an audience," and this contribution could lead the inquiry in another direction. Progressive education is, as Dewey warns, a "harder business" because a professor must be ready to follow the ideas of students and yet still create "a continuing line" of learning (Dewey, *Experience and Education* 79). For instance, the reference to "using reason" could lead to a discussion of the role of emotion in arguments and on to the three rhetorical appeals (instead of the rhetorical triangle as explained above). Thus a progressive teacher must be prepared to "take advantag[e]" of these "special occasions" for learning (Dewey, *Experience and Education* 78).

When the appeal to student experiences leads to the construction of knowledge, the first principle of progressive education is fulfilled. Dewey demands that teachers must lead students to what he terms an "interaction" between their experiences and the desired course content (*Experience and Education* 42). These interactions occur when an image of Bobby Knight or some diverse definitions of argument lead students to key concepts of rhetoric. Through an interaction, knowledge of the rhetorical triangle becomes the means for evaluating Knight's argument, or knowledge of the three appeals helps students examine the roles of reason and emotion in argumentation. These connections between present experiences and past knowledge make learning seem relevant to students, and they avoid the problem of knowledge being imposed in traditional education. Interactions prevent the "cast-iron result[s]" of traditional education (Dewey, *Experience and Education* 72). The principle of interaction precludes not only some of the flaws of traditional education but also the potential problem of permissiveness. As Dewey explains in *Experience and Education*, "the trouble with traditional education was not that it emphasized [subject matter] . . . but that it paid so little attention to [student experiences]" (42). By ignoring student experiences, traditional education "violated the principle of interaction from one side," but Dewey then warns that "this violation is no reason why the new [progressive] education [of the 1920s] should violate the principle from the other side" (*Experience and Education* 42). When interaction makes an "acquaintance with the past . . . the means of understanding the present" for students, the problem of permissiveness is overcome (Dewey, *Experience and Education* 78).

If the appeal to experience does not lead to such learning, the result is the permissiveness that plagued progressive education in the 1920s. Then the student-centered exchange on the meanings of "argument," for example, never challenges its participants to alter their initial opinions. In a permissive classroom, critical reflection does not follow self-expression. Let me stress that in *Experience and Education*, Dewey rejects such permissiveness explicitly and completely. Published in 1936, *Experience and Education* is Dewey's tour de force against lax permissiveness as well as rigid traditionalism. The "difficult task" of a progressive teacher is to "recognize in the concrete what [experiences] are conducive to" learning (Dewey, *Experience and Education* 30, 40). This recognition depends on a professor using the "organized subject matter" as "the goal toward which education should" be moving (Dewey, *Experience and Education* 83). Thus, Dewey opposes the very permissiveness with which he and the typical caricature of "touchy, feely" progressive education are sometimes but falsely associated.

There "is a decided difference between using" the subject matter, such as rhetorical concepts, as "the chief material of learning" and using the same concepts as the basis for "a continuing line" of learning, but the content of an argument course taught progressively will not differ significantly from that of a traditional one (Dewey, *Experience and Education* 79). Let me repeat, the pedagogical paths will differ, but the destination will not. The subject matter of many traditional textbooks, therefore, can be adapted to engage students in the progressive construction of knowledge. For instance, when White and Billings present the rhetorical triangle in *The Well-Crafted Argument,* they add that this triangle can be augmented with a fourth element. They add purpose to speaker, audience, and message in order to fashion a "rhetorical rhombus" (White and Billings 7). After explaining the additional corner, White and Billings emphasize the dynamic relationships among the four factors, but they do not ask students to weigh these alternative shapes of the rhetorical situation. A progressive professor, however, could ask whether purpose helps to clarify the relationship between argument and persuasion. In most arguments if one is trying to defeat a rival, the purpose includes trying to persuade the audience to accept one's position, as in a campaign debate. Yet as one tries to persuade, for instance, a friend to attend an event, is there always an argument against an alternative? One student might assert that this persuasion often includes an explicit argument against another option, such as "What are you just going to do instead? Stay home on a Friday night?" Another student might add that there always is an implicit argument against some alternative in most persuasions. A third student might disagree, and all three would be critically considering the relationship between argument and persuasion.

Other aspects of traditional textbooks can be converted to the nonfoundational construction of knowledge. As shown in *Everything's an Argument,* it is easy to align the three corners of the classic triangle with the three rhetorical appeals—writer-ethos, audience-pathos, and message-logos (Lunsford and Ruszkiewicz 35). Yet rather than just present this alignment, this convenient correspondence could be applied to the previous discussion of the rhetorical situation as three- or four-sided. Since there is no fixed foundation in Dewey's epistemology, a progressive professor could use the felt difficulty of the rhetorical rhombus vs. the triangle to encourage students to wonder, "Can the three appeals be expanded to four? Or does the correspondence of a triangle with the three appeals make it a better conception of the rhetorical situation?" As these queries suggest, all nonfoundational knowledge exists in the context of other beliefs. Altering one assumption can affect another in this epistemology without absolute certainty. This does not mean that there is no truth in this epistemology but only that there is a different basis for verification. According to Dewey, truth is not determined by a resemblance to some fixed foundation, such as Plato's forms. Instead an assertion proves to be true in its consequences, meaning when it predicts the outcome of a subsequent event. Or as William James liked to say, "truth happens" (89), and during this construction and verification of knowledge, Dewey insists that the influence of language must be examined.

EXAMINING LANGUAGE'S INFLUENCE

Most traditional textbooks skirt the examination of language's influence on our knowledge. For example, in *Everything's an Argument,* Lunsford and Ruszkiewicz explain *ethos* in terms of authority, values, motives, and language. They assert that a speaker should use "language that echoes" the discourse of one's audience (Lunsford and Ruszkiewicz 61). In *Thank You for Arguing,* Heinrichs elaborates on the role of language in establishing an effective *ethos.* He states that "a speaker should sound like the collective voice of his audience," but this echoing does not have to be purely imitative (Heinrichs 46). Heinrichs invokes Kenneth Burke to stipulate that "identification" requires the use of "speech, gesture, [and] tonality" familiar to one's audience so they can understand and appreciate one's character (47). Yet in neither the mostly traditional *Everything's an Argument* nor the more progressive *Thank You for Arguing* is the epistemological influence of language on knowledge addressed.

Unlike later antifoundationalists such as Jacques Derrida, Dewey does not deny the existence of a material reality and reduce knowledge to endless language play. There is a physical world "out there," but as we experience it, we have to construct knowledge from these events using language. I therefore have been referring to Dewey as a "nonfoundationalist" in order to distinguish him from the antifoundationalism of later postmodernists such as Derrida. According to Dewey's nonfoundational epistemology, there is no "direct appeal to nature," so language's influence on knowledge must be examined (*Experience and Nature* 180). Knowledge cannot be assumed to be "complete prior to language," nor can language be believed to "expres[s] thought as a pipe conducts water" (Dewey, *Experience and Nature* 141). Rather than imagine language to be a hollow medium, Dewey conceives of language as the discursive context that shapes our understanding.

He explains that experience "is dependent upon the extension of language" (*Experience and Nature* 143). Through language, experience is "overlaid . . . with the products of . . . past generations. . . . It is filled with interpretations [and] classifications . . . which have been incorporated into what seems to be fresh" thought (Dewey, *Experience and Nature* 34). These "interpretations [and] classifications" influence us "long before" we are aware of their effect (Dewey, *Reconstruction* 92). For example, a child learns terms such as "boy," "girl," "white," and "poor" long before they may influence his or her beliefs about gender, race, and class. Thus "the *ways* in which we believe [meaning language] . . . have a tremendous effect upon *what* we believe" (Dewey, *Experience and Nature* 15).

Using the example of *argument,* White and Billings provide a compelling example of language's "tremendous effect." They explain that the "traditional language of argument . . . is filled with militaristic metaphors: We *win* or *lose.* . . . We *attack* someone[e]. . . . We *marshall* evidence. . . . Even the seemingly neutral term of *debate* is of military origin (from *battre,* to do battle)" (White and Billings 134–35). However, they do not extend this example to address the epistemological importance of language in general. A progressive professor can ask students to offer their own examples of the agonistic assumptions of argument and, once again, work inductively to the general conclusion of language's influence on knowledge. Or a teacher could refer to some of the students' earlier agonistic definitions and images of argument and then ask, "Why do we often find it so easy to shift from a reasoned debate to an angry quarrel?" This question can lead to some of White and Billings's provocative examples of militaristic metaphors, and then a professor can press the larger point of language's influence, for example by citing George Lakoff and Mark Johnson from *Metaphors We Live By.*

Lakoff and Johnson too use argument as one of their examples and explain that the Western concept of argument is structured "in terms of WAR" as we try to defend a position and destroy an opponent (63). They assert, as their title suggests, that language is filled with metaphors, or Dewey's "interpretations [and] classifications," that structure our thinking. Although I have used this example in class, I have found that the concept of argument as an agonistic dispute is so deeply ingrained in Western culture that some students need to consider other examples in order to understand their immersion in language and its effects.

A progressive professor can ask students to consider the meaning of another central term of their subject, such as "rhetoric." As when a professor seeks students' definitions of argument, this request usually will elicit some uncomfortable silence at first. Next there may be some stilted references to "speaking well," "persuasive writing," "the art of argument," and then the troubling connotations of "empty talk," "inflated speech," and "mere rhetoric." Rather than be dismayed by these pejorative responses, a progressive teacher can ask students to consider the implications of the negative connotations. Students initially may be hesitant to respond, so a teacher can pose a leading question such as "Who do we usually accuse of mere rhetoric?" This query usually will yield two responses: politicians and, gulp, professors, but a brave professor can continue, "If we assume that politicians engage in empty talk and professors in inflated speech, what effect does this assumption about rhetoric have on our attitudes toward government and education?" The resulting apathy can be summed up with two phrases all too familiar to political campaigns and college campuses: "Why bother voting?" and "I'm getting by." Thus the often unspoken meanings of terms such as "rhetoric" and "argument" influence our thoughts and actions.

Next a progressive teacher can ask students to consider a more positive concept of rhetoric, such as Cicero's image of "a good man speaking well." These connotations of integrity and eloquence are appealing, but at least one student usually will inquire about the gendered reference to "a man." In addition to the standard explanation of Roman patriarchy, a professor can ask students, "To what degree do we still consider rhetoric as though it were a masculine endeavor?" This query will invite diverse responses, such as a connection of agonistic arguments to male aggression, the difficulty for some female speakers to be assertive, and yet the premium placed on deeds instead of words for action-oriented males. Like "rhetoric," the term "man" influences our thinking about gender "long before" we are aware of its "tremendous effect," and with diverse examples the larger point of language can be pressed: "we bring to the simplest observation a complex apparatus . . . of accepted meanings" (Dewey, *Experience and Nature* 180). In this case our concept of "rhetoric" and our notions of gender affect our assumptions about argument, who can argue, and how they argue.

When the examination of influential terms such as "rhetoric" and "argument" lead students to further understanding of this subject, the second pedagogical principle of progressive education has been fulfilled: "continuity" (Dewey, *Experience and Education* 33). According to Dewey's first principle as explained above, a learning situation should create an "interaction" between present experiences and past knowledge. With his second principle, Dewey looks ahead to the future consequences of an interaction. Using the term "continuity," Dewey insists that a truly educational activity also must lead "fruitfully . . . [to] subsequent experiences" (*Experience and Education* 28). For example, the initial discussion of argument and its images should motivate students to continue with the later analysis of its agonistic assumptions. Or, as I will explain below, the second examination of this influential term should create "a continuing line" to exploring less combative forms of argument, such as Rogerian consensus building. Traditional and permissive education both fail to fulfill the principle of continuity because too often they either alienate or amuse their respective students. Neither one encourages students to engage in subsequent learning.

To avoid the problem of permissiveness, a progressive teacher must engage in a "more difficult kind of planning" (Dewey, *Experience and Education* 58). A professor cannot prepare a lesson based solely on the subject matter and its "dictation," as in traditional education. Instead a professor must plan by considering three crucial questions:

1. How will the appeal to experience be made?
2. How are the students likely to respond?
3. How will the professor react to the responses in order to lead students to the construction of knowledge, the examination of language's influences, and ultimately, the achievement of greater agency?

A progressive teacher prepares for class by planning to create a learning experience and by anticipating the likely student responses. Yet once class begins, this professor also must be ready to practice what I like to term "prepared improvisation" because the actual student responses may head in one direction but not another. As explained above, the students' replies to a professor's question about argument, for example, may lead to the rhetorical triangle or the three appeals. The planning of a progressive professor must be flexible, but this daily improvisation also must be organized into a "continuing line" of learning. Or as Dewey asserts, "the office of the educator [is] to select those [experiences that] . . . stimulat[e] new ways of observation and judgment . . . [as well as] expand the area of further experience" (*Experience and Education* 75).

If a progressive educator can succeed in this more difficult and more provisional planning, the twin principles of interaction and continuity connect "the issues of the present" with "the achievements of the past," and once the present has been "enlarged to take in the past," it then can be "expanded into the future" (Dewey, *Experience and Education* 77). The examination of language can create exactly this interaction of present and past, and then the subsequent expansion into the future can lead to greater agency.

ACHIEVING INDIVIDUAL AGENCY

As Dewey asserts the "tremendous effect" of language, he must be distinguished from later continental thinkers such as Roland Barthes and Michel Foucault. Dewey does not declare the death of the author or locate the subject in a panopticon of oppressive ideologies. He grants that an individual can never transcend the mediation of experience by language, but he also insists that a particular belief can be foregrounded for analysis. For Dewey, discourse is not a postmodern prison house; instead language is "the tool of tools. . . the cherishing mother of significance" (*Experience and Nature* 154).

In Dewey's nonfoundational epistemology, all "events are subject to reconsideration and revision" through language because "their meanings may be indefinitely combined and re-arranged in [the] imagination" of individuals (*Experience and Nature* 138). This does not contradict Dewey's assertion that "experience is dependent upon the extension of language," as explained in the previous section (*Experience and Nature* 143). Dewey conceives of language with the same complexity as that of his "double-barreled" concept of experience. Language is a "social product" that "presages [particular] outlooks" (Dewey, *Experience and Nature* 143; Dewey, *Democracy* 46). Yet language also "continues to exist by transmission"—in fact, it "may be fairly said to exist in transmission" (Dewey, *Democracy* 5). During this transmission of language, an individual can alter as well as perpetuate various discourses. As language is altered, its consequences can be examined.

Dewey likens this process to "intellectual disrobing," and he elaborates, "We cannot permanently divest ourselves of the intellectual habits we take on and wear when we assimilate the culture of our . . . time and place. But the intellectual furthering of culture demands that we take them off, that we inspect them critically to see what they are made of and what wearing them does to us" (*Experience and Nature* 35). History is replete with examples of this critical inspection of particular beliefs. Eighteenth-century revolutionaries overthrew their monarchs, for instance, by reconceiving the basis of their political legitimacy. The opponents of England's King George and France's Louis XIV took "off" these monarchs' claims of divine-right rule and replaced this religious basis with the secular and more democratic legitimacy of citizen consent. More recently postmodern theorists disrupted foundational assumptions about authorship by substituting the term "subject" for the modernist concept of "individual" (Berlin 18). Traditional argument textbooks, however, rarely ask students to examine "the habits" they "take on" through the rhetorical concepts of their instruction. Yet a progressive professor can encourage students to "inspect them critically."

A progressive teacher can engage students in this Deweyan "disrobing" in order to "see what [discursive terms] are made of." As explained above, some students will find it hard to conceive of argument as anything other than an agonistic struggle, while others will desire a less confrontational alternative. From these felt difficulties, students can be encouraged to try on and "take . . . off" various kinds of arguments. Most traditional textbooks suggest this critical inspection of what "wearing" these multiple modes of argument "does to us." Traditional textbooks such as *The Well-Crafted Argument* usually present various kinds of argument. However, as White and Billings do so in chapters 3–5, they offer only cursory connections between them, such as "Toulmin argument has enhanced the dynamics of Classical argument" (134). This lack of connection is even more pronounced in *Everything's an Argument.* In the first chapter Lunsford and Ruszkiewicz present what really amount to thirteen different kinds of argument:

> Purposes of argument: to inform, convince, persuade, explore, decide, and meditate
> Occasions for argument: past/forensic, future/deliberative, and present/epideictic
> Kinds of argument: fact, definition, evaluation/causation, and action [stasis]. (5–27)

They, however, make only minimal connections such as linking "argument[s] that explore" to arguments that decide (12). Lunsford and Ruszkiewicz fail to make other connections across their categories, such as by linking an argument to decide with deliberative rhetoric about the future and/or a stasis argument about action.

The Well-Crafted Argument and *Everything's an Argument* do offer instances of the typical exigency of when each kind of argument can be used, such as a forensic argument in a courtroom (White and Billings 83) and a factual argument over the authorship of Shakespearean plays (Lunsford and Ruszkiewicz 208). Yet both these works never focus on one situation and ask students to discriminate between the uses of various kinds of arguments. They never encourage students to weigh the relative merits of each kind and to distinguish the most or least opportune time to employ each one.

A progressive instructor can engage students in this critical inspection of various kinds of arguments by asking them to employ and evaluate several at the same time. For example, groups of students can be asked to present, as I have tried, several prepared oral arguments and then reflect upon the kind of argument made by each group. One year, in a 200-level introduction to argument course, all of the arguments focused on Aldous Huxley's *Brave New World.* The forensic argument employed a stasis format (fact, definition, evaluation, and recommendation) in order to argue who is guilty for the climactic death of John the Savage; the Toulmin argument debated the licit use of the psychotropic drug soma; the Rogerian argument addressed the banning of "obscene" books such as *Brave New World* from public high schools; and the believing and doubting argument, based on the theory of Peter Elbow, considered to what degree American culture is fulfilling Huxley's predictions of a hedonistic and materialistic society. To illustrate the agency achieved through this assignment, I quote liberally from the fine efforts of two students: Justin and Samantha; and to address the benefits of a progressive approach, I also will describe the efforts of the entire class.[1]

In Justin's reflective essay on the multiple arguments presented in class, he quipped that the outcomes of these diverse forms could range from "a complete consensus to a possible fistfight." Although none of the student groups came to blows, Samantha observed that during the forensic argument, "It was apparent that members were getting angry." Justin realized that the believing and doubting arguments of his own group were "less confrontational. . . . Collectively, the entire [group chose] to believe, to . . . support the claims being made [then] to doubt, to search for errors that would disprove the claim being made." With these contrasts, Justin and Samantha were starting to discriminate between these two kinds of arguments.

After just ten weeks in this introductory course, Justin also demonstrated the insights that wearing the "intellectual habi[t]" of rhetoric could foster for him and his partner Samantha. Analyzing his own group's argument, he observed as follows: "Samantha brought up our . . . use of text messaging to demonstrate the uniformity of our society in comparison to *Brave New World.* . . . Samantha understood her audience [and] by including their beliefs . . . she got unanimous agreement. . . . The use of a tactical flaw reveals a weakness [in order to] win sympathy. . . . [By her] admitting she texts just as much as the members of her audience . . . they were able to identify with her more. . . . They had begun to trust her ethos."

Samantha likewise was able to analyze the rhetoric of her group's oral argument. She concluded, "Our success came from combining ethos, logos, and pathos. We built our ethos by showing . . . practical wisdom [and] bringing up childish television shows. . . . [We used these examples] to support the conclusion of immature [adult] behavior [through] inductive logic." Even better, Samantha was able to critique her group's effort through the further application of key rhetorical concepts. She explained, "Our group was least convincing when . . . [we were] doubting American society is degraded like [in] *Brave New World.* . . . [We] ended making a hasty generalization. . . . We had many reasons to believe our society was becoming like *Brave New World,* yet we decided, because we are repulsed by that society, we are not like it. . . . Looking back we could have provided more specific examples of what repulsed us in the text."

Samantha and Justin also were able critically to inspect the rhetoric of other groups with similar insights. On the forensic argument, Samantha found the group blaming the society for John's death more convincing. She explained, "When Kendall pointed out that John himself had said, 'I'm claiming the right to be unhappy' . . . Stacey countered by . . . ask[ing] us to see it all from John's perspective. I thought that suggestion was an effective rebuttal." Justin analyzed the Rogerian argument over banning books such as *Brave New World,* and he observed, "Diana eloquently argued that the *Brave New World* society valued sex as just sex, not love. . . . High school students may be influenced to not value long-term relationships and be ignorant of consequences, such as pregnancy. In response . . . Erica expressed her agreement that there are consequences to such sexual freedom. [Yet] after agreeing, she said that *Brave New World* serves as a warning. . . . Erica's agreement was an example of a concession . . . [and] by agreeing [and conceding] . . . in a Rogerian argument, both sides can work to reach a compromise that benefits both parties."

Justin then concluded on the various forms of arguments presented in class: "Rogerian arguments can involve both epideictic and deliberative arguments. In other words, both sides can come to an agreement concerning their shared values and then use that set of values to choose the best course of action for the future. . . . Rogerian arguments . . . eliminat[e] the selective blindness that other arguments value so [issues] can be debated . . . peacefully." Of course, other students expressed their dislike for the "messier" methods of a Rogerian or a believing and doubting argument; they favored the clear-cut steps of a stasis or a Toulmin argument. As the students defended their preferences, they all demonstrated that they had learned to try on and take off various kinds of arguments in order to inspect each one critically. After the first ten weeks of an introductory course on argument, they had begun the critical process of discriminating between them.[2]

I believe that the fine efforts of Justin and Samantha, in particular, demonstrate the achievement of greater agency in regard to rhetoric and argumentation. A skeptic may want to counter that bright students such as these would have fared just as well in a traditional classroom. Perhaps they would have. After taking lecture notes or reading a textbook chapter, they would have been able to think through and wrest control over the course content on their own. I concede that many top students do so every year.

What is far more difficult for me to present on this page is the response by the rest of the class, including some less able than Justin and Samantha. As these students prepared, presented, and analyzed their arguments, they too were engaged and enthusiastic. None of the oral arguments involved the listless efforts or droning voices of students going through the proverbial motions. I will not claim that every analysis was as insightful as the two samples presented, but every student was engaged in an hour-long peer response session as pairs of students commented on each other's drafts. Every final draft was at least a reasonably good effort, and several other students equaled the analyses of Justin and Samantha.

This outcome, of course, will not be guaranteed the next time I teach this course. The students may come to my class more set in the routines of traditional education: lecture, textbook, and test. It may be harder for me to make them understand the different expectations of a progressive classroom. The students may be less responsive to the appeal to experience, or they may be less willing to explore felt difficulties. Yet if I am tempted to revert to a traditional approach and tidy bricks of knowledge, I hope I will recall the thrills as well as the difficulties of progressive education. I will have to remember the moment when students wanted to explore whether every argument involves persuasion and its converse, or the class when Justin, Samantha, and their peers presented their arguments with conviction and commitment. I will have to believe that another group of students can be led to construct knowledge, examine language's influence, and achieve greater agency.

When we can avoid the twin perils of foundationalism and permissiveness, our pedagogical efforts and those of our students will be rewarded. These rewards will last long after the particular course has ended. The lasting benefits of teaching students to argue well using a progressive approach are that they will have been taught to be more engaged learners, more critical thinkers, more persuasive rhetors, and more active agents in a democratic society that desperately needs them. As Dewey asserts in *The Public and Its Problems,* "the improvement of the methods and conditions of debate, discussion and persuasion" is an "essential need" (208). As our nation now faces polarized politics, economic troubles, and international conflicts, this need is even greater. Dewey's seemingly simple theory may not be easy to implement, but it is worth pursuing.[3]

NOTES

1. These student papers are quoted with the explicit permission of their writers: Justin DiConzo and Samantha Edington.

2. For an example of greater agency achieved by a student in an upper-level rhetoric course, please see the essay published by Melanie Wilson in *Xchanges,* an online journal of undergraduate education. This essay developed from an assignment in a 300-level course on rhetorical theory that included primary texts, such as Plato's *Gorgias.* The assignment was for students to apply the classic debate over rhetoric and ethics to a contemporary example such as the corporate Web site of Philip Morris. Wilson analyzes the effort of Philip Morris to promote its company and fulfill the Master Settlement Agreement, which requires the dissemination of information on the health hazards of tobacco products. In terms of Dewey's progressive pedagogy, Wilson's work represents a continuity with her introductory study of argument, and her published paper demonstrates an interaction between classic rhetorical theory and a current case. Her postgraduation employment in the health-care industry may well involve a further continuity with her study of rhetoric and ethics. Wilson's paper "Rhetorical Analysis of a Corporate Website: Philip Morris, Ethos, and Ethics" can be found at http://infohost.nmt.edu/~xchanges/old_exchanges/6.1/wilson/wilson.html (accessed June 10, 2013).

3. In addition to acknowledging Brian Jackson for his editorial assistance, I also want to thank the members of my writing group who supported this essay to its completion: Irene Papoulis and Peter Elbow.

WORKS CITED

Berlin, James. "Poststructuralism, Cultural Studies, and the Composition Classroom." *Rhetoric Review* 11.1 (1992): 16–33.

Dewey, John. *Democracy and Education.* 1916.Reprint. New York: Free Press, 1967.

———. *Experience and Education.* 1938. New York: Macmillan, 1975.

———. *Experience and Nature.* Rev. ed. La Salle, Ill.: Open Court, 1929.

———. *How We Think.* Lexington, Mass.: Heath, 1933.

———. "The Need for a Recovery of Philosophy." In *Experience, Nature, and Freedom,* ed. Richard Burnstein, 19–69. New York: Bobbs-Merrill, 1960.

———. *The Public and Its Problems.* 1927. Chicago: Swallow, 1954.

———. *The Quest for Certainty.* New York: Putnam, 1929.

———. *Reconstruction in Philosophy.* Rev. ed. Boston: Beacon, 1948.

Freire, Paulo. *Pedagogy of the Oppressed.* New York: Continuum, 1993.

Heinrichs, Jay. *Thank You for Arguing.* New York: Three Rivers, 2007.

James, William. *Pragmatism and Other Essays.* New York: Pocket, 1963.

Kimpton, Peter. "Please Mind Your Language." *Observer,* February 3, 2008. Web (accessed September 5, 2008) http://www.guardian.co.uk/books/2008/feb/03/referenceand languages.features

Lakoff, George, and Mark Johnson. *Metaphors We Live By.* Chicago: University of Chicago Press, 1980.

Lunsford, Andrea, and John Ruszkiewicz. *Everything's an Argument.* 5th ed. New York: Bedford/St. Martin's, 2010.

White, Fred, and Simone Billings. *The Well-Crafted Argument.* 3rd ed. Boston: Houghton Mifflin, 2008.

Afterword

The Possibilities for Dewey amid the Angst of Paradigm Change

Gerard A. Hauser

In his lectures on biopolitics, Foucault discusses the advent of new problems confronting the state, beginning with the rise of industrialization in the seventeenth century and the accompanying mass migration of populations into urban centers. Hoards of people living in close proximity, no longer sustaining themselves through their own agricultural practices, and depending on the local municipality to provide basic services undermined the monarch's unilateral power. In its place, Foucault argued, a new paradigm for thinking about governance, called "governmentality," emerged. Governmentality marked a shift from the monarch's unchallenged power to decree who should die or be allowed to live as the basis for organizing the nation and maintaining order. With large segments of the population now living close to each other, the nation needed practices that addressed the new problems of maintaining order and the general welfare—problems of public safety, sanitation and public health, economic stability, and education. These were not problems that could be addressed through decree. Exploding populations in the great cities of Europe—London, Paris, Vienna—created an imperative to organize society by regulating bodies in order to ensure that needs of public safety, public health, employment, and education were met.[1]

These concerns provided the conatus for the Enlightenment's foment of political theorizing. Hobbes, Locke, Rousseau, Montesquieu, and Burke were leading voices in tackling the problem of how the state might best regulate bodies to ensure order and safety, prevent the ravages of plague, prepare its population to gain employment, and cultivate a marketplace that maximized economic opportunity. The regulatory imperatives to produce citizens whose practices met the needs of policing, sanitation and public health, education, and economic growth required mentalities, rationalities, and techniques to produce citizens whose practices would fulfill the government's policies. Thus there has been a shift from the monarch's power to make die and let live to the biopower of the state to make live and let die. The monarch's power to make die was exhibited on the scaffold through the device of the executioner's ax. It was localized, ritualized in the ceremony of the execution, and in its ceremonial character partial. Its staging of might jostled with the legal and moral need for justification, which revealed the monarch's limitations through its very performance. By contrast, the biopower of governmentality goes beyond the individual to the society, where it assumes responsibility for its well-being, or the responsibility to make live, on which the state's legitimacy rests.

Foucault, among others, has written at length about how this new paradigm has given us a biopolitics based on governmentality's inherent logic of biopower. The modern state has power to improve life, to prolong its duration, and to improve chances for economic well-being, avoiding accidents and compensating for life's failings. However, it does so by subjugating bodies to its policies in order to control society. In its regulations of the living, the state reclaims death through its power to let die as a necessity for society's well-being. Its more dramatic formulations, such as Agamben's (*Homo Sacer; State of Exception*), find biopower's reclaiming of death manifested in the death camps of Nazi Germany and the state of exception. Less dramatically but still effectively, biopower is exercised through policies regulating and selectively supporting education, access to public health, the economy, labor, foreign policy, and police protection, to name a few. The problems of governmentality that Foucault traces are real. The ways and means by which they are met lie at the center of a modern democracy. The dangers of biopolitics also are real, and how they are met makes a difference for the course of democratic society.

Others have traced in detail shifting paradigms for public policy in the United States (for example, Dodd; Friedman), and they support the conclusion that serious changes in models for maximizing social good were witnessed in the twentieth century. The period of laissez-faire, typified by President Coolidge's administration, gave way to a model of social welfare initiated by President Roosevelt's New Deal, which was later displaced by a return to a more laissez-faire–like model under President Reagan. As America moved into the twenty-first century, this model was and remains at the center of a deep and dividing debate in the United States and the world at-large over sustainable structures for maintaining economic growth, international and national safety, public and planetary health, and opportunity for personal and societal well-being. In this afterword I wish to look forward to consider where we go from here vis-à-vis the current political divide in the United States. *Trained Capacities* has explored the value of a Deweyan perspective in the context of democracy, society, and education; I wish to raise the question of whether Dewey remains relevant to the contemporary realities of governmentality in a technologically sophisticated society.

The diversity of the United States has historically produced deep differences over how democracy should be lived. James Madison wrote with prescience about this in *Federalist Paper No. 10*. There, Madison warned about the twin dangers of factions and tyranny of the majority that threatened the political balance of the newly forming nation. He was a political realist who recognized that deep differences were inevitable and could exert a destabilizing effect on politics. His solution was to swallow factions and a majority bent on trampling the minority's rights in the larger body of a representative assembly that had many members with short terms of office. This, he believed, would dilute the power of geographically located zealots and prevent a tyrannical majority from gaining an irreversible toehold on the American polity.

Madison's concerns have proved warranted. Factions have abounded through America's history, and political allegiances in congressional districts have lurched to opposite extremes as changing conditions and charismatic politicians catapulted different interests to preeminence. Changes in the ideological bent of political blocs also have precipitated movement left or right in the White House, Congress, and the Supreme Court. The U.S. system of checks and balances, however, has produced a mostly centrist course in public policy by taming the often-divided agendas of those in control of these branches of government. Moreover as paradigms of power, the role of the state, and the federal government's relationship to the governed have changed, paradigmatic differences and shifts in the United States, remarkably, have taken place without insurrection and bloodshed, with the notable exception of the Civil War. Instead the United States has displaced physical violence with asseverations of irremediable divides and performances of difference that render the prospects for meaningful political dialogue problematic.

These paradigmatic transitions reflect biopolitics through contorted rhetoric disengaged from the deliberative process that Dewey regarded as at the heart of democratic life. Instead of considering alternatives based on evidence that supports or denies predicted consequences, contemporary political rhetoric rests on the dialectically secured positions of progressive or neoliberal ideology that reduce political relations to a zero sum game. Bodies will be regulated; the question is, by which logic?

These transitional moments have discernible rhetorical features. They begin with factionalism growing in size and stridency. For example, Supreme Court decisions, such as *Brown v. Board of Education* or *Roe v. Wade*, gave rise to cries that the political fabric had been rent. Those on the losing side interpreted the decision as the signal issue that trumped all other political relations, forcing those on the prevailing side to mount a counteroffensive. In the case of *Brown*, the divisions solidified in the advocates of segregation rallying behind states' rights, while the civil rights movement intensified agitation for what eventually became the Civil Rights Law. With *Roe*, the prolife vs. prochoice divide has continued for forty years, with both sides using the decision as a template for political choice and linking it to either reinstating a political right (of the unborn) believed to have been trampled or protecting a political right (women's reproductive rights) from concerted onslaught by an organized and zealous opposition. These causes take root as they reflect the views of segments in society that are under assault and form as single-issue publics. The proliferation of this type of public is an indication that the existing paradigm is unable to contain society's differences. As these factions increase in number and size and aggregate along shared fault lines, the evidence becomes clearer that a paradigm shift is afoot.

The felt need to reverse a perceived trampling of one's political rights is typically accompanied by extreme rhetoric. Extreme rhetoric over political differences, in itself, is neither unusual nor an indicator of paradigm shift. However, as its treatment of the opposition becomes more seriously threatening, it can be an indicator of paradigm shift. When, for example, the opposition is vilified in ways that question its patriotism and ethics—as in the case of President Obama, whose native birth as a U.S. citizen was called into question by some on the far right, while others, with the avowed purpose of making him a one-term president, labeled his domestic policies as socialistic and his foreign policy as cowardly—the shadow of ad hominem attacks shrinks the available ground for policy debate while opening the gates for more dangerous appeals.

Personal vilification of opponents escalates when those who feel under assault believe the situation so dire as to require extreme measures, even to the point of calling for a revolution. The rhetoric of revolution, albeit not a literal call to arms against the government, does target those who govern. It usually justifies extreme measures on grounds of restoring the nation to its founding principles and at its far reaches includes violent rhetoric issuing calls for slaying the opposition. In recent times this manifestation of paradigmatic warfare was exemplified in the famous tweet by Sarah Palin, who, exorcised over passage of the Obama-sponsored health care reform bill in 2010, exhorted her followers, "Don't retreat, instead—RELOAD!" Palin then posted to her political action committee, Takebackthe20.com, images of twenty legislators who had supported this bill, including Arizona representative Gabrielle Giffords, in the crosshairs of a rifle sight. Tucson's Jesse Kelly, Giffords's Tea Party opponent, went even further. His campaign in 2010 hosted an event called "Get on Target for Victory in November." The description urged supporters to "Help remove Gabrielle Giffords from office. Shoot a fully automatic M16 with Jesse Kelly" (Hamsher). After an assassination attempt on Giffords, which nearly took her life and whose physical consequences eventually led to her resignation from the House of Representatives, proponents of "slaying the opposition" demurred that these were simply rhetorical figures, not literal calls for assassination.

Still, the rhetoric supporting "rhetorical" violence has its roots in political, and sometimes religious, fundamentalism that warrants revolution. For instance, rhetorical violence at points of transition invokes history to find foundational principles that support an absolutist interpretation of events and policies. Room for negotiation evaporates since the quest is for restoration of trampled rights. Sacred documents are invoked with fundamentalist interpretations that refuse to compensate for evolving historical circumstances and growing social complexity. An escalating rhetorical violence makes it challenging at best to conduct meaningful political dialogue since the appeals of those who are calling for a revolution are grounded in "truths" secured through the dialectical exercise of arriving at conclusions from first principles that then typically are decontextualized and go unexamined in public rhetoric.

The escalating extremism of the group that believes its rights have been trampled is not necessarily directed exclusively at the opposition party. Often it signals a struggle inside its own ranks for control over the direction of the group or even the political party itself. The struggle over regulation of business within the Republican Party eventuated in Teddy Roosevelt splitting off to form the Bull Moose Party. The struggle within the Democratic Party over segregation in the South led to southern Democrats forming a short-lived splinter party called the Dixiecrats, dedicated to the doctrine of states' rights and preserving the southern way of life, which was besieged by the federal government, especially with antisegregationist legislation and policies. The 1968 Democratic convention was torn by conflicts between mainline party support for Hubert Humphrey and the challenge of antiwar candidates Eugene McCarthy and George McGovern. The split spelled the end of New Deal democrats as the reigning force within the party. The challenge of conservative Barry Goldwater to the centrist Republican platform associated with President Eisenhower started a movement within the Republican Party to the right, eventuating in the presidency of Ronald Reagan based on a doctrine of free-market economics and social conservatism. Since Reagan's presidency, the rise of neoliberalism, with its resonant call for smaller government and, ironically, its effective alliance with the increasingly strident call of social conservatives for greater government regulation in areas of social life, has brought the United States to the point where it is clear that the revolution his presidency instigated has itself become a paradigm. Thirty years after his inauguration, the body politic in the United States again finds itself beset by factions. The number of fractures in the social and political fabric now at the heart of its current great political divide may be a sign that Reagan's neoliberalism has passed its zenith, thus signaling that the United States is once more in a time of paradigm shift.

STATE OF EXCEPTION

The discontent propelling the currently agitated state of American politics—discontent over perceived unfairness by the state in rewarding irresponsible bankers with bailouts, perceived unfairness in tax codes that require the wealthiest 1 percent to pay a lower rate than the rest of the country, the root causes of unemployment, the proper role of the federal government in funding social services, and a slew of social value issues that parse along absolutist lines based on religious conviction—cautions us not to assume that one biopolitical paradigm shall prevail over another. The so-called Reagan revolution solidified a conservative swing toward economic reform and reaffirmation of conservative social values under way since Barry Goldwater's unsuccessful presidential bid in 1964. It promised lower taxes and smaller government, reduced federal control and fiscal responsibility, while adopting policies that advanced a conservative doctrine of personal responsibility, commitment to dismantling the social welfare programs begun during the New Deal and expanded since, and championing the traditional family over individual needs and rights as the states' guiding values. Although there had been some challenges to this agenda, it continued to grow and solidify, especially in the prominence of conservative, often fundamentalist, Christian values as its motor, culminating with the presidency of George W. Bush in 2000.

Caution is necessary not to link biopolitics exclusively with one or another political philosophy. Both the Left and the Right advance biopolitical paradigms. The questions with respect to governmentality concern which course for regulating bodies will produce the most efficacious social, political, and economic results, and what forms of oppression accompany those policies. At the same time, and complicating the political landscape of the present day, the neoliberal analysis and resulting practices of the neoconservative (aka neocon) paradigm ushered in by Reagan took a radical swing on September 11, 2001. The terrorist attack and Bush's response recontextualized neocon initiatives with the state of exception.

The Italian philosopher Georgio Agamben has posited that the state of exception is the biopolitical outgrowth of biopower and that it has become the preferred mode of governmentality today. The state of exception is a political space outside law, akin to the state of emergency, in which the sovereign has the ability to act outside the constitution. This transcending of the law is justified in the name of the public good. Under the state of exception, the sovereign's word is law.

Following 9/11 the Bush administration further advanced this acquisition and consolidation of supreme power above legal restraint in the office of the presidency through the doctrine of the unitary executive. Under this doctrine the president controls the entire executive branch. In its strong forms, it argues that Congress has limited power to interfere with interexecutive decision-making. The Bush White House pushed the doctrine further to argue that neither Congress nor the federal courts had authority to tell the president what to do or how to conduct his office, especially in matters of national defense.

In the context of the war on terrorism, this was taken to mean that the president had the power to hold prisoners indefinitely without charge; to deny habeas corpus rights, even to U.S. citizens accused of involvement in terrorist activity; to conduct warrantless wiretaps; to violate international treaties prohibiting torture, to which the U.S. was signatory; and numerous other policies related to detention and suspension of rights in the name of national security. The iconic legislation legitimating this doctrine, ironically named so that its acronym became the USA

PATRIOT Act (aka Patriot Act, which stands for Uniting and Strengthening America by Providing Appropriate Tools Required to Intercept and Obstruct Terrorism Act of 2001), abridged basic First and Fourth Amendment rights with the added twist of an acronym insinuating that it was unpatriotic to dissent from its provisions compromise one's constitutional rights as a citizen. By wrapping policies, that under normal circumstances might have provoked outrage from the American electorate, in a rhetoric of fear, the Bush administration largely had its way. Most citizens supported his policies as necessary to combat an elusive and faceless enemy that might strike anywhere anytime.[2]

In the wider context of governmentality, the neocon paradigm found expression in the extraordinary number of signing statements by President Bush. Signing statements, which are issued at the time of signing a bill into law, indicate how the president interprets certain provisions, especially those that may be ambiguous, to guide executive agencies in its implementation, to indicate constitutional reservations about a bill in order to guide executive agencies by imposing limits in those areas that are suspect, or for rhetorical purposes, such as lauding the triumphant character of the legislation. The practice does not have constitutional authority; the president is given three constitutional alternatives for acting on a legislative item: veto it, sign it, or do nothing. However, presidents since James Monroe have engaged in the practice, and the Supreme Court has been ambiguous on the status of signing statements, although *Marbury v. Madison* (1803) usually is taken as establishing the Supreme Court's power to conduct judicial review. The practice was uncontroversial until recent times, when presidents began indicating that they would not enforce certain provisions. This use of the practice became widespread during the G. W. Bush administration when more than 750 signing statements are estimated to have been issued, some of which changed the intention of the law under the power of the unitary executive theory. For example, the signing statement that accompanied the Detainee Treatment Act of 2005 (H.R. 2863, Title X) prohibiting cruel, inhuman, and degrading treatment of detainees in U.S. custody stated, "The executive branch shall construe . . . the Act, relating to detainees, in a manner consistent with the constitutional authority of the President to supervise the unitary executive branch and as Commander in Chief and consistent with the constitutional limitations on the judicial power" (Bush). On the theory of the unitary executive, the president has the authority to not follow the mandates of legislation that would in any way supersede or constrict his prerogatives and powers as commander in chief. In short, this use of the signing statement is an iteration of the state of exception in which the president's word is law.

DEWEY IN THE CONTEMPORARY CONTEXT

Although factions are not new phenomena in American democracy, their proliferation in the present context exacerbates the problem of the public that John Dewey wrote about in 1927. In *The Public and Its Problems,* Dewey warned that the problem of the public arose from the proliferation of publics, each with its own agenda, issues, and ways of expressing its interests. As a result the public was in eclipse. Dewey's concerns, sparked by the balkanization of the public, focus on the challenge posed by diversity once the problems that intersect citizens' lives are no longer confined to locality. Problems of national scope lose the emotional and ethical bonds of attachment that define a community and bring those who feel the indirect consequences of decisions by others into political contact with other citizens who do not necessarily share their orientation or experience the problem in the same way.

Dewey's awareness of the problem posed by a vast nation, such as the United States, when bonds of local attraction lose their traction led him to frame it as a problem of communication. His analysis still rings true, and the problem is exacerbated by the realities of social, political, and economic life in the twenty-first century. In an age of globalized interconnections sustained through new media, the problem of difference is accelerated and the reality of mutual dependency hardens. For many, this reality poses a danger to core beliefs and values. When what might be common and shared is obscured by practices of others that seem to violate core beliefs, difference becomes threatening and trust becomes exceedingly difficult. Amid claims that Washington is broken and calls for fixing Congress, the foregoing suggests that the problem lies deeper. The fix is not in Washington or Congress (although they require fixing) but in the at once more local and pervasive problem of our inability to hear alternative perspectives and entertain the possibility that a cloud of ideological reifications has obscured our vision of the problems that confront the modern polity—public safety, public and planetary health, economic stability, and education. Its reifications have denied us a common language for finding common meaning and arriving at a common sense of the problems that define the common realities we confront. We still face Dewey's problem of bringing the many together and trying to make sense of their political conditions as one nation that can function in harmony despite its differences.

Change is not new. Though the haze of distance has encouraged us to regard the turbulence of war and the reality of social dangers of times past as counterbalanced by beliefs and structures that allowed confidence in some truths as shared and immutable, history shows that to be a fabulous perception more rooted in imagination than in fact. Still, the changes we face today are so many and so diverse that we seem to be set in a Hobbesian nightmare of all against all. Pick your poison—religion, politics, economics, the environment, health—and the divides in opinion seem beyond repair. Perhaps we see the world from a perspective that brings differences too close for us to focus on the whole picture and to ferret the underlying causes for the seeming intractable rhetorics of opposition that are rending our social fabric. As Jeremy Engels's observations on Dewey and Jefferson remind us, democracy requires belief in human decency. Without it democracy appears to be a politics of folly doomed at least to disillusion if not catastrophe.

That requirement seems to be under siege in U.S. politics today. Politics and democracy are not identical. However, insofar as politics has as its abiding concern an ongoing negotiation over how we shall act and interact, a breakdown of politics is equally a breakdown of democracy as a functionally viable form of governance. As the essays in this volume demonstrate, Deweyan democracy is predicated on the vision of communication of the sort that permits reasoned and reasonable consideration of public problems in order to reach an informed understanding of the issues and a responsible position on them. We are reminded by Lucy Knight's discussion of Dewey on war that, as far as Dewey's own practice was concerned, this perspective toward thinking and acting on public problems did not mean that communication would necessarily bring opposing perspectives to consensus. Dewey remained opposed to Addams on U.S. involvement in World War I. However, their disagreements were framed by mutual trust that each had a concern for a just and morally correct course of action regarding war.

The combination of forces molding U.S. politics today appears to conspire against the relevance of Dewey's vision. Models of governmentality in which biopolitical practices seem to mount assaults against freedom, regulate bodies in ways that are patently unfair in their consequences on who they will make live and who they will let die, and consolidate power in an executive that is above the checks and balances of the Constitution and whose word can function as law, especially in the arena of national defense, seem to lack trust in human decency. That message, certainly reflected in polling data that show the American public has little trust in Congress, has taken its toll on the level of social trust in the nation as a whole.

Since the 1990s at least, America's political motto seems to have followed the advice of the hit TV series *The X-Files,* in which FBI agents, in an ongoing quest to uncover a conspiracy in government, operated under the slogan "Trust no one." Despite the spike in social trust that occurred in the immediate aftermath of the 9/11 terrorist attacks, social trust has continued to decline. According to the latest available data in the General Social Survey (2006), response to the general question "Can people be trusted?" has declined steadily since 1970 from a roughly even split between trusters (46.3 percent) and mistrusters (50.0 percent) to a split of nearly two-thirds who are mistrustful (62.4 percent) vs. one-third trusters (32.3 percent). The General Social Survey also shows decline of trust in our institutions, including organized religion, while the Gallup Poll taken in September 2011 (Gallup.com) shows that 81 percent of Americans have little or no trust in their federal government to do what is right—and that includes any of the three branches!—with only 19 percent believing they can trust the government just about always or most of the time.

The incivility, bunker mentality, and ideological rigidity of America's political parties and, indeed, among sizable segments of the population have made political collaboration on national problems appear impossible. The toll these attitudes have taken on the spirit of national dialogue, along with the failure of public institutions —including not only the government but also churches, corporations, banks, and more—to exhibit even remote awareness of, not to mention concern over, the consequences of their personal gains for public costs, seems to define Dewey's relevance out of the game. That is a serious doubt; it poses a serious challenge to the democratic culture that Jackson and Clark announce as the subject of this volume, with dire consequences if unmet. It requires more than a fairyland response. I believe there is a line of thought in Dewey that might help us gain focus on what is needed to ameliorate our present discontents. If it does not provide a specific program of action, it at least offers a perspective toward what must be done.

One of the constant themes running through this volume has been Dewey's belief that experience is the core from which human belief and action spring. A primary experience necessary for a Deweyan and Madisonian democratic vision to flourish is that of mutual dependencies. This requires a citizenry capable, first, of having rhetorical experiences of diversity. Here I follow Dewey's lead from *Art as Experience,* where experience is conceptualized as "heightened vitality" (19). That is to say, the consequence of experiencing together, as happens through the rhetoricality of speaking, listening, viewing, sharing, and acting together, is to produce a more vital relationship. Rather than "announcing," rhetoric creates mutual experience between rhetor and audience (244). Moreover rhetorical experience does not have discernible practical, emotional, or intellectual *phases;* it is a *unity* akin to what Dewey finds in differentiating what we mean when we label the everyday as the "experience" of, say, work from an episode that stands apart and cannot be understood apart from the interaction of its several parts, as in the exclamation "That was *an experience*!" As Dewey instructs, "[In such an experience], its varied parts are linked to one another, and do not merely succeed one another. And the parts through their experienced linkage move toward a consummation and close, not merely to cessation in time. This consummation, moreover, does not wait in consciousness for the whole undertaking to be finished. It is anticipated throughout and is recurrently savored with special intensity" (55).

The experience of rhetoric I have in mind, inclusive of vernacular rhetoric's multiple modes, is a predominantly public experience. The unity of practical, emotional, and intellectual aspects of experience in the public realm resituates our focus from the consequences of public discourse and perhaps even from Aristotelian judgment and directs it instead to the priority of sharing the experience of participation in the rhetorical act itself. In Dewey's words, "the act itself is exactly what it is because of how it is done" (*Art as Experience* 109). Moreover, contra Aristotle's exclusion of performance from the essence of tragedy and the implications of that move for theorizing an art that might include spectacle, an experiential perspective considers performance as essential because it is theory producing. Applied to rhetoric, theory in this sense is not knowledge of abstract principles, which exist only hypothetically sans the rhetorical act. I believe this is what Jean Goodwin is pointing toward when she argues, in her essay in this book, that one need not be an insider, say an expert on issues related to agriculture, to arrive at a sense of how one's interests were involved and form a reasoned opinion on the proposals under consideration *provided* one's attention is actively engaged in the communication—discussion and debate—by those in the know. Rhetorically established principles emerge in performance, which determines the fashion in which they are manifested and invites mutual experience in their enactment. These are principles for living—for being, thinking, and doing, for sociality and community—rendered experientially concrete through shared participation in their articulation. At a time when we are captive to enclaved rhetoric, the aesthetics of artful communication, especially artful journalism and documentary filmmaking as well as the creative arts generally, offers a venue for shared experience of this sort.

Second, by focusing on rhetorical experience we also focus on the means for exciting the public imagination into an understanding of publics as multiple, as emergences from rhetorical interaction, as manifested in multiple ways in a plurality of public spheres each accommodating a montage of multiple messages and forms of expression. Why? Because rhetorical experience unites theory and practice in a way that creates bonds of publicness among persons as actors, among them as participants in a rhetorical ensemble. We create our identity as a public and articulate and enact the principles upon which our identity rests, through the moment-by-moment mutuality of rhetorical experience. In short, engaging in rhetoric provides the framework for mutual experience so essential for a public (as distinct from an interest group or an enclave of the wholly-knowing) to emerge. Insofar as these are experiences of diversity—of different perspectives that share bonds of interdependency and inflect alternative frames of reference—the conversation can change to include what we share in common and perhaps the actions that may have mutually acceptable consequences.

Third, this line of reasoning has implications for the ways publics form and can be reformed. It is not the case that a public is a public is a public. Not all publics are the same. Here I caution about the publics invited into being by politics of today, which seems more attuned to political spectacle than political judgment. It is a politics of overdetermination and suspicion that deploys rhetorical spectacle to ridicule rather than embrace diversity, that symbolically slays the opposition rather than refutes it. Publics constituted by political spectacle are not asked to apply standards of *utilia* for making pragmatic judgments, *justa* for making legal judgments, or *honesta* for making moral judgments. In the heated arenas of today's politically partisan public spheres—whether Tea Party rallies, cable TV political forums, political blogs, or partisan party primary debates—the wholly-knowing rail against their opponents in apocalyptic terms to an audience not asked to critically entertain that there might be another point of view on the matter. They constitute audiences conditioned to one-sided presentations and to admire verbal pugnacity and even reward it with TV ratings or votes. Even in the extensive presidential primary debates in the 2008 and 2012 campaigns, attacks against opponents for the party's nomination employed smear tactics with apocalyptic tones. Those who are adroit at "mixing it up" exhibit a form of argumentativeness that can charm and persuade through perverse displays of virtuosity, and attract the sort of admiration that gives them authority (or scorn that they have it). Without necessarily holding formal leadership or elected office with a record to defend, pundits, colorful commentators, and pugnacious spokespersons for a point of view can deflect captive viewers and listeners from weighing arguments and reduce them to a demographic drawn to the magnet of spectacular rhetoric. Their success both conditions a public to respond to the spectacle of verbal assault and encourages politicians to imitate the form. It makes for exciting television.

A case in point was the response of Newt Gingrich during the 2012 Republican primary debate in South Carolina to a question posed by CNN correspondent John King. King asked Gingrich whether he cared to respond to his ex-wife's claim that he asked her for an "open marriage." Gingrich's response was an excoriation of King and the press in general for asking that type of question in a presidential primary debate. Gingrich's reply, seamless in its performance of outrage, drew standing applause, and his ratings soared. The following week the format of the NBC debate did not permit audience response, which Gingrich strenuously protested was an infringement of free speech.[3] It also was a crimp on an accomplished political actor's style, where feeding off crowd responses and using crowd responses to infect the audience with a "we" feeling are essential ingredients for managing political spectacle. When we see displays of beauty, slick encomia of commerce, the antics of a pub crowd lustily cheering and hissing a poetry slam, or a studio audience moved to raucous displays of affirmation, we are no longer in the abstract region of discursive space in which we may reflect upon the developing scene. We are in a specific place, with a specific history, being invited and even provoked to respond in partisan ways, and susceptible to all of the inner turmoil and extravagance of feeling and expression that accompany such moments of engaging displays.

This is rhetorical experience, to be certain, but of a different sort than those geared to develop a sense of mutuality amid difference, encourage critical discussion of issues, and build bonds of social trust. A Deweyan vision of communication's role in a democracy points away from the agonistic rhetoric of attack and partisan persuasion and, in line with what William Keith and Robert Danisch argue in their essay in this book, toward the experience of community that comes from discussion aimed at exploring issues, finding solutions, and engendering collaboration. In addition to being an art of production, rhetoric also is a social practice. Dewey leads us to consider how effective engagement in a social practice both requires and produces an orientation. And orientation, as Scott Stroud has explored in his essay in this book, shapes our consciousness of objects, persons, situations, and actions in social life. A Deweyan sensibility toward rhetorical experience harkens to the clear assertions of Demosthenes and later the Romans that rhetoric comes alive in the experience of citizens through performance and its status is established in *actio*. The quality of *actio*, which is to say the rhetorical experience of participation in an ongoing negotiation over how we shall act and interact, defines the character and quality of our public life.

There is no quick fix for the problems of our polity. In part this is because the problems grow from structural flaws that run deep and require political will to advance the common good rather than gaining hegemony for a preferred ideology. We may hope that the Supreme Court will undo its 2010 decision on campaign financing, but that will require a court of different composition, which seems unlikely to occur for some time. Besides, the United States has a long history of brutal partisanship in its political campaigns, and since Lyndon Johnson's notorious Daisy ad raised the specter of nuclear holocaust were Barry Goldwater elected, mediated political campaigns at all levels have grown steadily more negative, nasty, and mean. Removing anonymity and limiting funding will not eliminate negative or deceptive ads. Or we may hope that there will be a spirit of fairness in congressional redistricting to undo the so-called "safe seats" created by unorthodox districting by the party in power to gain the advantage in future elections. But until states adopt nonpartisan systems for determining election districts, safe districts will continue in place and will encourage extreme perspectives in order for a person to be elected to public office.

There are, however, two forms of communication that may engage in the slow process of creating rhetorical experiences to produce a more demanding electorate, one that seeks something different from the status quo for political dialogue, one capacitated to reward or punish rhetorical behavior based on its relevance to substantive issues: news and interaction with strangers. Unless the public is informed of the facts, it cannot defend itself against the captivating spectacle of media presentations that dominate the mediated arenas where public problems are discussed. As Brian Jackson, Meridith Reed, and Jeff Swift observe in their essay in this book, getting the facts and discerning the quality of witnesses are essential for thinking experimentally about the consequences of proposed action. This requires artful presentation of the facts and the testimony of competent witnesses, presentations that connect facts and witnesses to the lives of citizens so that there is a foundation beyond the shifting emotional sands of partisan opinions.

Interaction with strangers is important because it provides the vehicle for taking the threat out of difference. The rhetorical experience that comes from encountering those who come from different backgrounds, hold different beliefs, and still encounter the same or similar problems discloses a basis for seeing different perspectives in human rather than ideological terms. It is a basis for building social capital and trust (see Coleman; Hauser and Benoit-Barné). The rhetorical experience of communicating with diverse partners is an important part of the individual's political formation. Dewey's commitment to "conjoint communicated experience," admirably explored in Keith Gilyard's tracing of Deweyan echoes in Du Bois's educational vision for African Americans (see Gilyard's essay in this book), stands against attitudinal and structural obstacles that fostered inattention to those on the margins, sequestering difference in safe enclaves and preying on fears that germinate in the soil of ignorance. Encounters with difference capacitate a person to experience interdependence as something more than an abstraction and therefore to engage in practical reason on contingent matters.

Rhetoricians can play a significant role in bringing such rhetorical experiences into being through our pedagogy. Our present discontents will be righted only through constant attention to and advocacy of a curriculum that includes developing rhetorical competencies.[4] It will require at least a generation of attention not only to speaking and writing classes but to all classes in which issues that are open to interpretation include opportunities, curricular structures, effective pedagogy, and concrete outcomes that develop deliberative skills and habits in our students, that involve them in contexts where they can have rhetorical experiences that excite their civic imagination to the advantages of collaboration, and that eventually set criteria of civic engagement that reach beyond their localities to the larger venues in which our political fortunes are decided. Tending to this agenda as Dewey might—in the ways explored by the thoughtful essays in this volume—with a concern for the place of rhetorical experience in critical thinking and civic performance may be slow going, but it can be transformative in our students' lives and, one hopes, eventually in the American polity.

NOTES

1. The burgeoning populations of London and Paris, Europe's great cities, are illustrative of the transformation that swept Europe as industrialization of its economies expanded. Both cities increased massively during this period. London's population in 1595 stood at 150,000; by 1632, 315,000; in 1700, about 700,000; and around 1750 it had reached 750,000. As Richard Sennett observes, these figures pale before the growth of London during the industrialization of the nineteenth century from 860,000 to 5 million. "But the people of the 18th Century didn't know what was to come. They could only see what had happened, and the city, especially after the great fire in the middle of the 17th Century, appeared to them to be becoming extraordinarily populous" (Sennett 50). The growth of Paris seems less stark—in 1637 at 410,000; in 1684 about 425,000; and in 1750 at 500,000—but we must bear in mind that the population as a whole in France was stagnant, if not in real decline, during this period. Inspection of the birth-to-death ratio of this period suggests that the growth in both cities was fueled from outside by urban migration from rural areas. Sennett tells us that the populations of these cities, both of which were commercial and soon to be industrial hubs, were increasingly composed of strangers of a special sort: "alone, cut off from past associations, come to the city from a significant distance" (51), who were now part of its economic, political, and social fabric.

2. I have discussed the Bush administration's rhetoric consolidating supreme power in the executive in *Prisoners of Conscience* (2012).

3. The success of Gingrich's response is all the more noteworthy as an example of political spectacle's power in that it aroused such a strong positive response from South Carolinians that he went from a 17-point deficit in the polls to a 12-point victory. Moreover this was

a response from voters reputed to be placing great emphasis on value issues in the primary. Gingrich was able to make villains of the media and John King for asking him about allegedly requesting permission from his then cancer-stricken wife to continue his affair with a woman he had been involved with for six years.

4. Three pedagogy groups working at the Alliance of Rhetoric Societies conference held at Evanston, Illinois, in 2003 developed far-reaching proposals for the ways we might reassert rhetoric education's centrality in the modern university. Spanning these was their call for ARS to *commission a manifesto recovering the value of rhetoric education as central to civic education.* Their recommendations may be found in Hauser "Teaching Rhetoric."

WORKS CITED

Agamben, Georgio. *Homo Sacer.* Trans. Daniel Heller-Roazen. Palo Alto, Calif.: Stanford University Press, 1998.

———. *State of Exception.* Trans. Kevin Attell. Chicago: University of Chicago Press, 2005.

Bush, George W. President's Statement on Signing of H.R. 2863. "The Department of Defense, Emergency Supplemental Appropriations to Address Hurricanes in the Gulf of Mexico, and Pandemic Influenza Act, 2006." December 2005. Web (accessed January 27, 2012) http://www.gpo.gov/fdsys/pkg/PLAW-109publ148/pdf/PLAW-109publ148.pdf

Coleman, James. "Social Capital in the Creation of Human Capital." *American Journal of Sociology* 94. S1 (1988): S99–S120.

Dewey, John. *Art as Experience.* 1934. Reprint, New York: Paragon, 1979.

———. *The Public and Its Problems.* 1927. Reprint, Chicago: Swallow Press, 1954.

Dodd, Lawrence C. "Political Learning and Political Change: Understanding Development across Time." In *The Dynamics of American Politics,* ed. Lawrence C. Dodd and Calvin Jillson, 331–64. Boulder, Colo.: Westview, 1994.

Foucault, Michel. *The Birth of Biopolitics: Lectures at Collége de France, 1978–1979.* Trans. Graham Burchell. 2004. Reprint, New York: Palgrave, 2008.

Friedman, George. *The Next 100 Years.* New York: Doubleday, 2009.

Gallup.com. "Americans Express Historic Negativity toward U.S. Government." *Gallup Politics,* September 26, 2011. Web (accessed January 29, 2012) http://www.gallup.com/poll/149678/americans-express-historic-negativity-toward-government.aspx

General Social Survey. "Trust." 2006. Web (accessed January 28, 2012), http://www3.norc.org/GSS+Website/Browse+GSS+Variables/Subject+Index/

Hamsher, Jane. "Giffords Opponent, Jesse Kelly, Held June Event to 'Shoot a Fully Automated M16' to 'Get on Target' and 'Remove Gabrielle Giffords.'" FireDogLake, January 8, 2011. Web (accessed January 30, 2012) http://firedoglake.com/2011/01/08/giffords-opponent-jesse-kelly-held-june-event-to-shoot-a-fully-automatic-m16-to-get-on-target-and-remove-gabrielle-giffords/

Hauser, Gerard. *Prisoners of Conscience: Moral Vernaculars of Political Agency.* Columbia: University of South Carolina Press, 2012.

———. "Teaching Rhetoric, or Why Rhetoric Isn't Just Another Kind of Philosophy or Literary Criticism." *Rhetoric Society Quarterly* 34.3 (2004): 39–54.

Hauser, Gerard A., and Chantal Benoit-Barné. "Reflections on Rhetoric, Deliberative Democracy, Civil Society, and Trust." *Rhetoric & Public Affairs* 5.2 (2002): 261–75.

H.R. 2863, Title X. 2005. Detainee Treatment Act of 2005. *Jurist,* December 31, 2005. Web (accessed January 27, 2012) http://jurist.law.pitt.edu/gazette/2005/12/detainee-treatment-act-of-2005-white.php

Palin, Sarah. "Don't Get Demoralized! Get Organized! Take Back the 20!" Facebook, March 23, 2010. Web (accessed January 29, 2012) https://www.facebook.com/note.php?note_id=373854973434

———. Twitter. "@sarakpalinUSA." Web. (accessed January 29, 2012) https://twitter.com/SarahPalinUSA

Sennett, Richard. *The Fall of Public Man.* New York: Vintage, 1978.

CONTRIBUTORS

GREGORY CLARK is a University Professor of English at Brigham Young University. His books include *Rhetorical Landscapes in America* (2004) and, with S. Michael Halloran, *Oratorical Culture in America* (1994). His recent work examines theories and practices of rhetorical aesthetics.

NATHAN CRICK is associate professor in the Department of Communication at Texas A&M University. His research draws from American pragmatism and classical Greek thought to develop a democratic social theory in which rhetoric is a medium of cooperative inquiry and aesthetic judgment.

ROBERT DANISCH is an assistant professor at Concordia University in Montreal, Canada. He is the author of *Pragmatism, Democracy, and the Necessity of Rhetoric* (2007). Currently he is working on a new book, *Completing the Linguistic Turn: The Promise of Rhetorical Pragmatism,* which critiques neopragmatism for failing to embrace rhetoric and recommends the development of a rhetorical pragmatism useful for improving American democratic culture.

JEREMY ENGELS is associate professor of communication arts and sciences and interim codirector of the Center for Democratic Deliberation at Pennsylvania State University. His research investigates the rhetorical foundations of democratic culture in the United States. His first book, *Enemyship: Democracy and Counter-Revolution in the Early Republic,* was published in 2010 in the Rhetoric and Public Affairs series at Michigan State University Press. His essays have been published in *Rhetoric & Public Affairs, Quarterly Journal of Speech, Rhetoric Society Quarterly, American Quarterly,* and *Communication and Critical/Cultural Studies.*

A native New Yorker, KEITH GILYARD has lectured widely on language, literature, education, and civic affairs. His books include the education memoir *Voices of the Self: A Study of Language Competence* (1991), for which he received an American Book Award; *Let's Flip the Script, an African American Discourse on Language, Literature, and Learning* (1996); *Composition and Cornel West: Notes toward a Deep Democracy* (2008); *John Oliver Killens: A Life of Black Literary Activism* (2010); and

True to the Language Game: African American Discourse, Cultural Politics, and Pedagogy (2011). He is currently a Distinguished Professor of English at Pennsylvania State University, University Park.

JEAN GOODWIN is associate professor of English and in the Speech Communication Program at Iowa State University. Her research focuses on the theory and pedagogy of civic argument. She has had a number of articles published in international journals, including *Argumentation, Philosophy & Rhetoric, Informal Logic, Studies in Communication Sciences,* and *Argumentation and Advocacy,* as well as essays in leading collections such as *Dialectic and Rhetoric: The Warp and Woof of Argumentation Theory.*

GERARD A. HAUSER is College Professor of Distinction in the Department of Communication at the University of Colorado. He is the author of *Vernacular Voices: The Rhetoric of Publics and Public Spheres* (1999), *An Introduction to Rhetorical Theory* (2002), and many other influential publications in rhetorical studies. Hauser is an NCA Distinguished Scholar, an RSA Fellow, and the winner of numerous awards. He is editor of *Philosophy & Rhetoric.* His current work examines the moral vernacular rhetorics of political prisoners.

BRIAN JACKSON is assistant professor of English and associate coordinator of university writing at Brigham Young University. A graduate of the University of Arizona, he teaches and writes about John Dewey, pedagogy, and American religious rhetoric. He lives in Provo, Utah, with his wife Amy and their four children.

DONALD C. JONES is associate professor of rhetoric and professional writing at the University of Hartford. His publications appear in *College English, Rhetoric Review, Pedagogy,* and the *Journal of Advanced Composition.* In addition to Dewey and pedagogy, his research interests include writing process theory and digital literacy.

WILLIAM KEITH is professor of communication at the University of Wisconsin-Milwaukee. He is the author of *Democracy as Discussion: Adult Civic Education and the American Forum Movement* (2007) and numerous essays on the rhetoric of science.

LOUISE (LUCY) W. KNIGHT is an independent scholar and Adjunct Professor in Communication Studies at Northwestern University. The author of *Jane Addams: Spirit in Action* (2010) and *Citizen: Jane Addams and the Struggle for Democracy* (2005), she has also published articles in the *Journal of Women's History, Gender & History,* the *Journal of Community Practice,* and *Affilia: Women and Social Work.* Her essays have been published in various collections, including Maurice Hamington, ed., *Feminist Interpretations of Jane Addams,* and Marilyn Fischer et al., *Jane Addams and the Practice of Democracy.* She has reviewed books for the *Wall Street Journal,* the *New York Times Book Review,* and the *Women's Review of Books* and writes for the History News Service, an op-ed syndicate. In 2000 she received a fellowship from the National Endowment of the Humanities, and in 2007 *Citizen* received the Russell P. Strange Memorial Award for best book on Illinois history from the Illinois State Historical Society.

WALTON MUYUMBA is a writer, critic, and associate professor of English at the University of North Texas. His most recent book, *The Shadow and the Act: Black Intellectual Practice, Jazz Improvisation, and Philosophical Pragmatism,* was published in 2009. He lives in Dallas, Texas.

MERIDITH REED received her M.A. in English from Brigham Young University, where her thesis focused on the aesthetic theories of John Dewey and Kenneth Burke. She teaches first-year writing and persuasive writing at BYU.

PAUL STOB is assistant professor of communication studies at Vanderbilt University. His work focuses on the relationship between rhetoric and intellectual culture and has appeared or will soon appear in *Philosophy & Rhetoric, Argumentation and Advocacy,* and *Rhetoric & Public Affairs.* He is currently finishing a book entitled "William James and the Art of Popular Statement."

SCOTT R. STROUD is assistant professor of communication studies at the University of Texas at Austin. He has published research on pragmatism's relation to rhetoric, criticism, and ethics in *Rhetoric Society Quarterly, Philosophy & Rhetoric, Western Journal of Communication,* and the *Journal of Speculative Philosophy.* His forthcoming book, *Pragmatism and the Artful Life,* addresses the relevance of Dewey's aesthetic theory for ethics and communication.

JEFF SWIFT is a Ph.D. student of communication, rhetoric, and digital media at North Carolina State University, where he studies the rhetoric of new media and teaches first-year writing.

INDEX

CPSIA information can be obtained at www.ICGtesting.com
Printed in the USA
LVOW12*0455080114

368508LV00004B/7/P